7.9.15

MW01706652

LA DIVINIA COMMEDIA • DANTE ALIGHIL...

General Books LLC™, Memphis, USA, 2012.

LA DIVINA COMMEDIA

The Divine Comedy

of

Dante Alighieri

A line-for-line translation in the rime-form of the original, by

Melville Best Anderson

BY WAY OF INTRODUCTION

As to the form and phrasing of this translation, a few explanations seem desirable. This is a line-for-line translation retaining the original rime-form,—*terza rima,* or triple rime. In using the expression "line-forline translation," it is not meant to imply that every line will be found in the translation in the exact place where it is found in the original. The substance of every sentence or paragraph presents itself to the translator as material to be freely rehandled in accordance with the exigencies of the rime and the requirements of English idiom. It will be found that the number of lines in every canto of the translation corresponds to that of the original. In conformity with the genius of our language and the practice of our poets, the Italian hendecasyllabic line is rendered by the normal English line of ten syllables. As almost every Italian word ends with a vowel sound, the feminine or double rime, involving a line of eleven syllables, is normal in that language. To what issue the attempt to transplant the Italian eleven-syllable line into English leads, has been shown by the experiment of Lee-Hamilton with the Inferno. Like other poets of our tongue, I have introduced the eleven-syllable lines here and there, sometimes in considerable numbers, with a view to special expressiveness.

With respect to the choice of the English triple rime, I will frankly admit that the late Professor Charles Eliot Norton very strongly, although very kindly, advised me against it. Certainly there was little to encourage one in the results attained by those who had previously attempted to render the Poem in this form. To argue that because no one had succeeded with *terza rima* in English, failure was necessarily a foregone conclusion, seemed to me a plain begging of the question. There was encouragement in the fact that Rossetti had succeeded beautifully in his translations of the minor poems in the original rime-forms, and that he, as well as Byron, had nobly rendered in triple rime the story of Francesca. In fact, the arguments against the attempt to translate Dante in the corresponding English meter were much on a plane with those raised against the attempts at the conquest of the Poles and of the Air. Twenty-one years ago, when I began this delightful labor, those conquests were still to make.

Twenty-one years is doubtless a long period to look forward to. Looking back, however, the time seems only too short, and I do not regret one hour of it. Should a friendly critic perchance admonish me that I ought to have tarried longer in Jericho, I should be inclined to agree with him. Parsons, a true poet, is said to have given a very much longer time to his brilliant experiment, leaving it after all only half done. Of the shortcomings of the present version I am, of course, more painfully aware than any one else can be. But I do think that in certain passages I have justified the choice of the triple rime as the form in which the translator can come nearest to the spirit and power of the great original. There were moments when I felt near the Master,—when he seemed to take the pen out of my hand and show me how the lines should read in English. Moments of happy, stimulating illusion, such as come to the translator as the supreme reward of fidelity!

To judge by much recent comment, Dante seems to be popularly known as the poet of the Inferno. In fact, persons who ought to know better have fallen into the loose habit of referring to the *Divine Comedy* as "Dante's Inferno."

The Inferno has perhaps a hundred readers, where the Purgatorio has a score and the Paradiso one or two. Yet the two latter Cantiche *Introduction* v contain passages transcending in beauty and in moral significance anything in the Inferno. And to speak of my translation, inasmuch as I naturally gained in mastery of my difficult instrument as I proceeded, I believe my rendering of the Paradiso to be both technically and poetically superior to my rendering of the Inferno. I should be sorry, therefore, if any disappointed reader should lay down my version without looking at some of the later cantos. If the *Divine Comedy* be regarded as the Poet's spiritual autobiography, surely the Inferno must be essentially preliminary. The true center of the Poem, so considered, is found in the thirtieth and thirty-first cantos of Purgatorio.

With respect to the marginal notes, I wish to say that they of course make no claim to anything like completeness, being intended only as an unobtrusive running commentary to help the reader to slip through, or *over,* certain perplexing passages, so encouraging him to achieve the rather unusual feat of reading the whole *Divine Comedy* through at a few sittings. It is believed that this can be comfortably accomplished in the long winter evenings of a single week. I once read my translation of the whole Inferno to a friend at a single unbroken sitting.

To the longer notes which have been appended to certain cantos, I wish here to add the two following. The first is with respect to the pronoun of direct address. This is throughout the time-honored pronoun of the second person, "thou," with its corresponding forms. By this Dante and Virgil address each other; by this Dante addresses so great a personage as the Lady Matilda. This ordinary use of "thou" sets in marked relief the occasional exceptional use of "you" as the singular pronoun of direct address. The use of "you" is intended as a mark of the ceremonious respect due to royalty or superior rank. This is emphasized by the Poet in the opening lines of Paradiso xvi. His use of "you" in that place in addressing his great ancestor is a sign of family pride, causing Beatrice to smile at the Poet's weakness. In Purgatorio xxxi, after Beatrice has assumed the remote and impersonal attitude of the judge, he uses this form in addressing her. He uses it out of reverence to Pope Adrian in Purgatorio xix. In the Inferno the Poet so addresses Farinata, the elder Cavalcanti, and Brunetto Latini, but not Pope Nicholas III. Wherever "thou (thy)" and "you (your)" are used in close connection, the reader may properly infer that different persons are thus referred to. For example, in Inferno xix, line 102, "thou" refers to Pope Nicholas, while in the next line but one "your" refers to the whole class to which he belongs.

The other note is with reference to the first line of the Invocation to the Muses, in the seventh line of the first canto of Purgatorio:

"Here let dead poesy arise again."

The commentators generally understand the words "dead poesy" to refer to the spiritual death which has been the subject of the Poem hitherto. But as our Poet teaches us to look in his verses for various phases of meaning (compare the famous letter to Can Grande), the question properly arises whether beside the allegorical, or moral, or anagogical meaning, there is not a meaning which, being on the surface, is not seen, for the very reason that we are searching for something deeper. That there is such an unnoted but rather obvious meaning is patent, as soon as one thinks of it. In the thirty-third canto of the Inferno, Poesy is certainly alive, passionately and powerfully alive in the highest degree. In the final canto, however, there is an intentional lowering of the temperature. Poesy seems *Introduction* vii benumbed with the chill of Cocytus. Dante cannot, like Milton, make his Satan a lofty and heroic figure. He is no Baudelaire to suffuse the flowers of evil with sickly grace and unwholesome sentiment. It is a picture of unredeemed ugliness, without the dramatic quality and the charm of imagery and allusion that make us fairly hold our breath while witnessing the horrible transformations in Inferno xxiv and xxv. Even at the very end of the canto the description of the ascent is studiously plain. Done with Hell and glad to banish it from our minds, we hasten forward to the world of light:

"Tomorrow to fresh woods and pastures new." n

Of special interest to the student of Dante are the handsome armorial shields of Florence and of her Patrician families. Drawings, in which colors are conventionally indicated by the arrangement of the lines, are here given of the arms of the Cavalcanti and of the Portinari; also of the Gianfigliazzi, the first of the four coats distinctly described in Inferno xvii. Of still greater interest are the two colored plates of the old and the new shield of the Commune of Florence, referred to at the end of Paradiso xvi. The old emblem, the lily argent on a shield gules, was retained by the Ghibellines, while the Guelfs in the middle of the century (1251) reversed the colors. These plates serve also as an illustration of the important and sublime passage in Paradiso xviii, where we are told how the bird-like spirits formed the mystic constellated Eagle from the M of the word TERRAM. Now the *fleur-de-lis* of Florence might very well have served an ancient manuscript illuminator as a highly ornate initial letter M. Regarding it as such, the reader will easily imagine the medial point of the letter to be developed, as the Poet describes, into the head and neck of an Eagle. In fact, the resemblance to the heraldic Eagle is striking. The Emblem may also be taken as an illustration of that passage in Purgatorio xxiii in which is recorded the quaint fancy that God stamped the word 0M0 (homo) on the face of man.

Inasmuch as my brief marginal notes pass without comment hundreds of names and allusions about which the reader may be curious, it is my pleasant duty to refer to a few of the abundant helps to the study of the Poet which exist in English. In the way of general criticism it happens that we have two essays worthy of the lofty subject, one by the English Dean, R. W. Church (Macmillan), and one by the American poet-critic, J. R. Lowell (Houghton Mifflin). In the whole wide field of Dante criticism, I have found nothing quite equal in their way to these two essays, which admirably supplement each other. Of the somewhat abundant comment that has recently arisen in connection with the commemorations of the Poet in this anniversary year, the most noteworthy essay that I have chanced to see is that of the eminent Italian thinker, Benedetto Croce, in the *Yale Review* (October, 1921).

Of editions of the Poet, the one published in the series of "Temple Classics" will be found on the whole most useful to the beginner. This contains a translation, facing the text, together with brief notes, useful maps, diagrams, tables, and pictures. The translation of the Inferno is the excellent one by John Carlyle. The other translations are less commendable, and the notes are too often wanting in urbanity.

In the way of a prose translation of the complete Poem, there is nothing quite equal to that by Charles Eliot Norton; and a whole library of information is *Introduction* ix packed into his terse notes, which are the fruit of lifelong study (Houghton Mifflin).

The notes to Longfellow's blank-verse translation are of a different character and are even more interesting. The progress of Dante studies, which has been very great during the past half century, has made many of Longfellow's interpretations obsolete. But as a body of literary parallels, Longfellow's notes should be in the hands of every reader (Houghton Mifflin).

The best edition of the text, with notes and arguments in English, is that by Professor C. H. Grandgent (Heath), who has made scholarly use of the works of the most recent Italian writers and investigators.

Fuller comment is given by H. F. Tozer, whose notes are published separately in three volumes by the Clarendon Press.

In the way of a handbook of historical and biographical information, there is nothing on the whole so good as the compact "Primer of Dante" by E. G. Gardner (Dent). It contains an analytic account of all the Poet's works, together with tables and diagrams and other information of value. Inexpensive and handy, it is the one book which I recommend to the reader as almost indispensable.

Perhaps the most important single book of reference for the student of Dante is the "Dictionary of Proper Names" by Paget Toynbee (Clarendon Press). This work contains some account of every one of the hundreds of persons introduced or referred to in the course of Dante's poems. Mr. Toynbee, who is now the most eminent living English Dante scholar, has had in hand for many years a general Dictionary to the language of Dante,—a work unhappily not yet completed.

It would give me deep pleasure to record here the names of friends who have helped me with advice and sympathy. As I have mentioned Professor Norton, it would be ungracious not to add that, although believing me to be just another "Childe Roland" at the Dark Tower, he gave me unstinted assistance, as his notes on the manuscript of some of my earlier cantos bear witness. As I think of other and nearer friends, who encouraged my first crude attempts and who are now with Dante and Beatrice, I recall the pathetic words of Goethe:

"Sie horcn nicht die folgemlen Gesatige,
Die Seelen, denen ich die ersten sang."
(Those spirits do not hear the present cadence,
Who kindled to the song that first I sang.)

Of the many friends still happily with us to whom I feel deeply indebted, I cannot forbear to mention here Mr. Edward Howard Griggs, without whose timely and active assistance this translation would certainly not have seen the light of this memorial year.

M. B. A.

CONTENTS

Inferno

Cakto *rtoz*

Contents xiii

INFERNO.

Proem: Rescue Of Dante By Virgil

« '? u When half the journey of our life was donei" (-« I found me in a darkling wood astray, *h j* Because aside from the straight pathway runo

—Ah me, how hard a thing it is to say A

G«" What was this thorny wildwood intricate *C* w"" Whose memory renews the first dismay!

Scarcely in death is bitterness more great £ jl But as concerns tlre good discovered there

Qe. The other things I sawwill I related

How there I entered I am unaware,

So was I at that moment full of sleep

When I abandoned the true thoroughfare.

But when I reacht the bottom of a steep

Ending the valley which had overcome

My courage, piercing me with fear so deep,,

Lifting mine eyes up, I beheld its dome,4

Already covered with that pfehet's light

Which along all our pathways leads us home.

Then was a little quieted the fright

That had been lurking in the heart of me

Throughout the passage of the piteous night.

And as the panting castaway, if he
Escape the wave and on the shore arrive
Turns back and gazes on the perilous sea,
Even so my spirit, still a fugitive,
Turned back to look again upon the shore
That never left one person yet alive.
My weary frame somewhat refresht, once more
Along the solitary slope I plied . So that the firm foot ever was the lower. *'. Just what sins* And lo! where but begins the mountainside, »,; *tjfyt3* A leopard.Ught and very swift of pace *Va puted. EUe-*And coVeredwith a gayly spotted hide, jgjjjj *fa'wolf* Never/Withdrew she from before my face; *is the type oj* Nay; rather blockt she so my going on r *Method!* '"/...'That oft turned my footing to retrace. *means.all'forms-*'It was about the moment of the dawn; *.t&eT'* Uprose the sun and paled the light benignvv
'Me *of others.* Of those fair stars which were beside him yonv *whthhe'tLt* When took they motion first from Love Divine: *frequently stig-*So the sweet season and the time of day *o'the1ore.* Caused me to augur as a hopeful sign *the allegory here* That animal with skin bedappled gay: *cannot be merely* Yet not so much but that I felt dismayed, *personal* i-V P»_vJ To see a lion intercept my way. ft--*$?Z* L' 3 /» .
It seemed to me that he toward me made »
With head erected and with hunger raving,
So that the very air appeared afraid: jkW-
, nd jijheswojfj made gaunt by every craving
Wherewith methought she heavy-laden went,
And much folk hitherto of joy bereaving;
She brought on me so much discouragement
. f" By terror of her aspect that perforce
I forfeited all hope of the ascent.
And as one, interrupted in his course
Of winning, when his fortune is undone
Is full of perturbation and remorse,
That truceless beast made me such malison,
And coming on against me pace by pace *c.'* o Baffled me back where silent is the.sm v'f'
While I was falling back to that low place, & ""
A certain person there appearance made,,
Whose lengthened silence argued feebleness. V"»
When him I saw in the deserted glade,
"Have pity upon me!" I imploring cried,
"Whate'er thou beest, whether man or shade."
Dante's choice of Virgil as his guide is a noble instance of that humanity which is above all creeds. The Roman poet is made the type of human reason and he therefore retires, in the Earthly Paradise, in favor of Beatrice who typifies "the good of intellect," i.e. the knowledge of God
"Not man,—a man once was I," he replied,
"My parents both were born at Mantua,
And were of Lombard blood on either side. *Sub Julio* was I born, though late the day,
And under good Augustus lived at Rome
When false and lying deities bore sway. I was a poet: that just hero whom
Anchises sired, I sang, who came from Troy
After the burning of proud Eium, But why dost thou return to such annoy,
Wherefore ascend not the delightful Mount,
Beginning and occasion of all joy?"— "Art thou indeed that Virgil, and that fount
Whence pours of eloquence so broad a stream?"
I made reply to him with bashful front. "O of the other poets light supreme,
May the long study well avail me now *Oja-* JtjX *% e f*
And the great love that made thy book my theme™ » »" Thou art my Master and my Author thou, o-w fc-sVflP"'
And thou alone art he from wnom results
The goodly style whereto my honors owe. Behold the beast that doth my steps repulse:
Come to my help against her, famous sage,
For palpitates my every vein and pulse."— f'-
"AnothfiT-jouriiey must thy steps engage," v1--" 1
When he beheld me weeping, did he say,
"Wouldst from this savage place make pilgrimage; Because this beast whereat thou criest, gives way
Never to any comer, but doth sore
Impede and harass him until she slay.
Malignant is she so that nevermore
The craving of her appetite is fed,
And after food is hungrier than before.-i;j--r
Many are the animals that with her wed, w"''
And there shall yet be more, until the Hound
Shall come and in her misery strike her dead.
The Hound is to be' a great national deliverer, such as Dante at one time hoped Henry of Luxemburg would be. Here be 1 seems to have in mind Can Grande della Scala, but the '. reference is pur i posely vague
His food shall not be either pelf or ground
But what is loving, wise, and valorous: *j.f'*
Feltro and Feltro shall his nation bound. *S:* t
That Hflmble Italy preserves he thus.
For which the maid Camilla bit the dust,
Turnus and Nisus and Euryalus.X V""1""" k,"".
out of every city shall he thrust I
That beast, until he drive her back to Hell
Whence she was first let loose by envious lust.
Wherefore for thee I think and judge it well

Thou follow me, and I will bring about Thy passage thither where the eternal dwell.

There shall thou hearken the despairing shout,
Shalt see the souls of yore, each woeful guest
Who craving for the second death cry out. tjafc'-

Shalt see thereafter those who are at rest

Amid the flame, because their wishes bend *ft'V'*
To make them, whensoever, of the blest.

If then to these thou wishest to ascend,

For this a worthier soul than I shall wait, Jv tV
And with her will I leave thee at The end:

Because that Emperor who there holds state,
Seeing I was a rebel to His law,
Wills that through me none pass His City-gate.

There rules HisXove, as everywhere His Awe; N.

There in His Capital He sits on high:
Happy His chosen who may nigh Him draw."—

"O Poet, I entreat of thee," said I,

"By that Divinity thou didst not know,
So this and greater evil I may fly,

That where thou saidst I may a pilgrim go,
And led by thee Saint Peter's portal find,
And those thou makest out afflicted so. "—

Then moved he on, I following behind.

Dante Distrusts His Worthiness II
Virgil Describes The Appeal Of Beatrice

Day was departing and the dusk: air

Loosing the living things on earth that dwell

From their fatigues; and I alone was there Preparing to sustain the war, as well ft?.

Of the long way as also of the woe, *V*

Which now unerring memory will tell, O Muses! O high Genius, aid me now!

O Memory who wrote down what I did see, J

Herein all thy nobility will show. J

Now I began: "Poet who guidest me,

Look to my worth if it be plenteous,

Ere to the hard pass thou confidest me. Thou tellest that the Sire of Silvius

Went to the everlasting world, while still &jt»u *.1.4*

Corruptible, and in the body thus.

But that the Adversary of every ill

Should grace him so, viewing the issue high

And who he was and what he should fulfill, Seems not unfit to the understanding eye:

For he was father of imperial Rome

Elected in the empyrean sky, Founding that city and her masterdom

In sooth, for see and sanctuary blest

Of those who after greatest Peter come. U"' And by that going, which thou honorest,

He heard of things whereon were consequent His victory and then the Papal Vest.
There afterward the Chosen Veggej went ("(v .

Thence bringing comfort to that Faith supreme Which of salvation is the rudiment.
But wherefore I? Who grants me such a dream?
iEneas am I not, nor am I Paul,

Nor to myself or others worthy seem.
Time: Evening of Good Friday, 1300 That the Roman Empire is a fundamental part of the Divine plan for human redemption is a principle in Dante's philosophy of history, as wuH be fuUy Cantos vi and xviii of Paradiso Not mere fine
.phrasing; no
one could despise it more
Whence, if I dare to yield me to thy call,
I tremble lest the going prove insane:
My words are to the wise,—thou knowest all."—
And like to those who chop and change again
„1UA-y On second thoughts, unwilling former will,
And make their fair Wgimvng wbnlly vajn,

Such became I on that benighted hill:

Since, taking thought, I canceled the emprise
I was before so eager to fulfill.
"If I have comprehended thy replies,"
j jlrrA Returned that shadow oLthe4efty mind,
"Thy soul in caitiff apprehension lies,

Which oftentimes so baffles humaku$u W-u
They turn like animal false sight perceiving,
Leaving emprise of honor all behind.

To free thee from this timid misconceiving,

Let me now tell thee what my coming meant,
And what I heard of thee that set me grieving.
I was with those who are in Limbo pent,
-, i.»« When a fair Lady from the blest abode

Called me, and her command was my consent..

More brilliant than the star her glances glowed;
And gently and serenely she began
With voice angelic, in her own sweet mode:

'O courteous shade, soul of the Mantuan

Whose fame endures today in human ear,
And will endure as long as motion can,

One dear to me and not to fortune dear,
Is on the desert hillside in his way
So hindered that he has turned back for fear,

And may, alas! be now so far astray

That I am risen for his relief too late,
From what I hear the Heavenly voices say.

Now go, and with thine eloquence ornate,

And what may serve for his escape from woe,
Aid him, lest I should be disconsolate.
The Blessed Spirit Appeals to the Castaway 7

Myself am Beatrice who bid thee go;
than Dante did.

Thence come I, whither to return I sigh; £0Lto *Y'Z*"

' ' *the perfect utter*

Love prompted me and makes me urge thee so. *anes ofthe truth:*

When I shall be before my Lord on high "" *% chV*

Often will I invoke for thee His grace. — *organ of human* Thereat she paused, and I began reply: *reason*

'O Lady by virtue of whom the human race

Doth in nobility all things excel
Within the Heaven that rounds the smallest space, *Jf "'* 7

To do thy bidding pleases me so well

The deed were laggard if already done:

There is no further need thy wish to tell. But tell me rather why thou dost not shun

Descending to this center from the sphere

So wide, whereto thou burnest to be gone.'— 'Seeing it is thy will so far to peer,

I will proceed to tell thee,' she replied,

'Why fam not afraid to enter here. Of those things only fear is justified

Wherein is power of harming less or much: At nothing else need one be terrified.

By Grace Divine have I been fashioned such

That pangs me not the misery of you,

Nor can the flame of all this burning touch.o«- In Heaven there is a gentle Lady who *y-'.-m-i The blessed Vir*

Berues this barrier whence I bid thee fare, *n"ame,* iL *that*

So that she bursts'on high stern judgmentthrough. *of Christ, recurs* She summoned Lucy'to her in her prayer JSgPTrf1"'

And said: "Thy faithful one now needs tnee so *Poem, may not*

That I commend him to thy tender care."— *Hshhsl*

Lucy, of every cruelty the foe, *Likewise God is*

Arose and came where I had not been long *mmdy as "An*

With Rachel, who was set there long ago. *other." Santa*

"Beatrice," she said, "God's very choral song, *rs%Z*

Why help not him who had such love for thee *blyin Purg. ix,*

That he forsook for thee the vulgar throng? *seems* to"" *been a saint to* Dost thou not hear him weep in misery? y ro«i By Death upon a flood wild as the sea?"—

None ever in the world so swiftly sped

Avoiding hurt or questing benefit,

As came I, after suchlike words were said,

Speeding me down from where the blessed sit,

Trusting thy noble speech whose modest lore

Honors thyself, and others hearing it. '—

After she this had spoken, she forbore,

And, weeping, turned her shining eyes away,

Wherefore to come she made me hasten more;

And, coming to thee even as she did pray,

I drew thee from that beast which up the fair..

Mountain, bereft thee of the briefer way.-Sf

What ails thee then? ah, why, why tarry there?

Why harbor in thy heart such cowardice?

Why not take liberty to do and dare,

When cherish for thee so much care as this

In Court of Heaven three Ladies benedight, #,» And mine own speaking pledges thee such bliss?"— jy (Jtven as the flowerets by the chill of night *l&ir* Bended and closed, when brightens them the sun

Uplift both stem and petal to the light,

So with my drooping courage I had done

Already, and began like one set free,

So much good daring to my heart had run:,

"O deep compassion of her who succored me!

And courteous thou, promptly obedient

To the true words that she addressed to thee!

Thy words have with such ardent longing bent

My heart to the adventure that, in troth,

I have returned now to my first intent.

Now go, for one will animates us both:

Thou leader and thou lord and master mild!"—

So said I; and he moving, nothing loath

I entered on the pathway deep and wild.

The Entrance i m ef' 9 HI

The Dire Inscription And The Dark River

"Through me the way is to the city of woe;C-r; r

Through me the way unto eternal pain;

Through me the way among the lost below. Justice commovjed my high Creator, when

Made me Divine Omnipotence, combined

With Primal Love' and Wisdom Sovereign. Before me nothing was of any kind

Except eterne, and I eterne abide: Leave, ye that enter in, all hope behind!"

On high above a gateway I descried, V

Written in dusky color, this device: ' ' '

Whence I: "The sense is dire to me, O Guide!" Then answered he, as of expert advice:

"Here must thou every fear perforce neglect,

Here must perforce be killed all cowardice. Now come we where I taught thee to expect

To look upon the woeful populace

Who have forgone the good of intellect.".. tvY '(j ''. Laying his hand on mine with cheerful face,

Whence I was comforted, he made me keep

Right on and inward to the secret place. Here lamentations, sighs, and wailings deep

Resounding, so the starless welkin fill

That, at the first, I could not choose but weep. Strange languages, discoursings horrible,

Accents of anger, histories of woes,

Smiting of hands, with voices hoarse and shrill, Make a tumultuous roar that swirling goes

Forever in that air of endless night,

Like to the sandblast when the whirlwind blows. And I, my temples girded with affright,

Said: "Master, what is this, and who may be

The folk who seem in such a woeful plight?"

"The melancholy souls," then answered he, *y* "Of those enduring this condition dire, *f* / Lived void of honor and of infamy.

r-V.S . They are commingled with that caitiff quire

Of angels, who nowise rebellious were,

Nor leal to God, but all for self-desire.

The Heavens to keep their beauty from impair,

Banned them, nor harbors them the deep of Hell. Because the damned some boast of them would bear."

"Master," said I, "what grievance is so fell

To these, that their lament should be so great?"

He answered: "I will very briefly tell.

These have no hope of death; and this their state

Of blind existence is degraded so,

They are envious of every other fate.

Report of them the world does not allow;

Mercy and Justice hold them in disdain:

Let us not speak of them, but look, and go."

And I beheld, on looking there again,

A whirling banner running swiftly on,

As scorning all delay; and such a train

Of people in pursuit of it that run,

Nothing but seeing could belief persuade

That ever Death so many had fordone.

And recognizing some, I saw a shade

In whom detected I that one of these *The Great Re-*Who cravenly the Great Refusal made.

!inmTkt Pope This was « sect of caitiffs. wno displease — *('destine V,* As now forthwith I understood and knew,—*trJaTtba-*Not God alone but al l His enemies. *My managed by* Wretches who never were alive, and who *f* A *hlSc-cZ?Boni-*W«e sorely stung upon their bodies nude *i/J faceVIII.achief* By hornets and by wasps that thither new. *Kj 0MepoeZcfUt* These caused their vs to stream with blood, *scorn and de-*Which, mixed with tears, was gathered at their feet

By vermin, foul and loathsome multitude.

nunciafion Charon 11

And now my glances, pushing further, meet

People upon the marge of a great stream;

Whence I: "Now tell me, Master, I entreat, What folk are these, and by what rule they seem

So eager on the passage to be gone,

As I distinguish by the feeble gleam.

" And he to me: "These matters shall be known. *-»*

Unto thee, when we stay from our advance w X«y

Upon the woeful marge of Aefaejpj," gfAr *-+)* Thereon with downcast eyes and modest glance,

Fearing my words were irksome to him, I

Far as the stream refrained from utterance. And lo! upon a bark approaching nigh,

One white with ancient tresses, passing old:

"Woe to:you wicked spirits!" was his cry. "Hope nevermore the Heavens to behold:

I come to lead you to the other bank,

Into eternal darkness, heat, and cold.

And thou, O living spirit, from the rank

Dispart thee, of these others who are dead."

And when he saw me not as one who shrank: ""Til" "Another way, by other ports," he said, »

"Not here, shalt come for ferriage to the shore:

Upon a lighter keel must thou be sped." "Vex thee not, Charon," said my Monitor:

"Thus it is willed where will is one and same

With potence to fulfill,—and ask no more." Then quieted the shaggy cheeks became,

Of him, the boatman of the marish dark,

Who round about his eyes had wheels of flame. But all those spirits, so forworn and stark,

Change color and their teeth are chattering, As soon as they the cruel accents mark.

God they blaspheme and their own sires, and fling

Curses on race and place and time and law

Both of their birth and their engendering.

Then, flocking all together, they withdraw,

Bitterly weeping, to the cursed shore

Awaiting each who holds not God in awe.

Charon, the demon, with the eyes that glow'r,

Beckoning to them, every one receives,

And smites whoever lingers, with the oar.

As in the autumn season when the leaves,

First one and then another, lightly fall,

, Till all upon the ground the bough perceives: */-mu*

Likewise the evil seed of Adam all

Fling them from off that margin one by one

At signals, like the bird at his recall.

Thus over the dusk water they are gone,

And ere they can alight on yonder strand

Forgathers a fresh throng on this anon.

"Son," said the courteous Master, "understand

That those who perish subject to God's ire

Are all assembled here from every land,

And ready are to pass the river dire,

Because Celestial Justice so doth goad

That very fear converts into desire.

No righteous spirit ever takes this road:

And hence, though Charon may of thee complain,

Thou knowest now the meaning of his mode."—

When he had ended, all the dreary plain
So trembled that, but calling it to mind,
The terror bathes me now with sweat again.
The land of tears gave forth a blast of wind
With lightning flashes of vermilion deep,
Whence consciousness I utterly resigned:
Then sank I like one overcome with sleep.

"Now go we down among the people blind" 13 IV

First Circle: Limbo; The Virtuous Pagans

A pealing burst of thunder loosed my sense
From chains of heavy sleep, and made me bound
Like one who is awakt by violence:
And, risen erect, on every side around
I moved my rested eye, and fixed my sight
To recognize the features of that ground.
True is it that I stood upon the height
Above the valley of the Abyss of Woe,
Which gathers roari of wailing infinite.
It was so dark, deep, cloudy, that although
My gaze upon the bottom I confined,
Not anything discerned I there below.
"Now go we down among the people blind,"
Began the Poet, pallid as the dead:
"I will go first, and follow thou behind. "
And I, observant of his pallor, said:
"How shall I come if thou afraid appear,
By whom I am wonted to be comforted?"
"The anguish of the people downward here,
Portrays upon my face," said he at this,
"That pjjy which thou deemest to be fear.
The long way urges: come, be not remiss."
Thus he set forth, and made me enter thus,
The foremost circle that begirds the abyss.
Here was no sound perceptible to us
Of wailing, only sighs and sighs again,
That made the eternal air all tremulous:
And this arose from woe unpanged with pain,(?& v
Felt by the great and thronging multitude
Of children and of women and of men.
"Askest thou not," resumed the Master good,
"What spirits these may be thou dost behold?
Now ere thou go, I wish it understood
Though these sinned not, their merit manifold
Doth not, for want of Baptism, signify,—
The portal of the faith which thou dost hold
They worshipt God but through idolatry,
Seeing they were to Christian ages prior:
And among such as these myself am I.
For such defects, and for no trespass dire,
Lost are we, suffering no more but so, *jrlt*
That without hope we languish in desire."""'
On hearing this, laid hold on me great woe,
For very worthy people knew I well,
Suspended in that Limbo there below.
"O tell me, Lord, O Master, speak and tell"
Began I, wishing full intelligence
About the faith that doth all error quell,
"Went ever any by self-merit hence,
Or by another's, to a blissful fate?"
And he, who understood my covert sense,
Made answer: "I was new unto this state,
When I beheld One come omnipotent,
With sign of victory incoronate.
The shade of our first father penitent, Jl
Abel his son and Noah, hence He drew; &
Moses the lawgiver obedient;
Patriarch Abraham, King David too; 0 *ifa*
Israel with his sire, with every son, t/""
With Rachel for whose sake such pains he knew,
And many more, and gave them benison:
And thou must know that earlier than these,
Never a human soul salvation won."
Not for his speaking, did our going cease,
But ever through the Jorest did we fare,—
The forest, I mean, where spirits were the trees.
We had not traveled far as yet from where
Wt My sleep befell, when I beheld ajblaze
iVT' Which conquered from the dark a hemisphere.

Dante Received among the Great Poets 15

U#»r'w' We still were distant by a little space, p % —"
Yet not so far but I discerned in part
That honorable people held that place. aO thou who honorest both science and art,
Who may these be that so great honor claim,
Thus set from fashion of the rest apart?" And he to me: "The honorable fame
Concerning them that in thy life doth ring,
Wins grace in Heaven that so advances them." Hereon I heard a voice thus heralding:
"Honor to him of poets loftiest! H-—
HisiEa3e returneth home from wandering." After the voice had ceast and was at rest,
Four mighty shades advancing did I see,
In whom nor grief nor joy was manifest. (_'-""' The Master good began to say to me:
"Mark him there, carrying that sword in hand,
Who, as their lord, comes on before the three: Tis Homer, sovran bard of every land,
Horace next after him, satiric wit,

Third Ovid, Li 1 can last of all the band. Since unto each doth, as to me, befit

The name the one voice sounded, in such wise Tney do me honorj and do well in it."

Thus gathered the fair school before mine eyes,

Of him, the lord of song the loftiest,

Who o'er the others like an eagle flies. When they had talkt awhile with him, the rest

To me with signs of salutation bent;

Whereat my Master's smile his mind expresst. They paid me honor far more eminent,

In that they made me of their brotherhood:

So I was sixth of them, the sapient. Toward the light we thus our way pursued,

Discoursing things whereof fits reticence,

Even as there to speak of them was good.

y) The gates of the We gained a castle's grand circumference, *tastle, con-*With seven lofty walls encircled round, _ *cewed an a mag-.,, Ikt nificent $Jni-*Bemoated with a brooklet for defense." *Wnwtal* This passed we over as upon dry ground:

*arts of the Triv-*Through seven gates I with those sages went;

tglcketarkj A meadow of & verdure there we found. *andtheQuadriv-*People were there of aspect eminent, *fZlSri-faT"" Wlih* evesthat moved majestical and slow: *tronomy'.munc).* Taciturn, but with voices sweetly blent. *These formed* A fe to One sjde wIthdrew we *me regular curriculum of the* Into an open place, and high and sheen, *schools, as being* m d y;ht feh y d / *the avenues* to. *ASmmml all human* There opposite, upon the enameled green, Vl *knowledge* Were shown to me the mighty souls, whom I

Feel inwardly exalted to have seen. J»jl, 1 saw Electra with much people.by,

Hector among them, and iEneas descried, And armored Caesar with the falcon eye.

Camill', Penthesilea, I espied;

Over against them King Latinus dwelled, , Lavinia, his daughter, by.h

I saw that BraTOs-Tarquin wno

his side.

Tarquin wno expelled; *J*

Lucrece, Cornelia, Julia, Marcia; then

Alone, apart, great Saladin beheld. *x "*

And when I lifted up my brows again,

The Magter I beheld of those who know, Sitting amid the philosophic train.

All look to him, to him all honor show:

Here saw I Plato, Socrates advance,

"4 Who nearer him before the others go;

Democritus, who puts the world on chance,

Anaxagoras and Diogenes I saw;

Dioscorides, collector good of plants;

Thales, and Zeno of the Stoic law;

Orpheus, Heraclitus, Empedocles,

Tully, and Linus, andlbioral Seneca;

"The word comes short of thought" 17

Euclid, geometer; Hippocrates,

Ptolemy, Avicen, Galen; him who wrought

The Commentary great, Averroes.*-r A &r-ML*

In full concerning all report I not,

For the long theme impels me forward: thus

Many a time the word comes short of thought.

The band of six gives place to two of us:

My sage Guide leads me by another way

Forth from the still air to the tremulous;

And now I come where shines no light of day.

V

Second Circle: Francesca Da Rimini

From the first circle thus I made descent

Down to the second, whose contracted rim

Girdles so much more woe it goads lament.

There Minos stands and snarls with clamor grim,

Examines the transgressions at the gate,

Judges, and sends as he encircles him.

Yea, when the spirit born to evil fate

Before him comes confessing all, that fell

Distinguisher among the reprobate,

Seeing what place belongs to it in Hell,

Entwines him with his tail such times as show

How many circles down he bids it dwell.

Always before him many wait; they go

All turn by turn to sentence for their sin:

They tell and hear and then are whirled below.

"O thou that comest to the woeful inn!"

As soon as he beheld me, Minos cried,

Leaving the act of so great discipline,

"Beware to enter, beware in whom confide,

Be not deceived by wideness of the door."—

"Why dost thou also clamor?" said my Guide,

"Bar not his going fated from before:

Thus it is willed up yonder where is might

To bring the will to pass, and ask no more."—

And now the notes of woe begin to smite

The hollow of mine ear; now am I come

Where I am pierced by wailings infinite.

I came into a place of all light dumb,

Which bellows like a sea where thunders roll

And counter-winds contend for masterdom.

The infernal hurricane beyond control

Sweeps on and on with ravishment malign

Whirling and buffeting each hapless soul.

"Blown with restless violence11 19

When by the headlong tempest hurled supine,

Here are the shrieks, the moaning, the laments,

Here they blaspheme the puissance divine.

I learned that to such sorry recompense

Are damned the sinners of the carnal sting,

Who make the reason thrall to appetence.

And as great flocks of starlings on the

wing
In winter time together trooping go,
So did that blast the wicked spirits fling
Now here, now there, now up, and now below:
Comfort of hope to them is never known
Either of rest or even less bitter woe.
And as the pilgrim cranes from zone to zone
Draw out their aery file and chant the dirge,
So saw I, and I heard them making moan,
Shadows who on that storm-blast whirl and surge:
Whence I: "Who, Master, are those tempest-flung, Round whom the black air whistles like a scourge?"—
"The first," said he, "that multitude among,
Of whom thou seekest knowledge more precise,
Was empress over many a tribe and tongue.
Abandoned so was she to wanton vice
That, her own stigma so to wipe away,
Lust was made licit by her law device.
That is Semiramis,—as annals say
Consort of Ninus and successor too;
Where governs now the Soldan, she held sway.
The next one, lo! herself for love she slew
And to Sichaeus' urn her faith dismissed;
Next wanton Cleopatra comes to view;
Now lookest thou on Helen, whose acquist
Brought evil years; and great Achilles see
Who found in Love his last antagonist.
Look, Paris, Tristan..." and he pointed me
A thousand shades, and named me every name,
Who in our life gave Love the victory.
, f.v,. When I had heard my Teacher many a dame Of eld enumerate, and many a knight, / ""-Pity assailed me and almost overcame.
I — "Poet," began I, "fain would I invite
Speech with those twain who go a single way
And seem upon the wind to be so light. "—
And he made answer: "Thou shalt mark when they
Draw near to us, and then adjure them by
The Love that leads them, and they will obey."-
Thereafter when a whirlwind swept them nigh
I lifted up my voice: "O souls forspent,
Come and have speech with us if none deny."—
As doves to the heart's call obedient
Are borne along to the beloved nest
On wide and steady pinions homeward bent,
So these came tow'rd us through the air unblest,
Veering from Dido and her multitude,
So tender and so strong was my request.
"O living creature full of grace and good
Who goest through the dusk air visiting
Us who left earth encrimsoned with our blood,
If friendly were the Universal King
We would be praying to Him for thy peace,
Seeing thou pitiest our suffering.
Whatever ye to speak and hear may please, *Ravenna, where* That will we speak and hear you close at hand, *Dante spent his* If t *&yfMe* the d as nOW cease toiler *years* in *the service or* The town where I was born sits on the strand *under the pro-*Beside the water here descends the pQ *tection qj ii3 lord, Guido* . In quest of peace, with his companion band.
as *tPz*'Lwe that in sentie heart is soon agiow o/ *Francesco.* Laid hold on this one for the person fair *faahtesf hef* Beref l me,and the mode is stil l my woe *grievous to her* Love that doth none beloved from loving spare, *Mh%* tf a To do him pleasure made my heart so f ain *chance* to *repent* That, as thou seest, not yet doth it forbear. *Francesca* 21
Love led us down to death together: Cain
Awaits the soul of him who laid us dead."—
These words from them to us returned again.
Hearing those injured souls, I bowed my head
And held it for so long dejectedly
That, "Whereon thinkest thou?" the Poet said.
When I could answer, I began: "Ah me,
How many tender thoughts, what longing drew
These lovers to the pass of agony."—
Thereafter I turned to them, and spoke anew:
"Francesca, all thy torments dim mine eyes
With tears that flow for sympathy and rue.
But tell me, in the time of the sweet sighs IBy what, and how did Love to you disclose The vague desires, that ye should realize?"— she to me: "It is the woe of woes
Remembrance of the happy time to keep
In misery,—and that thy Teacher knows. But if thy yearning be indeed so deep
To know the first root of a love so dear, I will do even as they who speak and weep.
One day together read we for good cheer
.J Of Love, how he laid hold on Launcelot:
Alone we were and without any fear.
Many and many a time that reading brought
Our eyes to meet, and blancht our faces o'er,
But only one point we resisted not.
When reading of the smile long-waited-for
Being kissed by such a lover chivalrous,
He, never now from me divided more, Kissed me upon the mouth, all tremulous...
Gallehaut was the book and writer too:
That day there was no reading more for us."— And while one soul was saying this, for rue
So wept the other, that I fainted all

For pity, even as dying persons do,
And fell, as would a lifeless body fall.

VI

Third Circle: The Intemperate

On coming to my senses, closed at sight
Deplorable of them, the kindred twain,
Pity for whom had overwhelmed me quite,
New souls in torment and new modes of pain
Wherever I am moving I behold,
Wherever I turn and look about again.
In the Third Circle am I, where the cold
Eternal cursed heavy rain doth flow,
In mode and measure ever as of old.
Thick hail and turbid water-drops and snow
Down through the darkling air forever fall;
Foul stench receives them on the ground below.
Cerberus, fierce and monstrous animal,
With triple gullet barks in currish wise
Above the people here submerged withal.
Greasy and black his beard, and red his eyes,
And belly big, and fingers clawed amain:
Clutching the spirits, he doth rend and slice.
Howling like dogs by reason of the rain,
They shelter one side with the other,—thus
Turn back and forth the reprobates profane.
The open-mouthed great dragon Cerberus
Displayed his fangs, what time he us descried:
No limb had he that was not tremulous.
And, spreading palms and fingers out, my Guide
Took earth up and, full-fisted, flung it right
Into those gullets ravenous and wide.
As dog that barks for craving appetite
Grows quiet setting tooth upon his food,
For but to gorge it doth he tug and fight,
So quiet grew those faces, filth-imbrued,
Of Demon Cerberus, who bellows so
The spirits would be deaf if they but could.

Prophecy of Ciacco 23

We passed above the shadows whom below
The heavy rain is beating, treading down
What seems a body, but is empty show.
Prone on the bottom lay they every one,
Except that sudden sat erect one shade
As soon as it perceived us passing on.
"O thou who through this Hell art led," it prayed,
"Recall me, if thou canst, to memory:
Or ever I was unmade, wast thou made. "
"Perchance," said I, "the anguish thou dost dree,
Doth from my memory thy form efface
So that, it seems, I never looked on thee.
But tell me who thou art, that in a place
So woeful liest, punished in such plight
That none, though greater, were so much disgrace."
"Thy city," he returned, "distended quite
With envy till the sack no more can hold,
Held me as hers, when life to me was bright.
Ciacco, ye citizens called me of old:
For the pernicious guilt of gluttony
The rain subdues me, as thou dost behold.
And, wretched spirit, not alone am I,
Since for like guilt these suffer, all and some,
Like punishment:" no more he made reply.
"Ciacco," I answered him, "thy martyrdom
Doth weigh me down to tears compassionate:
But tell me, if thou knowest, to what will come
The citizens of ie divided state?
If any one therein be just? and whence
Such mighty discord makes it desolate?"
And he to me: "After long turbulence
There will be bloodshed, and the rustics, they
Will drive the others forth, with much offense.
Thereafter it behooves them fall away
Within three suns, and the others rise again
Thanks to a certain one who trims today.

This prophecy refers to incidents in the bitter, fluctuating, dramatic struggle for mastery in Florence between the aristocratic Black Guelfs, captained by Corso Donati, and the Whites, led by the Cerchi,— whose rustic origin is so often referred to as to convince us that they retained some of the faults of breeding that stamp in all ages the newly rich.— The trimmer is Pope Boniface. Who the two just men are is matter of conjecture. We shall meet all but one of the celebrities referred to by name

Long while shall they a lofty front maintain,
Keeping the former, spite of tears and shame,
'Neath heavy fardels bended down amain.
The just are two, but none gives heed to them:
Envy and avarice and arrogance
Are triple sparks that set all hearts aflame."
Here ended he the sad deliverance.
And I: "Pray thee, instruct me further forth,—
I crave the guerdon of more utterance.
Of Tegghiaio and Farinata, men of worth,
Of Rusticucci, Arrigo, Mosca, tell,
And of the others who brought good to birth,
Where are they,—cause that I may know them well:
For great desire constrains me to descry
If Heaven may soothe them, or envenom Hell."
"They are among the souls of blackest dye,
Whom sins diverse down to the bottom weigh:
Thou mayst behold them, going down where they lie.

But when thou art in the sweet world, I pray
That thou wilt bring me back to human mind:
No more I answer thee, no more I say."
His straight eyes thereupon aslant inclined,
Awhile he scanned me; then did headlong fall
Down to the level of the other blind.
"No more," my Leader said, "he waken shall
This side of the angelic trumpet sound.
When shall arrive the judge inimical
Each one shall in his dismal tomb be found,
His flesh and outward figure reassume,
And hear what shall eternally resound."
So fared we onward through that filthy scum
Of shadows and of sleet, with footing slow,
Touching a little on the life to come.
Wherefore I questioned: "Master, will this woe
After the mighty Judgment grow amain,
Or less become, or burning be just so?"
Unrelenting Justice 25
"Turn to thy science," answered he again,
"Which holds&he more complete the thing, the more
It feels of pleasure, and the like of pain.
Though these accursed people nevermore
Reach true perfection, after that event
They look to be completer than before."
A circling course along that road we went,
Speaking far more than may repeated be;
Then came we to the point of the descent,
And here found Plutus the arch-enemy.
VII
Fourth Circle: The Parsimonious And The
'Prodigal
"Pape Satan Pape Satan aleppe!"
Thus Plutus' clucking voice beginning went;
And that benignant Sage, experienced
In all things, said for my encouragement:
"Fear not, for any war that he may wage
Shall not prohibit thee the rock's descent."
Then to that bloated visage turned my Sage,
And said: "Accursed wolf, be not so loud!
And be thou gnawed within by thine own rage.
Not without cause this going is allowed:
Thus it is willed above where Michael
Wrought vengeance for the deed of whoredom proud."—
As ocean-faring sails, which the winds swell,
Would fall entangled should the mainmast crack,
So to the ground the cruel monster fell.
Descending into the Fourth Gap, we track
Still farther that declivity of woe
Which doth our universal guilt ensack.
Justice Divine! can any there below
Heap up such penalties and travail new? And why does guilt of ours consume us so?
As on Charybdis yonder surges do,
Each against other shattering its crest,
So here the folk their counter-dance pursue.
Here saw I people more than all the rest
Who from each quarter, with a howling din,
Were trundling burdens by main force of breast.
They clash together, and then both begin
The counter-movement, rolling back again, Shouting: "Why throw away?" and "Why hold in?"— *Transient Farce of Getting and Spending* 27
So on both sides they circle to regain
The point opposed, along the dismal mew,
Still shouting their opprobrious refrain:
Then as along his semicircle drew
Each one to the other joust, he wheeled withal.
And I, who felt my heart as stricken through,
Said: "Master mine, now tell me, who may all
These people be? and on our left-hand side
These shaven crowns,—were they all clerical?"—
"All these were in the first life," he replied,
"Of mind so squinting that the middle route
Of measured spending could not be espied.
With voice exceeding clear they bark this out,
When to the two points of the circle come,
Where counter-crime compels them turn about.
These heads bereft of hair were, all and some,
Priests, popes, and cardinals, whose practices
Show avarice in sovereign masterdom."
Then said I: "Master, among such as these
There surely must be some I ought to know,
Who were defiled with these iniquities.
"
And he to me: "Vain thoughts combinest thou:
The purblind life that made them sordid there
Bedims them to all recognition now.
To the two buttings will they ever fare;
Out of the sepulcher will these arise
Close-fisted, even as those with scissored hair.
Ill-giving and keeping ill have Paradise
Bereft them, and in such a scuffle joined:
No beauteous phrase to grace it I devise.
How transient is the farce, here mayst thou find,
Of goods committed unto Fortune, son,
Whence buffet one another humankind.
For all the gold the moon looks down upon,
Or that did ever in the world ejdst,
Could of these weary souls give rest to none."
Cropt hair is a symbol of lavishness. "He has spent his whole substance, even to the hair of his head" (Italian saying) Fortune, re-"Master, now tell me more," did I insist: *aTdL "inidli-*"This

Fortune whereunto thou dost allude, *gence whose* What is she, with the world's wealth in her fist?
brintZJL1? And he to me: "O foolish human brood, *mighty and exalt* What ignorance is this wherein ye pine! *theof low* Now let my judgment of her be thy food._
He whose transcendent wisdom is divine,
Fashioned the skies, and gave them those wk guide
That every part to every part may shine,
So equally do they the light divide;
Likewise for earthly grandeur did ordain
A common regent, who, as times betide,
Might work vicissitude of treasures vain,
That they from people and from kindred pass,
Beyond all human prudence to restrain.
Whence rules one race, another cries 'Alas!'
Obeying her decree, the circumstance
Whereof is hidden, like the snake in grass.
Your wisdom can no counterstand advance:
She looks beforehand, judges, and pursues,
As do the other gods, her governance.
Her permutations have not any truce:
Necessity makes her precipitate,
With frequent turns of luck at fast and loose.
Such is that one against whom people prate
Who rather ought to praise her, doing amiss
To deal in blame and to vituperate.
But she is blest and takes no heed of this:
With other primal creatures jocundly
She rolls her wheel, rejoicing in her bliss.
Now go we down to deeper misery:
Already sinks each star that made ascent
When I set forth,—no loitering may be.
"
Across the circle to the bound we went,
Above a bubbling fountain that careered
Down through a gully where it found a vent.
The Sordid Fen 29
The water far more dark than perse appeared:
And as the dusky waves companioned us,
We entered downward by a pathway weird. A marish, Styx by name, this dolorous
Rivulet fosters when its waters flow
To foot of the gray slope precipitous.
And standing there intently gazing, lo!
I saw a folk bemired upon that fen,
All of them naked, and with look of woe. Each smote his fellow with the hand, and then
With both the feet and with the chest and head,
Rending with teeth and rending once again. "Now seest thou, son," the kindly Master said, *The Wrathful*
"The souls of those whom Wrath did overquell:
And I would also have it credited
That underneath the water people dwell
Who sigh, and make it bubble at the brim,
As wheresoe'er it turn, thine eye may tell. Fixt in the ooze, they murmur forth this hymn:
'Sweet sun-rejoicing air did we respire
Sullenly, drowned in sluggish vapors grim: Now lie we sullen here in the black mire.'
They gurgle in their gullets this refrain,
Because they cannot speak with words entire." Thus, in wide compass round the filthy fen,
Between the dry bank and the bog we passed,
Scanning the guzzlers of the puddle: then We reacht the bottom of a tower at last.
and the Sullen Filippo Argenti, of the great house of the Adimari, a VIII
Fifth Circle: The Wrathful
Long while before (I say continuing)
We reacht the bottom of that tower so high,
Our gaze upon its top was lingering
By reason of two lights we could descry;
And other signal gleamed far opposite,
So far away it hardly caught the eye.
Turned to that Sea of Wisdom infinite,
I said: "What means this? what may answered *b:*
By yonder beacon? and who kindled it?"
"The thing we await thou mayst already see
Over the turbid waves," he answered, "so
The marish-vapor hide it not from thee.
"
Cord never shot an arrow from the bow
That ran so swift a course athwart the air,
As o'er the water at that moment, lo!
I saw a little bark toward us fare,
Under a single boatman's pilotage,
Who shouted: "Now, fell spirit, art thou there?"
'Phlegyas, Phlegyas," replied to him my Sage,
"This time thou shoutest vainly: it is meet
Thou have us but to pass the ferriage."
As one who listens to some foul deceit
That has been done him, and resents it sore,
Such became Phlegyas in his gathered heat.
Embarking thereupon my Monitor
Caused me to take my station at his side,—
And only then the boat seemed laden more.
When I was in the wherry with my Guide,
The ancient prow upon the passage sped,
More than with others furrowing the tide.
While we were running through the channel dead,
Arose before me one whom mud did steep:
"Who art thou, coming ere thy time?" he said.
And I: "Though come, I stay not in the deep: *swaggering, in*
But who art thou who art grown filthy so?" Stota

And he: "Thou seest that I am one who weep." *with silver* Then I to him: "With weeping and with woe

Accursed spirit, tarry here for aye:

For thee, all filthy as thou art, I know. "— Then stretcht he forth both hands, the boat to stay:

But him my wary Master from us pressed,

Crying: "Away, with the other dogs, away!" Then said: "Indignant soul!" as he caressed

My bosom with embrace, my cheek with kiss,

"Blessed be she that bore thee 'neath her breast! A person arrogant on earth was this;

His memory is graced with nothing kind:

So likewise here his shade in fury is. Up there how many who are in their mind

Great kings, shall wallow here in mire like swine, Leaving a horrible report behind."

"Much should I like," said I, "O Master mine,

To see him in this hellbroth dipt and dyed,

Before we issue from the marsh malign." And he to me: "Thou shalt be satisfied

Ere comes the shore to view; it is not fit

That such desire of thine should be denied." Short while thereafter I beheld him smit

By that bespattered folk with stroke so fell

That still I praise and thank my God for it. "At Philip Argenti! at him!" all did yell:

That spirit Florentine exasperate

Turned on his very self with tooth and nail. We left him there, nor more do I narrate:

But lamentation smote mine ears upon,

Whence I look forward with mine eyes dilate. And the good Master said: "Now, O my son,

The city named of Dis is nigh at hand,

With heavy citizens, great garrison. " *The reference to* And I: "Already in the valley stand *Z cZpiuto?* Its mosques, O Master, and to me they show *the Infernal* Vermilion, as if issuing from the brand." *fzszjJu* And he made answer: "The etemai eiow *the elaborate* Of inward flame kindles that ruddy glare, *IS-SZiSi* A-thou perceivest in this Hell below." *Heaven and* Then came we into the deep fosses, where *if Goslandthose* They compass round that town disconsolate: *of Lucifer,* The walls appeared to me of iron there.

featrTof Not without making first a circuit great, *Dante's art. To* We came unto a place where loudly cried *tdM Chtt* The boatman: "Get ye out, here is the gate." *tian the mosque* I saw above the portals and beside,

Irii&dfiEEJ" Thousands rained down from Heaven, who wrath *Thus Bell has* ful said: *"mfofAe* aWho is this man that, never havin& died, *"college" of the* Is going through the kingdom of the dead?" JSSSflSJ And my sage Master signaled he would fain *goes so far as to* Talk with them privately.—Thus they were led *ZtinluZn.* A little tG abate thdr 8"»t *», of the Church to* And cried: "Come thou alone; let him go back

Sri Waohas made boid to enter this domain *Christ and* Alone shall he retrace his reckless track: *ItnTof* (Cto Let mm attempt it; *r* thou here shalt stay *xxxiv)* Who hast revealed to him a land so black."

Imagine, Reader, what was my dismay

At hearing that accursed language: for

I felt that I could never find the way.

"O my beloved Leader, thou who more

Than seven times hast made me safe, and hast

Rescued from peril deep," did I implore,

"Do not forsake me thus undone at last;

And if the going farther be denied,

Let us retrace our steps together fast."

And that Lord who had thither been my Guide,

Answered: "Fear nothing, for the way we go

By Such is given, none turneth us aside.

Wait here, and let thy soul, forwearied so,

Be fed with better hope and comforted:

I will not leave thee in the world below. "

And thus the gentle Father forth is sped,

There leaving me who in conjecture dwell;

For Yes and No contend within my head.

What he proposed to them I could not tell;

But long he had not tarried with them, when

Back inwards all went scurrying pell-mell.

The gates they shut, those enemies of men,

On my Lord's bosom, who, excluded thence,

With tardy steps returned to me again.

His eyes were on the ground, of confidence

His forehead shorn, and amid sighs he spake:

"Who has denied me the grim tenements?"

And then to me: "What though my wrath awake,

Be not dismayed, for I shall find the way,

Whatever obstacle within they make.

This insolence is nothing new, for they

Displayed it at less hidden gate of yore,

Which stands unbolted to this very day.

Thou sawest the deadly writ above the door;

And now descends the steep upon this side,

Passing without a guide the circles o'er,

One who shall fling the city open wide." *Virgil's repulse here seems to shadow forth a spiritual crisis so terrible thai the noblest human reason is unavailing. There are dreadful gates where the wisest can only cast his eyes to the ground. In tin, middle of the next Canto the Poet emphasizes the importance of the allegory in this crucial passage* IX

Sixth Circle: The Furies And The Angel.

The cowardice that blancht my outward hue

On seeing my Conductor back repair,
The sooner checkt in him his color new.
As listening, he stopt attentive there,
Because the vision not far forth could roam Through the thick murk and through the darkling air.
"Yet we must gain perforce the masterdom,"
Began he: "Nay but... so great help was sent...
Oh, long it seems until that Other come!"—
I plainly saw how what at first he meant,
He sought with after thoughts to cancel through
In phrases from the former different.
But still his language roused my fear anew,
For in the broken phrase I traced a scope
Perchance more harmful than he had in view.
"Into this hollow, down the dismal slope
Comes ever any one from the first grade
Whose only punishment is crippled hope?"
So questioned I; and this reply he made:
"Rarely does any out of our abode
Journey, as I am doing, to this glade.
Once previously, indeed, I took this road
Conjured by that Erichtho void of grace
Who erst their bodies to the shades bestowed.
My flesh was bare of me but little space,
When she compelled me enter yonder mure,
To draw a spirit forth from Judas' place.
That is the lowest round, and most obscure,
And farthest from the all-circling Heaven: the path
I know full well: therefore be thou secure.
This marish, breathing forth the fetid scath,
Begirds the woeful city of the dead,
Where now we cannot enter without wrath."
I bear not now in mind what more he said,
Because so fast were riveted mine eyes
To that high tower with summit glowing red,
Where on a sudden up erect arise
Infernal Furies three of bloody dye,
Who have the limbs of women and their guise;
Bright green the hydras they are girded by;
Little horned serpents pleated in a braid
Like tresses round their cruel temples lie.
And recognizing every cruel maid
Of her, the Queen of everlasting woe,
"Behold," he bade me, "the Erinyes dread.
This is Megaera on the left, and lo!
Alecto weeping yonder on the right;
Tisiphone is between," he ended so.
Each with her talons rips her breast; they smite
Upon themselves with palms, so loudly wailing
That close I press the Poet in affright.
"Medusa come, with stone his body scaling,"
All shouted looking downward; "to our bane
Avenged we not on Theseus his assailing."
"Turn round, and let thine eyes close shut remain:
For should the Gorgon come, and shouldst thou see,
There would be no returning up again."
Thus said the Master; and thereafter he
Turned me, nor trusted to my hands alone,
But also with his own blindfolded me.
O ye who hold sane intellect your own,
Consider needfully the hidden lore
Whereon the veil of the strange verse is thrown!
And now there came the troubled waters o'er
A crashing clangor of a fearful kind,
Whereat were trembling yon and hither shore:
Not otherwise it was than when the wind,
By dint of adverse heats grown wild and high,
Tosses the forest boughs, and unconfined

It seems to be agreed that the Furies represent pangs of conscience. But what is the Got gont Some say, Doubt, which turns the heart to stone; others malce it an emblem of the hard ening effect of Despair. The modern psychoanalyst might term it the Medusa-complex, and bring about the opening of the gate without the intervention of the Messenger of Heaven. But his coming is one oj the high points of the Poem

Shatters, and dashes down, and sweeps them by:
Superbly whirls along in dust and gloom,
Making the wild beasts and the shepherds fly.
He loosed mine eyes: "Across that ancient foam
Be now the nerve of sight directed yond,"
He bade me, "where most pungent is the fume."
As frogs before their serpent-foe abscond,
All slipping through the water in retreat
Till squatted on the bottom of the pond,
So saw I thousands of lost spirits fleet
Away before a Certain One who plied
Over the Stygian ford with unwet feet.
He often fanned that fetid air aside,
By waving the left hand before his face,
And only with that trouble seemed annoyed.
Well I perceived him sent from Heavenly place,
And turned me to the Master, who made sign
That I stand quiet and my knees abase.
Ah, how he seemed replete with scorn condign!
When with a little wand he touched the gate
It opened,—nor came any to confine.
"O abject race, from Heaven how alienate!"
Began he, standing on the horrible sill,
"How harbor ye this insolence so great?
Wherefore recalcitrate against that Will
Which from its purpose never can be shut,
And which has many a time increased

your ill?
What profits it against the Fates to butt?
For this your Cerberus, as well ye ween.
Is going yet with chin and gullet cut."
Then he turned back along the way obscene
Speaking no word to us, but did advance
Like one constrained and urged by care more keen
Than that of him soliciting his glance.
And we went forward to the City of Dis,
Secure after the holy ordinance.
We entered without arms or armistice:
And I, because I had desire to know
The state of them lockt in such jail as this,
Being within, cast round mine eye; and lo!
On either hand a spacious plain was shown
Replete with cruel torment and with woe.
Even as at Aries, where ponds the river Rhone,
Even as at Pola near Quarnaro Bay
Which bathes Italia's limitary zone,
Sepulchers strew the ground in rough array:
Here upon every hand it was the same,
Except that here more bitter was the way:
For scattered in among the tombs was flame,
Whereby such utter heat in them arose
That never craft can more from iron claim.
Their lids were lifted all, and out of those
Were issuing such dire lamenting cries,
As told of wretched ones and full of woes.
"Master," said I, "what people on this wise
Finding within these burial-chests their bed,
Make themselves audible with woeful sighs?"
"Here the arch-heretics," to me he said,
"With followers of every sect are pent:
More than thou thinkst the tombs are tenanted.
Like unfo" like are here in burial blent,
And heated more and less the monuments."
Then, when he to the right had turned, we went
Between the tortures and high battlements.

At Aries the Rhone no longer "ponds," aSf though Us tendency to do so is manifest in La Camargue, a little below. A few relics of tiie ancient cemetery are still to be seen there. But in the Great War Italy has finally regained its boundary on the Gulf of Quarnaro, beyond Pola Dante exhibits the great heretics, as he does the virtuous pagans, with frank admiration. The lofty figure of Farinata is portrayed with the same sympathy, not to say partiality, with which Milton draws his imposing Satan. The poets attitude is much the same in the ease of Ulysses Canto xxvi)

Sixth Circle: Farinata Of The Uberti

My Master now along a hidden track
Between the city rampart and the fires,
Goes forward, and I follow at his back.
"O Virtue high, that through these impious gyres
Dost wheel me at thy pleasure," began I,
"Speak to me,—give content to my desires.
The people in the sepulchers that lie,
Might they be seen? With lifted covers burn
They ever, and no one keeps guard thereby."
"All will be shut within, when they return
Back from Jehosaphat," thereat he said,
"Bringing their bodies from the burial urn.
Herein with Epicurus have their bed
His followers one and all, who represent
The spirit with the body to be dead.
But soon shalt thou within here have content
As to the question which thou hast proposed,
And to the wish whereof thou'rt reticent."
And I: "Good Leader, I do not keep closed
My heart from thee, except that words be few:
Nor hast thou me now first thereto disposed."
"O Tuscan, thou who goest living through
The city of fire, speaking becomingly,
May it please thee stay thy steps in this purlieu!
The fashion of thy speech proclaimeth thee
A native of that land of noble pride
Which haply suffered too much harm from me."
Suddenly in such accents some one cried
From out one of the coffers; startled now,
I drew a little closer to my Guide.
Whereat he said: "Turn round; what doest thou?"
"Lo! Farinata, standing at full height:
And thou canst see him all from belt to brow."
Upon his countenance I fixt my sight;
And he was lifting up his brow and breast,
As looking upon Hell with great despite. My Leader pusht me to his burial-chest
Among the tombs with bold and ready hand,
"Be chary of thy words!" was his behest. When at the bottom of his tomb I stand,
Awhile he eyes me; then, with some disdain,
Inquires: "Who were thy fathers in the land?" And I, to be compliant wholly fain,

Conceal it not, revealing to him all.
He slightly lifts his brow, then speaks again: "Fiercely to mine were they inimical,
To me, and to the cause I had at heart,
And therefore twice I scattered them withal." "Though banisht, they came back from every part,"
I answered him, "both once and yet anew;
But yours have never rightly learnt that art." Then, alongside of him, arose to view
A shade uncovered to the chin; and bent t Upon the knees, I think it upward drew. It peered all round about me, as intent
To look for some one who escaped its ken;
But when expectancy was wholly spent, Weeping it said: "If through this sunless den,
Thou goest because of lofty genius,
Where is my son, and why not with thee then?" "Of mine own self," said I, "I come not thus:
He, waiting yonder, leads, of whom perchance
Your Guido held regard contemptuous." His words, and of his pain the circumstance,
Had told his name already: otherwise
My answer would have had less relevance. Suddenly starting up erect, he cries:
"How sayst thou, *held?*—And does he live no more?
Does the sweet light not fall upon his eyes?" *The personage by the side of Farinata is the father of Guido Cavalcanti. Guido, who was Dante's intimate friend, seems to have belonged to that Florentine type of Ac lofty-minded, cultivated, able, somewhat skeptical Patrician, of which Lorenzo d Magnifico is the most conspicuous example. The broken spirit of the elder Cavalcanti here sets the superb figure of Farinata in relief The bloody battle of Montaperti, near Siena, in 1260, where the Florentine Guelfs were utterly put to rout by the Sienese and the Florentine Ghibellines under the leadership of Farinata*
Then he, aware of some delay before
My answer I returned, incontinent
Fell back again, and stood forth nevermore.
But that great-hearted one for whose content
I had remained, no change of aspect made,
Neither his neck he moved nor flank he bent.
"And if,—" resuming what before he said,
"They ill have learnt that art,—if this be so
It more torments me than this fiery bed.
But fifty times shall not rekindled show
The visage of the Lady reigning here,
Ere thou the hardness of that art shalt know.
And so the world may sweet to thee appear,
Say why the statute of that people runs
So pitiless against my kindred dear?"
"The havoc and the massacre that once
Stained," I replied, "the Arbia-water red,
Are causing in our fane such orisons."
And sighing thereupon, he shook his head:
"Not I alone in that, and in no case
Should causeless with the rest have moved," he sai#
"But I it was, when in that other place
To wipe out Florence one and all agreed,
Alone defended her with open face."
"Ah! so may ever rest in peace your seed,"
Entreated I, "pray loose that knot for me,
Which doth my judgment at this point impede.
It seems that ye prophetically see
What time brings with it, if I hear aright,
And as to present things act differently. "
"We see, like him who has imperfect sight,
The things," said he, "that are remote from view,
So much still shines for us the Sovran Light:
When they draw nigh, or are, quite canceled through
Our vision is; if others bring it not,
Unto your human state we have no clew.
The Poet Disturbed by Forebodings 41
Whence thou canst comprehend that blotted out
Will be our knowledge, from that moment when
The portal of the future shall be shut."
As conscious of my fault, I said: "Now, then,
I wish that you would tell that fallen one
His son is still conjoined with living men.
And if just now I rendered answer none,
Tell him it was because my thoughts were tied
Still by that error which you have undone."
Already was recalling me my Guide:
Wherefore more hurriedly did I request
That spirit tell who else therein abide.
"With thousands here," he said to me, "I nest:
The Second Frederick herein is pent,
And the Cardinal: I speak not of the rest. "

He hid himself; and thereupon I went
Toward the ancient Poet, pondering
That word which seemed to me maleficent.
He moved along, and then, thus journeying, t Inquired of me, "Why art thou so bestirred?"
Whereat I satisfied his questioning,
t memory preserve what thou hast heard
Against thyself," that Sage adjured me so,
Lifting his finger;—"and now markBfcord!
When thou shalt standing be in the swUiPow
Of her whose beauteous eye on all is bent,
From her the journey of thy life shalt

know."
Then turned he leftward: from the wall we went,
Striking across toward the middle by
A pathway leading to a pit that sent
Its loathsome stench ascending even so high.
The Emperor, of whom Dante often speaks and whom he admired greatly; and the Cardinal Ottaviano of the Ubaldini, who said when abovl to die: "If there he a sold, 1 have lost mine a thousand times for the Ghibellines." He had looked at the Gorgonl XI
Classes Of Sins And Distribution Of The
Damned
Upon an eminence with margin steep,
Formed by rock-masses in a circle rent,
We came above a still more cruel deep.
And here, by reason of the horrible scent
That was belched forth from the profound abyss,
Behind the lid of a great monument
We stood aside, and saw inscribed on this:
"I hold within Pope Anastasius
He whom Photinus led to go amiss."—
"We must delay our going down, that thus
A little more familiar to the sense,
The dismal blast no longer trouble us."
The Master thus; and I: "Some recompense
Do thou devise to balance this delay,
Lest time be lost."—"My very thought!" he assents
"My son, within these rocks," began he say,
"From grade to grade three lesser circles wind,
Like those above from which we come away.
All swarm with cursed souls of humankind:
But Hjhl' sight alone suffice from hence,
Learn P&nd wherefore they are thus confined.
Of every malice that gives Heaven offense,
Injury is the aim; such aim again
Grieves others or by Fraud or Violence.
But because Fraud is man's peculiar bane,
God loathes it more; and so the fraudulent
Are placed beneath, assailed with greater pain.
The whole First Circle is for the violent:
But since to persons threefold force is done,
In triple rounds it has apportionment.
To God, to neighbor, and to self, can one
Do violence: I say, their property
And them,—as thou shalt hear made clearly known
By violence, death and grievous wounds may be
Dealt to one's neighbor; to his goods and rights
Injury, arson, and rapacity:
Whence homicides and each who wrongly smites,
Marauders and freebooters, all their train
The foremost rondure plagues in various plights.
A. man may lay a violent hand again
On self and on his goods: wherefore below
In the second rondure must repent in vain
Whoso deprives him of your world, whoso
Gambles and dissipates his affluence,
And comes to grief where he should jocund go.
The Deity may suffer violence
With heart's denial and with blasphemies,
Which Nature scorn, and His beneficence:
And hence the smallest rondure signet-wise
Stamps Sodom and Cahors, and all of those
Who, speaking from the heart, their God despise
That Fraud whose gnawing every conscience knows,.
tA man may use on others who confide,
Or on them who no confidence repose.
s latter method seems but to divide
The link of love that in our nature is:
Whence in the Second Circle therejfce
Wizards, hypocrisy, and flatteries, Hr
Cheating, and simony, and thievishness,
Panders, and the like filth, and barratries.
In the other mode there lies forgetfulness
Of love which nature makes, and furthermore
Of what begets especial trustfulness:
Whence in the Smallest Circle, at the core
Of the whole universe, and seat of Dis,
Whoso betrays is wasted evermore."
"Master, thy reasoning of the abyss
Runs clear," said I, "denning what belongs
To place, and to the folk possessing this.
But tell me: of the fat lagoon the throngs,
Those the rain beats upon, those tempest-led,
Those who encounter with such bitter tongues,
Wherefore are they within the City red
Not punisht, if the wrath of God they bide?
If otherwise, then wherefore so bestead?"
"Why wandereth thine intellect so wide
Beyond the wonted mark?" he said, "or what
Hath thine attention elsewhere occupied?
Hast thou the tenor of those words forgot
Wherewith thine Ethics thoroughly explain
The vices three that Heaven endureth not,—
Incontinence, and malice, and insane
Bestiality? and how incontinence
Less angers God, and less doth censure gain?
If thou consider well this evidence,
And what they are recall to memory,
Who up outside are bearing punishments,
Thou wilt discern why they divided be
From all these felons, why God's hammers smifc
Upon them somewhat less avengingly."
"O Sun! thou healer of all troubled

sight,
So gladdens me thy bringing truth to view,
That By no less than knowledge is delight
Yet turn aJR, back," said I, "pursue
Thy argument that usury offends
Divine beneficence,—that knot undo."
Posophy," said he, "if one attends,
Not merely in one passage has defined
How Nature in her origin descends
From art Divine, and from the Master Mind;
And if unto thy Physics thou refer,
After not many pages wilt thou find
That your art, as it can, pursueth her,
As the disciple doth the master; so
That your art is God's grandchild, as it were.
Usury neither of Nature nor of Art 45
To these twain, if thy memory backward go
To Genesis where it begins, perforce
Must men their life and their advantage owe.
Since usurers adopt another course,
They Nature and her follower disdain,
Because they draw their hope from other source.
But follow, for the journey am I fain:
The Fishes on the horizon writhe by this,
While wholly over Caurus lies the Wain,
And yonder far descends the precipice." *This is an daborate way of saying that it is an hour or two before sunrise. The Fishes are on the morning horizon, the Ram (with the sun) just below it, the Wain (Septentrion, "Dipper") is with the Northwest wind (Caurus)* XII
Seventh Circle: Ring 1. Those Violent
Against Neighbors
The place we came to that we might descend
Was alpine, what beside was on that bank
Was such that it would every eye offend.
Such as that rock-fall which upon the flank
Struck on the Adige, this side of Trent,
Whether by earthquake or support that sank;
For, from the summit whence the ruin went,
Down to the plain, the cliff has fallen between, So from above there might be some descent; *The Minotaur,* Such was the causeway into that ravine: *symbol of mo-*Ad on the border of the rugged brow *lence, the more bestial for being* The infamy of Crete was prostrate seen, *half human. The* That was conceived in the fictitious cow: *symbolic unum of Pasiphae and* He bit himself, when eyes on us he laid, *the buU U twice* Subdued within by anger. "Haply thou," *referred to in ,,.,...*
Purg. xxvi. My Master sage toward him shouting said, *The Minotaur* "Believest here the Duke of Athens, who A *is the fit guar-*B *dian of the en-*Up in the world of mortals struck thee dead? *tTtc-mo?HM rB* Monster, begone! for guided by no clew
where sins of Given by thy sister, comes this man below,
testMit aT"re ut passes "y, your punishments to view." *.punished.* Just as the bull that feels the deadly blow, TM(Breaks from his halter, and not very far *also by Shake-*Can move, but merely plunges to and fro: *speare* domg I beheld the Minotaur. "Run," cried my Master, who the passage showed,
"While he is raging, hasten down the scar."
Thus downward we, our way pursuing, trode
That dump of stones, which often as I went
Moved 'neath my feet, so novel was the load.
I musing passed. And he: "Thou art intent
Perhaps upon this ruin, sentineled
By that brute wrath, now rendered impotent.
S"ow I would have thee know, that when I held
My first course hither to the deep abyss,
This mass of rock had not as yet been felled.
But certainly, discern I not amiss,
A little ere He came who mighty prey
From the upper circle levied upon Dis,
The deep and loathsome valley every way
So trembled, that the Universe, I thought,
Was thrilled with love, whereby there are who say
The world was many a time to chaos brought:
And in that moment, here and elsewhere, thus
Upon this ancient crag was ruin wrought.
But fix thine eyes below; for neareth us
The river of blood, wherein all boiling be
Who were by force to men injurious."
0 wicked, blind, and mad cupidity,
That in our brief existence spurs us so,
And in the eternal steeps so bitterly!
1 saw a wide moat curved into a bow
And such that it doth all the plain embrace,
According as my Guide had let me know.
Between it and the precipice did race
Centaurs in file with arrows, as of yore
It was their wont on earth to follow chase.
Seeing us coming down, they moved no more:
And three detacht themselves from out the row,
With bows and with long arrows, chosen before.
And from afar one shouted: "To what woe
Descending thus the precipice come ye?
Tell it from thence; if not, I draw the bow."
My Master answered: "Our reply will be
To Chiron yonder at close quarters made:
Thus ever rash thy wil, the worse for thee!"
"That one is Nessus," nudging me he said,
"Who died because of Dejanira fair,
And for himself, himself his vengeance paid.
He who said so was Empedocles. Possibly Dante means to hint that love in Hell would be, locally at least, a dis-

organizing force The Centaurs, like the Minotaur, half beast and half human, are equally appropriate watchmen here

And gazing on his breast between the pair,
Is mighty Chiron who Achilles taught:
Pholus the wrathful is the other there.

By thousands go they round the fosse about,

Piercing with darts whatever soul withdraw
From out the blood, more than its crime allot."

Nearing those fleet wild animals, we saw

Chiron take up a shaft and with the notch
He ruffled back his beard behind his jaw.

When his huge mouth he had uncovered, "Watch!
Are ye aware," thus to his mates he said,
"That he behind moves whatso'er he touch?

Not so are wont the footfalls of the dead."

And my good Leader, level with his breast
Where the two natures are together wed,

Replied: "Indeed he lives, and by behest
Alone I show him thus the dark defile:
Necessity, not choice, impels the quest.

From singing Alleluiah paused awhile

One who commits to me this office new;
He is no robber, I no spirit vile.

But by that Virtue which gives motion to
My feet along so wild a thoroughfare,
Give us for escort any one of you,

That he may show us where to ford, and bear
This man upon his back across the tide:
For 'tis no spirit that can walk the air."

"Turn about, Nessus, so to be their guide,"

Said Chiron, round upon his right breast bent:
"If other troop encounter, warn aside."

Together with the trusty guide we went
Along the boiling of the crimson flood,
Wherein the boiled were making loud lament.

I saw who plunged there to the eyebrows stood:

"Once these," the Centaur great took up the tale,
"Were tyrants steept in pillage and in blood.

The ruthless wrongs they wrought they here bewail:
Here Alexander, fell Dionysius who
Made woeful years in Sicily prevail;

A.nd yonder brow with hair so black of hue
Is Ezzelin; that other, fair of face,
Obizzo of Este, whom his bastard slew

Up in the world, to truly state the case."—
Then turned I to the Poet, and he said:
"Give him the first and me the second place."

A little farther on the Centaur led

And paused above a folk whose evil fate

Plunged them throat-high within that boiling red.

He showed a shade alone and separate,

Saying: "That spirit cleft within God's breast
The heart that still by Thames they venerate."

Then saw I people who with head and chest
Wholly uplifted from the river stood;
And many I recognized among the rest.

Thus evermore grew shallower that blood
Until it only cookt the feet: and lo!
Here was our passageway across the flood.

"Just as thou seest the boiling river grow

Still lower on the farther side, and lower,"
The Centaur said, "so I will have thee know

That on this other, with a circling shore

Its bottom sinks, until it makes its way
Where tyranny must groan forevermore.

Justice divine here goads that Attila
Who was a scourge upon the earth, and stings
Pyrrus and Sextus, and milks forth for aye
From Rinier of Corneto tears, and wrings
Hot tears from Rinier Pazzo,—Riniers twain
Who on the highways wrought such plunderings."
Back then he turned and passed the ford again.

Of the violent here the two moat interesting to us are Ezzelino da Romano, called a "firebrand" by his sister, the blessed Cunizza, whom we shall meet in the Heaven of Venus; and Guy de Montfort, who slew in church at Viterbo the young English prince, Henry of Cornwall, innocent victim of vendetta xni

Seventh Circle: Ring 2. The Suicidal Wood

Not yet had Nessus gained the farther side,
When we began to pass a forest through,
Wherein not any path could be descried.

Not green the foliage, but of dusky hue;

Not smooth the boughs, but gnarled and intricate;
No fruits therein, but thorns with poison grew.

Those fierce wild animals that hold in hate

Tilled lands 'tween Cecina and Corneto, no
Thickets infest so dense and desolate.

Hither the loathsome Harpies nesting go,

Who drove the Trojans from the Strophades,
With direful prophecy of coming woe.

Broad wings, and human face and neck have these,
And feet with claws, huge belly feathered all;
They utter rueful cries on the weird trees.

"Ere yet," the Master good began withal,

"Thou tread the Second Round, consider well
That here thou shalt employ the interval

Until thou comest to the sand-waste fell.

So look aright, and there shall be descried

Things thou wouldst not believe, if I should tell."

Thereat I wailings heard, on every side,

And person who might utter them saw not:

Whence stood I still, completely mystified.

I think now that he thought perhaps I thought

That through those trunks so many voices came

From people who from us concealment sought.

Wherefore thus said the Master: "K thou maim

Of any of these plants one little spray,

The thoughts thou hast will all be rendered lame."

Lifting my hand a little then, away

A branchlet from a mighty thorn I tore;

Then did the trunk of it, lamenting, say:

Pier delle Vigne 51

Why rendest thou?" Thereafter, dark with gore,

Began again to cry: "Why mangle me?

Hast thou no spirit of pity then? Of yore Men were we, and each now is turned to tree:

Well might thy hand have shown itself more kind,

Though souls of veritable serpents we." As out of a green brand, which burns behind,

And from the other side the drops exude,

The while it sputters with the escaping wind: So from that broken sliver words and blood

Were flowing forth together: whence I let

The tip fall down, and like one frighted stood. "O wounded soul!" my Sage replied, "if yet

Before he had been able to believe

What he has only in my numbers met,

Thou wouldst not this offense from him receive;

The wonder of the thing made me advise

His doing that whereat myself I grieve. But tell him who thou wast, so that in guise

Of some amends, he yet may vindicate

Thy fame on earth, where he again shall rise." The trunk: "Thy honeyed words hold out such bait,

I cannot choose but speak; then let it be

Not burdensome if I expatiate. I am that one who held the double key *The shade of*

Of Frederick's heart, and, turning both ways, knew SSS'

To lock and loose with such suavity, *confidant of the*

His confidence from others I withdrew: Ksbsto

To that high trust fidelity I bore, on *able and elo*

Losing my vigor and repose therethrough. JgJjJ *Ls*

The harlot who yet never from the door *may still be*

Of Caesar's dwelling turned her wanton eyes, *Itis 'outofhcrm*

The curse and bane of courts forevermore, *age to him as a*

T *a* J 11 J ±. i. *stylist thai*

Inflamed all minds agamst me; in such wise *Daante*

Inflamed, they made Augustus flame again, *him teU his*

So that glad honors turned to dismal sighs. *ornate a manner*

My spirit, through her temper of disdain,

Deeming by dying from disdain to flee,

Made me, though just, to self-injustice fain.

I swear by the new rootlets of this tree

That to my Lord, whose worth I honored so,

I never forfeited fidelity.

If one of you to earth returning go,

Let him the memory of me restore,

Still lying prostrate under Envy's blow."—

When he a little to discourse forbore,

The Poet said: "Let not the moment go,

But speak and ask him what thou wouldest more."

And I to him: "Do thou entreat him show

Whate'er thou thinkest may content my will,

For I cannot, for pity of his woe."

Whence he resumed: "So may the man fulfill

What thou hast prayed for, and full willingly,

Imprisoned spirit, may it please thee still

To tell us in what way the soul may be

Bound in these knots; and tell, if licit, too,

If ever any from such limbs breaks free. "

The trunk a mighty suspiration blew,

Whereon that wind was changed to voice like this:

"Brief the reply that shall be made to you.

When the fierce spirit separates amiss

From out the body whence itself has torn,

Minos consigns it to the seventh abyss.

It falls into the forest, where no bourn

Is chosen for it, but where chance may throw,

Here it sprouts up, as doth a grain of corn;

Doth to a sapling and a wild tree grow:

The Harpies, browsing then its leafy crest,

Cause woe, and give a window to the woe.

We shall go seek our bodies like the rest,

But with them never to be re-arrayed:

For 'tis not just to have what we divest.

The Black Dogs of the Wood of Phlegeihon 53

Here shall we drag them, and the forest glade

Shall see our bodies hanging dismally,

Each on the thorntree of its injured shade."

We were attentive still unto the tree,

Thinking that haply it would tell us more,

When a tumult overtook us, so that we

Were like to one aware of hunt and boar

Approaching to the place where he had stood,

Who hears the branches crash the beasts before.

And lo! on the left hand, two spirits nude
And scratcht, fleeting along so furious
They broke through every barrier of the wood.
The first: "Now hurry, hurry, Death to us!"
And the next, who thought himself in speed outdone,
Was shouting: "Lano, not alertly thus
Thy legs did at the jousts of Toppo run."
And haply for his breath too short he found,
A thicket and himself he grouped as one.
After them, filling all the forest round,
Were running ravening bitches black, and fleet
As, after slipping from the leash, the hound.
In him who cowered down their tushes meet,
All into pieces rending him: again
They bear away those limbs dilacerate.
Taking me by the hand, my Leader then
Led forward to the bush, with many a sigh
Lamenting through its bleeding wounds in vain.
"0 James of Sant' Andrea," was its cry,
"Of making me thy screen what is the good?
For all thy wicked life what blame have I?"
The Master said when he beside it stood:
"Who wast thou that, through wounds so numerous
Art blowing forth thy woeful words with blood?"
"0 souls that hither come," he said to us,
"To view the shameful havoc that from me
Has rended all away my foliage thus,

It was a characteristic popular superstition at Florence that the continual strife that raged there was due to the jealousy of the ancient patron god, Mars. The present Baptistry, the old Cathedral, was pretty certainly built on the foundation of an ancient temple of Mars. Compare the significant reference to the maleficence of the mutilated statue of the god on the Ponte Vecchio (Par. xvi, near end of canto)

Gather it up beneath the wretched tree.
Mine was the town that her first patron for
The Baptist changed: and for this reason he
Will plague her with his art forevermore.
And, were it not that still of him remain
Some features where men cross the Arno o'er,
Those citizens who built the town again
Upon the ashes left by Attila,
Would have performed the labor all in vain.
With mine own house I made myself away." *The Steady Rain of Fire 55.* XIV
Seventh Circle: Ring 3. Defiers Of God
Because for native country reverent,
Perforce I gathered up the scattered leaves
And gave them back to him, whose voice was spent. Thence came we to the boundary which cleaves
The Second Rondure from the Third, where dread
Mode of eternal justice one perceives. To show the new things clearly, be it said
That we arrived upon a desert plain
Which banishes all plants from off its bed.. The woeful wood enwreathes it, as again
The dismahmeat encloses that around:
Here, hard upon the verge, did we remain. An arid and dense sand composed the ground,
Nor was it formed and fashioned otherhow
Than that of old where Cato footing found. Vengeance of God! O how much oughtest thou
By every person to be held in awe
Who reads that which was manifested now! Manifold flocks of naked souls I saw
Who all did woeful lamentations pour,
And they seemed subject unto diverse law. Supine were lying some upon the floor,
And some were sitting all together bent, And others went about forevermore.
The more were those who round about there went,
And fewer those who lay in torment low,
But had their tongues more loosened to lament. Above that waste of sand, descending slow,
Rained everywhere dilated flakes of fire,
As upon Alps, without a wind, the snow. As Alexander, where the heat is dire
In India, upon his host beheld
Flames fall, as far as to the ground entire;
Whereat he with his legions was compelled
To trample down the soil, for better so
The flames, remaining single, could be quelled:
Such was descending the eternal glow;
Whereby, like tinder under steel, the sands
Were kindled for redoubling of the woe.
Forever tossing were the wretched hands
Now hither and now thither without rest,
Fanning fresh burning off in counterdance.

"Master," began I, "thou who conquerest
All things except the stubborn demon train
That from the gate against our entering pressed,
Who is the mighty one that in disdain
Lies scowling, nor appears the fire to dread,
So that he seems unripened by the rain?"—
And that same one, perceiving what I said
In question to my Guide of him, did shout:
"What once I was alive, that am I dead.
Should Jupiter his blacksmith weary out,
From whom the sharpened thunderbolt he tore
Wrathful, and me upon my last day smote;
Or weary out the others o'er and o'er
MongibeUo is In Mongibello at the stithy swart,
fTMtmnZ7here Crying,'Help, help, good Vulcan,' as of yore *the Cyclopes had* On Phlegra's battlefield; and should he dart *their forge* His bolts at me with vigor multiplied,
That vengeance never should make glad his heart."
My Leader then with so much strength replied
That I had never heard his voice so great:
"O thou Capaneus, just because thy pride
Remains unquencht, the woefuller thy fate:
No torment save thy very rage would be
Unto thy fury pain proportionate!"
Then with a better look he turn'd to me:
"That one was of the seven monarchs who
Laid siege to Thebes; he held and seemingly
Holds God in scorn, and gives contempt to view:
But, as I said to him, his spiteful mood
Is for his breast adornment very due.
Now follow me, and let thy heed be good
Not on the burning sand thy feet to set,
But keep them ever back, close to the wood."
In silence came we where a rivulet
Gushes from out the wood: a rill so red
That thinking of it makes me shudder yet.
As from the Bulicame there takes head
A brooklet which the sinful women share,
So this ran down across the sandy bed.
The bottom and both shelving bank-sides were
Hardened to stone, and the margins at the side:
Whence I perceived our passageway was there.
"Among all other things by thee descried
Through me, since entering within the gate
Whose threshold unto no one is denied,
Thine eyes not anything yet contemplate
Noteworthy as the present stream, which quite
Doth all the flames above it suffocate
This language of my Leader did incite
Petition from me that he let me taste
The food for which he lent the appetite.
"In the mid-sea there lies a country waste," Thereon he said, "that bears the name of Crete,
Under whose king the world of old was chaste.
There is a mountain, Ida, once the seat
Of laughing waters and of leafy shades
Today it lies deserted and effete.
Once Rhea in this faithful cradle laid
Her son; and to conceal him should he raise
His voice to weep, caused clamors to be made.
A tall old man within the mountain stays,
Who doth his back to Damietta hold,
And upon Rome, as in a mirror, gaze:
Bulicame: name of a hot mineral spring at Viterbo, from which water seems to have been conducted to the houses of unfortunate women The tall old man in the cavern of the Cretan Mount Ida seems to symbolize historically the human race facing westward, its tears supplying the rivers of Hell
His head is fashioned of the finest gold,
And of pure silver are the arms and breast,
Whence to the fork he is of brazen mold;
Thence downward all is iron, of the best,
Save the right foot of terra cotta, and more
Doth he on that than on the other rest.
Every part, except the golden ore,
Is broken by a cleft where tears distill,
And, gathering, perforate that cavern floor.
They fall cascading to this valley,—fill
And Acheron and Styx and Phlegethon;
Then flow along this narrow channel, till
They come where there is no more going down:
They form Cocytus,—that pool shalt thou know
By seeing: so be here description none.
"
And I: "If thus the present brooklet flow
Down from our world wherein its source is found.
Why does it only on this border show?"
And he to me: "Thou knowest the place is round;
And though thou comest from a distant place,
Still to the left toward the bottom bound,
Thou dost not yet the circle fully trace:
Wherefore if something novel comes to view,
It ought not to bring wonder to thy face.
"
"Where found is Phlegethon," said I anew,
"And Lethe? for of one thou'rt silent, Lord,
And sayest the other to this rain is due."
"Thy questions please," he said, "in every word,

Although the crimson brook's ebullience
Might well the answer unto one afford.
Lethe shalt see, but from this fosse far hence,
There where to lave themselves the souls repair,
When guilt has been removed by penitence."
Then added he: "The time is come to fare
Out of the wood: take heed thou follow me:
The banks, not burning, form a thoroughfare,
And all the space above from flame is free." *Brunetto Latini 59* XV
Seventh Circle: Ring 3. Dante Meets A Great Teacher
Now bears us over one of the hard banks,
And fumes above the brooklet, shading well,
Shelter from fire the water and the flanks.
As Flemings, who 'twixt Bruges and Wissant dwell,
Fearing the flood tides that upon them run,
Throw up the dike the ocean to repel,
And as by Brenta does the Paduan,
His villas and his villages to spare
Before Carinthia ever feels the sun:
Of like formation those were fashioned there,
Though not so high nor of so broad a base
The Master made them, whosoe'er he were.
We were so distant from the forest chase
By this, that I could never have descried
The spot, though backward I had turned my face;
And now we met along the margin side
A company of spirits coming by,
Who each peered at us, as at eventide
Beneath new moon, we one another spy;
And they were puckering their brows at us
Like an old tailor at the needle's eye.
By such a family inspected thus,
Well-known I proved to one of them, who caught
My garment's hem, and cried: "How marvelous!"
And when he stretcht his arm, a glance I brought
To bear so fixt upon his branded hue,
That his scorcht countenance prevented not
His recognition by my inner view;
And to his visage bending mine anigh,
I answered: "Ser Brunetto, is it you?"
"My son," he said, "be not displeased if I,
Brunet' Latini, backward with thee fare
A little way, and let the train go by."
Brunetto Latini was a distinguished citizen and man of letters who had powerfully influenced Dante in the tatter's earlier years. Brunetto's principal work was written in French,—"Le Lime dou Tresor"-a compilation of encyclopedic character held at that time in high esteem
"That is," I said to him, "my urgent prayer;
And if you wish me sit with you, I fain
Will do it, if it please my Leader there."
"O son," he said, "whoever of this train
But pauses, lies thereon a century low,
Without a fan when pelts the fiery rain.
Therefore pass on: I at thy skirts will gp,
And then rejoin my fellows, who lament,
While faring onward, their eternal woe.
"
I durst not from the causeway make descent
Level to walk beside him, but did bow
My head, and walkt as walk the reverent.
"What fate," began he, "or what fortune now
Leads thee down hither ere thy final day?
And who may this one be that shows thee how?"
"Up in the clear life yonder," did I say,
"Or ever yet my age was fully come,
I went within a valley far astray.
But yestermorn I turned my face therefrom:
This one appeared to me returning there,
And leads me now along this pathway home."
"If following thy star thou onward bear,
Thou canst not fail of glorious port," he said,
"If well discerned I in the life so fair:
And but that I was far too early dead,
Beholding Heaven so unto thee benign,
I would thee in the work have comforted.
But that ungrateful populace malign,
Who came of yore down from Fiesole,
And savor still of mountain and of mine,
For thy good deeds will be thy enemy;
And rightly: for 'mid crabbed sorbs confined,
Befits not the sweet fig to fructify.
Old rumor in the world proclaims them blind;
A people envious, arrogant, and hard:
Take heed thou from their manners be refined.
Dante Faces the Future Serenely 61
Fortune reserves thee honor and reward,
Such that both parties yet will hungry go
For thee: but far from goat shall be the sward.
Let the Fiesolan beasts their litter strow,
Bending themselves; nor let them touch the blade,

If ever any on their dunghill grow,
Wherein may yet revive the holy seed
Of Romans,—those therein still resident
When it became such nest of evil deed."
"If all my prayer had found accomplishment,"
Replied I to him, "not yet would you be
From human nature placed in banishment:
For I have held in loving memory
Your kind paternal image, and now yearn
For you, who in the world instructed me
From hour to hour how man becomes eterne:
And while I am alive, it is but right
Men in my words my gratitude discern.
What you relate about my course, I write,
And keep—with other text—for Lady, who,
If I attain her, can the gloss indite.
Thus much would I have manifest to you,
That if so be my conscience do not frown,
I am ready, whatsoever Fortune do.
Not newly is such hansel paid me down:
Therefore let twirling Fortune ply her wheel /
At pleasure, and his mattock ply the clown." /
Thereat my Master, back upon his heel
Turning toward the right, upon me bent
His eyes; then said: "Who notes it, listens well!"
Nor speaking less on that account, I went
With Ser Brunetto on, and question made
Of his companions known and eminent.
"To know of some of them is well," he said,
"Of others best be silent, for the time
With so much speaking were too quickly sped.
Know then, in brief, that all were clerks, sublime
In their renown, and men of letters great,
On earth polluted with the one same crime.
Priscian goes with yon troop disconsolate,
And Francis of Accorso; who observes
Such vermin, might have seen that reprobate
Who, by the Servant of each one who serves,
Was banned from Arno to the Bacchiglion',
Where he laid by his ill-excited nerves.
Of more would I relate, but going on
And speech can be no longer, for I see
New smoke from the great sand uprising yon.
A people comes with whom I may not be;
My Treasure' be commended to thy love,—
There still I live: more ask I not of thee.
"

Then he turned back, and showed the action of
Those at Verona who cross-country run
To win the cloth of green, and thereabove
Appeared the winning, not the losing one.

Souls in Torture Concerned for Florence 63 XVI

Seventh Circle: Ring 3. Three Great Citizens Of Florence

was already where we heard a sound
Such as the bees make in the hive, a hum
Of water falling into the next round;
Chen did three shades together running come,
Quitting a passing company that went
Beneath the rain of the sharp martyrdom.
Approaching, in this cry their voices blent:
"Stop thou, who by thy garb appearst to be
Some one from out our city pestilent."
kVhat sores flame-branded on their limbs, ah me!
Still recent ones and ancient, met my view:
It grieves me for them yet in memory.
Their cries attention from my Teacher drew,
Who turned his face to me and said: "Now stay:
To such as these all courtesy is due;
And if it were not for the fiery spray
The nature of the place darts, I should feel
That thou wert better hurry, and not they."
They re-began to dance the ancient reel
Soon as we paused, and, drawing near us so,
All three resolved themselves into a wheel.
As champions stript and oiled are wont to do,
Who for their grip and for their vantage look,
Before they ever bandy thrust and blow:
Thus, wheeling round, not one of them forsook
The sight of me, so that in counterchase
The neck and feet continual journey took.
"Ah! if the misery of this shifting place
Make us and our desires contemptible,"
Began one, "and our black and blistered face,
Let our renown incline thy mind to tell
Who art thou that, with such security,
Trailest along thy living feet through Hell?
He treading in whose steps thou seest me,
Excoriated though he be, and nude,
Was higher than thou thinkest in degree.
The grandson was he of Gualdrada good;
His name was Guido Guerra: much he planned
Astutely, and his sword was likewise shrewd.
The other who behind me treads the sand,
Tegghaio Aldobrandi is, whose fame
Ought to be grateful in the upper land.
And I, thus put upon the cross with them,
Was Jacob Rusticucci: that I grieve,
Truly my savage wife is most to blame.
"

If from the fire I could have had reprieve,

I should have flung me down to them below,
And think my Teacher would have given me leave
But since I should have parcht and burnt me so,
Terror availed to check the kindly thought
Which prompted me to their embrace to go.
"Contempt," then I began, "indeed 'twas not,
That your condition thrilled me with, but rue
So deep that it will not be soon forgot,
When this my Lord spake words to me, wherethrough
The expectation was within me stirred
That people might be coming such as you.
I am your fellow-townsman; every word
That told your honored names and actions all,
With love I ever have rehearst and heard.
I go for the sweet fruit, leaving the gall,—
Fruit by the truthful Leader promised me:
But to the Center first I needs must fall. "
"So may thy limbs long while directed be
By living soul," that one thereon replied,
"And so may thy renown shine after thee,
Tell whether courtesy and valor abide
Within our city as of wont, or thence
Banisht and altogether thrust aside?
For William Borsiere, who laments
Of late with us, and goes with yonder train,
Speaks that which much our misery augments."
"The upstart people and the sudden gain
Excess in thee and arrogance have bred,
O Florence, as thou findest to thy bane!"—
Thus cried I out aloud with lifted head:
And holding this for my reply, the three
Lookt at each other, as when truth is said.
"If otherwhile so little costs it thee
Others to satisfy," all answered then,.
"Happy thou, speaking with impunity.
Whence if, escapt this place of gloom, again
Returned to see the starry heavens fair,
I Thou shalt rejoice to utter, 'I have been,'
Pray speak of us unto the people there."
Now break they up the wheel, and as they part,
Their nimble legs appear to wing the air.
It is not possible "Amen" could start
From tongue as quick as their evanishment:
Wherefore it pleased my Master to depart.
I followed, and but little way we went,
Before so near us was the water's sound,
That, for all speaking, scarce were hearing lent.
Even as that stream which holds its proper ground
The first, from Monte Viso to the sea
Eastward, upon the Apennine's left bound,—
Stillwater called above, before it be
Precipitated to its lower bed,
But of that name is vacant at Forli,—
Above Saint Benedict from the mountain head
Goes bellowing down a single waterfall
Where for a thousand there were room instead:
Thus, leaping downward from a scarped wall,
We heard that tinted water make such din,
That it would soon have stunned the ear withal.

Monte Viso (Chaucer's "Vesulus the colde") is at the head of the Po. The river here referred to, the Montone, was the first river north of the Apennines which had an independent course to the sea. Dante makes his references an element of poetry, as after him did Milton The cord is supposed to be the girdle of St. Francis, who intended it as an emblem of the binding of the vyild beast of the body. The old commentator, Iliiti' states that Dante teas once a member of that order of Franciscans called from the cord. Cordeliers. So the celebrated Guido da Montefeliro, who tells his dramatic story in Canto xxvii

I had a cord that girt my garment in,
For with it I had once thought requisite
To take the leopard of the painted skin.
As soon as I had loosed it from me quite,
To the commandment of my Guide submiss,
I reacht it to him, coiled and wound up tight.
Whereon he turned toward the right, and thisy
A little out beyond the verge, did fling
Down into that precipitous abyss.
"Now surely it must be that some new thing,"
I said within, "answer the signal new
Which thus the Master's eye is following.",
Ah me! how cautious should men be and do
Near those who witness not alone the deeds,
But with their wisdom to the thoughts look through!
He said to me: "What I expect must needs
Come upward soon, and what thy dreams now ask
Must soon be such that very eyesight heeds."—
Aye to that truth concealed beneath false mask,
A man should close his lips, if in him lies,
Lest he, though blameless, should be brought to task;
But here I cannot: by the harmonies
Of this my Comedy, Reader, I swear,
So may their grace be lasting, that mine eyes
Saw through the gross and gloomy atmosphere
A shape come swimming up, of such as be
To every steadfast heart a thing of fear:
As he returns who sometime dives, to

free
The anchor-fluke, lest vessel come to harm
On reef, or aught else hidden in the sea,
Who draws his foot in, and flings up his arm.

The Monster Geryon 67 XVII

Seventh Circle: Ring 3. The Wonderful Flight Downward

"Behold the beast with pointed tail, whose guile
Doth mountains cleave and walls and weapons rend;
Behold him who doth all the world defile."
So spoke to me my Leader and my friend;
And that it come in shoreward beckoned it,
Near where the trodden marbles make an end.
Then forward came that filthy counterfeit
Image of Fraud to land its head and bust,
But drew not up its tail from out the pit.
Its face was like the face of person just,
So outwardly benignant was its hue,
But like a serpent all the rest outthrust.
Paws shaggy to the armpits it had two;
And many a painted nooselet, many a quirk
The back, the breast, and both the flanks bestrew.
Never was cloth by Tartar woven or Turk,
More variously colored, warp and woof,
Nor yet such tissue did Arachne work.
As along shore the wherries lie aloof
At times, in water part and part on land;
And as the beaver in his hunt's behoof
Doth yonder 'mid the guzzling Germans stand:
So lay that worst of beasts along the stone
That forms the margin fencing in the sand,
All quivering in the void the tail was thrown,
Twisting aloft the point of it, that bare
A venomed fork as in the scorpion.
"Now," said my Leader, "it behooves us fare
Somewhat aside, far as that maledight
Wild beast which couches on the border there."
So therefore we, descending on the right,
Ten steps along the outer border pace,
The sand and flakes of fire avoiding quite.

These are the cognizances, respectively, of the Florentine families Oianfigliazzi and Ubriachi, and of the Paduan family, Scrovigni, all degraded by the inordinate practice of usury. A drawing of the first of these shields is prefixed to this Cantiea

As soon as ever we have reacht the place,
A little farther on the sand I see
A people sitting near the empty space.
"Of this third round," the Master said to me,
"That thou mayst cany full experience,
Go now, consider what their manners be.
Out there concise must be thy conference:
I will persuade this brute his shoulders strong
To lend us, against thy returning thence.
"
Thus farther yet, and all alone, along
That seventh circle's utmost head, I go
Thither where sit the melancholy throng.
Out of their eyes is bursting forth their woe:
Now here, now there, with hands they agonize
Against the flames, against the soil aglow.
Dogs in the summer do not otherwise,
Now with the paw and presently with snout,
At bite of fleas, of gadflies, or of flies.
When I had singled certain faces out
Of those on whom the woeful fire is shed,
Not one of them I knew; but slung about
Each neck perceived a pouch, emblazoned
With certain hue and certain cognizance,
And therewithal, it seems, their eye is fed.
And as, among them looking, I advance,
Beheld I *Azure* on a wallet *Or,*
Bearing a lion's mien and countenance.
And as the sweep of vision onward bore,
Another bag, blood-red, beheld I now
Display a goose, as butter white, and more.
Then one upon whose wallet white a sow,
In brood and azure, was in blazon set,
Exclaimed: "Here in this ditch what doest thou?
Now get thee gone: and since thou'rt living yet,
Know that my townsman, Vitaliano, here
Upon my left-hand side a seat shall get.

Descent astride Geryon 69

A Faduan with these Florentines, mine ear
Ofttimes they deafen, crying in each close,—
'Let him come down, the sovran cavalier
Who with the triple-beaked budget goes!'"
Here pursing up his mouth, he made display
Of tongue, like cattle when they lick the nose.
And apprehensive lest my longer stay
Displease him who had bid me little bide,
I turned me from those weary souls away.
On back of that fell beast I found my Guide
Already mounted, and he said: "Take care
That thou be steady and unterrified.
Now must we needs descend by such a stair:
Mount thou in front, for I between will sit,
So that the tail do thee no harm whate'er."
Like one about to have the ague fit
Of quartan, blue of nail, all shuddering
At shadow, catching but the sight of it,—

Such I became, on hearing such a thing;
But his monitions wrought in me £bat shame
Which makes brave servant before noble king/
I set myself upon that monstrous frame:
"Clasp me!" I tried to say, but utterance
Refused to come, though I believed it came.
But he who otherwhile in other chance
Assisted, with his arms surrounded me
As soon as I had mounted. "Now advance,
O Geryon! ample let thy wheelings be,"
He bade, "and slow be thy descending here;
Remember the new load that burdens thee."—
As draws a little vessel from her pier,
So, backing, backing, thence did Geryon draw;
And when he felt that he was wholly clear,
Turned tail to where before his breast I saw,
And tail outstretching, moved it like an eel,
And gathered in the air with play of paw.
No greater fear, I ween, did any feel,
When Phaeton, abandoning the rein,
Branded the sky, as still the nights reveal;
Nor when poor Icarus perceived each pen
Fall from his flank the molten wax withal,—
"Thy way is wild!" his father shouted then,—
Than mine, when I beheld me to be all
Adrift in air, and saw extinguisht so
Every sight but of the animal.
He swims along, slow undulating, slow,
Wheels and descends,—this could I but surmise
By wind upon my face, and from below.
Already on the right I heard arise
Out of the cataract a frightful roar,
Whence I outstretcht my head with downward eyes.
Thereon the precipice dismayed me more,
For burning did I see and moaning hear,
Whereat my thighs gripped closer than before.
Now I discerned, what first did not appear,
The sinking movement and the wheeling, by
Great woes from every quarter drawing near.
Like falcon, overlong enforced to fly,
That without spying either bird or bait,
"Ah me, thou stoopest!" makes the falconer cry,
Then settles weary whence it sped elate,
Alighting, after many a circling round,
Far from its lord, aloof, exasperate:
So Geryon set us down upon the ground,
Hard by the bottom of the cliff rough-scored,
And disencumbered of our weight, did bound
Off and away, like arrow from the cord.

Malebolge 71 xvin
Eighth Circle: Pouch 1. Panders And Seducers. Pouch 2. Flatterers

There is in Hell a region all of stone,
By name Malpouches, of an iron hue
Like the precipitous encircling zone.
Right in the middle of the fell purlieu
There yawns, exceeding deep and wide, a Pit c—
Whose structure I shall tell in order due. _. /!".
A rounding girdle thus remains of it - "-
Between the Pit and the high rocky steep, —
And in its bed ten vales divided sit.,. .*S-r*
Of like configuration was that deep
As otherwhere, for safeguard of the wall,
Several moats begird a castle-keep:
Such an appearance had these valleys all;
And as from thresholds of such fortalice
Run to the outer rampart bridges small,
So from the bottom of the precipice
Struck across banks and moats bridgeways of stone,
Converging and cut short at the abyss.
In this place, from the back of Geryon thrown,
We found ourselves: then did the Poet go
Toward the left, and I behind moved on.
On the right-hand discovered I new woe,
New torments and new wielders of the thong,
Full filling the first Malpouch there below.
The sinners naked at the bottom throng:
This side the middle come they facing me,
Swifter, beyond, they stride with me along.
The Romans thus, in year of Jubilee,
To make the people pass the bridge devise,
By reason of the countless company,
So that on one side all direct their eyes
Toward the Castle and Saint Peter's fane;
On the other toward the Hill their passage lies.

Ghisola (or Ghislabella) was his sister, whom he persuaded to become the mistress of the Estc, the powerful lord of Ferrara

"Sipa" was the Bolognese form of the present subjunctive of the verb meaning "to be." The modern form is said to be "sepa." Bologna lies between the two rivers Reno and Savena

Hither and yon along the gloomy lane,
I saw horned demons with great whips, who dealt
Behindward on them furious blows amain.
Ah! how these made them after the first pelt
Lift up their heels! then truly waited none

Until the second or the third he felt.
While I was going on, mine eyes by one
Encountered were; and instantly I said:
"For sight of him I have not hungry gone!"
Wherefore to make him out my feet I stayed;
And my kind Leader, slackening his pace,
Consented to some steps I backward made.
And that scourged spirit, lowering his face,
Bethought to hide, but with small benefit;
I saying: "Thou that dost thine eyes abase,
Must, if those features are not counterfeit,
Venedico Caccianimico be:
But what brings thee to such a smarting pit?"
"Unwillingly I tell, though forced," said he,
"By thy explicit speech which brings the old
Foregone existence back to memory.
To do the Marquis pleasure, I cajoled
Fair Ghisola,—in whatsoever way
The shameful tale be peradventure told.
No lonely Bolognese I weep here: nay,
For rather do we so this region fill,
That not so many tongues are taught to say
Sipa 'twixt Reno and Savena; still
If thou wouldst have me pledge or proof subjoin,
Recall to mind our avaricious will."
While he spoke thus, a demon on the loin
Lasht him, exclaiming: "Pander, get thee gone!
There are no women here for minting coin."
I now rejoin mine Escort: whereupon
With footsteps few we come where we discern
A craggy bridge that from the cliff was thrown.
Jason the Seducer 73
Ascending this full easily, we turn
Upon its jagged ridgeway to the right,
Departing from those circling walls eterne.
When came we where a gap beneath the height
Yawns for the sinners driven by the thong,
My Leader said: "Lay hold, until the sight
Strike on thee of another misborn throng,
Of whom thou hast not yet beheld the face
Because they still have gone with us along."
From the old bridge we viewed the file, apace
Who neared us on the further side below,
And whom the scourges in like manner chase.
Without my asking, the Good Master so
Addrest me: "Yonder mighty one behold,
Who seems to shed no tear for all his woe:
How kingly in his bearing, as of old!
'Tis Jason, who by prowess and by guile
Despoiled the Colchians of the Fleece of Gold.
He skirted once the coast of Lemnos isle,
After the merciless women unafraid
Devoted all their males to death ere while.
There, with love-tokens and fair words, the maid
Hypsipyle did he betray, that one
Who first, herself, had all the rest betrayed.
And there he left her, pregnant and alone:
Such guilt condemns him to such martyrdom,
And for Medea too is vengeance done.
With him go such deceivers all and some:
Of the first valley let so much suffice,
And of those by its vengeance overcome."—
Already had we reacht the place where lies
The narrow path across the second dike,'
Which buttress for another arch supplies.
Thence heard we people whimper plaintive-like
In the next pocket, and with snorting roar
Of muzzle, with their palms upon them strike.
It is hardly The banks were with a mold encrusted o'er SXC£ fiy vapore from *hdaw* that on them rest, *thetic reader*
With both the eyes and nostrils waging war.
t'lTSl The bottom is so hollowly deprest *more delicate* There is no room to see, except one go
mfrXd'than Up wnere tne arching bridge is loftiest. *Dante. Bui it is* Thither we came, whence in the ditch below *ZSrSZjk* I saw folk weltering TM excrement *Hell vrithout* That out of human privies seemed to flow. *mZlTZcen-*
While I was looking down with eye intent, *Uy, as here and* I saw one head so smeared with ordure all, *Call* xiT 0/ K clerk or layman 'twas not evident.
"Wherefore so greedy art thou," did he bawl,
"At me more than the filthy rest to stare?"
"Because," I answered, "if I well recall,
I have already seen thee with dry hair;
Alessio Interminei of Lucca, late
Wast thou: whence singled out from others there."
And thereon he, belaboring his pate:
"To this has plunged me down the sycophance
Wherewith my tongue was never satiate."
Hereon my Leader said to me: "Advance
Thy face still further forward, till thou bring
Thine eyesight full upon the countenance
Of that uncleanly and disheveled thing,
Who scratches yon with nails smeared filthily,
And now is standing up, now cowering.
Thus is the harlot Thais seen of thee,
Who answered once her minion when he said:
'Dost greatly thank me?'—'Nay, stupendously.'

And herewith let our sight be surfeited. "

More Shameful Prostitution 15 XIX

Eighth Circle: Pouch 3. Simoniacal Popes 0 Simon Magus, O disciples vile!
Ye who the things of God, which ought to be
The brides of righteousness, lo! ye defile
For silver and for gold rapaciously;
Now it befits the trumpet sound your doom,
Because in this third pouch of Hell are ye.
Already had we on the following tomb
Mounted, to that part of the bridgeway whence
It doth the middle-moat quite overloom.
Wisdom Supreme! of art what evidence
In Heaven, Earth, and the Evil World is found,
And ah! how justly doth thy power dispense!
1 saw upon the sides and on the ground,
With many a hole the dark stone drilled, and all
Of one dimension, and each one was round.
None ampler seemed to me, nor yet more small,
Than those that in my beautiful St. John
Are made to the baptizers for a stall;
And one of these, not many years agone,
I broke for one who stifling would have died:
Be this a seal to undeceive each one.
Thrust forth from every opening, I descried
A sinner's feet, and saw the ankles twain
Far as the calf: the rest remained inside.
The soles of all were both consumed amain,
And so with flames the joints were quivering
No ropes and withies would have stood the strain.
As flame of oily things is wont to cling
Alone upon the face exterior,
So here from heel to point 'twas flickering.
"Master," said I, "who is that one who more
Infuriate writhes than his companions there,
And whom a redder flame is licking o'er?"

One of the legal punishments of that implacable period was the "planting" thus of the perfidiovs murderer. Dante's similitudes imply, of course, familiarity on the part of the reader of his time with the scene referred to. The customs, habits, sports, arts, affairs of all kinds from which he draws images have greatly changed,.to that we have to use more imagination in reading him The references to the Church as the Lady, or the Bride of Christ, and by extension of the Pope as the Vicar of Christ, are so frequent that comment is, in most cases, superfluous

And he to me: "If thou wilt let me bear
Thee down by yonder cliff that lies more low,
From him of him and of his crimes shalt hear."
"Thy pleasure, lord, is mine, and thou dost know
That I depart not from thy will," I said,
"And knowest my unspoken thought, I trow."
Thereon the fourth embankment did we tread,
Turned, and descended leftward from the bank
Down to the narrow, perforated bed.
The Master good not yet from off his flank
Deposed me, till he brought me to the hole
Of him who so was weeping with his shank.
"Whoe'er thou art, thus planted like a pole
Top downward," then began I, "do thou strive
To speak out, if thou canst, O wretched soul!"
My posture was the friar's, at hand to shrive
The false assassin, who, when planted, tries
To call him back, still to remain alive.
"Art thou already standing there?" he cries,
"Art standing there already, Boniface?
By several seasons, then, the writing lies..
And art thou glutted with that wealth apace, *t*
For sake whereof thou didst not fear betray
The Lady beautiful, and then disgrace?"—
Such I became as people brought to stay
Because an answer from the mark seems wide,
As if bemockt, not knowing what to say.
"Say to him quickly," hereon Virgil cried,
"T am not he thou thinkst, I am not he!'"
And as enjoined upon me, I replied.
The spirit writhed his feet exceedingly;
Then sighing, and with voice disconsolate,
Said to me: "What then wan test thou of me?
If thou desire so much to know my state,
That for this cause thou hast the bank traversed,
Know, I was vested with the Mantle Great.
True son of the She-bear, I had such thirst
Insatiate to advance the Cubs, mine own,
That wealth above, and here myself, I pursed.
Beneath my head the others down are thrown,
Preceding me in simony, and all
Flattened along the fissures of the stone.
Down thither shall I likewise drop withal,
When comes that other whom I thought to meet
What time I let the sudden question fall.
But longer now do I already heat
My footpalms, standing here inverted thus,
Than he shall planted stay with ruddy feet:
For after him a Pastor impious
Shall come from Westward, fouler in his deed,

Such as befits to cover both of us.
New Jason will he be, of whom we read
In Maccabees: and pliant as that lord,
Will he who governs France give this one heed."
I know not if foolhardy was my word,
But I made answer only in this key:
"I pray thee tell me now how rich a hoard
Saint Peter paid into the treasury,
Ere gave Our Lord the keys to his control?
Nothing in truth He askt save 'Follow me!'
Nor Peter nor the rest did levy toll
Of gold or silver, nor Matthias grant,
For the lost office of the guilty soul.
Then stay, well punisht, and be vigilant
In guardianship of the ill-gotten gold
That made thee against Charles so arrogant.
And were I not forbid to be so bold,
Because of reverence for the Keys Sublime
Which in the happy life thou diddest hold,
Still harsher language would befit my rime:
Pastors, your greed afflicts the world; it brings
Good underfoot, and it uplifteth crime!
The ex-Pope Nicholas III who is speaking was an Orsini, whose cognizance was the "orsa" ("ursa," she-bear) Referring to
Clement V, thc
Frenchman,
tool of Philip
the Fair. See 2
Maccabees,
iv and v
This donation of Constanline was at a later time proved to be fictitious. Dante lived before historical sources were critically analyzed. Milton's translation of this apostrophe will be remembered
Of you the Evangelist had prefigurings,
When her that sits the waters did he view
Committing fornication with the kings:
She with the seven heads begotten, who
From the ten horns her sign and sanction bore
Long as her spouse delight in virtue knew.
A god of gold and silver ye adore;
And from the idolaters how differ ye,
Save where they one, a hundred ye implore?
Ah, Constantine, to what iniquity
Gave birth—not thy conversion—that domain
Which the first wealthy Father took from thee!"
And while I sang to him in such a strain,
Whether that frenzy or that conscience bit,
With both his foot palms struggled he amain.
I think my Leader well applauded it,
He listened still with look of such content
To the clear accents which the truth befit.
Thereon to take me up, both arms he bent,
And when he had me wholly on his breast,
Remounted by the way of his descent;
Nor did he tire of holding me thus pressed,
Till up the summit of the arch he bare,
Which crosses from the fourth to the fifth crest.
Here he laid down his charge with tender care,
Tender, for rugged was the crag and steep,
That goats had found a toilsome passage there:
Thence was disclosed to me another deep.
Looking and Walking Backward 79 XX Y
Eighth Circle: Pouch 4. Diviners.
Origin Of Mantua
New punishment must needs by me be dirged,
And in a twentieth lay the theme pursued
Of the first Song, which tells of the submerged.
I now was wholly in an attitude
To peer down into the disclosed abyss,
Which was with tears of agony bedewed,
And through the circling vale I saw at this
A silent, weeping folk, who onward pressed
As pace in this our world the litanies.
As lower down on them my sight did rest,
Each wondrously distorted seemed between
The chin and the beginning of the chest:
For every visage had been twisted clean
Round to the loins, and backward they must go,
Since looking forward had forbidden been.
Thus utterly distorted by some throe
Of palsy, some one may have been perchance;
I never saw, nor think it can be so.
Imagine, Reader, so God's sufferance
Permit that, reading, thou be edified,
How I could keep unwet my countenance,
When near at hand our image I descried
Contorted so, the weeping eyes did wet
With tears the hinder parts where they divide.
Truly I wept, leaned on the parapet
Of the hard bridge, so that mine Escort said:
"Art thou among the other fools even yet?
Here piety lives on in pity dead.
Who is a greater reprobate than one
That grieves at doom divine? Lift up thy head,
Lift up thy head, and do thou look upon
Him earth engulfed before the Theban's sight,
Whereat all shouted: 'Whither dost thou run,
The soothsayer Amphiaraus, in the course of the expedition of the Seven against Thebes, was swallowed up by the earth. Dante gets the tale from the poet Siatius, whom we shall meet in Purgatory The Poet's visit to the beautiful Lunigiana named from the ancient Etruscan and Roman hum) at the foot of the marble snow of the Carrara Moun-

tains, is commemorated in the lovely eighth canto of Purgatorio This long digression, geographically so vivid and accurate as to the origin and situation of Mantua, is one of the few passages not vitally—at least not obviously—connected with the scheme of the whole. No other long poem has so few such excrescences, whose "moral is in being fair"

Amphiaraus? Why forsake the fight?'
From plunging downward he was only stayed
By Minos, who lays hold on every wight.
Mark how hi3 shoulders to a breast are made!
Because he wished to see too far before,
Forever backward doth he look and tread.
Tiresias see, who altered semblance wore
When from a male he was made feminine,
While all his members transformation bore;
And afterward he had to strike again
With wand the intertwining serpents two,
Ere he regained his plumage masculine.
With back to this one's belly is Aruns, who
In mountain land of Luni (on whose height
Drudges the Carrarese who dwells below)
Had once a cavern among marbles white
For his abode, from which he could behold
Ocean and stars with unobstructed sight.
And sbe whose locks unfilleted enfold
Her bosom from thy sight,—the hairy coat
O'er all her skin on the other side unrolled,—
Was Manto, who through many countries sought,
And after tarried where I had my birth:
Whereof to please me take a little note.
After her father had from life gone forth,
And Bacchus' city came to slavery,
This woman for a long time roamed the earth.
There lies a lake up in fair Italy,
At bottom of the Alps that fence Almain,
Tyrol above,—Benaco names that sea.
I think a thousand founts the Pennine drain
Of water which within that lake is pent,
Garda and Val Camonica between.
There is a middle place where he of Trent
Or Brescia pastor, or the Veronese,
Might give his blessing, if that way he went.
Peschiera, fair and mighty fortalice,
Sits where lies lowest the surrounding shore,
To front the Brescians and the Bergamese.
There whatsoever cannot tarry more
In bosom of Benaco, down must flow
And make a river through green meadow floor.
The waters gathering head, as Mincio,
No longer called Benaco, flow apace
Far as Governo, falling into Po.
Coursing not far, they find a level place
Where in a wide lagoon they stagnant spread,
And where in summer oft is noisomeness.
Passing that way, the Virgin, never wed,
Perceived a tract of land amid the fen,
Wholly untilled and uninhabited;
And there, to shun all intercourse with men,
Stayed with her servants, arts of magic plied,
Lived, and there left her empty body then.
The people, who were scattered far and wide,
Thereafter gathered in that place, which lay
Defended by the marsh on every side.
O'er those dead bones the city builded they,
And, after her who first had chosen the place,
Called it, without more omen, Mantua.
Denser therein was once the populace,
Ere ever Casalodi witlessly
From Pinamonte suffered such disgrace.
Hence if thou ever hear, I monish thee,
My city given foundation different,
Let falsehood not defraud the verity."—
"Master, thy reasons are so evident,
And so lay hold of my belief," said I,
"That others were to me but embers spent.
But tell me, of the people going by,
None seest thou worthy of note? for to their woe,
Only to that, returns my inner eye."—

Referring to a bloody coup d'itat in the course of which Pinamonte first duped and then expelled the lord of Mantua, Count Casalodi The Man in the Moon was popularly Cain carrying a bundle of thorns, the sorry "fruit of the ground" that lie harvested. The sky is of course invisible in Bell, but Dante will not forgo his astronomical allusion. The moon is one day past the full and sinks into the sea south of Seville (taking Jerusalem as the point of observation). That is, it is about G A.m.

Whereon he answered: "He whose

beard doth flow
Down from his cheeks upon his shoulders dun,
Was, what time Greece of males was emptied so
That in the cradles tarried almost none,
An augur, and with Calchas gave the sign
To cut, in Aulis, the first cable,—one
Eurypylus,—thus in a certain line
My lofty tragedy records the name:
Well knowest it thou who knowest each verse of mine.
That other, in the flanks so light of frame, /
Was Michael Scott, and of a truth he knew
Of magical deceptions well the game.
Guido Bonatti view; Asdente view,
Who now would wish his leather and his awl
Had held him,—all too late repents he too.
See wretched hags who let the needle fall,
The spool and distaff, for divining fain,
With herb and image working spells withal.
But come, for with his thorns already Cain
Doth hold of both the hemispheres the bound,
And yonder under Seville touch the main,
And only yesternight the moon was round:
Thou shouldst recall, for she did thee no wrong
One certain time within the wood profound."
While thus he spake to me, we moved along.

Bosses and Grafters 83 XXI *V*

Eighth Circle: Pouch 5. Barrators

Discoursing thus of matters different
Whereto my Comedy cares not to hark,
Holding the height, from bridge to bridge we went,
But halted other vain laments to mark
In Evil-pouches, other cloven den;
And there I saw that it was weirdly dark.
As in the Arsenal of Venice, men
Boil sticky pitch in winter, which they use
To make their vessels water-tight again
When unseaworthy; some perhaps may choose
To build anew,—some make it their concern
To caulk ribs buffeted in many a cruise;
Some hammer at the prow, some at the stern,
Some fashion oars and others cordage twine,
And some to mend the jib or mainsail turn:
Thus not by fire, but by an art divine,
Boiled clammy pitch down there, which every side
Smeared over the embankments that confine.
I saw it, but naught else therein descried,
Except the bubbles which the boiling raised,
As all heave up and then compress subside.
While thither downward steadfastly I gazed,
"Beware! beware!" my Leader thus began,
And drew me forth from where I stood amazed.
Thereat I turned, like one in haste to scan
The very thing which it behooves him flee,
And whom incontinently fears unman,
So that he puts not off his flight to see:
And there I saw a demon, black as night,
Run up the bridge behind my Guide and me.
Ah, how ferocious was he to my sight,
And in his action how unpitying,
With open wings and on his feet so light!

Dante here gives some pregnant hints about Lucca, as he elsewhere does of Siena and many other famous cities intimately known to him. Santa Zita is patroness of Lucca; the Holy Face is an ancient image of Christ still venerated in the Cathedral there; the Serchio flows near the city wall. Bonturo is excepted as who should say,—all grafters except Boss Tweed

His shoulder, which was high and tapering,
A sinner with both haunches sat astride:
That fiend the tendons of the feet did wring.
"Maltalons!" pausing on our bridge, he cried,
"One of the elders of Saint Zita, ho!
Down with him, while I go for more beside
Unto that city furnisht with them so:
Barrators all except Bonturo,—if
You offer money, make they Yes of No. "
He flung him down, and on the flinty cliff
Then wheeled about: ne'er gave so hot a chase
A loosened mastiff, running down a thief.
That sinner plunged, and aired his back apace;
But demons, lurking there the bridge below,
Cried: "No invoking here the Holy Face!
Here swim ye not as in the Serchio:
Therefore take heed, unless thou mean to try
Our grapples, not above the pitch to show."
Then, pricking him with hundred prongs, did cry:
"Here must thou dance about in covert guise,
That, if thou can, thou swindle on the sly!"
Cooks make their sculbons do not otherwise,
When with their hooks they plunge the carcass clean
Down in the caldron, that it may not rise.
Then said the Master good: "Lest it be seen
That thou art with me, do thou downward cower
Behind a block, that thou mayst have some screen;
And what though wrong may seem to overpower,
Be not afraid, for I these matters know,
Having been in such wrangle once before."

Beyond the bridge's head then did he go,
And when he reacht the sixth embankment's crest
He had full need a steadfast front to show.
With such a stormy fury manifest
As when dogs rush upon a beggar man,
Who, where he halts, makes quickly his request: *Among the Demons* 85
Thus from beneath the bridge those demons ran,
And turned against him every hook and rake;
But, "None of you be felons!" he began:
"Ere with your forks ye loose upon me break,
To listen to me send ye forward one:
Then as to tearing me your counsel take. "
All shouted out: "Be Malacoda gone!"
And halted: whereupon one forward goes,
Saying, "What can it skill?" as he came on.
"And dost thou, Malacoda, then suppose,
Thou wouldst have found me," said that Lord of mine,
"Safe hitherto, however ye oppose,
Without propitious fate and Will Divine?
Let me pass on, for Heaven has sent behest
That I show some one else this road malign."—
Thereat so fallen was his haughty crest,
That, letting fall the grapple at his feet,
"No striking now!" he shouted to the rest.
"O thou!" exclaimed my Leader, "from thy seat
Where crouching on the craggy bridge dost hide,
Now unto me securely make retreat."
Wherefore I moved, and promptly sought his side;
But all the devils sprang toward me so
I trembled lest the compact were defied.
Even thus I saw the soldiers long ago,
By compact from Caprona issuing,
Exhibit fear amid so many a foe.
With all my body I drew up to cling
Unto my Leader close, nor turned mine eye
From off their look, which was not promising.
Forks leveled, they kept saying: "Shall I try
And touch him up upon the hinder side?"
"Yes, nick it into him," was the reply.
But that one who was talking with my Guide,
Turned about quickly and commanded thus:
"Bide quiet, Scarmiglione, quiet bide!"
The arch was shattered when Christ after the Crucifixion descended into Hell. It is now, therefore, mid-forenoon of the Saturday after Good Friday, 1300
These are humorous travesties of names of Florentine families which Dante regarded as fair game. To this day Florence is noted for family names which seem humorous or ironical
Then: "There's no thoroughfare," he said to us,
"Across this bridge, because the sixth arch lies
Now on the bottom, wholly ruinous:
If going forward still to you seem wise,
Along the present bank ye journey may;
Hard by there doth another bridgeway rise.
Later by five than this hour yesterday,
Twelve hundred six and sixty years their line
Completed since here broken was the way.
Thither I'm sending some of these of mine
To see who airs him in the pitchy den:
Go with them, for they will not be malign.
Alichino and Calcabrina, forward then,
And thou Cagnazzo," he began to add;
"And Barbariccia, do thou lead the ten.
Libicocco and Draghignazzo come," he bade,
"Tusked Ciriatto and Graffiacane too,
And Farfarello and Rubicante mad.
Explore all round about the boiling blue;
Let these be safe to the next bridging way
Spanning the dens, a craggy avenue."—
"Alas, my Lord, what see I?"—did I say;
"Go we alone and without escort now;
If thou art able, none for me, I pray!
If with thy wonted heed observest thou,
Dost thou the gnashing of their tusks not hear,
And see them threaten mischief with their brow?"-
And he to me: "I would not have thee fear;
Let them gnash with their tushes at their will,
They do it for the parboiled wretches there."—
Upon the left-hand margin turned they still;
But each began by thrusting tongue to lump
The cheek, as signal to their leader ill,
Whereat he made a trumpet of his rump.
Swimmers in the Pitch 87 XXII
Eighth Circle: Pouch 5. Comedy Of The Devils
I have seen horsemen into battle go,
And when on dress parade, and striking tent,
And scurrying to anticipate the foe;
And foragers who on you made descent,
O Aretines, and many a mounted scout,
Running of tilt and clash of tournament,

With boom of bell and blare of trumpet shout,
With castle beacons and with drums of war,
And instruments from home and from without:
But never yet to bugle so bizarre
Did I see horse or foot set forward thus,
Nor ship by any sign of land or star.
On went we, the ten demons guiding us:
Ah, the fell company! but in the fane
With saints, in tavern with the gluttonous.
Intent upon the pitch did I remain,
To see the whole condition of the moat
And of the people in their burning pain.
Like dolphins when to sailors they denote,
With arching body bounding into sight,
That they look sharp to keep their ship afloat:
So ever and again, for easement slight,
Some sinner would present his back outside
And hide it fleeter than a flash of light.
And as *at"* marge of flooded moat abide
The frogs, and let the nose alone protrude,
So that their feet and other bulk they hide:
Thus upon either hand the sinners stood;
But fast as Barbariccia came their way,
They disappeared beneath the boiling flood.
I saw (whereat my heart quakes to this day)
One lingering thus—as it will often chance
That while the frogs are diving, one will stay:
Him Gramacane, standing near, with lance
Hookt in his pitch-entangled locks, updrew,
So that he seemed an otter to my glance.
(The names of all and sundry of that crew,—
So had I noted them when they were picked
And listened when they called,—by this I knew.)
"O Rubicante, see that thou inflict
Thy talons on his back and soundly flay!"
Shouted together all the maledict.
And I: "Endeavor, Master, if thou may,
To learn what luckless spirit thus doth lie
To clutches of his enemies a prey."
My Leader up beside him drawing nigh,
Demanded whence he came, and this his word:
"Born in the Kingdom of Navarre was I.
My mother placed me servant to a lord,
For she had borne me to a worthless blade,
Destroyer of himself and of his hoard.
Of good King Tybalt then retainer made,
In barratry attained I mastership,
Wherefore down here hot reckoning is paid."
And Ciriatto, each way from whose lip
A tusk, as of a boar, protruded long,
Gave him to feel how one of them could rip.
The mouse was fallen evil cats among,
But Barbariccia locked him in embrace,
Saying: "Stand off from him, while I emprong!"
Then to my Master turning round the face,
Added: "Ask on, if thou wouldst have him show
Yet more, before the other fiends deface."
"Now of the other sinners, dost thou know,"
My Leader said, "any Italian here
Beneath the pitch?" And he: "Short while ago
I quitted one who was their neighbor near;
Would I were still with him in cover laid,
So neither claw nor grapple should I fear."
"We bear too much!" then Libicocco said,
As with the hook he caught his arm amain,
And, rending, bore away a sinew-shred.
And Draghignazzo for a grip was fain
Down at the legs; whence their Decurion
With grim demeanor turned and turned again.
When they were somewhat pacified anon,
My Guide inquired of him, without delay,
Who ruefully his wound was gazing on:
"Who was that soul from whom, as thou dost say,
I11 parting madest thou to come abroad?"
"'Twas Friar Gomita," answered he straightway,
"He of Gallura, adept in every fraud,
Who had in hand his master's every foe,
And dealt so with them that they all applaud:
Taking the cash, he suavely let them go,
So says he; by no petty standard clever
In office jobbery, but hugely so.
Don Michael Zanche of Logodoro ever
Keeps him boon company; Sardinia draws
Them on to wag their tongues that weary never.
But look! I fear that other fiend because
His teeth are gnashing; I would add a word,
But for my scurf he seems to whet his claws."—
To Farfarello turning then, who stirred
His eyes asquint as if for striking home,
Their master marshal said: "Off, wicked bird!"—
"If ye would see or hearken all and some,"
The frightened spirit re-began thereon,
"Tuscans or Lombards, I will make them come.
But the Maltalons must be well withdrawn
Lest my companions their vendetta fear,

And I, not stirring from this spot, for one
That I am, will make seven more appear
By whistling, which, when one of us gets out,
Is customary signal with us here."
Gallura and Logodoro are two of the four provinces into which the Pisans divided Sardinia. Michael Zanche was victim of an atrocious crime recorded at the close of Canto xxriii. We meet a just and gentle magistrate of Gallura in Purg. viii
Cagnazzo at these words perked up his snout,
Wagging his head, exclaiming: "Hear the thing
The knave to fling him down has thought about!"
Whence, fertile in device, he answering
Said: "Over-knavish am I, it is true,
When I procure my friends more suffering."
Alichino could not hold, but counter to
The others, said to him: "If thou depart,
I shall in no wise galloping pursue,
But shall above the pitch on pinions dart:
Leave we the ridge, a shelter be the shore,
And see what match for us alone thou art!"
Reader, new sport is presently in store!
Bended their eyes the other way all these,—
He foremost who had been most loath before.
Selected well his time the Navarrese,
Planted his foot-soles firm, and in a flash Leapt, and releast him from their purposes. *Alichino,* Whereat they all with self-reproaches gnash, ST *mggZi-m*
He most who made them so discomfited; *had enabled the* And he leapt forward, yelling: "Not so rash!"
But little it availed: fear faster fled
Than wing could follow; down he dove amain,
And on, with upturned breast, the demon sped.
Not other fashion is the wild duck fain
Dive nimbly down, when draws too nigh the hawk,
Who, ruffled, wrathfully flies up again.
But Calcabrina, furious at the mock,
Followed behind him flying, in delight
At this escape, the scuffle not to balk.
And when the barrator had vanished quite,
His claws upon his fellow turned,—whence yond
Above the moat they grappled for the fight.
But the other was a sparrow-hawk full fond
To claw him well, and both together went
Plump to the middle of the boiling pond.
Navarrese to escape Demons Brought to Grief 91
The heat caused sudden disentanglement;
But all the same they had no power to soar,
So wholly did the pitch their wings cement.
Barbariccia, woeful with the rest, made four
Incontinently on their pinions glide,
With hooks and all, far as the other shore;
Down to their posts they dart on either side
And stretch their forks toward the limed pair
Who were already cookt within the hide:
And thus we left them in embroilment there.
A frog, while towing a rat across a stream, dives; but seeing the commotion a kite swoops upon both
Eighth Circle: Pouch 6. Hypocbites Under
Copes Of Lead
Silent, alone, and uncompanioned, so
Went we, the one before and one behind,
As on their way the Minor Friars go.
Upon the tale of Esop now my mind
Was fixt, by reason of the present fray,
Where of the frog and mouse we fabled find:
For not more similar are Ay and Yea
Than this to that, if with attention due
The outset and the end we rightly weigh.
And even as thoughts on other thoughts ensue,
Now out of that was born another: thus
My former terror double in me grew.
For I was thinking: "These because of us
Are flouted, damaged, and at naught are set,
So that, methinks, they must be furious.
If rancor should their evil purpose whet,
They will come after us, more pitiless.
Than dog when snapping up the leveret.
"
Already did I feel my every tress
Stiffen with terror, while I backward peer
Intently, saying: "Master mine, unless
Thou quickly hide thyself and me, I fear
Maltalons, for they hard upon us tread:
I so imagine them, I feel them near."
"If I were fashioned out of glass and lead,
I could not catch thine outward lineament
More quickly than thine inward now," he said.
"Even now thy thoughts among my own were blent,
With similar action and with similar face,
So that of both I made one sole intent.
If but the dexter bank so slope to base
That we may down to the next pocket go
We shall escape from the imagined chase.7
He had not yet made end of saying so,

When I beheld them come with wings spread wide,
Not far away, with will to work us woe.
Then caught me up full suddenly my Guide
(Even as a mother wakened by a shout
To see the flames enkindled close beside,
Who snatching up her little son runs out,
And, having less for self than him regard,
Tarries not even to wrap a smock about),
And from the ridge of the embankment hard
Glided face upward down the rocky shore
Which on that side the adjacent valley barred.
So swift through sluice slipt water nevermore
The wheel of any bankside mill to run,
Even when nearest to the floats, as bore
My Master me, that border land upon,
Lying securely claspt upon his breast,
Not merely as his comrade but as son.
Scarce did his feet upon the bottom rest,
Ere our pursuers were upon the hill
Above us; but all fear was now supprest:
Because the Providence Supreme, whose will
To the Fifth moat their ministry ordained,
Denies all power of leaving it and skill.
Down here we found a painted folk, who gained.
Their circling ground with steps exceeding slow,
Weeping, and weary in aspect, and constrained
They had on mantles with the hoods drawn low4
Before their eyes, and fashioned by such law
That in Cologne monastics wear them so.'
Gilded without, they dazzled them who saw;
But were within of lead, so loaded down.
That those of Frederick were light as straw
0 everlasting mantle, heavy gown!
We went along in their companionship
Leftward once more, hearing their dreary moan:

Geoffrey, Archdeacon of Norwich, had a cope of lead put over his head and shoulders, in which he was starved to death for whispering the news of the excommunication of King John. Evidently that heavy penalty was not invented by Frederick II

But with the weight forspent, that fellowship
So slowly came, that overtook we new
Pilgrims at every movement of the hip.
Wherefore unto my Leader I: "Now do
Find some one not unknown by name or deed
And thus advancing, let thine eyes rove too."
And one who gave the Tuscan accent heed,
Cried to us from behind: "O ye who race
Thus through the dusky air, now stay your speed!
Perchance thou'lt get from me the wished-for grace."—
Whereat my Leader turned and said: "Now stay,
And then proceed according to his pace. "—
I stopt, and by their look saw two betray
Great eagerness of spirit to advance;
But the load hindered, and the crowded way.
Having come up, awhile with eye askance
They gaze upon me, but their words control;
Then say between themselves, exchanging glance:
"He seems alive by action of his jole:
And by what privilege, if they are dead,
Go they divested of the heavy stole?"
To me then: "Tuscan, to the college led
Of the sad hypocrites, do not thou scorn
To tell us of thy origin," they said.
Then answered I: "In the great city born,
I by the river of fair Arno grew,
And have the body I have always worn.
But who are ye whom I behold imbrue
With tear-distilling sorrow thus the cheek?
And what the pain that glitters so on you?"
And one replied to me: "Of lead so thick
The orange hoods are, that without surcease
The weights thus cause their balances to creak.
Jovial Friars were we, and Bolognese,
I Catalan, he Loderingo named,
And by thy town together for its peace
Taken, where but a single man is claimed
By custom; and it still may be descried
Around Gardingo how we should be blamed."
"O Friars, your iniquities..." I cried,
But went no further, for there struck my sight
One on the ground with three stakes crucified.
Beholding me, he writhed with all his might,
Blowing into his beard with many a sigh:
But Friar Catalan, who saw his plight,
Said to me: "That staked felon thou dost eye,
Counseled the Pharisees that it was meet
That one man for the populace should die.
He is laid naked and across the street,
As thou beholdest, and has first to note
Of all who pass, how heavy weigh their feet.
His father-in-law is staked within this

moat,
And so the others of that Parliament
Which for the Jews was seed of evil fruit."
Virgil thereafter I beheld intent
With wonder on that spirit crucified
So vilely in eternal banishment.
Then to the Friar: "Be it not denied,
So please you, if it be legitimate,
To tell if He upon the right-hand side
Some passage, that we may go out that gate
Without constraining any angel swart
To come, and from this bottom extricate."
"Still nearer than thy hope," said he, "doth start
A bridgeway from the belt of the abyss,
Spanning the cruel valleys overthwart,
All save that, broken, it bespans not this:
Ye can ascend the wreck that heaps the ground,
And lies aslope, flanking the precipice."
With bended brow in meditation bound,
My Leader stood, then said: "In wicked wise
He told the way who hooks the sinners yond!"
During the year when these two were partners in the mayoralty of Florence the palaces of the great Ghibelline family of the Uberti were razed. The Gardingo was anciently a Longobard fortress, standing about where now is the Palazzo Vecchio and its Square Caiaphas and Annas. Virgil, here representing Rome, would not understand
The Friar: "At Bologna many a vice
I heard laid to the Devil, there among
That he's a liar and the father of lies."
Then went my Guide with larger strides along,
While wrath somewhat perturbed his aspect sweet:
Whence I departed from the burdened throng
After the prints of the beloved feet.
XXIV
Eighth Circle: Pouch 7. The Robbers And
The Serpents
In that young year-time when the sun his hair
Tempers beneath Aquarius, and when
The nights already tow'rd the southland fare,—
The hoarfrost on the greensward copies then
His sister's image white, but by and by
Abates the dainty temper of his pen,—
The husbandman, who sees starvation nigh,
Rising and looking out, beholds the plain
All whitened over, whence he smites his thigh:
Returning in, doth to and fro complain
Like one who cannot mend his wretched case;
Then out he comes and picks up hope again,
Beholding how the world has altered face
In little while, and catching up his crook
Drives forth his sheep to pasturage apace:
Thus when I saw perturbed my Master's look
Did I lose heart, and thus the balm applied
Suddenly from the wound the ailment took.
For when we reacht the ruined bridge, my Guide
Turned round and fixt me with that kindly glance
Which first I saw beneath the mountain side.
He spread his arms out, and, as laying plans
Within himself, first viewed the ruined fell,
Then laid his hold upon me to advance.
Like one who labors and considers well,
Seeming forever to provide anew,
My Leader, lifting me toward the swell
Of one crag, had another rock in view,
Saying: "Now clamber over that one, but
Try first if it be firm to grapple to."
No way was this for one in mantle shut,—
For scarcely we, he light and I pusht on,
Were able to ascend from jut to jut.
This is not the only passage where Dante shows himself familiar with mountain climbing. He had clambered over the weary heights between Lerici and Turbia (Purg. Hi), and perhaps over the Alps more than once. The allegory here is that of the difficulty of renouncing a course of dissimulation
And were it not that in that quarter, one
Ascent is shorter than the other, I know
Nothing of him, but I had been fordone.
But since upon a slant Malpouches go
All to the entrance of the lowest Pit,
So must the site of every valley show
One bank upreared above the opposite:
We clomb, however, the last craggy stair
At length, which from the ruined cliff is split.
My lungs so utterly were milkt of air
When I was up, no farther could I get;
Nay, sat me down on first arriving there.
"Thus now behooves that sloth aside be set,"
The Master said, "to fame we never come
Sitting on down nor under coverlet,
Which wanting, whoso goes to his long home
Leaves of himself on earth as little trace
As smoke in air or in the water foam.
Up then, thy panting overcome apace,
With spirit that will every battle dare
Unless the heavy body deep abase.
Behooves thee yet to climb a longer stair:
Suffices not that forth from these we went;
If thou hast understood, now forward fare."
Then up I rose, and showed my breath less spent
Than 'twas indeed, and said: "Go on once more,-
Look, if I be not strong and confident."
Upward we took our course, the bridgeway o'er,
A craggy, difficult, and narrow way,
And far, far steeper than the one before.
Speaking I went, no faintness to betray,
When out of the next moat a voice I

heard
1ll suited aught articulate to say.

Of what it said I do not know a word,

Though now atop the arch that crosses nigh;
But he who spake appeared to anger stirred.
Burning of Vanni Fucci 99

I had bent downward, but no living eye

Could through the darkness to the deep attain:

"Master, contrive to come," said therefore I, "To the next dike, the inner wall to gain;

For even as hence I hear, but cannot heed,

So peering down I shape out nothing plain." To this he said: "No answer is of need

Except the doing, for the fit request

Should tacitly be followed by the deed."— The bridge we now descended from the crest

Where with the eighth bank it united stood,

And then to me the pouch was manifest: And there I saw so terrible a brood

Of serpents, of diversity so great,

That the remembrance still freezes my blood. Let Libya with her sand no longer prate:

Though Amphisbcena, Cenchres, Phareae,

Chelydri, Jaculi, she generate, So many plagues, of such malignity,

She never showed, with Ethiopia wide,

Nor with the land that borders the Red Sea. Amid these, cruelly that multiplied,

Were running naked and affrighted folk

Hopeless of heliotrope or place to hide. *Heliotrope,*

Serpents the hands of these behind them yoke, *a mineral, possi .. ',. oly bloodstone,*

With head and tail transfix them through the lorn, *which so turned*

And into knotted coils before them lock. *the sun's rays . that the wearer*

And lo! at one who loitered near our coign *became invisible*

Of vantage, sprang a snake and pierct him through

Just where the collar and the shouldets join. Never was I so quickly written, or O,

As he took fire and burnt, and he was doomed All into ashes dropping down to go;
And then, when thus upon the ground consumed,

The dust drew of itself together there,

And suddenly that former shape resumed.

And even thus, the sages great declare,
The Phoenix dies and then is life astir
Again, on reaching her five-hundredth year;

Lifelong no grain nor grasses pasture her,
But tears of incense and amome alone,
And her last winding-sheet is nard and myrrh.

As one who falls, he knows not how, and prone
Upon the ground by force of demon lies,
Or other stoppage that enfetters one,

Who, when he rises, looks around, with eyes
Wholly bewildered by the mighty throes
Which he has undergone, and looking sighs:

Such was that sinner after he arose.
0 Power of God, how just art thou to men, That showerest for vengeance down such blows!

"Who mayst thou be?" my Leader askt him then;

Whence he replied: "I rained from Tuscany

Short while ago into this cruel glen.
Life of the brute, not man, delighted me,

Mule Vanni Fucci, bestially propense: Pistoia was my den, and fittingly."
I to my Leader: "Let him not slip hence,

And ask what crime here thrust him down so low: 1 knew him man of blood and insolence." The sinner feigned not, hearing me speak so,

But full upon me bent his face and thought,
And colored with shame's melancholy glow;

Then said: "It grieves me more that I am caught
In misery which I must now display,
Than when I from the other life was brought.

To thy demand I cannot say thee nay:

I am put down so deep as this because
I robbed the Chapel of the Fair Array,—

And falsely to another imputed 'twas.

But that thy joy in such a sight abate
If ever thou escape these gloomy jaws,

Open thine ears and listen to thy fate::,
Pistoia shall be thinned of Blacks at first;
Then Florence men and manners renovate.

Mars out of Magra's vale with thunderburst
Arises, in black clouds embosomed round,
And with a storm impetuous and curst,

A battle shall be fought on Picene ground;

Whence sudden shall the mist be riven, so
That every White thereby receives a wound.

And this I have foretold thee to thy woe." *The thunderstorm of war from the Valley of the Magra (Ltsvzgiana) is Moroeilo Malaspina, uhose". family received.' and protected' Dante in 1S06. There is a noble tribute to this family at the end of Purg, viii .An-.insulting gesture called by Ancient Pistol '"the fig of Spain" The serpents in this and the preceding canto are of course symbolic of the stealthy nature of the crime which they punish*

"..-.;"; "' XXV

Eighth Circle: Pouch 7. Transformations Of;. The Five Patrician Thieves

As soon as those his words concluded were,

His hands with both the figs the thief upbends,
Yelling: "Have at thee, God; at thee I square!"

From that time forth the serpents were my friends,
For one of them did then his neck entwist,
As who should say, "Herewith thy speaking ends!"

Another, coiling, riveted each wrist,
Clinching in front of him to such degree,
He could not any longer jerk the fist.
Ah, why, Pistoia, dost thou not decree
To burn thyself to ashes and so fall,
Since thy ill deeds outdo thine ancestry?
Throughout the dark infernal circles all,
I saw no spirit Godward flaunt such pride,
Not him who fell at Thebes down from the wall.
He fled away, all further word denied;
Then saw I come a centaur, full of spleen:
"Where is, where is the callous wretch?" he cried.
Harbors so many serpents not, I ween,
Maremma, as he had his back along
As far as where our lineaments begin.
Behind the nape, upon the shoulder clung
A dragon with his pinions wide outspread:
On every one he meets his fire is flung.
"That one is Cacus," then my Master said,
"Who in the cavern of Mount Aventine
Has made full many a time a pool blood-red.
He goes not with his brothers in one line,
By reason of his wily practice, when
He stole the neighboring great herd of kine:
Wherefore his crooked actions ended then
Beneath the blows of Hercules, who plied
Perhaps a hundred,—but he felt not ten.
"
While thus he spake, and that one past us hied, .
Lo! underneath us came there spirits three *"W*
Whom neither I perceived, nor yet my Guide,
Until they shouted to us: "Who are ye?"
Whereby our story to a stand was brought,
And them alone thereafter heeded we.
And now it happened (for I knew them not),
As it is wont to happen, that one shade,
To name another by some chance took thought,
Exclaiming: "Where can Cianfa still have stayed?"
Whence I, to make my Guide attentive so,
Upward from chin to nose my finger laid.
If thou to credit what I say art slow
Now, Reader, need there be no wonderment,
For I, who saw, can scarce consent thereto.
The while I raised my brows on them intent,
There darted a six-footed serpent out
In front of one, and grappling with him blent.
With middle feet it claspt his paunch about,
And flung the forward ones his arms around;
Then gashed both cheeks of him the gaping snout.
With hinder feet outspread the thighs it bound,
Thrusting its tail between them, and behind
Upward extending it, the loins enwound.
So never did the barbed ivy bind
A tree up, as the reptile hideous
Upon another's limbs its own entwined.
They clave together,—hot wax cleaveth thus,—
And interfused their colors in such wise
That neither now appeared the same to us:
Just as in burning paper doth uprise
Along before the flame a color brown
Which is not black as yet, and the white dies.
The other two each shouted, looking on,
"O me, Agnello, how thou alterest!
Lo, thou'rt already neither two nor one!"
The manner in which Dante gradually gathers, by attentive listening to their talk, the names of four of the five Florentine thieves, is an example of his unobtrusive art. The gesture with the finger beside chin and nose is frequent in Italy "Property was Already the two heads had coalesced,
ThaTtheseif was ' Whereby two faces seemed to be compelled
not the same. Into one face, wherein were two supprest.
mdouMname Now the two arms from strips quadruple swelled;
Neither two nor The thighs and legs, the chest and belly grew
callgil" To members such as never man beheld.
("The Phoenix All former aspect there was canceled through:
Uen ' Two and yet none the shape perverted showed,
And such with tardy steps away it drew.
As the eye-lizard, under the great goad
Of dog-day heat, from hedge to hedge again
Darts like a flash of light across the road:
So, tow'rd the bellies of the other twain
Darting, a little fiery serpent went,
Livid and tawny like a pepper-grain.
And in that part whence first our nourishment
We draw, it one of them transfixt, then down
In front of him fell back, and lay distent.
The pierct one gazed, but language uttered none:
Nay, rather yawned and never stirred a limb,
As if with fever or with sleep fordone.
He eyed the reptile, and the reptile him:
One from his wound, the other from its snout
Smoked fiercely, and the smoke commingled dim.
Be still now, Lucan, where thou tellst about
Wretched Sabellus and Nasidius,
And wait to hear what now shall be shot out!
Of Arethuse be still, Ovidius!
If, fabling, he converts her to a fount,
Cadmus to snake, I am not envious:
Because two natures never front to front
Has he transmuted, so that both forms grew
Each o'er the other's substance paramount.

In such wise answered each to each the two,
That to a fork the serpent cleft his tail,
And the stricken one his feet together drew.
Snake and Man Exchange Shapes 105
The legs compacted, and the thighs as well,
In such a manner that in little space
The juncture left no mark discernible.
Now in the cloven tail the form we trace
The other forfeited; the former's skin
Elastic grew, the other's hard apace.
I saw the arms drawn through the armpits in,
And the reptile's two short feet becoming long
By so much as the arms had shortened been. Thereafter the hind feet together clung
To form the member that a man conceals,
And to the wretch from his, two feet were sprung. Now while the smoke with a new color veils
The one and the other, causing hair to spring
On one, which from the other part it peels, One rose, and fell the other groveling,
Though turning not aside the cruel glare t
Whereunder each his face was altering. 1.
The erect one drew his where the temples were, f
And from stuff overmuch that thither went,
Ears issued from the cheeks, hitherto bare:
And what, not running back, remained unspent,
Sufficed to form a nose unto the face
And give the lips their fit apportionment. £.
He that lay prone, thrust forward his grimace,
And then his ears into his head are drawn *U.*
As draws the snail his feelers into place. Lastly the tongue, which heretofore was one *f*
And fit for speech, is cleft, and the cloven kind
In the other closes: and the smoke is gone. The soul thus with a reptile form combined,
Exploding hisses fled the valley through,
And the other, sputtering, remains behind: Then, turning to the snake his shoulders new,
Said to the third: "As I along this way
Have crawling run, will I have Buoso do."
The seventh ballast did I thus survey
Shifting, reshifting: here let novelty
Excuse me, if my pen go aught astray.
And notwithstanding that mine eyes might be
Somewhat bewildered, and my mind the same,
Those could not flee away so covertly
But that I plainly saw Puccio the Lame:
And of the three companions did he keep
His form, alone of those at first who came;
The other, O Gaville, thou dost weep!
Note
The last line refers to the only one not named, possibly out of consideration for the Cavalcanti family, to which he belonged. The spirited peasantry of the little village of Gaville had killed the scoundrel, and now weep the vendetta wreaked upon them by the family.
Dante Takes to Heart the Lesson 107
XXVI
Eighth Circle: Pouch 8. Fraudulent CounSelors: Ulysses
Rejoice, O Florence, since thou art so great,
Thy wings are beating land and sea around,
And even in Hell thy name is celebrate.
Among the robbers five like these I found,
Thy citizens,—whereat comes shame to me,
Nor do thy honors greatly thence abound.
But if near dawning dream be verity,
Within short while from now shalt thou perceive
What Prato, if no other, craves for thee.
If it must be, let come without reprieve; erene the mind when of the worst aware *.)*
The older I become, the more 'twill grieve.
We parted thence, and up along the stair
The spur-stones made before for our descent,
My Guide remounted now, and drew me there.
And as the solitary way we went
Amid the crags and splinters of the span,
The foot without the hand had been forspent.
Then sorrowed I, and sorrow now again,
When I direct my thought to what I viewed,
And curb my genius from the course it ran,
Lest it from Virtue turn to truanthood;
So that if favoring star or higher grace
Have given me aught, I forfeit not that good.
During that season when from us his face
He least conceals whose light the world doth fill,
What time the fly unto the gnat gives place,
The peasant who is resting on the hill
Sees many a firefly down along the dale,
Perhaps where he doth gather grapes and till:
With flames so many the eighth pit of Hell
Was everywhere agleam, as I beheld
On coming where I saw the bottom well.
And even as he whom bears avenged of eld
Looked on Elijah's parting chariot
When straight the way to Heaven the horses held:
For with the eyesight could he follow not
So that aught other than the flame was seen
Flitting aloft, a fading cloudy spot:
Thus moved along the throat of the ravine
Each flame, for none of them the theft unlock,
Though every flame a sinner wraps

within.

I stood to look upon the bridge of rock,
Erect, so that, did not a jut prevent,
To make me fall had been no need of shock.

And when my Leader saw me thus intent,
He said: "The spirits in the fires abide,
Each swathed within the burning element."

"Through hearing thee, my Master," I replied,
"Am I more certain; but what thou dost say
I had surmised and would have asked, O Guide,

Who is within that flame which comes this way,
Whose cloven top seems rising from the pyre
Where once Eteocles with his brother lay?"

"Ulysses pines," he said, "within that fire,
And Diomed; thus neither goes alone
In punishment, as neither went in ire:

And in their flame together do they groan
The ambush of the horse, whence was to come
The noble seed by the old Romans sown;
There weep the guile whereby, though dead and dumb,
Deidamia still Achilles wails;
And there they pay for the Palladium."
It is hard not to "If they within those sparks can tell their tales,"
fhfZdlslM-n Said I, "O Master, much! pray *thee,* pray *bearing of* Until my prayer a thousandfold avails, *Dante, despite* That thou refuse not to me *tQ . las yearning,* , » *from direct* Until the horned flame comes hither nigh: *speech with the* Thou seest h what des;re I Jean that way »

"Thy prayer deserves all praise," he made reply,
"And therefore I accept it; none the less
Take heed thou to thy tongue all speech deny:
!Leave me to speak, for I already guess

What thou desirest. Seeing that these were Greek,
Perhaps they might be shy of thine address."

After the flame with the divided peak

Had come where time and place to him seemed due,
I heard my Leader in this manner speak:

"O ye, within one fire remaining two,
If I deserved of you in b'fe, if I
Or much or little merited of you

When in the world I wrote the verses high,
Do not move on, but one of you declare
Whither, being lost, he went away to die."

One horn, the mightier of the ancient pair,
With murmuring began to quiver then,
Even as a flame made weary by the air.

Waving the summit back and forth again,

Thereafter, like a speaking tongue, the flame
Flung forth a voice and spoke as follows: "When

Of Circe I had taken leave,—the same

Who held me near Gaeta a year and more,
Ere yet iEneas gave it such a name,—

Nor tender love of son, nor pity for
My aged father, nor affection due
That should have cheered Penelope, o'erbore

The ardor that was in me to pursue

Experience of the world, that I might be
In human vices versed and virtue too:

But I put forth on the deep open sea

With but one vessel, and that little train
Which hitherto had not deserted me.

Both of the shores I saw as far as Spain,
Morocco, and Sardinia's isle, and so
The other islands bathing in that main.
Greeks. Likewise Petrarch, although a halfcentury nearer to the Renaissance, never mastered the language of Homer. Both looked, like Moses from Pisgah, to the land of heart's desire The noble tale of Ulysses, as well as the preceding splendid series of images, is in refreshing contrast to the horrible scenes we have witnessed. Dante owes nothing to Homer, whom he could not read. It is interesting to contrast Tennyson's ornate rehandling of this plain tale

I and my company were old and slow

When in upon that narrow pass we bore,
Where Hercules set up his bounds to show

That man beyond might venture nevermore.
Here left I Seville back upon the right,
And had left Ceuta on the other shore.

'O brothers,' said I, 'who are come despite
Ten thousand perils to the West, let none,
While still our senses hold the vigil slight

Remaining to us ere our course is run,
Be willing to forgo experience
Of the unpeopled world beyond the sun.

Regard your origin,—from whom and whence!
Not to exist like brutes, but made were ye
To follow virtue and intelligence.'

With this brief speech I made my company
So keen to go, that scarce to be denied
Would they have been thereafter, even by me.

And having turned the stern to morning-tide,
For the mad flight we plied the winged oar,
Steadily gaining on the larboard side.

Night saw the constellations more and more
Of the other pole, and ours at such descent
That it rose not above the ocean-floor.

Five times rekindled and as many spent

The light beneath the moon did wane away, Since to the passage of the deep we went, *The mountain is* When there appeared to us a mountain, gray *Ojtotpu* i" With distance, and upreared a loftier brow *tory. The age of* Than I had ever seen until that day.
the great wyag-yje j0yed, but joy soon turned to weeping now, *ers was yet* flW" *m tant, and any*-For out of the new land a whirling blast *ihmg could be* Arose and struck the vessel on the prow— *imagined, for* # # i i i *the other*

»ide of Thrice with the waters all, it whirled her fast; *the world was as* The frth upheaved the stern and sunk amain *unknown as is* r *the other side of* The prow, as pleased Another, till at last *the moon* The Qcean had aboye ug closed agam» xxvn

Eighth Circle: Pouch 8. Gdido Da Monte-
Feltro And Pope Boniface Viii

The flame became erect and quiet now
To speak no more, and now was passing on,
Nor did the gentle Poet disallow;
When after it there came another one
Which made us eye its summit, whence found vent
A vague and indistinguishable tone.
As the Sicilian bull, which with lament
Of him was first to bellow ('twas his due!)
Who gave it fashion with his instrument,
Bellowed with voice of every victim new,
So that, for all it was of brazen plate,
Yet it appeared with anguish stricken through:
Thus, having at their source not any gate
Nor "outlet from the fire, into its mode
Of speech were turned the words disconsolate.
But afterward, when they had found a road
Up through the point, transmitting it the same
Quiver in passing which the tongue bestowed,
We heard it say: "O thou at whom I aim
My voice, who spakst the tongue of Lombardy,
Saying,—'Now go, no more I urge, O flame!'
To pause and speak be irksome not to thee,
What though I come a little late withal:
Thou seest, although I burn, it irks not me.
If from that sweet Italian land thou fall
But now into this world of blinded souls,—
For thence I came with my transgression all,—
Say, have they peace or war, the Romagnoles?
For I was from the mountains there between
Urbino and the range whence Tiber rolls."
Still was I bended down, with eager mien,
When now my Leader touched me on the side,
Saying: "Speak thou,—Italian he has been."

The brazen bull in which were roasted alive the victims of the tyrant Phalaris, wlio first tested it upon its maker,—very properly, subjoins Dante The Polenta family from, which had sprung Francesco, and which was to be Dante's best shield Forli, where a French army had suffered bloody defeat by the person addressed The Malatesta of Rimini, the bloody, treacherous tyrants to whose fangs poor Francesca had been thrown Faenza and Imola, as well as Cesena, are named by their rivers. As in the case of Forli the cognizance of the ruling family is mentioned Quido da Montefeltro, the astute Christian, is contrasted to his disadvantage with the noble pagan Ulysses. There is another contrast between Quido and his son Buonconte in Purgatory (Canto »). These are three of the longer tales in the Poem

And I, well knowing what should be replied,
Began to speak to him with ready mind:
"O spirit, thou who there below dost hide,
Never was thy Romagna uninclined
Within her tyrants' hearts to battle-play;
But now I left no open war behind.
As many a year, Ravenna stands today:
The eagle.of Polenta so doth brood
That with her wings she covers Cervia.
The town that gave proof of long fortitude,
And in a bloody heap the Frenchmen threw,
Beneath the Green Paws finds herself again.
Verruchio's ancient Mastiff and the new,
Who ill disposal of Montagna made,
Still flesh their fangs where they are wont to do.
Lamone's and Santerno's towns are swayed
Under the Lioncel of the white lair,
From summer to winter time a renegade
And she whose flank is bathed by Savio fair,
Even as she lies between the plain and mount,
Lives between tyranny and freedom there.
Now who thou art thyself do thou recount:
Be not more stubborn than another, pray,
So may thy name long in the world hold front."
After the fire in its peculiar way
Had roared awhile, the pointed tip was quaking
Hither and thither, and the breath did say:
"If I supposed myself as answer making
To one who ever could return on high
Into the world, this flame should stand unshaking:
But since none from this yawning cavity
Ever returned alive, if truth I hear,
Fearless of infamy, do I reply.
I was a man of arms, then Cordelier,
Hoping to make amends, begirded so:
And this my hope was coming true, no fear,

Boniface Absolves Guido 113
But for the Priest Supreme, betide him woe!
Who put me back into my sins of old;
And how and wherefore I would have thee know.
"While I was yet a tenant of that mold
Of bone and pulp my mother gave, my bent
Was ever of the fox, not lion-bold.
I knew all wiles and ways to circumvent,
And plied the craft of them with such avail
That to the ends of earth the rumor went.
When I began to feel the years prevail,
Arrived that time of life when one had need
To coil the tackle up and take in sail,
What pleased before, now grieved me: so with heed
To penance and confession I withdrew;
Ah, hapless! and it had availed indeed.
The Prince of the new Pharisees, in view
Of Lateran, having a war in hand,—
And fcot with Saracen, and not with Jew,
For all his enemies were Christian, and
Not one of them at-Acre's fall was nigh,,
Nor yet a trader in the Soldan's land,—
Neither his Holy Orders nor his high
Office regarded, nor that cord of mine
Which used to make more lean those girt thereby
But as within Soracte, Constantine
Besought Sylvester heal his leprosy,
Likewise, his fevered pride to medicine,
Did this man seek out as physician me:
Counsel he craved, and I deemed silence just,
Because his language drunken seemed to be.
At length he said: 'Let not thy heart mistrust;
Henceforward I absolve thee: teach me how
To level Palestxina with the dust.
I have the power to shut, as knowest thou,
And open Heaven: whence double are the keysj
Which my foregoer held not dear enow.
'
regc *So the King in Hamlet reasons: "May one be pardoned and retain the offense?"*
Constrained me weighty arguments like these,
To such a point that silence seemed unfit:
'Father, since thou assurest me release
From that transgression which I must commit,
Long promise with short keeping,' so I said,
'Will make thee triumph in thy lofty Seat.'
Saint Francis came for me, when I was dead;
But shouted one of the black Cherubim;
'Convey him not, nor wrong mefor instead
He must go down among my minions grim,
Because he gave the counsel fraudulent,
From which Eime forth I have been dogging him.
For none can be absolved but he repent,
Nor can a man repent and will withal,
For contradictories do not consent'
Alas for me! 0 how I trembled all
What time he took me, saying: 'Can it be *"j»* ij
Thou didst not think that I was logical
Ty
Down unto Minos then he carried me,
Who twined with eightfold tail his stubborn frame,
And, after he had gnawed it furiously,
Said: "Tis a sinner for the thievish flame':
Whence, where thou seest me, am I forlorn,
And, going thus attired, bemoan my shame."
When he had thus his testimony borne,
The flame with anguisht utterance withdrew,
Twisting about and tossing the sharp horn.
We passed along, my Guide and I, up to
The next arch of the viaduct, whence showed
That moat of Hell wherein is paid their due
To those who, severing, make up their load.
XXVIII
Eighth Circle: Pouch 9. Sowers Of-Discord
Who ever in words released from laws of rime
Could fully of the blood and wounds report
That now I saw, though telling many a time? Every tongue would certainly fall short,
Because the heart and speech of humankind
Have little compass to contain such hurt. Could ever all the people be combined
Who in Apulia wept their blood poured out
Upon the fateful land time out of mind By Trojans, and in that long war, the rout
Which issued in the mighty spoil of rings,
As Livy writes, whose word we cannot doubt; With those who bore the brunt of buffetings
Resisting Robert Guiscard; and that horde
Whose bones the plowshare to this day upflings At Ceperano, where each Apulian lord
Proved faithless; and at Tagliacozzo's field
Where aged Erard conquered without sword: And all their mutilated limbs revealed,
It would be naught to that dismemberment
In the ninth pouch obscenely unconcealed. No cask that middle board or stave forwent
Was ever cleft so wide as one I saw
Ript from the chin clean down to fundament: Between the legs hang down the viscera;
The pluck appears, the wretched sack I see
That turns to ordure what goes in the maw. While I am all intent upon him, he

Observes me, and both hands in breast he plants, *rar e ry*

Saying: "Behold how I dismember me; How mangled is Mohammed! In advance

Of me goes Ali uttering his woe,

Cleft chin to forelock in the countenance.

Trojans for Romans; the rings picked up on the field of Cannos; Robert Guiscard, Norman conqueror of Apulia; Ceperano is perhaps a mistake of the poet, the only great battle of the campaign referred to is Benevento (Purg. Hi), where Manfred was deserted by the Apulians; Tagliacozzo, where young Conradin, nephew of Manfred, was captured, was gained by the prudence of the Frenchman Fra Dolcino wished to lead men back to apostolic simplicity and was cruelly punished after having made a brave fight

And all the rest thou seest here did sow

Scandal, while living, and schismatic feud,

And therefore are they cleft asunder so.

A devil is behind us, who with crude

Cleavage is carving, to the edge of sword

Putting each member of this multitude,

When we have circled round the path abhorred;

For lo! the gashes reunited are

Ere we revisit that infernal lord.

But who art thou who musest on the scar,

Perchance because reluctant to go hence

To punishment, self-sentenced at the bar?"—

"Death has not reacht him yet, nor has offense,"

My Master answered, "to this torment led;

But to procure him full experience,

It is my bounden duty, who am dead,

To lead him down through Hell from round to round:

As I speak with thee, this is truly said."

More than a hundred, when they heard this sound,

Stood still within the moat at me to peer,

Forgetting in their wonder every wound.

"Well then, to Fra Dolcin this message bear,

Since thou, perchance, wilt shortly see the sun,

That if he would not quickly join me here,

Let him be armed with food, or be undone

By the Novarese, because of stress of snow:

Else were their victory not so lightly won."

When he had lifted up one foot to go,

Mohammed spoke to me such words as those,

Then stretcht it to the ground, departing so.

Another, who with slitted gullet goes,

And who withal has but a single ear,

And close beneath the eyebrows cleft the nose,

Stopping for wonder with the rest to stare,

Opened before that mutilated throng

His gullet, which was crimson everywhere,

Curio, Mosca, Bertran de Born 117

And said: "O thou by pangs of guilt unwrung,

Whom up in Latin country long ago

I saw, unless undue resemblance wrong,

Remember, Pier da Medicina's woe

If thou return to see the lovely plain

That from Vercelli slopes to Marcabd.

And speaking then to Fano's worthiest twain,

Ser Guido and Ser Angiolello, say

That, if our foresight here be nothing vain,

With sack and stone shall they be cast away

;Out of their ship, by a fell tyrant's guile,

And perish hard by La Cattolica.

From Cyprus westward to Majorca's isle,

Saw never Neptune so great outrage done

By pirates or Argolic folk erewhile.

That traitor who sees only with the one,

And lords the city, sight of which one here

Would be delighted never to have known,

Will summon them in parley to appear;

Then so will deal that neither vow shall be

Required against Focara's wind, nor prayer."

And I to him: "Show and declare to me,

If thou wouldst fain that word of thee be brought,

Him who deplores that sight so bitterly. "

Therewith on a companion's jaw he caught,

And with rude hand the mouth he open rent,

Crying: "This is the wight, and he speaks not;

This, this is he who, being in banishment,

Quencht doubt in Caesar, saying: 'To men prepared

Delay was ever found a detriment.'"

Oh, how disconsolate to me appeared,

With tongue asunder in his gullet lopt,

Curio, who in his speech so greatly dared!

And one whose hands from both his wrists were chopt,

The stumps uplifting so athwart the gloom

That blood upon the face defiling dropt,

This tyrant who sees but with one eye is Malaiestino, now tyrant of Rimini, where Curio had advised Cassar not to delay his advance on Rome. Focara is a squally headland on the Adriatic near La Cattolica, between Rimini and Fano Mosca of the Lamberti clan was he who advised the murder of young Buondelmonte, to which the origin of the great feud of the Guelfs and Ghibellines was attributed by tradition. See Paradiso xvi This Provencal poet was the friend oj Henry, called the young King, eldest son of Henry II of England

Cried out: "To memory let Mosca come,

Who said, alas! 'A thing once done is sped!'

Which was to Tuscan people seed of doom."

"And death to all thy kin," I adding said:

Whereon he went like person crazed

with rue,
Heaping up sorrow upon sorrow's head.
But I remained to look upon that crew,
And saw a thing I should feel insecure
Even to tell without assurance new,
If Conscience did not wholly reassure,
That good companion which emboldens man 1
Beneath the conscious helm of being pure. *I*
I truly saw, and seem to see again
A headless body going by, as passed
The others of that melancholy train;
And dangled by the tresses holds he fast
The severed head, which like a lantern shows,
And groans, "Woe me!" gazing at us aghast.
Of self he made himself a lamp,—and those
Were two in one, and one in two were they;
How that can be, Who so ordains, He knows.
Arriving just below the bridging way,
The arm with head and all uplifted he,
To bring the nearer what he had to say,
Which was: "Now see the grievous penalty,
Thou who to view the dead dost breathing go,
If any be as great as this one, see!
And that thou mayst bear tidings of me, know,
Bertran de Born am I, who counsel fell
Did craftily on the young king bestow,—
Made son and father each to each rebel:
Not upon Absalom and David more
With wicked promptings wrought Ahithophel.
Because I parted those so bound of yore,
Woe worth the day, I carry now my brain
Cleft from its source within my body's core.
Thus retribution doth in me obtain."
XXIX
Eighth Circle: Pouch 10. Counterfeiters
Of Metals
U.
The many people and strange wounds did steep
Mine eyes with tears, and made them drunken so
That they were craving, but to stay and weep. -
But Virgil asked me: "Whereon gazest thou?
What may it be that still thy sight beguiles
To rest upon sad mangled shades below?
Thou wast not wont to do so otherwhiles:
Consider, wouldst thou make the count complete,
The valley circles two and twenty miles,
And now the moon is underneath our feet;
Brief is the time vouchsafed us for the way,
And more to see than here thy glances meet."
"Hadst thou but heeded," did I answering say,
"The reason why my gaze was bended there,
Perchance thou wouldst have granted longer stay."
Already did my Leader forward fare,
I following while making my reply,
Subjoining then thereto: "Within that lair
Whereon so steadfastly I bent mine eye,
Methinks a spirit of my blood complains
About the crime that costs down there so high."
Then said the Master: "Baffle not thy brains
Henceforth with anxious thought concerning this;
Mind other thing, although he there remains:
For him I saw beneath the pontifice
Menacing thee with finger vehement;
Geri del Bello named in the abyss.
But thou wast at that moment all intent
On him who once held Hautefort,—thus the name
Thou heardst not, nor didst look, until he went."
"Dear Guide, the violent death that on him came,
For which," said I, "unpaid remains the score,
By any one a partner in the shame,
The' fnljn'ljers of four different kinds (alchemists, impostors, debasers of coin, malicious liars) are afflicted with disguising or deforming diseases. As everywhere, there is some congruity of punishment and sin. Here, as at the close of the next canto, Virgil takes Dante to task for being too deeply absorbed. Dante's apparent adhesion to the un-Christian custom of the vendetta is one of the several inconsistencies between creed and sentiment, without which he would not be like all the rest of us Undrained malarial regions. The Tuscan Maremma, so often referred to, is the wild moorland country near the seaboard southwest of Siena. The river Chiana stagnated in the region between Tiber and Arno, where Lake Trasimene lies. The Arno, indeed, once flowed into the Tiber. The region is now drained
Made him indignant; whence he passed before
Getting speech with me, if I guess aright,
And so has made me pity him the more. " /
Thus we conversed as far as the first height
Which from the bridge the neighbor valley shows
Quite to the bottom, were there but more light.
When we were over the last cloister-close
Of the Malpouches, so that to our view
All its lay brothers could themselves disclose,
Strange lamentations pierced me through and through,
Which had their arrows barbed with pity all:
Whence with my hands I shut mine ears thereto.
If from Chiana's every hospital,
'Twixt July and September, all the sick,
Maremma's and Sardinia's withal,

Were in one trench together crowded thick:
So woeful was it here, and such a scent
As out of putrid limbs is wont to reek.
Upon the final bank we made descent
From the long bridge, and still did leftward fare;
And then my vision, growing keener, went
Down tow'rd the bottom of the pocket, where
The High Lord's handmaid, Equity condign,
Punishes falsifiers apportioned there.
It was no greater sorrow, I opine,
To see Egina's people all infirm,—
What time the atmosphere was so malign
That animals, down to the little worm,
Fell stricken, and the ancient people then,
As poets for a certainty affirm,
Were from the seed of ants restored again,—
Than now to see, throughout that dim abode,
Languish in ghastly stack the souls of men.
They lie across the paunch, the shoulders load,
Of one another, and some creeping round
Shifted their place along the dismal road.
The Leprous Alchemists 121
Step after step we went without a sound,
Looking, and listening to the sick ones, who
Could not lift up their persons from the ground.
I saw, on one another leaning, two
(As pan is propt against a pan to dry)
All scab from head to heel: I never knew
A stableboy so eagerly to ply
The currycomb because his master watches,
Or one who keeps awake unwillingly,
As each of these incontinently scratches
Himself with biting nails, for frenzy mad
Of itching, which no other succor matches.
So was the tetter which their bodies clad
Flayed from them, as from bream knife scrapes the scales,—
Or other fish, if any larger had.
"O thou whose every finger thee dismails,"
So did my Guide to one of them begin,
"And sometimes makest pincers of thy nails,
Say if there be among those here within
Any Italian, so suffice thee thus
Thy nails forevermore upon thy skin."
"Italians both, whose plight so hideous
Thou seest," weeping, one replied; "But tell,
Who art thou that dost ask concerning us?"
My Leader answered, "Down from fell to fell
I with this living man am traveling,
And I came purposing to show him Hell."—
Thereat the mutual trestle sundering,
That couple turned round to me tremblingly,
With others who by echo heard the thing.
The gentle Master then drew close to me,
Suggesting: "To thy mind expression give."—
And as he willed, began I: "So may be
Your fame in the first world not fugitive,
Fading from human mind without a trace,
But may it under many a sun still live,
Examples of fashionable, ostentatious spendthrifts. Cloves imported from the far East at enormous expense. Siena gay, elegant, rich, was the garden in which such seed took root. The club was of young men of fashion who tried to see which one could run through his fortune most swiftly and merrily. They were eminently successful and their fame is still alive in their beautiful city It is interesting to find in our Shakespeare an echo of Dante. He calls Julio Romano the ape of nature
Declare me who ye are and of what race:
Do not, I pray, the revelation dread
Because of the foul punishment's disgrace."
"I was an Aretine," one answering said,
"Siena's Albert cast me in the fire;
But what I died for nowise hither led.
'Tis true I said, as did the whim inspire,
That I could wing the air in flight: whereon
He, who had little wit, but fond desire,
Would fain be taught that cunning, and alone
For I made him no Daedalus, made me
Burn at the stake, through one who called him son
But Minos damned me down for alchemy,
Which in the world I practiced, to the clutch
Of the tenth pouch and last, nor erreth he."
Then to the Poet I: "Was ever such
A foolish gentry as the Sienese?
Surely not so the French, by very much!"
The other leper, hearing words like these,
Spoke up: "Except me Stricca, resolute
For temperance in spending, if you please;
And Niccold, the first to institute
The costly application of the clove
Within the garden where such seed takes root;
Except the club where Caccia d'Ascian strove
To squander his great wood and vinery,
And Abbagliato his vast wit to prove.
But that thou know who thus doth second thee
Against the Sienese, now sharpen so
Thine eye that well my face responds, and see!
I am the shadow of Capocchio
Who did by alchemy false metals shape;
And, if I well descry thee, thou shouldst know
The curious skill that made me Nature's ape." *Examples of Insanity* 123
XXX , Eighth Circle: Pouch 10. Master Adam Of Brescia And Sinon Of Troy

In time when Juno had so angry grown
For Semele, against the Theban strain,
As she had more than once already shown,
Then Athamas was stricken so insane
That he, his very wife encountering,
Burdened on either hand with children twain,
Cried out: "Spread we the nets for capturing
The lioness and whelps upon this ground";
Then, stretching forth his claws unpitying,
He took the one Learchus named, and round
Whirled him, and round, and dasht him on a stone:
Herself, then, with her other charge, she drowned.
Again when Fortune had so overthrown
The arrogance of Trojans all too brave,
That king and kingdom were alike undone,
Poor Hecuba, a wretched captive slave,
When she had looked on dead Polyxena,
And afterward, beside the ocean wave,
The body of her Polydorus saw,
Barked like a dog, out of her senses then;
So grief had wrung the soul of Hecuba.
But never furies came to Theban ken,
Or Trojan, of so much ferocity
In goading brutes, much less the limbs of men,
As in two pallid, naked shades saw I,
Running along and biting in such kind
As does the boar when loosened from the sty.
One seized upon Capocchio, and behind
His neck-joint fixt a fang so murderous
It made the solid rock his belly grind.
Said the Aretine, who stood there tremulous:
"That goblin's Gianni Schicchi, and insane
He goes about to mangle others thus."
"Oh!" said I, "so the other may refrain
From planting fangs in thee, let me persuade
Thee tell who 'tis ere it dart hence again."
And he to me: "That is the ancient shade
Of Myrrha, who in her abandoned mood
Illicit love unto her father made.
Coming to sin with him, she understood
To take an alien form; as who withdrew
Yonder, to win the queen mare of the stud,
Made bold Buoso Donati to indue
In counterfeit presentment, making will
And testament in legal order true."
And when the rabid pair had passed, who still
Had riveted my gaze, I turning eyed
The other malefactors starred so ill.
One fashioned like a lute I then espied,
If only at the groin were amputate
The thighs, just at the point where they divide.
The heavy dropsy which doth so mismate
The limbs with ill-concocted humor thin,
That face and loin are disproportionate,
Compelled him so to hold his lips atwin
As hectics do, for out of thirst he bent
Upward the one, the other tow'rd his chin.
Casentino, "O ye exempted from all punishment
JgJJf *$"* In this grim world and why I do not know,"— *Amo, above* So he began,—''Ah! look and be intent *b% etwo'ctinTof* Upon the mode of Master Adam's woe: *Apennine and* Living, I had enough of what man wills, *t%! % Xonu And* now one droP of water crave *helowFaHerona. See* The rivulets to Arno from the hills *anT%T"* Descending through the Casentino green, *Alvernia, where* Cooling and freshening their little rills, *feivX'Z*-Ever and not TM.va. in, by me are seen,.
mata, overlooks Because their image is more withering
Than the disease that makes my visage lean.— *the Casentino Self-Pity and Unrepentant Hate* 125
Rigorous Justice with its goading sting,
Takes vantage of the very region where
I sinned, to give my sighs a nimbler wing.
There is Romena, where the coin that bare
The Baptist's image did I counterfeit:
For which I left my body burnt up there.
But could I Alexander's wretched sprite,
Or Guido's, or their brothers', down here see,
For Fontebranda I would not give the sight.
One is already in, if truthful be
What the mad shades that circle round me say,
But since my limbs are tied, what steads it me?
If yet enough of nimbleness had they
To carry me an inch a hundred year,
Already had I started on the way
To seek him 'mid this squalid rabble here,
Although eleven miles the round deploy,
Nor less than half a mile across appear.
Through them in such a family am I:
'Twas they who instigated me to stamp
The florins with three carats of alloy."
"What wretched two," said I, "lie, scamp by scamp
Together, hard upon thy right confine,
Reeking, like to wet hand in winter's damp?"
And he replied: "I found them here supine,
When to this trough I rained; they've moved no more
Since then, nor ever will they, I opine.
She, who false witness against Joseph bore,
He, Sinon the false Greek from Troy: intense
The fever is that makes them reek so sore."
And one of them, who seemed to take offense
At being mentioned in a mode so mean,
Fisted forthwith his hidebound corpulence,

Which rumbled, as it were a tambourine;
But Master Adam planted in his face
An elbow no less vigorous, I ween,
*The florin had on one ride the image of John the Baptist and on the other the Florentine lily. This and the Venetian ducat were the standard gold coins of those ages. As the credit of the Republic depended upon the faith that all the world had in its money, to tamper with the coin amounted to treason Counts of Romena who, being in debt, employed Master Adam, the famous Brescian expert, to debase the florin. The picturesque ruin of Romena, and the nearly dried-up Fontebranda that supplied it with water, are still there. That region and others, which in Dante's time were well-wooded and well-watered, are now denuded of forest and relatively arid In the 9th ditch the circumference is 2% miles (beginning of Canto xxix). The Pit is therefore a rap-*Saying to him: "Though I be held in place *idly narrowing* Because of my obesity of loin, *funnel, enor-. " mously wide at* I have a limber arm for such a case." *the top*
"When going to the stake," did he rejoin,
"Thou madest not so free with it, perdy;
But so, and more, when thou wast making coin."
"Thou sayest true," the dropsied made reply,
"Thou didst not witness to the truth so well
When of the truth they questioned there at Troy."
"Told I false tale, false coinage didst thou tell,"
Said Sinon, "for one fault am I undone,
But thou for more than other fiend of Hell."
"Bethink thee of the horse, thou perjured one,"
The sinner of inflated belly cries,
"That the world knows it, be thy malison."
"Thy malison the thirst that cracks and dries
Thy tongue," the Greek said, "and the filthy swill
Which makes that paunch a barrier to thine eyes."
"Thy mouth is gaping open to thine ill
As usual," thereon the coiner said,
"For if I thirst and flux my belly fill,
Thou hast the fever and the aching head;
To lap the mirror of Narcissus, few
The words of invitation thou wouldst need."
While I was listening absorbed,—"Now do
Go staring on!" the Master said to me,
"A little more and we shall quarrel too."
Now when I heard him speak thus angrily,
I turned me round toward him with such shame
That still it circles through my memory.
And even as he who of his harm doth dream,
And, dreaming, doth to be a dreamer sigh,
Craving what is, as if it did but seem,
Such, without power of utterance, grew I:
Longing to bring, I brought excuses in,
Yet did not think myself excused thereby.
Virgil Keeps Dante's Heart Pure 127
"Less shame would purge away a greater sin
Than thine has been," at this the Master cried, "Therefore disburden thee of all chagrin; And count that I am ever at thy side,
If it fall out again that Fortune place
Thee where in such a brabble people bide:.Because desire to hear the like is base.") XXXI
Descent: The Giants Towering Around The Pit
One selfsame tongue first bit these cheeks of mine,
Suffusing both of them with bashful blood,
And then held forth to me the medicine.
Achilles' lance, as I have understood
(He had it from his sire), was wonted so
To give first evil guerdon, and then good.
We turn our backs upon the vale of woe,
Up by the bank that girdles it around,
And without any speech across it go.
Here less than night and less than day we found,
Whence little way before my vision went;
But now I heard a mighty horn resound
So that it would have made all thunder faint:
Whence, running counter to it, on one spot
Mine eyes were turned, and wholly now intent.
After the dolorous defeat was wrought
That lost to Charlemagne the blest array,
A blast so dreadful Roland winded not.
Not long I held my head bended that way
When many a lofty tower appeared to rise;
Whence I: "What is this city, Master, say?"
And he replied to me: "Because thine eyes
Traverse the darkness through too wide a space,
Befalls that fancy wanders in such wise.
Well shalt thou see, arriving at that place,
How from afar the sense deceived may be:
Whence somewhat forward spur thyself apace."
Taking me by the hand then tenderly,
"Ere yet," continued he, "we farther go,
So that the truth appear less strange to thee,
Not towers are these, but giants, must thou know,
And in the Pit about the bank are they,
From the navel downward, one and all below."
As when the mist is vanishing away,
Little by little through the blotted air
The gaze shapes out whatever hidden lay:
So, through the dense and darksome atmosphere
Piercing, while ever nearer to the bound,
Forsook I error to encounter fear.
For, as with circling mural turrets crowned
Montereggione stands, from the orifice

Emerged half figures, turreting around
The margin that encircles the abyss,
The horrible giants whom Jove from the sky
Still with his thunder threatens, not amiss.
I could the face of one by now descry,
Breast, shoulders, and of belly portion great,
And either arm depending by the thigh.
Certainly Nature, ceasing to create
Such living beings, showed exceeding sense
These ministers of Mars to abrogate-
And if of elephant and whale repents
She nowise, he who subtly looks will find
Of justice and discretion evidence:
Because where the equipment of the mind
Combines with force and malice criminal, *f* No bulwark can be made by humankind. /His face appeared to me as huge and tall
As is Saint Peter's Pine-cone there at Rome,
With the other bones in due proportion all:
So that the bank, which was an apron from
His middle down, showed upward of his size
So much that, boasting to his hair to come,
Three Frisians would have made it good nowise:
For I beheld of him thirty full palms
Down from the place where man the mantle ties.
"Rafel mai amech zabi almi,"
The mouth ferocious began bellowing,
To which are not befitting sweeter psalms.

Montereggione still stands, as here described, a circular iurreted wall surrounding a village, a few miles north of Siena, of whose domains it was once a strategic point

An enormous antique cone, some ten feet high, of gilded bronze, now in the Garden of the Vatican

To him called out my Leader: "Stupid thing!
Stick to thy horn; contrive to make it serve
Thine anger, or whatever passion sting.
Search at thy neck and there wilt thou observe
The cord that makes it fast, O soul confused!
And see the horn thy mighty breast becurve."
And then to me: "He hath himself accused;
This one is Nimrod, through whose evil mood
One language in the world is not still used.
Leave him, for empty speaking were not good:
Since every language is to him the same
As his to others, of none understood."
We therefore journeyed on, with constant aim
Toward the left, and at a crossbow shot
We found one far more fierce and huge of frame.
The master smith to bind him know I not,
But he was holding out his left hand bound
In front of him, the right behind drawn taut
By a cable chain, which held him so enwound
From the neck down, that on the part displayed
As many as five coils begirt him round.
"This arrogant soul was bent," my Leader said,
"To try conclusions with almighty Jove,
Whence in such fashion is his meed repaid.
His name is Ephialtes; he did prove,
When giants frighted gods, his force immense:
The arms he brandisht never will he move."
And I to him: "I would, if naught prevents,
That of the measureless Briareus
These eyes of mine might have experience."
"Antaeus shalt thou see," he answered thus,
"Hard by, articulate, unfettered,—he
To bottom of all bad shall carry us.
'Tis a far cry to him thou wouldest see;
Made fast is he, and fashioned like this one,
Save that his features more ferocious be."
Earthquake aforetime there was surely none
Of force to rock a turret as when grim
Ephialtes sudden shook himself thereon.
I feared death never as I did from him,
Nor need had been of more beyond the dread,
Had I not seen his gyres on every limb.
Farther along we then our footsteps sped,
And reached Antaeus standing forth ells five
Above the rocky verge, without the head.
"O thou who sawest the fateful valley give
Glory to Scipio, and on that day
When Hannibal and his host turned fugitive,
Didst bring a thousand lions for thy prey;
And through whom, hadst thou with thy brothers been
At the high battle, some still seem to say
The sons of Earth had won the palm therein:
Be not disdainful now to carry us
Down where the winter locks Cocytus in.
Make us not look to Typhon nor Tityus;
This man can give what here ye are craving for:
Wherefore stoop down, nor curl thy muzzle thus.
He in the world can yet thy fame restore:
For still he lives and waits long life, unless
Grace call him to herself his time before."
The Master thus; and he in eagerness

Took up my Leader in those hands outspread
Whence Hercules once felt the mighty stress.
And when he felt their pressure, Virgil said:
"Come hither, that I may enclasp thee quite";
Then of himself and me one fardel made.
Such as the Carisenda seems to sight
Of one beneath its leaning, when a cloud
Goes over, and the tower hangs opposite:
Just so Antaeus seemed to me who stood
Watching to see him lean; and it was then
I could have wished to go by other road.
Carisenda (or Garisenda) is one of a pair of leaning towers standing side by side at Bologna. This is 160 feet high; the other, which slants less, 320. Perhaps the Carisenda was once as high as its mate. Dante's choice of this, rather than of the more beautiful and famous tower at Pisa, is one of many reasons for thinking him to have been a student at Bologna. The writer has tested the vividness of the comparison under the slant both of this tower and But lightly down he laid us in the fen
The impression That Lucifer with Judas prisons fast:
is strong that Nor lingered there thus leaning, but again *the tower is-n* j i .1. *falling* Kose up and up, as in a ship the mast. *The Violent against Kindred* 133

XXXII

Ninth Circle: Caina; Antenoha

Had I such harsh and grating rimes as must
Be most in keeping with the dismal Pit
Where all the other crags converging thrust, I would press out the juice of my conceit
More perfectly: but since 'tis otherwise
Not without fear I come to speak of it: Because it is no frolic enterprise
To plot the ground of all the universe,
Nor for a tongue that *Mama* and *Papa* cries. But be those Ladies helpers in my verse,
Who helpt Amphion Thebes to close and keep,
That from the fact the word be not diverse.
0 dwellers in the unrecorded deep, Rabble beyond all others born amiss,
Better had ye on earth been goats or sheep!
When we were down within the dark abyss
Beneath the giant's feet, but far below,
And yet I gazed at the high precipice,
1 heard it said to me: "Look how thou go:
Let not thy soles betrample as they pass
The heads of weary brothers full of woe." Whereat I turned, and saw there a morass
Before and underfoot, and frost thereon
Made semblance not of water but of glass. The Austrian Danube never laid upon
Her current in the winter, veil so thick,
Nor, far beneath the freezing sky, the Don, As here there was: so that if Tambernic *Tall, rocky*
Or Pietrapana had tumbled there amain, *veas*
Not even the border would have given a creak. And even as frogs, that they may croak, remain
With muzzle out of water, when in dream
The peasant-maiden often gleans again:
Even so, as far up as where blushes stream, The woeful shades in the ice were pinched and blue,
Setting their teeth in tune to the stork's theme.
Each one of them held down the face from view,
By chattering teeth their chill may be divined,
And by the eyes how bitter is their rue.
Now, looking round about awhile, I find
Down at my feet, two forms so closely pressed
The tresses of the head are intertwined.
"Tell, ye who thus together strain the breast,"
Said I, "who are ye?" And their necks they bent,
And when their faces tow'rd me were addressed,
Their eyes, whose humor still within was pent,
Brimmed over at the lids, whereon the frost
Bound fast the tears between, and lockt the vent.
No clamp from board to board yet ever crossed
That held so firmly: whence, like he-goats twain, Together butted they, in anger lost. One, from whom frostbite both his ears had ta'en, Exclaimed, with visage ever bended down, *Sons of Count* "Why so to mirror thee in us art fain?
the Valley of the "thou wouldst have these two to thee acknown, *Bisenzio near* The valley whence descends Bisenzio *wZTilledeach* Their father Albert's was, and was their own. *other quarreling* They issued from one body; thou mayst go
tance '" Questing Cai'na through, and find no shade
Deserving more in gelatine to show:
According to the Not him in breast and shadow open laid
Lancelot?when By one and the same blow from Arthur's hand;
King Arthur's Focaccia not; nor him who with his head *3ouTofWMorAred* So hedges me, I can no view command,
the sunlight And who was Sassol Mascheroni hight:

fice!puncturing, tnou De Tuscan, well dost understand. *as Dante puts* But that no further speeches thou invite,
the body Know, I was Camicion de' Pazzi, and here
Expect Carlino to excuse me quite."
Then I beheld a thousand faces leer
Curlike with cold: whence shudders o'er me thrill
Forevermore, at every frozen mere.
While we were going tow'rd the Center still,
Whereto all gravity converges down,
And I was trembling in the eternal chill:
Whether by will, or fate, or fortune done,
I know not; but among the heads somehow
I struck my foot full in the face oS one.
Wailing he yelled at me: "Why tramplqst thou?
Unless to double vengeance for the day
Of Montaperti, why molest me now?"
And I: "Now, Master, make a little stay,
That I through him may rid me of a doubt:
Then shalt thou haste me as thou wilt away."
My Leader stopt; and I, now turned about
To him, still bitterly blaspheming there,
Said: "Who art thou on others crying out?"
"Nay, who art thou," he answered, "who dost fare
Through Antenora, and dost others smite,
So that, wert thou alive, 'twere ill to bear?"
"AliVeTamT if fame be thy delight,
It may be dear to thee," did I respond,
"That I with other notes thy name indite. "
"I crave the contrary of those beyond:
Begone, and pester me no more," he whined;
"Small skill hast thou to natter on this pond."
Then, laying hold upon his scalp behind,
"It shall needs be thou name thyself," said I,
"Or not a hair upon thee shalt thou find. "
"What though thou strip me bald," he made reply,
"I will not tell thee who I am, nor show,
Maul thou my head to all eternity."
I had his hair in hand already, so
That more than one tuft had been pluckt away,
He yelping, with eyes riveted below,
My kinsman Carlino (a Florentine Benedict Arnold) is so much worse thai I shall appear innocent. The others, — "let us not speak of them" This is Bocca of the Abati, who, at the crucial moment of the battle of Montaperti, the most cruel defeat Florence suffered in the time of the Republic, cut off the hand oj the Florentine standard-bearer. To this choice example of traitorhood Dante devotes more than thirty dreadful lines
When one cried out: "Bocca, what ails thee? nay
Enough! let jawbones chatter till they burst,
But must thou bark? what fiend is at thee, pray?"—
Whereat I said: "Thou traitor thrice accurst,
From this time forth I want no speech of thee,
For to thy shame true tale shall be rehearst."
"Begone, and babble what thou wilt," said he,
"But, going hence, fail not discourse to hold
Of him who had the tongue just now so free.
He is lamenting here the Frenchman's gold:
T saw him of Duera,' canst thou note,
'There where the sinners lie out in the cold.'
And should they ask thee other anecdote,
Him at thy side there name in thy reports,
The Beccheria,—for Florence cut his throat.
Gianni de' Soldanier, I think, consorts
With Ganelon, and Tribaldello yon
Who while men slept unbarred Faenza's ports."
Already we away from him were gone
When, frozen in one hole, beheld I two
So that one head was hood to the other one:
And even as people bread for hunger chew,
The uppermost upon the one below
Set teeth where brain and neck together grew.
Not otherwise once Tydeus gnawed the brow
Of Menalippus, in his rage malign,
Than skull and other parts gnawed this one now.
"0 thou who showest by so bestial sign
Hatred to him whom thou devourst," said I,
"Tell me the cause, upon this pledge of mine,
If thou complainest with good reason why,
That I, with both acquainted, and his guile,
May yet requite thee in the world on high,
If this my tongue be not dried up erewhile." *The Tower of Hunger* 137
XXXIII
Ugolino And His Children In The Tower
That sinner lifted from the foul repast
His mouth up, wiping it upon the hair
Behind the head whereon I looked aghast;
Then he began: "Thou wilt that I declare
Desperate grief that wrings the heart of me,
Even in the thought, before I lay it bare.
But if my words a seed of infamy
May sow unto the traitor whom I gnaw,
Speaking and tears together shalt thou see.
I know not who thou art, nor by what law
Thou comest down here; but a Florentine,
On hearing thee, it seemed to me I saw.
Thou hast to know I was Count Ugolin,
And this Archbishop Roger: why so fell
A neighbor am I, let me tell his sin.
That I, in his good faith confiding

well,
By his devices was in prison flung
And done to death, there is no need to tell.
But what thou hast not heard from any tongue,
That is, how cruelly my life was reft,
Shall hear, and know if he have done me wrong.
A narrow cranny in the dungeon cleft
Whereto for me the name of Famine clings,
And where to languish others shall be left,
Had shown me already through its openings
Many a moon, when the bad dream had I,
That tore away the veil of coming things.
This man seemed master of the hunting cry,
Hounding the wolf and wolflings tow'rd the mount
That shuts out Lucca from the Fisan eye.
With eager sleuthhounds gaunt and trained to hunt,
Had he Gualandi on before him sent,
Sismondi with Lanfranchi, to the front.
After brief coursing, sire and sons forspent
Appeared to me, and all the while they fled
I saw their flanks with whetted tushes rent.
When I awoke before the dawn was red,
I heard my children in their slumber cry,
For they were with me there, imploring bread.
Hard must thy heart be, if thou dost not sigh,
Only to think of my forebodings drear;
What wouldst thou weep for, if thine eyes are dry?
The hour that used to bring our food drew near,
And now they had awakened from their sleep,
And each one from his dream was full of fear:
When I heard, sounding through the horrible keep,
The nailing of the doorway: all for woe
I gazed into their face in silence deep.
I wept not,—stony seemed my heart to grow,
They wept; and Anselm said, dear little one,
'Father, what ails thee? Ah, why lookst thou so?'
Still shed I not a tear, made answer none
Through all that day, nor all the following night,
Till rose upon the world another sun.
And when a feeble glimmering of light
Was shed into the woeful jail, ah me!
And faces four displayed my own to sight,
I bit on both my hands for agony.
And, thinking that I did it under stress
Of ravenous hunger, rose they suddenly:
'Father,' they said, 'our pain will be far less
If thou wilt eat of us; thou hast begot
This flesh,—relieve us of its wretchedness,.'
This made me calm, lest they be more distraught;
That whole day and the next, none made a sign:
Ah, cruel earth! why didst thou open not?
And after the fourth day began to shine,
My Gaddo flung him down before my knee,
Crying: '0 why not help me, father mine?'
And there he died: and there I saw the three,
As thou seest me, fall one by one all through
The fifth and sixth days: whence betook I me,
Now blind, to groping on them, and for two
Whole days called to them, after they were gone:
Then hunger did what sorrow could not do."
Having said this, with eyes askance drawn down,
That miserable skull he grappled dumb,
With teeth strong as a dog's upon the bone.
Ah, Pisa! of the folk opprobrium
In the fair country where the *si* doth sound,
Since neighbors lag in punishment, let come
Caprara and Gorgona, shifting ground,
And choke up Arno's channel, quite across,
That every living soul in thee be drowned.
For if folk tax Count Ugolin with loss,
By treachery to thee, of places strong,
Shouldst not have put his sons on such a cross.
Thou modern Thebes! their youth made free from wrong
Uguccion and Brigata, and withal
The two already mentioned in my song.
Yet onward went we, where the icy pall,
Rough swathing, doth another people keep,
Not downward bended, but reverted all.
The very weeping there forbids them weep,
And finding on the eyes a barrier, woe
Turns inward to make agony more deep:
Because the first tears to a cluster grow,
And, like a visor crystalline, upfill
The whole concavity beneath the brow.
And though, as in a callus, through the chill
Prevailing there, all sensibility
Had ceased its function in my visage, still
I felt some wind, so now it seemed to me:
"Master, who moveth this?" I therefore said,
"Is not all vapor quencht down here?"
Whence he: *Italian was the "lingua di si" (language, originally, of "sic" for "yes) just as Provencal was the "langue d'oc" ("hoc" for "yes"), whence the name of the great region of Languedoc Caprara and Gorgona, islands off the mouth of Arno. Looking down the river from the Leaning Tower on a clear day, they do seem to block the outlet*
"Speedily art thou thither to be led
Where shall thine eye to this an an-

swer find,
Seeing the cause wherefrom the blast is shed."
And of the wretches of the frozen rind »
One shouted to us: "O ye souls so fell
That the last station is to you assigned,
Lift from my visage up each rigid veil,
That I may vent the sorrow in a trice,
Which swells my bosom, ere the tears congeal."
"Tell who thou art," I said, "I ask this price:
If thee therefore I do not extricate,
May I go to the bottom of the ice."
This gentleman And he: "Fra Alberigo I of late, to *whom Dante* "He of the fruit of the in garden. *had, by an . = ambiguous oath,* I here am getting for my fig a date., *promised a* "Already," said I, "art thou here below?" *courtesy, had murdered tvm of* And he made answer: "How my flesh may thrive *his kin at his* There in the upper world, I do not know. *dinner table, the* t i i *signal to the* This Ptolomea hath such prerogative *assassins being:* That oftentimes the soul falls to this place *Bring in ike .... fruit! Obviously* Ere ever Atropos the signal give. *Dante here acts* And that more willingly from off my face. *in harmony with "" what he con-*, Thou now remove away the glazen tears, *ceives to be the* Know that as soon as any soul betrays, *Divine Justice. ,_,,. n i Let Hie betrayer* As I betrayed, forthwith a fiend appears *feel in his own* d *iges* ner body, therein governing *person what,. „ treachery is likel* Throughout the revolution of her years.
Headlong to such a cistern doth she fling;
And haply still above the trunk is shown
Of yonder shade behind me wintering.
To thee, if just come down, he should be known:
Ser Branca d'Oria: and many a year
Since he was thus lockt up, is come and gone."
"I think," said I, "that thou deceivst me here:
For Branca d'Oria not yet is dead,
But eats and drinks and sleeps and dons his gear."

In Hell ichile Still on Earth 141
"Into the moat of Maltalons," he said,
"Up there where boils the sticky pitch away,
Had Michael Zanche's spirit not yet sped,
When this one left a devil in full sway
In his own body, and one next of blood
Who served him as accomplice to betray.
But now reach here thy hand, as understood,
Open mine eyes": my hand I reacht not forth,)
And courtesy it was to be thus rude.
Ah, men of Genoa! with aught of worth
At variance, and full of vices all,
Wherefore are ye not scattered from the earth?
For with Romagna's soul most criminal
I found one such of you, that for his meed
His soul bathes in Cocytus, yet withal
His body seems alive in very deed.
/ XXXIV
Ninth Circle: Judecca. Passage From Lucifer To The Light *"Vexflla Regis* "Tow'rd us the banner of the King of Hell *prodeunt in*-Advances; therefore forward bend thine eyes," *jernt v*
My Master said, "if thou discernest well."
As, when thick fog upon the landscape lies,
Or when the night darkens our hemisphere,
A turning windmill seems afar to rise,
Such edifice, methought, did now appear:
Whereat, by reason of the wind, I cling
Behind my Guide,—no other shelter near.
jJVV' Already (and it is with fear I sing)
T I found me where the shades all covered show
Like straws through crystal faintly glimmering.
Some stand erect, others are prone below;
One here head up, soles uppermost one there;
Another face to foot bent, like a bow.

When we had made our way along to where
I was to see, as pleased my Master good,
The Being that once bore the semblance fair,
He halted me, and from before me stood,
Saying: "Behold Dis, and the place behold
Where thou must weapon thee with fortitude!"
How faint I grew thereat, and icy cold,
Ask me not, Reader, to declare in speech: All language would fall short if it were told, uj' Devoid of life, yet death I did not reach:
XxSf Think for thyself, if wit suffice therefor,
What my condition was, bereft of each.
He, of the woeful realm the Emperor,
Emerged midbreast above the ice-field yon, w And liker to a giant I, than bore
The giants with his arms comparison:
Consider, with respect to such a limb,
How huge that whole which it depends upon.
The Worm at the Care of the World 143
If (lie were fair onc%! as he now is grim,
And raised hislbrow against That One who made, Well may all woe have fountainhead in him. O what a wonder, when upon his head Three faces to my sight were manifest!
The one in front, and it was fiery red;
The other two with this one coalesced
Just o'er the middle of each shoulder, while
They all conjoined together at the crest:
The right-hand face appeared to reconcile
With yellow, white; the left was such of hue v
As folk who come whence floweth down the Nile.
Vast wings came forth, beneath each visage two,
Such as were fitting to a bird like that:
Sails of the sea so broad I never knew.
They bore no feathers, but as of a bat
Their fashion was; and flapping them

he stood
So that three winds proceeded forth thereat,
Whence frozen over was Cocytus flood.
The cadent tears were trickling from six eyes
Over three chins, to mix with drooling blood.
At every mouth his tushes heckle-wise
Upon a malefactor champ and tear,
So that he thus makes three to agonize.
To him in front the bite could not compare
Unto the clawing, for at times the hide
Dilacerated, left the shoulders bare.
"That soul up yon, most sorely crucified,
Is Judas the Iscariot," said my Lord,
"His head within, he plies his legs outside.
Of the other two, whose heads are netherward,
Brutus it is who hangs from the black jole:
Look how he writhes and utters not a word!
The other Cassius, stalwart-seeming soul.—
But now another night is darkening;
We must depart: for we have seen the whole."
About his neck I, at his bidding, cling:
And he of time and place advantage takes:
And soon as wing is wide apart from wing,
Lays hold upon the shaggy flanks, and makes
His way from shag to shag, descending by
The matted hair among the frozen cakes.
When we were come to that point where the thigh
Revolves, exactly where the haunches swell,
My Guide, with effort and distressful sigh,
Turned round his head to where his footing fell, And like one mounting, grappled to the hair, *Possibly some* So that, methought, we back returned to Hell.
arfsaZrbtdl "Keep fast thy hold' because by such a stair'" *willing to be told* The Master said, panting like one forspent, *that the Point in* "Forsaking so great evil, must we fare." *QUCsliOtl tods ZflG Center of the* Out through the crevice of a rock he went, *Earth, so that we* And t it b mk then Il *are now under " the southern* Planting his feet, his steps toward me bent. *pZrg8' I* Kfted up mine eyes, thinking to see *toward which we* Lucifer, just as I had seen him last, *Ing "osT.' -And* saw him with his leSs upturned to me. *Jerusalem, we* And what perplexity now held me fast,
ZSm'SZ of dullards fancy who have notion none
time. It would What point it was I had already passed.
Xtf S "Rise Up " the Master said, "thy feet upon: *so that twenty-*The way is long, and difficult the road, *SalLeTfo The And* now *to* middle *tierce* returns the sun." *passage from the* It was no palace chamber where we stood, *fooToj* fte" But Io! a natural dungeon vault was this, *mountain of* Wanting in light and without footing good.
SzfZ' ft "Before *I* pluck myself from the y88' *all, we ought to* Master," when risen to my feet I said, *%at%Zt?wi:* "Talk th me somewhat, lest I judge amiss. *are not, as in* Where is the ice? and how is This One stayed *%Z&Ld* Thus upside down and how, in moments few, *-stops by the way* The sun from even to morning transit made?"
"Thou still believest thee," he said thereto,
"Yon-side the Center, where I gript the hair
Of the fell Worm that pierces the world through.
So long as I descended wast thou there:
Soon as I turned, the point we overran
Whereto all weights from all directions bear:
Thou'rt come beneath the hemisphere whose span
Is counterposed to that which doth embrace
The great dry land, beneath whose cope the Man
Was slain, pure born and without need of grace:
Thy feet upon a little disk abide
That for Judecca forms the counter face.
Here it is morn when yonder eventide:
And still doth This One stand as fixedly
As ere he made a ladder with his hide.
Down out of Heaven upon this side dropt he,
And all the land that here of yore arose
Was veiled, through terror of him, with the sea,
And joined our hemisphere; and some suppose
Perhaps that land today on this side found
Fled up from him, and left this empty close."
There is a place below, whose further bound
From Beelzebub far as his tomb extends,
By sight unnoted, but betrayed by sound
Made by a rivulet that here descends
A crannied rock, which it has gnawed away
With gently sloping current, as it wends.
My Guide and I upon that hidden way
Entered, returning to the world of light:
And without caring for repose to stay,
He first, and I behind him, scaled the height,
Till a round opening revealed afar
The beauteous things wherewith the heavens are bright:
Thence came we forth to re-behold each star.
The land of the southern hemisphere shrank away from him as he fell, and, after he was planted in the Center, the ground forming the island and mountain of Purgatory fled up from him, leaving that passage open Each Cantica closes with the word "stelle," stars. This the stubborn English rime cannot always manage to the letter PURGATORIO
The Dawn Of Easter
Sets sail the little vessel of my mind
And henceforth better waters furrowing
Leaves such a cruel ocean far behind
And of that Second Kingdom will I

sing
Wherein the human spirit, purged of stain,
Grows worthy to ascend on heavenward wing.
Here let dead poesy arise again,
O holy Muses, since I am your own,
And here Calliope uplift her strain,
Companioning my singing with that tone
Whence the poor Magpies felt so stricken through
That they were desperate of pardon grown.—
The tender oriental sapphire hue
Suffusing the calm heaven from midmost height
To the first circle down, so pure and blue,
Cheered up mine eyes with long-unfelt delight
Soon as I issued forth from the dead blur
That had afflicted both my heart and sight.
The planet fair that is Love's comforter
Lit with her smiling all the eastern skies,
Veiling the Fishes then escorting her.
Turning toward the right, I fixed mine eyes
On the other pole, thereby four stars discerning,
Ne'er seen by man save first in Paradise.
The heaven appeared enraptured with their burning:
Clime of the northland, O how widowed thou,
Since these have been withholden from thy yearning!
When from their view I could avert my brow,
Glancing a little toward the north, that shone
Where the bright Wain had sunk from sight ere now,
147
Scene: An island in the Southern Ocean, at foot of a loftier Teneriffe Time: The action begins before dawn Easter Sunday, A.d. *1300 Characters: All, save the pilgrimpoet, shades of the dead Virgil and Dante appear 01 the plain sloping from seashore to mountain-cliff As he is facing toward the dawnstar, the four symbolic stars are near the South Pole. These "sacred stars" which appear again in Canto xxxi probably symbolize the four Pagan or Cardinal virtues of Prudence, Justice, Fortitude, Temperance The shade of Cato of Utica, warden of this region outside of Purgatory. Examples of other just Pagans, who appear among the redeemed, are given in Paradiso xx*
Near me appeared an elder all alone,
Worthy of so great reverence by his mien
That more to father owes not any son.
Long was his beard, with grizzled streaks between,
And like thereto the crown of hair he wore
Fell to his breast in double tresses sheen.
Beams of the holy luminaries four
Adorned his face and so great luster shed,
I saw him as though the sun had been before.
"Who are ye, against the darkling river fled
From out the eternal prison void of day?"—
Moving those venerable plumes, he said.
"Who was your lantern or who led the way
Issuing forth from the abysmal gloom
That makes the infernal valley black for aye?
Are broken thus below the laws of doom?
Or has in Heaven gone forth some new decree
That ye, being damned, to my rock-caverns come?"
Straightway my Leader laid his hold on me,
And what with word and hand and signal, brought
To posture reverent my brow and knee;
And then replied: "Of myself came I not:
A Lady has descended from the sky,
And I assist this man as she besought.
But seeing that thy questions signify
The will for further truth about us twain,
I could not find it in me to deny.
This man saw not his final evening wane,
But by his folly was so near thereto
That little time was left to turn again.
I was sent thither where he lay perdue
In rescue, as I said, nor was there road
But this which I am striving to pursue.
To him all circles of the lost I showed;
And now I am intending to display
Those spirits who are purged beneath thy code.
How I have brought him would be long to say:
Comes Virtue from aloft, enabling me
To give him sight and speech of thee today.
Now look upon his coming graciously;
He goes in quest of freedom, boon how dear
Knows that man who with life has paid her fee.
Thou knowest it, for death did not appear
Bitter to thee in Utica, there leaving
The vesture that great day to be so clear.
No law eternal by our act is cleaving,
For this man lives, nor Minos is my lord;
But I am of the circle where are grieving
Marcia's pure eyes, as though they still implored
That thou wouldst hold her thine, O holy breast:
For her love, then, thy grace to us accord.
Let us throughout thy seven kingdoms quest:
Thee by report to her will I requite,
If word of thee below thou sanctionest.
"—
"Marcia was aye so winsome in my sight
Long as I tarried yonder," he replied,
"That doing all her will was my delight.
Now can she, from beyond the baleful tide,
Move me no more, by law which took effect
When I passed over from the further side.

But if a Lady of Heaven prompt and direct
As thou hast said, thy bland persuasion hush,
Sufficient answer for her sake expect.
Go then and see that with a simple rush
Thou gird this mortal, washing in such wise
His face that for no soilure it may blush:
For it were unbecoming that with eyes
Beclouded, he appear before the Prime
Angel who is of those of Paradise.
This islet, ere the slope begins to climb,
About the margin where the billow heaves,
Is fringed with rushes in the oozy slime.
Symbolic cleansing and girding of Dante. The reed is symbol of humility: Dante's besetting sin, as we shall see, is pride
No other plant, of such as put forth leaves
Or harden, could survive there, since not bent
To every buffet that the stalk receives.
Put all returning here from your intent;
The sun, now rising, will instruct you how
To take the Mount by easier gradient. "—
So vanisht he; and I, uprising now
Without a word, and firmly taking stand
Close to my Leader, bent on him my brow.
"Follow my footsteps, son," was his command,
"Let us turn backward, for from here this lea
Slopes to the lower limit of the land."—
Now did the shadowy hour of morning flee
Before the dawn, so that from far away
I caught the gusty ripple of the sea.
We walked the lonely plain as wander they
Who turn back to the pathway lost, and who
Until they find it seem to go astray.
When we had reached that region low where dew
Contends with sun, nor in the chilly air
Disperses while the beams are faint and few,
Softly upon the tender herbage there
Both of his outspread palms my Master placed;
Whence I, who of his purpose was aware,
Lifted my grimy cheeks, with tear-stains laced;
There to my features he restored that hue
Which by the spume of Hell had been effaced.
Cf. tlie fate of Then to the lonely seashore came we two,
CTjwie», *Inf.* Which never yet upon its waters found
One mariner who afterward withdrew.
Here as that other bade, he girt me round:
O miracle! that such as from the earth
He culled the humble plant, quick from the ground
Whence it was pluckt, it came again to birth.

II

The Angel Pilot

The sun by now to that horizon came
The arc of whose meridian is at height
Just at the point above Jerusalem:
And, circling opposite to him, the Night
Was issuing forth from Ganges with the Scales
Which fail her hand when she exceeds in might;
So, where I was, the cheek that glows and pales
Of fair Aurora, sallowed with the ray
Of orange, because age on her prevails.
Beside the sea we pondered on the way
Like folk who, lingering still along the shore,
Hasten in heart and in the body stay;
And as, a little while the dawn before,
Mars reddens through the vapor baleful-bright
Low in the west above the ocean-floor,
I saw, — O may it bless again my sight! —
A luster coming on across the main
With speed unparalleled by any flight.
And when I let mine eye awhile remain
Detached from it, to question of my Guide,
Larger and brighter now it showed again.
Then there emerged to view on either side
A whiteness indistinct, and down below
Little by little another I descried.
My Master uttered not a word, till lo!
The first white spots appeared as wings to shine,
Then, when he surely did the Pilot know,
He cried: "Make haste, make haste, the knee incline,
Fold hands, —it is God's Angel! thou shalt use
Henceforth to see such ministers divine.
Look, how doth he all human means refuse,
Scorning device of sail or oar, nor drew
Aught but his wings upon so far a cruise;

Contrast the opening of Inf. ii

The sun is rising here at Purgatory, night is falling at Jerusalem, it is midnight on the Ganges. Cf. the diagram, Temple Primer of Dante, p. 147. And cf. the beginning of Canto xxvii

Psalm 1U. This passage refers, says Dante, by allegory to Redemption, morally to Conversion, anagogically to the departure from earthly slavery to eternal freedom. Cf. letter

to Can Grande,
§7
The Ram being
vrith the Sun on
the horizon, the
Sky-goat wQl be
in the Zenith

Look, look how heavenward he holds them true,
Fanning the welkin with those plumes eterne
Which do not molt as mortal feathers do!"—

Then, near and nearer come, might I discern
The Bird of God more dazzling than before,
Until mine eyes that with the blaze now burn

Fall down undone. But he drew near the shore
On pinnace light and rapid, — such an one
The water swallowed nothing of the prore.

Astern the Pilot stood, and benison

Celestial showed upon his face devout:
A hundred and more spirits sat thereon.

"When Israel from Egypt issued out,"

They chanted as with single voice the lay,
With what there afterward the Psalmist wrote.

When sign of holy cross he made them, they

Flung themselves one and all upon the strand,
And swiftly as he came he swept away.

There huddled they together close at hand
Gazing about, like strangers to the place
Endeavoring new things to understand.

The sun was shedding everywhere his rays,
And with the arrows of his radiance now
Did Capricorn from middle-heaven chase,

When the new people lifted up their brow
Toward us, saying: "If expert ye be
In faring up the Mountain, show us how."—

And Virgil said: "Ye deem perchance that we
Have some experience to guide us here,
But we are also pilgrims as are ye.

We came before you, and not long whilere,

By road so rough and hard that the ascent
But sport henceforward will to us appear."—

The spirits, among whom the whisper went

That I was still a living and breathing one,
Turned deadly pale for very wonderment.

Casella 153

And as, to hear good tidings, people run

To reach the olive-bearing messenger,

And not a man appears the throng to shun, So one and all the happy spirits there

Fastened upon me hungrily their view,

As if forgot the quest to make them fair. And I saw one of them who forward drew

To my embrace with love so manifest

That I was influenced the like to do.
O insubstantial souls in shadowy vest!

Thrice did I clasp my hands behind that shade

And drew them back as often to my breast. Wonder, I think, was on my face portrayed;

Whereat it only smiled and drew away

While I pursued in hopes it would have stayed. In mellow tones he gently said me nay,

And knowing him thereby, did I implore

That he for speech a little while would stay. "As loved I in the mortal flesh of yore,

So loosed I love thee still," he answered clear,

"I stay then; but why pacest thou the shore?"— "To this place where we are, Casella dear, *Of this friend*

To come once more I make this pilgrimage; *Dantfimdin*

But why is so much time bereft thee here?"— *the milder*

And he: "No injury can I allege, *fi/ titoU*

If he who takes up when and whom he please *knoum more*

Somewhile denied to me the ferriage, &" gjJ£

For of right will his own is made. Yet these *Three months*

Three happy months accepts he verily *inee Christmas* inn. i..-.i n *when the Jubilee*

Whoever longs to enter, with all peace; *year of peace*

Whence I, who had just now betaken me *and pardon had*

Where Tiber water savors of the brine, *'"gun*

Have been received by him benignantly. That is the goal where now his wings incline;

For at that outlet ever gathers what

Falls not perdue to punishment condign."—

And I: "If novel law abolish not

Practice or memory of the song of love
That used to solace all my yearning thought,
I pray thee grace me with the comfort of
Thy song, for in the body traveling
So far, my heart is weary here above. "—

The first line of "Love, deep within the spirit reasoning,"
thihaDante So sweetly he began to sing
it tnus *analyzes in his* That still the dulcet tones within me ring.
3W«' *Tkird* Mv Master and *I* and that unanimous
Company with him drew such rapture thence
As if no other care encumbered us.

Still hung we on that music in suspense,

When lo! that stately elder: "Laggard crew
Of spirits, what portends this negligence?

Think what, delaying, ye neglect to do!

Speed to the Mount to slough the film," he cried,
"That lets not God be manifest to you. "—

As pigeons that are feeding side by

side
And pecking at the darnel or the ear,
Quiet and strutting not with wonted pride,
If aught whereof they are afraid appear
All of a sudden let alone their food
Because of being assailed by greater care,
So saw I that newly-landed multitude
Forsake the song and scurry tow'rd the height
Like them who go but wot not where they would:
Nor any less precipitate our flight.
Bodies of the Shades 155 m
Antepurgatory
While sudden flight was all dispersing thus
That flock of spirits through the countryside
Toward the Mount where reason searches us, I drew up close to my Companion tried;
And how without him had I kept the course?
Who up the mountain would have been my guide? He seemed to me disturbed with self-remorse:
O soul of honor, tender conscience good,
How little fault to have such bitter force! After his feet the hurry had subdued,. That of all action mars the dignity,
My mind, which hitherto in durance stood, Eagerly rendered its attention free;
Then turned my sight toward the Hill, supreme
Of peaks emerging skyward from the sea. Behind us flamed the Sun, whose ruddy gleam
Before me broke in the configurement
Formed on me by the stopping of its beam.
I turned, in terror of abandonment
Dante for the
Sidewise and half around, become aware *& mf secs his shadow*
The ground was shadowed only where I went. Then turning round to me, my Comforter
Began: "Why givest thou suspicion room?
Dost thou not think I, guiding, with thee fare? Already it is evening at the tomb
Where lies the body of me that cast a shade:
Naples received it from Brundusium.
Now if no shadow is before me made,
Like wonder in the heavens dost thou behold,
Whose rays are not by one another stayed. The Power who will his workings not unfold
Makes bodies apt to suffer, as we do,
Torments arising both from heat and cold.
The Riviera from Turbia (near Nice) to the Gulf of Spezia was traversed by a mountain-path
One Substance, in Three Persons, travels through
Illimitable ways, where it were wild
To deem that human reason might pursue.
Be to the fact, O mortals, reconciled,
For, had ye power to see all things and learn,
No need had been for Mary to bear child.
And ye have seen without fulfillment yearn
Those whose desire would have been satisfied,
Which now is given to them for grief eterne.
Of Aristotle and Plato I speak, — beside
Many another."—Here his brow he bent,
Deeply perturbed, and further speech denied.
Meanwhile toward the mountain-foot we went:
A cliff so steep that nimble legs would be
Of small avail attempting such ascent.
The way between Turbia and Lerici
Most lonely and deserted were a stair,
Compared with that, accessible and free.
"Where slopes the mountain, who can tell me where,"
The Master murmured, staying his advance,
"So that the wingless foot may clamber there?"—
And while he, casting down his countenance,
Was questioning his mind about the way,
And up along the rock I ran my glance,
Behold, off to the leftward, an array
Of spirits all in our direction bound,
Though seeming not, so slow of pace were they.
"Lift up thine eyes, good Master, and look round,"—
Said I, "some who may help are coming yon,
If yet thy wisdom at a loss be found."—
We moved along a thousand steps or so,
Finding that company as far by this
As a good thrower with his hand could throw,
When at the foot of the high precipice
Gathered they all, compact and circumspect,
Gazing like men who fear to go amiss.
"O ye who ended well, O souls elect!"
Virgil began, "in name of that sublime
Peace which, I think, ye one and all expect,
Tell us if it be possible to climb
The Mountain somewhere by a slope less bold:
For irksome to the wise is loss of time. "—
As sheep are wont to issue from the fold
By one and two and three, the rest pursue
Meekly, and eye and muzzle downward hold,
And what the first one does the others do,
And if she stop all huddle at her side,
Nor question why, the quiet silly crew:
So moving now toward us I descried
The column-leaders of that happy flock,
Modest in face, in action dignified.
When those in front beheld my body block
The light upon my dexter hand, whereby
The shadow stretched from me toward the rock,

They halted and withdrew somewhat more nigh
Those following behind, and all the rest
Did in like manner, without knowing why.
"I frankly tell you, without your request,
This is a human body that ye see,
As by the broken light is manifest.
Then do not wonder, but persuaded be
That not by heavenly Power unwarranted
To mount this barrier endeavors he."—
The Master thus; and that good people said:
"Then turn about and enter in before,"
And with the backs of hands the signal made.
"Whoever thou mayst be," did one implore,
"While pressing forward, hither turn anew:
Consider if thou sawst me there of yore. "—
I turned to scan him, and there met my view
Fair features and of gentle mien and blond,
Although one eyebrow had been cloven through.

By the shadow knowing Dante to be in the body The pregnant and pathetic lines that follow deal with the treatment of the last Uohenstaufen who reigned in Italy by Pope Clement IV, obsequious to the conqueror. To feel its full significance the reader should know much more of the facts, both political and ecclesiastical, than can be told in a note Treating the body as that of an excommunicated ruler

And when I ventured humbly to respond
With a denial, "Look!" —and he laid bare
Above his breast a sanguinary wound.
"Manfred am I," said he with smiling air,
"Grandson of Empress Constance: whence I pray
Thee go, returning, to my daughter fair,
Mother of both the monarchs who bear sway,
One in Sicilia, one in Aragon,
And tell her truth, whatever else they say.
When these two mortal stabs had quite undone
My body, yielded I with tears contrite
To Him who willingly gives benison.
Horrible were my sins, but Infinite
Bounty has arms of an embrace so broad
That it accepts whoever turn to it.
And if Cosenza's Pastor, who at nod
Of Clement went to hunt me down, had known
How to peruse aright this page in God,
Even now were of my body every bone
At the bridgehead near Benevento trenched,
Beneath the safeguard of the heavy stone.
Now scattered by the wind, by the rain drenched,
Beyond the kingdom hard by Verde's flow,
Whither he carried them with tapers quenched.
By curse of theirs no soul can perish so
But that Eternal Love for them may bloom
While hope one particle of green can show.
True is that such as die beneath the doom
Of Holy Church, though they at last repent,
Must here outside the precipice find room,
Full thirtyfold the time that they have spent
In their presumption, if to briefer span
Good prayers do not reduce such banishment.
Hereafter pray rejoice me, if thou can,
Revealing to my gracious Constance dear
How thou hast seen me and alas! this ban:
For much those yonder may advance us here."— IV

The Ascent Of The Mountain Begun

When an impression of delight or dole
Works on some faculty of ours, and thus
Wholly that faculty absorbs the soul,
It seems of other force oblivious;
And this is counter to that erring thought
Which would enkindle soul on soul in us.
Therefore, when hearing or when seeing aught
That draws the soul's attention potently,
Time passes by, and one perceives it not;
For that which notes it is one faculty,
Another that which holds the soul intent:
This is preoccupied, and that is free.
Hereof I made a true experiment
Listening in wonder to that spirit fair;
For now the Sun had fully made ascent
Fifty degrees, and I was not aware,
When came we where those spirits to us cried
With one accord: "Look, your desire is there!"—
The hedger oft an opening more wide
Blocks with a forkful of his brambles, when
Toward the vintage grapes are purple-dyed,
Than was the passage where ascended then
My Leader and I after, we alone,
While all that flock of souls were lost to ken.
You mount San Leo, drop to Noli down,
And of Bismantova you scale the height
With only feet; but here must wings be grown,—
I mean swift pinions that are fledged for flight
With great desire, behind that Leader, who
Was giving me hope and holding but a light.
Hemmed in on either hand we mounted through
The cloven rock; the ground whereon we trode
Made work enough for feet and hands to do.

The Timaeus of Plato expounds the theory of a mortal and an immortal soul So that it is now

about nine
o'clock
So he does in
Italy today
More than 46 Looking eastward in the southern hemisphere

When at the verge of the high bank we stood
Aloft upon the open mountainside,
I asked: "Which way pursue we, Master good?"-
"Be wary of thy foothold," he replied;
"Win with me up the mountain till we find
One who may prove to be a skillful guide."—
So soared the peak, it left the sight behind,
And steeper far the slope than line away
From middle quadrant unto center inclined.
Weary was I when I began to pray:
"Dear Father, O turn hitherward and see
How I am left alone unless thou stay!"—
"My son, draw up as far as here," said He,
Pointing me to a ledge just overhead
Circling on that side all the acclivity.
So sharply spurred me on the words he said,
That I crept after him with might and main
Until the terrace was beneath my tread.
There to sit down awhile we both were fain,
Facing the East whence we had made ascent;
For, looking back, a man takes heart again.
Mine eyes at first to the low shores were bent,
Thereafter lifted to the Sun, whose glow
Struck us from leftward, to my wonderment.
The Poet well perceived me gazing so
Upon the Car of Light with wonder, where
It entered between us and Aquilo.
Whence he: "If Castor and if Pollux were
Companions with that mirror which sheds back
The light divine to either hemisphere,
Thou wouldst behold him blaze in Zodiac,
Unto the Bears revolving still more nigh,
Unless the sun should quit his ancient track.
If thou wouldst understand the reason why,
With centered thought imagine Zion-hill
On earth set over against this mountain high,
So that they both have one horizon still And hemispheres diverse; then wilt thou see,
If to take heed thine intellect have skill,
How the highway that Phaeton, ah me!
Knew not to course, must pass upon that side
This mountain, and this side of Zion be.
"—
"Truly, my Master, never yet," I cried,
"Saw I so clearly as I now discern,
Since of the mark my wit seemed ever wide,
That the mid-circle of the heaven supern,
Equator in a certain science known,
And which doth still 'twixt sun and winter turn,
Is distant, for the reason thou hast shown,
Northward from here as far as once the Jews
Beheld it looking tow'rd the torrid zone.
But if it please thee well, I fain would choose
To know how far we clamber; for so high
Rises the Hill, that sight in vain pursues.
"—
"This mountain slope is such," he made reply,
"That low beginnings ever painful seem;
The toil decreases climbing tow'rd the sky.
But when it comes about that thou shalt deem
Climbing as easy as to ship and crew
Seems gliding with the current down the stream,
Then is the end of this hard road in view;
There may thy weary limbs expect repose;
More I reply not, knowing this for true.
"—
No sooner had he said such words as those,
Than sounded out a voice near by: "Perchance
He'll have to sit before so far he goes!"—
Both of us, turning at this utterance,
Saw at the left a stone of massive size
Which neither had perceived at the first glance.
Thither we drew apace, till met our eyes
Persons behind the rock, with shadow blent,
Lying along as one in idlesse lies.
Jerusalem is conceived as at the antipodes of Purgatory. The course of the sun must therefore be north of Purgatory and south of Jerusalem. See the beginning of Canto ii
And one of them, who seemed to me forspent,
Was sitting, and was clasping both his knees,
Holding his face deep down between them bent.
"Look, Master mine," said I, "if one of these
Seems not more overcome with lassitude
Than if his sister had been slothful Ease.
"—
At this he bent to us, and understood,
Moving his visage up along his thigh,
And said: "Now up, for thou hast hardihood!"—
Then showed he features that I knew him by,
And my still panting breath impeded not
My going to him; and as soon as I
The send of Had reached him, he uplifted but a jot
Belacqua Fair-His b and murmured: "Seest thou how the Sun
water), an old friend of O'er thy left shoulder drives his chariot?"—
tiumYimfoient s laz n"en and phrase compactly spun *of temperament,* Relaxed my lips to show a little glee; *ter-isTc FUrZ* "Belacqua," I began, "from this time on *tine shrewdness* I grieve no more for thee; but answer me, *of wit*

Why sitst thou here? Awaitest thou a Guide?
Or has thy wonted mood recaptured thee?"—
"Brother, what use in climbing?" he replied;
"The Bird of God, at threshold of the gate,
Would not admit me to be purified.
First Heaven must needs as often circulate
Round me outside, as it in life had done,
Since I delayed repentance till too late;
It is noon in If earlier aid me not some orison *her9JmeVthe* 'Breathed forth from soul with living grace at core; *other hemi-*What boot is other prayer, unheard up yon?"— *Goes5Zm* Aheady went the Poet up before, *Morocco, is in* Saying: "Come on now: look, the Sun is bright *nXufustbfgin-*On the meridian, and at the shore *ning in Morocco* Morocco lies beneath the foot of Night. "—

Tragic Deaths Of Three Noble Souls

Now from those shades departing, I betook
Myself my Leader's footmarks to pursue,
When one behind me, pointing, shouted: "Look,
The sunbeam seems not to be shining through
Leftward from him below; and more by token
He seems to bear him as the living do!"—
I turned about to look when this was spoken,
And saw them gaze at me for marvel — yea
At me, and at the sunbeam that was broken.
"Why is thy mind diverted from the way
To make thee loiter?" said my Master kind;
"What carest thou up here how whisper they?
Come after me and let them speak their mind;
Stand like a tower unwavering and stout
Against whatever buffets of the wind.
For he who thinks about it and about
Falls short, forever thwarted of his aim,
Since one thought by the next is canceled out."
I said, "I come!" — how answer else for shame?
And said it with that flush which may restore us
To pardon, if we worthily lay claim.
Behold now people who, short way before us
Across the Mountain passing, as they go
Sing *Miserere* verse about in chorus.
Seeing my body interrupt the flow
Of sunlight, and enshadowing the plain,
They changed the singing to a long hoarse *Oh!*
And in the form of messengers came twain
Running toward us from that multitude,
Desiring knowledge of our state to gain.
"Ye can go back," replied my Master good,
"To those who sent you forth, and certify
That this man's body is true flesh and blood.
A lower slope of the mountain. Early afternoon of the first day perhaps, that these souls had neglected action through "some craven scruple of thinking too precisely on the even?
And if to see his shadow made them shy
As I suppose, let this reply suffice:
Him let them honor, profiting thereby. "—
So swift-enkindled vapors to mine eyes
Never the sunset clouds of August clove
Nor flasht at fall of night across the skies,
But these in briefer time returned above;
And, there arrived, with the others tow'rd us wheeled
Like squadron without rein that forward drove.
"Many are these who crowd on us afield,"
The Poet said, "to make thee one request;
Yet go right on and, going, hearing yield."—
"O pilgrim soul who goest to be blest
With those limbs fashioned in thy mother's mold,
Stay but a moment!"—cried they as they pressed.
"Look if thou sawest one of us of old,
That thou to earth mayst tidings of him bear:
Pray why dost thou go on? pray why not hold?
We all were slain by violence whilere,
And sinners till the final hour of grace;
Then light from Heaven made us so well aware
That, penitent and pardoning, apace
We quitted life at peace with the Most High,
Who heartens us with yearning for his face."—
"Although I scan your lineaments," said I,
"Not one do I recall; but pray ye speak,
If aught to please you in my power there lie,
And I will do it, happy spirits meek,
By hope of peace which, following up the Hill *Jacopo del Cat-*Behind such Guide, from world to world I seek."— *TSuSZ.* Andonebegan: "We.all »trustingstm *man of Fano,* In thy good service, nor need oath attest, *pStyaZa,-*K only weakness do not cancel will; *dm in the pay* Whence I, who speak alone before the rest,— *Azzo "und'of* "tnou *shafo* look upon that land one day, *Ferrara* Between Romagna and that of Charles,—request *Buonconte and la Pia* 165
That thou of courtesy for me wilt pray
In Fano, so that there be orisons
To help me purge my heavy sins away. Thence came I; but the gashes wherethrough once
Issued the blood wherein I had my seat,
Were dealt to me among Antenor's sons, There where I fancied safest my retreat:
The Este had it done, who held me then
In anger more by far than justly meet.
But had I fled toward La Mira, when

At Oriaco by pursuers found,

Still were I yonder among breathing men. I ran to the marsh; the mud and reeds around

So hampered me I fell, and there saw I

My blood become a pool upon the ground."— "Ah, by that yearning," did another sigh,

"Whereby to the High Mountain drawest thou,

Do thou aid mine with pious sympathy. I was of Montefeltro, merely now *Buonconte da*

Buonconte; heeds me none, not even Joan, *Montefeltro, son*

Whence among these I go with downcast brow. — *captain who*

And I: "From Campaldino lost alone ?"? " *"f. ,.. xxm. Dante*

By chance wast thou, or violence malign, *himself fought*

So that thy burial place was never known?"— ? *f*

"Oh," said he, "runs athwart the Casentine *(1S89)*

A stream called Archiano, rising o'er? *«mtmst* .. r *between the story*

The Hermitage, aloft m Apenmne. *of the son and*

There where it answers to that name no more TMrf *f* /atf'.
is marked with
Came I with throat empierced, as I fled
artistic intention

On foot along the plain, marked with my gore. There eyesight failed me, and the prayer I said

Paused on the name of Mary; there I fell,

And there my flesh remained untenanted. The truth I speak among the living tell:

God's Angel took me: 'Why wilt thou be stealing

Mine own, thou son of Heaven?' cried he of Hell;

'With his immortal art thou skyward wheeling;
That part I forfeit for one little tear;
But with the other use I other dealing. '—

Thou knowest how gathers in the atmosphere

That vaporous moisture, soon to water turning
By the chill pressure of the upper sphere.

That Evil Will, for evil only yearning,

Endowed with native power intelligent,
Joined and moved cloud and wind with fell discerning.

Thereafter, when the day was fully spent,

From Pratomagno to the Great Yoke fills
With fog the valley and veils the firmament

And into water the teeming air distills;

Down through the gullies comes the fallen rain,—
All thirsty earth could drink not,—and the rills

Into great torrents gathering amain,

Headlong toward the royal river bore

With such a rush that weir and dike were vain.

Wild Archiano found my body frore

Hard by his outlet, sweeping it inert
Into the Arno, and from my bosom tore

The cross I made me, conquered by the hurt;

Whelmed me along by many a bank and shoal, Then with his shingle covered me and girt."— *Pia, of the great* "Ah, when thou turnest to an earthly goal, *house of the* snalt have restecl frora the weary way,"— *by a faithless* The second ceasing, followed a third soul,— *husband from* "Remember me, who am Pia, when thou pray; *his castle-crag* 1 *in the wilds of* Siena made me, by Maremma undone: *the Tuscan* jje k wno ringed me, ringless till that day,

Espousing me with gem and benison. "— *Can Prayer Alter God's Decree?* 167 VI

Dante The "stormy Voice" Of Italy

When breaks the game of hazard, he who lost *First day, mid*

Remains behind in sorrow, and essays *fffk'jkik*

The throws again, thus learning to his cost; *of the mountain*

With the winner all the others go their ways:

One in advance, one plucks him from the rear,

And for reminder one beside him stays. He hastens,—all soliciting his ear,—

His hand goes out to some, who leave him free,—

And from the pressure of the crowd gets clear. So I, amid that thronging company,

Was turning to them here and there my face,

And making promise, extricated me.
The Aretine who in the grim embrace

Of Ghin di Tacco perisht, with them stood,

And the other who was drowned while giving chase. There prayed, with hands in suppliant attitude,

Frederick Novello, and that Pisan son

Who proved the good Marzucco's fortitude. I saw Count Orso, and the soul of one

Bereft of life by spite, as he averred,

And envy, not for any trespass done,— Pier de la Brosse, I mean: and by this word

Be warned the Dame of Brabant to take heed

Lest she for this consort Math baser herd. As soon as I was from these shadows freed,

Whose one prayer was that other prayer benign

Them on the way to holiness might speed, Thus I began: "It seems, 0 light of mine, *JEneid vi, 376*

In one text thou expressly questionest

That orison may bend decree divine;
And yet these people only this request:

Can it be possible their hope is vain?

Or is to me thy word not manifest?"—

And he responded: "What I wrote is plain,
And not fallacious is the hope of these
If one consider it with reason sane,

For Top of Judgment stoops not when the pleas
Of burning love do in a moment what
These do who here await the slow decrees.

And in the instance where I tied that knot,
Prayer did not counterbalance the defect,
Since, from God disunited, prayer was

not.

Howbeit, waive decision in respect

To doubt so deep, till she interpret this, Who shall be light 'twixt truth and intellect. *In the Earthly* Be assured that here I speak of Beatrice: *Paradise* jjer snalt thou see aDove) upon the crown

Of this same Mountain, smiling and in bliss."

And I: "Lord, let us hasten to be gone, For I am not as hitherto forspent, And look, the hill now casts a shadow down."-

"As much as possible of the ascent,

Will we perform today," responded he, "But other than thou thinkest is the event.

Ere thou canst climb up yonder, thou wilt see Return that light so hidden that its ray Is interrupted now no more by thee.

But see! there is a spirit making stay

All, all alone, and looking tow'rd this side; It will point out to us the speediest way. "—

We thither came. O Lombard soul, what pride And lofty scorn thine attitude exprest, And thy slow-moving eyes how dignified!

As we came on he proffered no request,

But let us go our way, calmly surveying In manner of a lion when at rest.

Steadily drew up Virgil tow'rd him, praying

Direction where ascent might best be made; But he, no word by way of answer saying,

News of our life and of our country prayed.

And when thereto the gentle Guide began,— "Mantua —" upleaped that all-secluded shade

From where before he stood: "0 Mantuan, I am Sordello of thy city!" — said he, And to embrace of each the other ran.— *Is*

Hostel of woe, ah, servile Italy,

Vessel unpiloted in a great storm, No Lady of provinces, but harlotry!

Eager that noble spirit was and warm

To welcome there his own compatriot, So did the sweet name of his city charm!

While now in civil tumult are distraught Thy living citizens, —at daggers drawn Those whom one wall incloses, and one moat.

Make search around thy seaboard, wretched one, And after in thy bosom look again, If anywhere within be unison!

What boots Justinian adjust the rein

If ever empty be the saddle? Without Such bridle not so black would be the stain.

Ah, gentry, ye that ought to be devout And let but Caesar in the saddle sit, Nor leave unheeded what God pointed out,

Look well to this wild beast, consider it, Ungoaded by the spur how fell it grows Since ye laid hand upon the bridle-bit!

O German Albert, who to such as those Yieldest this wild unruly animal, And oughtest to bestride her saddlebows,

May from the stars upon thy issue fall

Just judgment, and be it strange and manifest Such that it may thy follower appall!

Thy father suffered, and thou sufferest,

Held back up yonder by the greed of you, The garden of the Empire go to waste. *Political chaos of that age Of what avail the Law without a power to enforce? The claim of the clergy to temporal power Albert, ton of the Emperor Rudolph, absentee King of the Romans Warring fami-*Come look at Capulet and Montague, *lGhiMHnefe* Monaldi and Filippeschi, careless prince,

These dreading that which those already rue. *The count) of* Come, cruel man, and see thy nobles wince *greAldobran-*Under oppression, cure their hurts, — nay come *desco family,* See Santafiora how secure long since! *rfssefbyfna* Come hear the outcries of thy weeping Bome *(cf. Canto xi)* By day and night, a widow and alone: "My Caesar, why forsakest thou thy home?"

Come, see thy people, how their love is grown; And if for us thou have no sympathy, Come and take shame to thee for thy renown.

And if it be allowed me, Jove most High, Thou who for us on earth wast crucified, Is otherwhere averted thy just eye?

Or is it discipline thou dost provide

In thy deep counsel, for some useful plan To our perception utterly denied?

Swarm in Italian towns the tyrant clan, And a Mareellus comes incipient In every churl who plays the partisan.

My Florence, thou indeed mayst be content

With this aside, — thy withers are unwrung, Thanks to thy people all so provident.

The bow of justice is but slowly strung

By many, who let no random arrow fly: Thy people have justice pat upon the tongue.

Many would put the public burden by, But answers eagerly thy populace Unbidden: "Shoulder to the wheel!" they cry.

Good reason hast thou to take heart of grace: If sooth I say the facts do not conceal, Thou wealthy and thou wise and thou at peace!

The Athenian and the Spartan commonweal,

Long famed for art and law, gave feeble proof Of civil life to what thy deeds reveal, *Fickleness of Florence* 171

Who with such foresight weave in that behoof, That reach not to the middle of November

The filmy threadlets of October's woof.
How often hast thou changed (canst thou remember?)
Law, coinage, offices, time out of mind,
And usage, renovating every member.
And were thy memory not so short or blind,
Thou wouldst see thyself in that sick woman, fain
A little rest upon her couch to find,
Who would by tossing ward away her pain.

VII

The Negligent Princes *Late afternoon*
After the courtly and glad greetings now
&%$et"' Again a third time and.a fourth
& the mountain-Sordello drew back saying: "Who art thou?"—
"Ere to this Mount turned any soul of man
Worthy to rise with God to be enskied,
My bones were buried by Octavian.
Virgil am I; and for no crime beside
Not having faith, went I from Heaven astray."—
So forthwith made reply to him my Guide.
Like one encountering upon his way
Some sudden wonder which he stands before,
Doubting, believing, saying *yea* and *nay,*
Sordello stood; then bowed his forehead lower,
Turning to greet my Leader with embrace
More humble, where lays hold the inferior.
Cf. the eulogy "0 glory," exclaimed he, "of the Latin race,
'inTi' Through whom our language showed its worth so
well,
0 praise eternal of my native place,
What merit shows thee or what miracle?
If I be worthy held thy news to know,
Say from what cloister comst thou, if from Hell?"—
"Through all the circles of the world of woe
Am I come hither," — so he made reply,
"Moved by a power of Heaven whereby I go.
Omitting, not committing, forfeit I
Sight of the Dayspring where thy longings rise,
And which was known by me too tardily.
There is a place below not otherwise
Tormented save with gloom, where the laments
Are uttered not in wailing but in sighs;
There I abide with little innocents
Bitten by fangs of Death and all undone
Ere yet exempt from man's maleficence;
Inf. i No Ascent by Night 173
There I abide with those who put on none
Of the three holy virtues, yet who knew
The others, following guiltless every one.
But if thou knew and can, afford some clew
To us, whereby we may arrive apace
Where Purgatory has beginning true.
"—
He answered: "We are bound to no fixed place;
I lawfully may wander up and round,
And join you as guide for my allotted space.
But look! the day declining to the bound,
And we are powerless to ascend by night;
Then let us think of pleasant resting-ground.
Souls dwell secluded yonder to the right:
Unto them will I lead if thou consent,
Nor will acquaintance be without delight."—
"How so?" was askt, "if any made ascent
By night, would he be then inhibited
By another, or would want of power prevent?"—
"Look!" and the good Sordello's finger sped
Along the ground, —"the sun being parted hence
Thou couldst not even cross this line," — he said;
"Not that there else would be impediments
To going up save shades nocturnal, — they
Would trammel up the will with impotence.
One might indeed in darkness downward stray,
And make the tour of the whole mountain-ring,
While the horizon prisons up the day.
"—
Then said my Master, as if wondering:
"Now lead us on whither, by thy report,
We may have some delight while tarrying."—
Thence on the Mountain was the distance short
When of a hollow I became aware,—
Valleys down here are hollowed in such sort.
"Yonder," proposed that shade, "let us repair
Where inward-curving slopes a dell surround,
And dawning of new day await we there."—
Philip HI of France and Henry I of Navarre; the "plague of France" is Philip the Fair; the stalwart King is Peter of Aragon, husband of the Constance of Canto Hi
Now level and now steep, a pathway wound
That led us to a margin where the height
Half falls away before that hollow ground.
Gold, silver fine, scarlet and pearly white,
Clear Indian wood of azure loveliness,
Or fresh-flaked emerald would be less bright
Than were the grass and flowers in that recess:
In color each of these would be outdone
As by the greater is outdone the less.
Nor yet was Nature a mere painter yon,
But did from thousand odors sweet distill
A subtly blended fragrance known to none.
Salve Regina, with such chanting thrill
The souls on bloom and greensward there at rest,
Concealed before by hollow of the hill.
"Before the faint sun settle to his

nest,"

The Mantuan said who made us thither swerve,

"Do not my guidance among these request.

From vantage of this bank ye will observe

The features and the acts of all and some,

Better than down among them in the curve.

He highest placed, to whom seems burdensome

That he neglected what he ought, for song

Upon the lips of others finds him dumb,

Was Rudolph, Emperor, who feels the prong

In unhealed wounds, fatal to Italy,

While healing through another tarries long.

The next, who seems his comforter to be,

Governed the country whence the waters spring

Moldau bears Elbe, Elbe to the sea,—

His name was Ottocar, far better king

As babe, than bearded Wenceslaus, his child,

In luxury and idlesse battening.

That small-nosed one, with him of aspect mild

So close in counsel, as seems manifest,

Died fleeing and left the fleur-de-lis defiled:

Look there, how he is beating at his breast!

And yonder at his sighing partner glance'

Who on his palm has laid his cheek at rest.

Father and father-in-law of the plague of France

Are these, — they know his vicious life and lewd,

And hence the grief that pierces like a lance.

He who so stalwart seems, whose song in mood

Accords with that of him of virile nose,

Wore girt the cord of every manly good;

And if the youth who yonder doth repose

Behind him had long governed in his stead,

Worth would have passed from vase to vase in those;

This of the other heirs cannot be said:

While James and Frederick the kingdoms sway,

None has the better share inherited.

Not often rises up through branch and spray

Prowess of man; it is the Will Divine

In order that from Him the gift we pray.

My words apply as well to the aquiline

As to his fellow-singer, Peter: this

Do now Apulia and Provence repine.

Matcht with the seed the scion goes amiss,

By how much Constance still her spouse may praise

More than can Margaret and Beatrice.

Look at the monarch of the simple ways,

Harry of England, sitting there alone:

Better the issue that his branches raise.

That one of them whose eyes are upward thrown

Is Marquis William, humblest among these,

For whom Alessandria and her war make moan

Both Monferrato and the Canavese."—

He of the virile nose is Charles I of Anjou, who defeated Manfred at Benevento Dante rates Peter, husband of Constance, far above Charles of Anjou, husband of Margaret, and Beatrice,— whose children are much worse than he. These degenerate sons of Peter and Charles are mentioned again notably in Par. xix. Harry of England is Henry III, father of Edward I, one of the greatest of medieval Kings. Marquis William is the good but unfortunate ruler of Montferrat (in Piedmont) vm

Happy Interview With Departed Shades *Nightfall in the* Now was the hour that melts the heart anew

K£ In voy&gers TMth yearaingfor the shore *wait the prince* The day beloved friends have said adieu,

And the new pilgrim feels the pang once more

Of love, on hearing from the far-off land

Bells that belike the parting day deplore,

When I began no more to understand

His words, on seeing a soul among them there

Uprisen, who craved a hearing with its hand.

It joined both palms and lifted them in air,

Fixing its eyes toward the orient,

As saying to God, — "I have no other care!"—

"Before the close Te hicis ante in notes so sweetly blent

gf'to *HaTn* Came from *tilose* HPs devout, all my concern *good Catholics,* Lapsed and was lost in rapturous content.

telalt TerZfof that soul' the ««« their tuTM *the day* With sweet devotion did the hymn pursue, Holding their eyes upon the wheels supern.

To truth here, Reader, sharpen well thy view,

For verily so thin becomes the veil That it is easy passing inward through.

I saw that gentle army in the dale

Silently gazing afterward on high As if in expectation, meek and pale:

Then issuing and descending from the sky

Two angels with two swords whence flames were gleaming,

But broken and deprived of points, saw I.

As green as tender leaflets freshly teeming,

Their raiment, beaten and blown by pinions green,

In airy wafture was behind them streaming.

Above us one took post with guardian mien,

The other alighted on the further marge

So that the people were contained between.

Their blond heads saw I clearly, but surcharge

Of radiance concealed each glorious face

Baffling my vision with a light so large.

"From their embosoming in Mary's grace,"

Sordello said, "to guard the vale these two

Come, for the Serpent will arrive apace.

"—

Whence I, because nowise the way I knew,
Strove by the trusty shoulders to remain
Close sheltered, for I felt me frozen through.

"Now go we down," Sordello said again,
"And with the mighty shades exchange replies:
To bid you welcome will they all be fain."—

Three paces peradventure might suffice
For my descent; and one did gazing pore
Upon me, as in hope to recognize.

Already was the air endarkened more,
But not so that between his eye and mine
It failed to show what it had lockt before.

Tow'rd me he comes and I to him incline:
Noble Judge Nino, happy was my case
When I beheld thee not of the malign!

Silent between us was no word of grace;
Whereon he askt: "How long since camest thou
Through the far waters to the Mountain's base?"

"Oh!" said I, "out of dismal caves below
This morning come, in the first life am I,
But hope to gain the other, going so."—

As soon as ever heard they my reply,
Sordello and that spirit backward drew
Like startled folk whose impulse is to fly.

One turned to Virgil, and the other to
A soul there seated: "Conrad, look, the Lord
Has willed through Grace a wondrous thing to do!"-

Then turned to me: "By thanks thou must accord
To Him for special grace, who doth so hide
His own first motive that it has no ford,

Judge Nino Visconti, Pisari governor oj the Province of Galium, Sardinia Sordello has been preoccupied with Virgil, and, the sun being behind the Mountain, Dante's shadow was not visible Bis widow had married one of the Visconti of Milan, whose cognizance was the Viper Symbolizing the Christian virtues, as the four mentioned in Canto i symbolize the Pagan virtues o everyday life This incursion of the Serpent into the abode of the dead is.purely allegorical

When thou shalt be beyond the billows wide,
Say to my Joan that she for me implore
Where answer to the pure is not denied.

I think her mother cares for me no more,
Since she has laid aside her wimples white
Which she, poor thing, shall yet be craving for.

By her example may be seen aright
How brief the fire of love in woman's breast
Unless rekindled oft by touch or sight.

Less fair an emblem for her burial chest
The Viper leading Milan to the field,
Than would have been the Cock, Gallura's crest!"-

While he was speaking thus, his face revealed
That upright zeal wherewith the heart may be
Aflame, and in due measure stampt and sealed.

Ranging the heavens my eager eyes could see
Only the place where most the stars are slow,
As in a wheel nearest the axletree.

"Son," said my Guide, "at what art gazing so?"
"At those three starry torches," I replied,
"Wherewith the hither Pole is all aglow. "-

"Low are the splendid stars on yonder side,
Those four thou sawst at early dawn today,
And in their places these are now enskied."—

Sordello seized him as he thus did say,
Exclaiming: "See our enemy advance!"
With finger guiding him to look that way.

At that part where the little valley slants
Devoid of barrier, crept a Snake along,—
Such offered Eve the bitter food, perchance.

The evil streak the grass and flowers among,
With head reversed like beast that licks its fell,
Came undulating on with dartling tongue.

I did not see and cannot therefore tell
How the celestial hawks their stations left,
But saw the motion of each sentinel.

Reeling the air by their green pinions cleft,
The Serpent fled; both wheeling up as one
The angels lighted, having barred the theft.

The shade, that close beside the Judge had drawn
When he exclaimed, had not removed its eyes
Cleaving to me till that assault was done.

"So in the taper lighting to the skies
The wax of thy free will may not abate
Until thou reach the flowery Paradise,"

Began he, "canst thou tidings true relate
Of Valdimagra, or of region nigh,
Tell it to me, for there I once was great.

Conrad the Malaspina called was I;
The elder not, although from him descended;
My love of kindred here I purify."—

"Oh," cried I, "through your land I never wended,
But where in Europe dwells one so forlorn
As never to have heard their fame commended?

Renown and honor that your house adorn
Proclaim the land, proclaim her every lord,
So that he knows who never reacht that bourn.

And by my pilgrim hope I give my

word

Your honored kindred do not strip away

The virtue of the purse and of the sword.

Chartered by custom and by nature, they

Though the bad leader warp the world aside,

Alone go straight, and scorn the evil way."—.

And he: "Now look,—seven times shall not abide

The sun, returning back within the bed

The Ram's four feet now cover and bestride,

Ere this opinion, courteously said,

With better nails than hearsay hammered home,

Shall pierce the very middle of thy head,

Unless arrested be the course of doom."— *Dante ioas the honored guest of the Malaspina in the Lunigiana in 1S06* IX

The Symbolic Gate

Now did the mistress of Tithonus hoar

Show at the eastern window, clad in white, Forth from the arms of her dear paramour; *The lunar* Her brow was glittering with jewels bright *AuTnl th?TM"* Set *m e* figure *o* that monster *cd stellation of the* Which strikes at people with his tail; and Night *Scorpion* Had two already of the paces told

Wherewith she rises where our steps were stayed, And the third hour began her wings to fold, *The other four,* When I, on whom something of Adam weighed, *having cast off* Conquered by slumber, sank upon the lawn *t/LC ITlflBritflTlCfj from Adam, ap-*Where all we five the nightly vigil made.

parentlydo not Upon the hour when, very near to dawn, *just before dawn* Begins the twittering swallow to repine, *are deemed pro-*Perchance in memory of her woes foregone, *phetic or in some rirl ,,,. _ way true* When anxious thoughts less narrowly confine,

And when the pilgrim soul, from flesh more free, Is in her visions very near divine, *The reference to* Then poised aloft did I appear to see *aaUow lcaRs* ea£e, w1 8o plumage, in my dream, *the tragic story* With open wings, intent to swoop at me; *of Procne (the* ijyj I was m that place, or so did seem, *nightingale) ana* r *Philomela (the* Where Ganymede was torn from mends away, *swallow). Cf.* Up to the synod of the gods supreme.

19-21 "Perchance this bird strikes here," I seemed to say, "Only by habit, and from otherwhere

Scorns with his claws to carry up the prey."—

Methought then, having wheeled a little there,

He, terrible as thunderbolt, descended

And snatcht me upward to the fiery sphere.

There he and I seemed with the burning blended,

And so the imagined fire seemed scorching me

That of necessity my sleep was ended.

Even as Achilles shuddered once, when he

Found himself gazing round with wakened eyes,

Not knowing in what quarter he might be,

What time his mother him, her sleeping prize,

From Chiron in her arms to Scyros bore,

Whence later the Greeks took him,—in such wise

I shuddered when fled sleep away before

The face of me; and pallid did I stand,

Even as a man with terror stricken frore.

My Comforter alone was near at hand;

The sun above two hours had made ascent,

And I was facing now toward the strand.

"Fear nothing," was my Lord's admonishment,

"Be reassured, for we are in good state;

Relax not, but be every sinew bent.

Now art thou come to Purgatory-gate:

Lo there the cliff that closes round it, lo

The entrance where it seems to penetrate.

At dawn of day a little while ago,

As slept thy soul within thee on the bed

Of flowers that deck the meadow down below,

A Lady came, and T am Lucy,' said;

'Let me take up this sleeper; it is meet

That so he be upon his journey sped.'

With the other noble forms in that retreat Sordello stayed; she took thee, and with day

Came upward, and I came where fell her feet.

She laid thee here; that open entranceway

With her fair eyes first having pointed out,

Together then with sleep she went away."—

Like one who wins assurance after doubt,

And into confidence converts his fear

When truth is known, so did I change about;

And when my Leader saw me free from care,

He started up along the cliff again

Toward the height, and I pursued him there.

Awakening two hours after sunrise, Dante learns that his dream was indeed symbolically true The Door of Purgatory, the Warder, and the three symbolic steps. Allegorically, the steps are Confession, Contrition, Love. Anagogically they may represent, first the white purity of Christ; second, the cross of Christ breaking and malring contrite the black heart; third, the redeeming blood of Christ. The Adamant: the sure foundation (Par. xxix, 111). The Angel is the priest. The Seven P's, the mortal sins.

The Keys, those given to St. Peter

Reader, thou seest how I exalt my strain,
And therefore do not hold it strange if by
More cunning art I now the theme sustain.
We reached a point, as we were drawing nigh,
Whence what first seemed a wall that had incurred
A fissure, now threw open to the eye
A door, and steps beneath, first, second, third,
For access to it, all diverse of hue,
And a gate-keeper who yet spoke no word.
And as I opened more mine eye thereto,
I saw him sitting on the upper stair,
Such in the face I could not bear the view.
He held a sword whereof the blade was bare,
Which shed a sheen so dazzling to our viewing
That oft in vain I raised my glances there.
"Stand there and tell what aim ye are pursuing;
Where is the escort?"—he began to say,
"Beware lest coming up be your undoing!"—
My Master answered him: "This very day
A Lady of Heaven, aware how to proceed,
Bade, 'Thither go, there is the entrance-way!'"—
"And may she all your steps with blessing speed,"
Rejoined the Gate-keeper in courteous tone,
"Come to our stair then, as it is decreed. "—
Thither we came: a great white marble stone
Was the first stair, so polisht and so terse
That in it was my very image shown.
The second, tinct of deeper hue than perse,
Was rugged rock, scorcht with corrosive stain,
And cloven through both lengthwise and traverse.
The third, which from above thrusts down amain,
Seemed to me porphyry, as luminant
As red blood spirting from a master-vein.
Upon this last one both his feet did plant
Th' Angel of God, who sat the threshold warding,
Which seemed to me of stone of adamant.
Up the three steps, mine own good will according,
Drew me my Guide, and said: "Humbly request
That he unlock, admittance thus affording."—
Devoutly fell I at the footpalms blest;
For mercy craved the opening to me;
But first I smote me thrice upon the breast.
With sword-point he inscribed the letter P
Sevenfold upon my forehead: "Once inside,
Take heed to wash away these wounds,"—said he.
Ashes, or earth which has been digged and dried,
Would match the hue of his habiliment,
And, drawn from underneath it, I descried
Two keys, one gold, one silver instrument;
Now with the white, then with the yellow too,
He plied the gate until I was content.
"Should either key the fastening not undo,
Within the wards inadequately plying,"
Said he to us, "blockt is the passage through.
More dear is one, the other one relying,
Ere it unlock, on passing craft and wit,
For this one brings the knot to its untying.
Peter, who gave them, said 'twere better fit,
When people at my feet were prostrate lain,
To err by opening than shutting it."—
He pusht the portal of the holy fane:
"Enter," said he, "this knowledge with you bringing,—
Whoso looks backward goes outside again."—
And when upon their sockets were set swinging
The pivots of that consecrated door,
Hinges of metal stout, sonorous ringing,
Not so discordant seemed, nor did so roar
Tarpeia, when away from her was rended
The good Metellus, whence grew lean her store.
I turned away, and the first note attended: *Te Deum laudamus* on mine ear was stealing
In voices with sweet music interblended.

The silver symbolizes the knowledge of human nature which enables the priest to judge of the genuine nature of the penitence; the golden, the power of absolution According to the poet Lucan, the Tarpeian rock bellowed when Ccc &ar put aside the Tribune and violated the treasury. The reason why the door of Purgatory creaks is mentioned at the beginning of the next canto

Then listened I with such a raptured feeling
As often overcomes the soul down here,
When sing the people to the organ pealing,
And now the words are muffled, now ring clear.

Note to first line page 182

The sensitive reader will not fail to feel the singular loftiness of the style. The scenery wherein the falling asleep and the awakening of the Poet are framed; the imagery of the lunar aurora in the great constellation of the Scorpion; the dim imaginations of his dream and the contrast between its seeming violence and the placid action which it shadows; then the effect of Virgil's narrative upon Dante's mind and mood,—all these circumstances form a symmetrical avenue of approach, flanked by the converging lines of the dream and its answering reality. Hitherto we have been delayed outside the Christian Acropolis, first in the plain by the seaside, then upon the lower slopes of the Mountain; now we draw near to the mystic Propyheum. Invited by the courteous Gatekeeper, we are drawn with our good will up the three symbolic steps. The first of these may be taken as an emblem of the white purity of Christ wherein we behold, as in an accusing mirror, the stains which we have come to purge away. The second step, dark and rough and scorched, of massive stone cracked lengthwise and across, brings the broken and contrite heart in contact with the Cross of Christ; while perhaps the third, which seemed porphyry flaming like blood from a master vein, denotes acceptance on the part of the pilgrim of the redeeming blood of Christ. The Bird of God who sits above the threshold of adamant typifies the Priest receiving confession by authority of the Church. Here should be borne in mind the Poet's explanation in his letter to Can Grande of the various ways in which his poem may be read: it has meanings literal, moral, allegorical, anagogical,—now this meaning and now that one shining out, and sometimes two or three different meanings dazzling the reader with their iridescence. Thus here the threshold of adamant is a member of an architectural structure, while allegorically it refers to the solid foundation upon which Christ built the Church, morally to the steadfastness appropriate to the confessor, and anagogically (as Torraca suggests) to the light of Grace.

The purpose of the invocation is, in the light of these'considerations, clear. The reader will not have failed to note how habitually Dante descends at the close of a canto to some moral exhortation, some bitter invective, some piece of satire; and the loftier the theme of the canto the more studiously homely is the phrasing of such descent to earth. There is such a descent to the language and needs of little people (mulierculae) at the close of the preceding and of the succeeding canto. Such descents are more frequent as we go up and on. But in this canto there is no descent, and the Poet challenges the reader not to wonder if he uses more art to support the exalted matter of his song.

iclination *i* . The Marvelous Carved Walls
When once within the threshold of the gate.
Which souls disuse through evil incbhat
To make the crooked pathway appear straight,—
I felt it closed by its reverberation: «. "

And if I had turned back mine eyes thereto, '-
What for the fault were fitting exculpation? Lr-"
A fissured rock were we ascending through, C—
Which did to this side and the other sway *t*
As waves advancing and receding do. ',U-,
"Now must a little skill come into play,
In keeping close, now here," my Leader said,
"Now yonder, to the side that curves away."—
So scantily our steps were making head
That the moon's waning disk had time thereby
To settle down to rest within her bed,
Before we issued from that needle's eye.
But when we reached a free and open land
Above, where gathers back the mountain, I
Being weary, both uncertain on which hand
The way led, stopped we, not to go amiss
By roads more lonely than through desert sand.
From where the void borders the precipice
To base of the high cliff ascending sheer,
The human form thrice told would measure this;
And, as I winged my glances far and near,
Now to the leftward, now toward the right,
Still did this cornice such to me appear.
Our feet had not yet moved upon the height,
When that sheer cliff around us, there become
Too steep for climbing, proved of marble white
And decked with carvings past the masterdom
Not only of cunning Polycletus,—nay,
Nature herself had there been overcome.

Second day: middle of the forenoon. On the first of the seven terraces, that where the Sin of Pride is expiated

The hinges creak, therefore, because "strait is the gate, and few there be that find it"; and the symbolism is sustained by the loneliness of the way upon which they enter. In the narrow pass where the walls undulate, the poets are careful to go straight ahead. "The evil love of souls which makes the crooked way seem straight," implies familiarity with the poet's belief, to be fully developed later, that all actions, good or bad, are prompted by love of the good

*This first sub-*The Angel who proclaimed on earth the sway *ih'Th* peace long ages sighed to constitute, *ter of the gospel* Which swept the ancient ban of Heaven away, *of Luke, has of* Before us stood w£tli truth so absolute *course been since* . » 1 *the time of* Carved in the acting of the gracious theme, *Dante*

a favorite That it appeared to be no image mute" *one with paint-rsr" ers. Almost* You'd swear that he cried "Hail!" for how misdeem *greZ "mastrs"* When there WaS imaged forth that Lady dear *has made a* Who turned the key to open Love supreme?
lovely picture of «Behold the handmaid of the Lord is here!"— *the Annunciation* Such was the language by her mien attested,
Clearly as figure stampt in wax is clear.
"Attend not to one part alone,"—requested
The kindly Master who was holding me
On that side where the human heart is nested;
Whereat, my glance removing, did I see
Next beyond Mary, and toward the Guide
Who urged me on, another history
Set in the rock; whence, turning to that side,
I passed by Virgil and drew nigh alone,
So that it might the better be descried.
2 Samuel vi, There in the living marble carved, were shown
The cart and kine the holy ark that drew,
Whereby we fear an office not our own.
People were grouped about the foreground, who,
In seven choirs, made my two senses say,
One, "They sing not," the other, "Yes, they do."
And likewise, where the marble did portray
The smoke of incense, eyes and nostrils bore Discordant witness both of yea and nay. a *Samuel vi,* The lowly Psalmist, high-girt, on before
The sacred vessel, bounded in the dance,
And, doing so, was less than king and more.
Michal was figured, looking on askance
From window of great palace opposite,
Perturbed and scornful in her countenance.
12-16
From there the movement of my feet was slight
Till I could scan another tale anigh,
Which, beyond Michal, gleamed upon me white.
Herein was historied the glory high
Of the princely Roman who, beneficent,
Moved Gregory to his great victory:
Trajan, the emperor, hereby is meant;
And a poor widow to his bridle clung
In attitude of grief and of lament.
He seemed to ride with many a knight, among
A trampling throng; eagles of golden hue
Above him streaming to the wind seemed flung.
"Avenge me, Sire!"—amid that retinue
Appeared that wretched mother to implore,
"For my slain son my heart is stricken through."
"Be patient," answered her the Emperor,
"Till my return."—And she, with urgent moan
Replied: "How, Sire, if thou return no more?"—
Then he: "Whoso shall sit upon my throne
Will do it."—And she: "What boot shall be to thee
Another's bounty, if thou stint thine own?"—
"Now be thou comforted," consented he,
"For ere I go my duty must I do,
So Justice wills, pity restraining me."—
That Being who can look on nothing new
Produced that visible speech engraven yon,
Unknown here, therefore novel to our view.
While I delighted me to look upon
These portraits of humility so fair
And dear, considering Who this had done,
"Lo, many people, but with footsteps rare,"
Murmured the Poet, "on this side of us;
These will direct us to the lofty stair."—
Mine eyes, that were intent on gazing thus,
Turned round toward him, loath to be delayed,
To see new objects still solicitous.
It toas believed that Trajan was removed from Hell and redeemed in answer to the prayers of Gregory the Cheat. Cf. the great place given to the just Emperor in Paradiso xx Dante attributes to the reader that Sin of Pride which he acknowledges to have been his own (as will appear later)
I would not have thee, Reader, shrink dismayed
From thy good purpose, though thou come to know
How God ordains it that the debt be paid.
Take heed not to the fashion of the woe;
Think on what follows; at the worst take thought
Beyond the Judgment Day it cannot go.
"Master," began I, "what I see seems not
Persons approaching us with motion slight,
But sight is so at fault, I know not what. "—
And he replied to me: "So dire a plight
Doubles them down with punishment condign,
That I could not at first believe my sight.
But closely look till vision disentwine
What yonder comes beneath those bowlders bent:
Already canst thou see how all repine. "—
O ye proud Christians, wretched and forspent,
Infirm in vision of your inward eyes,
Who in backsliding steps are confident,
Perceive ye not how we from worms arise
To form the fair angelic butterfly
Which unto judgment undefended flies?
Why is the spirit in you puft on high,
Since ye are ungrown insects at your best,
Defective grubs that undeveloped die!
As ceiling or roof timbers often rest
On corbels, carved to indicate the strain
In figure quaint, contorting knee to breast,—

Whence out of the unreal, real pain
Is bred in him who looks,—beneath such stress
Did I see these, on giving heed again.
True is it, they were bowed down more and less
As more or less upon their backs they bore,
And he whose look seemed most to acquiesce,
Weeping, did seem to say: "I can no more!"— XI
The Proud Made Humble
"Our Father, Thou who dwellest high in Heaven,
Not circumscribed, save by the Love immense
That to Thy first creation Thou hast given,
Praised be Thy name and Thy omnipotence
By all created beings, emulous
To render thanks to Thy sweet effluence.
Let peace from Thine own kingdom come to us,
For with all reach of soul that in us lies
We cannot win it, if it come not thus.
As Thine own holy angels sacrifice
Their will to Thee, while they Hosannah sing,
So let men do with penitential sighs.
This day to us our daily manna bring,
For in this desert rough, in utter dearth,
We backward go when most endeavoring.
As we forgive to every one on earth
The wrongs we bore, so graciously do Thou
Forgive us, and look not upon our worth.
Put not to proof before our ancient foe
Our power of will, so easily undone,
But liberate from him who spurs it so.
We make, dear Lord, this final orison
Not for ourselves, because there is no need,
But all for dear ones left behind us yon. "—
Beseeching for themselves and us good speed,
Those heavy-laden shades went their slow way
Under such loads as oft from dreams proceed,
And with unequal anguish circled they
Wearily that first cornice of the Hill,
Purging the soilure of the world away.
If good for us be spoken yonder still,
What may be done and said for them down here
By those who have a good root to their will?
Morning of the second day The prayer "Deliver us from the Evil One" is no longer needed, but is made for us who are still subject to fall. How then should we remember them *when we pray!*
Surely we ought to give them aid to clear
The stains they carried hence, that light and chaste
They issue forth upon the starry sphere.
"Ah, so may justice and may pity haste / To disemburden you and speed your wing
Whither your heart's desire is wholly graced,
Tell us which passage to the stair may bring
Us soonest, and if more than one there be,
Show that where least is need of clambering:
For in the flesh of Adam comes with me
This person, by the burden so opprest
That, although willing, he mounts charily."—
The answer to these words, wherewith addrest
Those weary souls my Leader and my Friend,
Came back, from whom was yet not manifest;
But it was said: "If to the right ye wend
With us along the cliff, ye shall be shown
A passage where the living could ascend.
And if I were not hampered by the stone
Taming my neck, erewhilc imperious,
So that perforce I hold my visage down,
Then would I scan that one, not named to us
But still alive, to see if him I knew,
And make him of this burden piteous.
Once one of To a great Tuscan Sire my birth is due,
those great William Aldobrandesco: I know not
counts of banta Fiora mentioned Whether his name was ever known to you.
%Th ttied (. ancient blood, and prowesses that wrought *having a castle*
My forebears, so my vanity beguiled,
for every day in rpl of Qur common mother losing thought, *tlic year*
At all men with high arrogance I smiled,
So that I died, as know the Sienese,
Where he was And knows in Campagnatico each child.
"""'' Humbert am I; nor harmed my haughtiness
Me only, but all those my kinsmen bred
Are dragged in consequence to deep distress.
Vanity of Artistic and Literary Fame 191
And here I cannot choose but bow my head
Beneath this load till satisfied be Grace,—
Since not alive I did it, with the dead. "—
Listening to him, I bended down my face;
And one of them beneath the weight they brook
(Not he who spoke) twisted himself apace
And saw me and recognized and called, his look,
Albeit with effort, at my figure aimed
Which going withal their crouching posture took.
"Art thou not Oderisi,"—I exclaimed,
"Glory of Gubbio for that art of thine
In Paris now 'illuminating' named?"—
"Brother," said he, "the leaves more smiling shine
By Franco of Bologna's brush made

fair:
His now is all the boast, eclipsing mine.
I had not been so courteous over there
While living, for the yearning strong in me
For excellence, which was my utmost care.
Here of such pride is paid the penalty;
And had I not, while free to sin, been fain
To turn to God, even here I should not be.
O glory of the human powers, how vain!
Brief seasons to the summit verdure yield
If no beclouded era supervene.
Thought Cimabue to possess the field
In painting; now is Giotto in request
So that the elder glory is concealed.
So did one Guido from the other wrest
The palm in language; there may be, who knows?
One born to drive both eagles from the nest.
Worldly renown is windy breath that goes
Now hither and now yon, and changes name
According to the quarter whence it blows.
If old thou strip thy flesh, shall then thy fame
Be much more glorious than hadst thou died
While pap and prattle still thy lips became,
The "pride of the artist Guido Guinicelli, whom we shall meet in Canto xxvi, and Guido Cavalcanti, whose father we met in Inferno x. The third poet is dmibtless Dante himself. With delicate sdf-betrayal he thus illustrates that he was not exempt from "that last infirmity of noble mind"
A thousand years to come? a briefer tide To all eternity, than wink of eye
To circle round the Heaven most slowly plied. *The lord of the* With him who little road doth occupy sSf *f* Before me, ran8 all Tuscany of yore,
Though few for him now in Siena sigh
Where he was master once, and overbore
The rabidness of Florence, prostitute
At present, even as she was proud before.
As color of the grass is your repute
Which comes and goes; He makes it yellow and sere
Who summons from the earth the greening fruit."—
And I: "Thy truthful words make lowlier
My spirit, and abate my swelling pride:
But who is he of whom thou spokest here?"—
"That? Provenzan Salvani," he replied,
"Put here because presumptuous to hold
All Siena underfoot. So since he died
Has he been going, and ever as of old
Unresting goes; with such coin he atones
Who in the other life has been too bold. "—
And I: "If every spirit who postpones
Repentance till he reach life's utmost rim
Cannot, unaided by good orisons,
Ascend the Mount, but must an interim
Equal to all his life remain below,—
How has the coming been vouchsafed to him?"—
And he: "When living in the greatest show,
Upon the Campo of Siena fain
Was he to stand and all respect forgo:
For, wishing to deliver from the pain
Of Charles's prison house, a friend, he there
Compelled himself to quake in every vein.
Dante is also to I say no more, of darkling words aware; ii But shortly will thy neighbors bring about *upon the charity* That thou the pregnant comment canst prepare. *of strangers* This action from those limits 1 1 out»_ *Examples of Pride Brought Low* 193 xn
The Pictured Floor
Abreast, like oxen going in a yoke,
I with that heavy-laden soul went on,
By the kind Teacher's leave. But when he spoke:
"Now it behooves us leave him and be gone;
To ply the bark with sail and oar is best
Here, far as possible, for every one,"
Upright, prepared for walking, I redressed
My body, howsoever inwardly
My thoughts remained both lowly and depressed.
I had moved on, and followed willingly
The footsteps of my Master, and so fleet
We went as showed us light of foot to be,
When said he: "Cast thine eyes down; it is meet,
In order well the pathway to beguile,
To look upon the bed beneath thy feet."
As, that their memory remain awhile,
Earth-level tombs above the buried show
The carven traces of their former style,
Whence tears for them there often freshly flow
Through pricking of remembrances, that stir
Only the tender-hearted: even so
Beheld I, but of semblance gooduer
There, in accordance with the Workman's worth,
Figured the way along that mountain-spur.
I saw on one side him of nobler birth
Than any other creature, swift as light
Fall like a thunderbolt from Heaven to Earth.
I saw Briareus, smitten by the bright
Celestial dart, with chill of death subdued,
Heavy upon the ground there opposite.
I saw Thymbraeus, Pallas, Mars, who stood
In armor round their Father, and they were

Gazing at members of the giants strewed.

The time is near noon of the second day: the place further to the right around the Terrace of the Proud. The symmetrical rhetoric corresponds with the formal arrangement of the pictures. Carven tombs in the pavement of the church are common in Italy; but the most notable example of a pictured floor is in the Cathedral of Siena (the "graffiti"). Any reader with a Bible and a dictionary can look up the examples Series of stanzas beginning alike are frequent: e.g. , the three beginning with the word "Love" in Francesco's story (Inf. v), and the more elaborated series in Paradiso

I saw, at foot of his great labor, stare
Bewildered Nimrod, where on Shinar plain
Lay those who with him had been haughty there.
0 Niobe, with eyes how full of pain,
Portrayed upon the path I saw thee too,
Between thy seven and seven children slain!
O Saul, how on your proper sword did you
There lifeless upon Mount Gilboa show,
That felt thereafter neither rain nor dew!
O mad Arachne, I beheld thee so,
Half spider, wretched on the ruin wrought
Upon the web thou wo vest to thy woe!
0 Rehoboam, here thy form does not
Appear to threaten, but fulfilled with fear,
Snatcht from pursuers by a chariot!
Showed the hard pavement, too, what guerdon dear
Alcmseon made unto his mother once
The ill-predestined ornaments appear; Showed how upon Sennacherib the sons
Fell in the temple, where, when he was slain,
They left him without any orisons;
Showed how great ruin and what cruel pain
Wrought Tomyris, when she to Cyrus said:
"Thy thirst for blood with blood I slake again"; Showed how in panic the Assyrians fled
As soon as Holofernes was undone,
And showed the remnants of that victim dead.
1 saw in caves and ashes Ilion:
O Troy, thy state how low and pitiful
Showed in the sculptured imagery yon!
What Master could with brush or graving-tool
Those lines and shades so deftly have bestowed,
To make the cleverest wit cry "wonderful"?
The dead seemed dead, alive the living showed:
Better than I, saw not who saw the true,
All that I trod while bent above my road.
Now lift your haughty looks, insolent crew
Of sons of Eve, nor glance ye at the ground
To see the wicked way that ye pursue!
More of the mount by us was circled round,
And the sun's course now far more nearly spent,
Than deemed my spirit, which was not unbound,
When he who ever vigilantly went
Before me, "Lift thy head," began to say,
"The time is past for going thus intent.
Lo! yonder is an Angel in array
To come toward us: lo! returning seen
The sixth handmaid from service of the day.
Adorn with reverence thine act and mien,
That he may gladly speed our way on high:
Think that this day will never dawn again."
Well wonted to his monishing was I,
On no account to squander time; and thus
He could not on that theme speak covertly.
Toward us came the being beauteous,
Vested in raiment white, and in his face
Such as appears the dawn-star tremulous.
His wings he opened, opened his embrace,
Bidding: "Approach, for hard by is the stair,
And from henceforward ye ascend apace.
To these glad tidings the response is rare:
Born to soar up, why are ye overthrown,
O human race, at every puff of air?"
He led us to where cloven was the stone; Here with his wings did on my forehead smite,
Then promised me secure the going on.
As beyond Rubaconte, to the right,
Where sits the temple built to overlook
The well-directed city, the sharp flight
Of that ascent less pantingly we brook
By means of stairways fashioned in the days
Safe for the bushel and the audit-book;
So here the mountainside a little stays
Its dizzy drop from the succeeding round,
But high rocks either side the pathway graze.
As we are turning thither, voices sound,
"Blessed the poor in spirit!"—sweet concent
Such that to tell it words could not be found.
Ah me, these entrances how different
From that Infernal! for with anthems here
One enters,—there below with wild lament.
We were ascending now the holy stair,
And now I seemed to walk with lighter spring
Than even on the level plain whilere:
Wherefore I questioned him: "What heavy thing
Has been uplifted from me, Master, say,
That now I go almost unwearying?"
He answered: "When the other P's that stay,
Though indistinctly, on thy forehead still,
Shall, like the one, be canceled quite away,
Thy feet will be so subject to good will,
Not only will they not be wearied out,
But feel delight to be urged up the hill."
Then did I as do those who go about

Hooded they know not how, till by and by The beckonings of others make them doubt; *The touch of the* Wherefore the hand is raised to verify, *hJt'alaTone And* the thin£ *t* seeks,thus Ending aid *symbolic P from* To supplement the office of the eye; *the poef, brow* go found the gngers 0f my right outspread, Six only of the letters that erewhile
He of the Keys had graven on my head:
And this my gesture made the Leader smile.
Lashes of the Scourge of the Envious
197 XIII
Sapia Of Siena
We now were at the summit of the stair, *Early afternoon*
There where the mount that heals as one ascends jf *second day.*
Is cut away the second time.—And there *Envious*
A terrace round about the hillside trends
In the same manner as the former one,
Save that more suddenly its contour bends. Shaded or graven form appeared there none:
So bare the bank, and so the pathway showed
With but the livid color of the stone.
"If to inquire of people we abode
Still here," the Poet said, "I fear perchance
It would too much delay our choice of road." Then fixing on the sun a steady glance,
And centering his movement on the right,
He caused his left side round it to advance. "O Thou, confiding in whose kindly light
I enter the new pathway, lead," he said,
"For leading here within is requisite.
The world thou warmest, lamping overhead;
If other reason urge not, by thy smile
We ought forever to be onward led."
As far as here we reckon for a mile,
So far there did we on our journey move
By dint of ready will, in little while;
And tow'rd us were heard flying thereabove
Spirits invisible, with courteous
Persuasion, bidding to the board of Love. The first voice that went flying onward thus,
With loud proclaim cried out: "No wine have they," *Mary at the*
Repeating it long after passing us. *marriage at*
And ere, far off, it wholly died away,
I heard another that was flying by, *Pylades, wiih "I* am Orestes,"—nor did this one stay. *his friend*
"O Father mine, what voices these?" said I;
And while I questioned, did a third one urge,
"Love him that uses you despitefully. " *The Envious are* And he: "This round doth castigating purge *scourged by* The sin of £ d from I are , *voices of unself-' ish love. Tlie* On that account the lashes of the scourge.
to1£vy"isCfZknd Another sound must have the bridle rein, *voiced at the* And thou wilt hear it, if I well surmise, *close of Canto xiv* Q,. evef thou the Pass of Pardon gain
But through the air intently fix thine eyes,
And thou shalt see along this avenue
People, all sitting where the rocks arise. "

Then opened wider than before my view,
Taking in shades in front, with mantles on
That did not differ from the stone in hue.
And when we had a little farther gone,
I heard a moaning: "Mary, for us pray!"
To Michael and Peter and all the saints a moan.
I cannot think there walks the earth today
A man so hard as not to have been stung
With pity at what I saw beside the way:
For when I drew so nearly them among
That all their actions became manifest,
Out through mine eyes full bitter tears were wrung.
In haircloth mean I seemed to see them drest;
Each lent his shoulder unto him behind,
And all supported by the cliff did rest.
Thus at indulgences the poor and blind
To crave their needment by the portal wait,
Each with his head upon the next reclined,
That others may be made compassionate
Not by the sound of words alone so soon
As by their looks that no less supplicate.
As profits not the blind the sun at noon,
So to the shades who sat where I have said,
The light of Heaven will not confer its boon;
For pierces all their lids an iron thread,
And sews them up, as to a savage hawk
Is done, since it will not be quieted.
Methought it unbecoming so to walk
Beholding others while concealed from view;
Whence turned I, with my counsel sage to talk.
"What the mute wished to utter, well he knew,
Whence did he not my questioning abide,
But said: "Speak to the point; let words be few."
Virgil was walking with me on that side
Whence one may fall, because a parapet
To girdle round the terrace is denied.
Upon the other side of me were set
The pious shades, who through the suture dread
Strained forth the tears until their cheeks were wet.
To them I turned me, and, beginning, said:
"O people sure to see the lofty Glow
Whereto your longing thoughts are wholly led,
May Grace soon loosen all the soilure so
From off your conscience, that descending clear

Through it the stream of memory may flow,

Tell me,—for welcome will it be and dear,—

If soul Italian here among you be;

It might be well for him that I should hear."

"Citizens all, O brother mine, are we

Of one true city; but be this thy word,—

One who a pilgrim dwelt in Italy."

By way of answer, this, methought, I heard

A little farther on than where I stood;

Whence I directed me yet thitherward.

Among the others there, one shadow showed

A waiting look; should any ask "How so?"

It lifted up its chin in blindman's mode.

"O soul, subdued that thou mayst upward go,"

Said I, "if thou it be that answerest,

Vouchsafe that I thy name or country know."

No dividing lines of race or tongue or land or color

"I was a Sienese, and with the rest,"

She answered, "here I cleanse my life unfit,

Weeping to Him to come and make us blest.

Sapient was I not, though named of it

Sapia; greeting with far greater glee

Another's bane than mine own benefit.

And that thou think me not deceiving thee,

Hear whether I was foolish as I tell

What time the years were sloping down with me.

The defeat of One day the men who in my country dwell

'euiefa Joined battle near to Ctll6 With their foes« *Provemano Sal-*While I was praying God for what befell.

HW Routed were they, and felt the bitter woes *hnea* Of fugitives; beyond comparison My joy, on witnessing the chase, arose:

So that, uplifting my bold face thereon,

I cried to God, 'Henceforth I fear Thee not!'

As doth the blackbird for a little sun.

Upon the utmost verge of life I sought

For peace with God; and e'en yet would I be

Nowise by penitence of debt disfraught,

Had it not been that, out of charity

Grieving, with supplications holiest,

*Peter the comb-*Pier Pettinagno still remembered me.

maker, to unu-But who art thou that *eomest* making quest *.molly honest as . . to be still remem-*About our state, with unimpeded eye *bered in Siena* I believe, breathing reasonest?" *Dante confesses* "Mine eyes will be withheld," I made reply, *'tU.Jfing* "But briefly here, for small offense done when

With Envy they were yonder turned awry.

My spirit, too expectant of the pain

They suffer underneath, is terrified;

That load already weighs on me amain. "

And she to me: "Who then hath been thy guide

Up here among us, if return is meet?"

"He with me who is silent," I replied;

Desire for Good Report on Earth 201

"And living am I; whence do thou entreat

Of me, O chosen soul, wouldst have me yon

Yet move in thy behalf my mortal feet."

"O strange is this to hear!"—she said thereon,

"And of God's love to thee a happy sign;

Whence aid me sometime with thine orison.

And I implore by most desire of thine, If thou shalt tread the Tuscan earth anew,

That thou make good my fame with kindred mine.

Seek them among that futile people, who

Place hope in Talamone, forfeiting

More hope than when the Dian they pursue;

But the admirals will lose a greater thing."

Talarrume was a malarial seaport which the Sienese tried to develop; the Dian an underground stream they tried to tap. The Sienese "admirals" are like those of Switzerland. For other references to this fascinat' ing city, see Cantos v and xi, and Inf. xxix XIV

Degeneracy Of Tuscany And The Romagna *The Terrace of* "Who is this that, ere Death have given him wing, *midiffZL.* Doth.circling round ab.out our mountain go, *second day* Shutting his eyes at will, and opening?"

"I know not who he is, but he, I know,

Is not alone: ask thou, who art more nigh, And greet him gently, that he answer so." *Speakers: Guido* Thus, leaning each to each, held colloquy *Rirderiada* wo spi"ts' sitting on the right hand there; *Calboli* Then, to address me, with the face on high,

One said: "O soul, that dost already fare

Tow'rd Heaven, yet planted in the body thus, For charity console us, and declare Whence and who art thou; for so marvelous This grace of thine appears unto our eyes, As must a thing yet never known to us." *Course of the* And I: "In Falterona there doth rise *tZlTsotce* A brook, mid-Tuscany meandering, *to the sea* Whose course a hundred miles do not suffice.

From thereupon do I this body bring:

To tell you who I am were speech in vain,

Because my name does not yet widely ring."

Then he who first had spoken said again:

"Thou speakst of Arno, if I picture well

The meaning of thy words within my brain."

Whereto the other: "Why did he not tell

The very word we know that river by,

But keep it back as something horrible?"

And the shadow that was questioned made reply:

"I know not, but indeed 'tis fitting for

The very name of such a vale to die.

For from its fountain,—where the waters pour

So amply from that rugged mountain chain

Torn from Pelorus, seldom teeming more,

As far as where it renders up again

That which the heaven absorbs from out the flood,

Wherefrom the rivers have their

flowing train,— Virtue is driven like a serpent brood,
The enemy of all, or through mischance
Of place, or scourge of evil habitude.
Whence so disnatured are the habitants
Of that unhappy vale, it would appear
That Circe had them in her maintenance. Among foul hogs, of acorns worthier
Than other viands made for use of men,
It first directs its puny thoroughfare;
Curs it encounters, coming downward then,
More snarling than their power gives warranty,
And turns from them its muzzle in disdain; The more it flows on downward swellingly,
The more the dogs grown wolves discovers this Accursed ditch of evil destiny;
Finds then, descending many-a deep abyss,
Foxes so fraudulent they never fear
To be entrapt by any artifice.
Nor do I curb my tongue lest others hear:
And good for this man to remember well
The things true prophecy is making clear. I see thy grandson, who becomes a fell
Hunter of those wolf-creatures, and dismays All who along the cruel river dwell.
He vends their flesh while it is living,— slays
Them afterwards, as would a wild-beast hoar;
Many of life deprives, himself of praise. From the grim wood he issues red with gore,
Leaving it such not thousand years will show
That river-bank rewooded as before."
As at announcement of impending woe,
The hearer's face betrays his troubled mood,
From wheresoever peril threaten; so
The Romagna, bounded by Po, Reno, Apennine, Adriatic
I saw that other soul, in attitude
To listen, grow perturbed and full of teen,
When that prophetic word he understood.
The language of the one, the other's mien
Made me desire to know the names they bore;
Whereof I made request, with prayers between.
Thereat the spirit that spoke to me before,
Began again: "Thou wilt not do the same
Favor to me that thou art craving for;
But if God will that forth in thee should flame
Such grace, I will not as a niggard do:
Know then, Guido del Duca is my name.
So Envy did the blood of me imbue,
That, had I seen a man grow joyful there,
Thou wouldst have seen me tinged with livid hue.
From my own sowing reap I such a tare:
Why set your hearts, O human progeny,
On what ye are permitted not to share?
This is Rinier, of the house of Calboli
The glory and the honor; from their blood
Has sprung no heir of his nobility.
'Twixt Po and mountain, Reno and the flood,
His family is not the only race
Stript of integrity and gentlehood;
For in these bounds replete is every place
With poisonous scions, so that late and slow
Could ever tilth eradicate their trace.
Henry Mainardi and good Lizio,
Pier Traversar', Guy di Carpigna, where
Be they, O Romagnoles, who bastard grow?
When will Bologna now a Fabbro bear?
Faenza a Bernardin di Fosco when?—
Of humble family the noble heir.
Tuscan, let not my tears amaze thee then,
When Guy da Prata I recall to mind,
With Hugh of Azzo as he lived with men,
Degenerate Houses of the Romagna 205
And Frederick Tignoso and his kind,
The Traversara, the Anastagi (those
Two houses in their lineage declined!),
The knights and ladies, labor and repose,
That kindled in us love and courtesy,
Where every human heart so wicked grows.
O Brettinoro, why dost thou not flee,
Seeing that, not to be corrupted, go
Many to exile with thy family?
Well does Bagnacaval being barren so,
But Castrocaro ill, and bent to spawn
Such breed of counts, still worse does Conio.
Will do well the Pagani, when is gone
Their Demon from them; but not so that pure
Can ever the report of them live on.
O Hugh of Fantolini, now secure
Thy name is, which no fear may entertain
Of sons degenerating to obscure!
Now, Tuscan, go thy way, for I am fain
Rather to weep than our discourse pursue,
So has it left my spirit wrung with pain. "
That those dear souls could hear when we withdrew,
We were aware; and therefore confident
Their silence made us of the avenue.
When we became alone, as on we went,
A voice came counter to us that did say,
Even as when lightning cleaves the firmament:
"Every one that findeth me, shall slay;"
All of a sudden thereupon it passed,
As thunder with the storm-rack rolls away.
Soon as our ears had truce from such a blast,
Behold another of so loud a tone,
It seemed the thunderclap that follows fast:
"I am Aglauros, who became a stone!"
Backward instead of forward, at that sound

I stepped, and pressed the Poet hard upon.
The studious reader will lockup these forgotten great in Toynbee's entertaining Dante Dictionary This Devil ought to be remembered for his sonorous name: Maghinardo Pagani da Susinana. Tie was lord of Faenza and Imola. Dante gives him three lines in Inferno xxvii H9-51) Cain Apparently for coveting her sister's handsome lovsr The bridle-bit or
Now was the air grown quiet all around;
check-rein of d he to me. "That was the galling bit *Canto xiti, W,* i i i
Which ought to keep a man withm his bound.
But ye accept the baited hook, and it
Draws you toward the Adversary old,
Whence curb or call doth little benefit.
The Heavens are calling to you, and unfold
Their never-fading beauties to your view
Which ever fixt upon the earth ye hold;
Whence the All-seeing One is scourging you." *Ascent to the Terrace where Wrath is Purged* 207 xv
Treasure In Heaven: Visions Of Forbearance
As much as shows, between the dawn of day
And when the third hour closes, of the sphere
That like a child is evermore at play,
So much seemed left the sun of his career
Toward the night, remaining to be run:
There it was vespers, and 'twas midnight here.
The rays were striking full our face upon,
For so we circling round the mountain went
That we were going toward the setting sun;
When yet far more I felt my forehead bent
Beneath the splendor that did on it smite,
And the strange matters were my wonderment:
Wherefore I made a visor to my sight,
Lifting my hands above these brows of mine
So as to temper the excess of light.
As when on glass or water sunbeams shine,
Then in the opposite direction dart,
Ascending in a corresponding line
To that of their descent, and so depart
Equally from the plummet line away,
As demonstrate experiment and art;
So I felt smitten by a flashing ray
That seemed reflected full in front of me,
Wherefore mine eyes could not endure to stay.
"What is it, Father dear, whence cannot be
Sufficient shelter for my sight," said I,
"And coming on toward us seemingly?"
"Marvel thou not if dazzle yet thine eye
The family of Heaven," he answered. "Tis
A messenger inviting us on high.
In short while to behold such things as this
Will not be irksome to thee, but delight
So deep that Nature holds no sweeter bliss."
Late afternoon of second day. The sphere is surely not the Ecliptic but the visible heavens, our sky, conceived as always in happy, innocent activity Vespers is the time from 3 to 6 P.m. *At 3 in Purgatory it would be midnight in Italy Ascent to the Terrace of the Wrathful Guido del Duca: lines 86, 87 of Canto xiv*
When we had reacht the Angel benedight,
His glad voice said: "From here thou enterest
A stair than others far less steep of flight."
Departing thence, we mounted now, and *Blest*
Are the compassionate, did it intone
Behind us, and *Rejoice, thou conquerest!*
My Master and myself, we two alone,
Were going up, and, going, I took thought
How from his words to gain some benison;
And turned me to him, thus inquiring: "What
Could he have meant, the spirit Romagnole,
Speaking of sharing as permitted not?"
Then he: "Of his own greatest sin, that soul
Conceives the harm; whence let it not surprise
If he rebuke it, that there be less dole.
For inasmuch as your heart's treasure lies
Where through companionship ye lose a share,
Doth Envy work the bellows for your sighs.
But if love for the most exalted sphere
Should make your aspiration upward turn,
Ye would not harbor in your breast that fear;
Because the more there yonder be who yearn
To murmur 'Ours,' the more has each, and more
Of charity doth in that cloister burn."
"I am further from contentment than before
I ceased from being silent," then I said,
"And more of doubt within my mind I store.
How can a single boon, distributed,
Give many holders wealth more unconfined,
Than if it be by few inherited?"
And he: "Because thou centerest thy mind
Only on earthly things, thy inward sight
Is, in the plenitude of brightness, blind.
That inexpressible and infinite
Boon up above there, so to love out-

flows,
As to a lucid body runs the light.
Partnership in Spiritual Goods 209
Much as it finds of ardor, it bestows;
So that, however spread the flame of love,
Above it the Eternal Bounty grows.
And the more people set their hearts above,
The more love well there, and more love is wrought,
And mirrors each to each the bliss thereof. And if my reasoning appease thee not,
Thou shalt have Beatrice to cancel through
Both this and every other craving thought. Obliterated of thy wounds are two:
Only endeavor that, the same as these,
The five may soon be healed by feeling rue." As I was fain to say, "Thou dost appease,"
Behold! another Circle did I gain,
And eager eyes compelled me hold my peace. There suddenly I felt me overta'en *Three visions of*
By an ecstatic vision, whence beguiled, EST.
I saw a crowd of people in a fane; *Wrathful*
And at the door a Lady, with the mild *The Virgin*
Mien of a mother, seemed to say this thing: *Motlier*
"Ah, why hast thou so dealt with us, my child? Thy father and myself, lo! sorrowing
Were seeking thee."—As here she ceased to speak,
That which had first appeared was vanishing. Another then appeared, adown whose cheek
Those waters coursed that grief distills, when great
Resentment upon others it would wreak: "If Master of the town that such debate
Caused to the gods about its name," said she,
"And whence doth every science scintillate, Upon that bold embrace avenge thou thee,
That clasped our daughter, O Pisistratus!" *Pisistratus,*
Her lord benign and gentle seemed to me fcrf *Athem*
To answer her with temperate manner thus:
"What shall we do to them who wish us ill,
If they who love us are condemned by us?" *The stoning of* Then I saw angry folk aflame with will
St. Stephen To slay a yOuth by stoning, raising cries
Hoarsely to one another: "Kill him, kill!"
And saw him bowed to earth, and now he lies
Under the weight of Death, yet, thus undone,
Still making gates to Heaven with his eyes;
Lifting to the High Lord his orison,
With look such as unlocks our sympathy,
For pardon to his slayers every one.
Soon as returned my spirit outwardly
To things external to it, which are true,
Did I my not erroneous errors see.
Thereon my Leader, who could see me do
Like one disputing slumber's masterdom,
Exclaimed: "What ails thee? canst not stand? go to!
For half a league and farther art thou come
With eyes veiled over, and with legs that sway,
Like one with wine or slumber overcome."
Then said I: "O my gentle Father, pray
Listen to me, and I will tell thee what
I saw, when thus my legs were ta'en away!"
"A hundred masks upon thy face would not
Avail to shut thy mind from me," he said,
"However trivial might be thy thought.
What thou hast seen was that thou mayst be led
To ope thy heart to waters of repose
That pour from the eternal fountainhead.
I did not ask 'What ails thee?' as do those
Who only look with inattentive glance
When reft of consciousness the body shows,
But asked that vigorous thy foot advance:
Thus it behooves to spur the laggard, slow
To put to proof returning vigilance."
Still forward through the vesper did we go,
Straining as far as possible the eye
Against the late and shining rays; and lo!
Benighting Effect of Wrath 211
By slow degrees toward us coming nigh *The symbolic*
A cloud of smoke, as gloomy as the night, *smoke of wath*
Nor was there any place of shelter by:
This of pure air bereft us and of sight.

XVI

Lawlessness Of The Temporal Power Of The Clergy

Terrace of the The gloom of Hades and of shades that shroud *Wrathful. Late* Every star beneath a barren sky, *afternoon of the" " second day* As much as can be overcast with cloud,
Made never veil so thick unto mine eye
Nor of so rough a tissue to the feeling,
As did that smoke we there were covered by,
From the closed eye all vision quite concealing;
Whereat mine Escort sapient and tried
Offered me help, his shoulder tow'rd me wheeling.
Even as a blind man goes behind his guide,
And lest he haply stumble against aught
Might hurt or kill him, does not go aside,
So faring through that bitter fume, I caught
The accents of my Guide, who did but say:
"Take care that we be separated not!"—
Voices I heard, and each appeared to pray
That might in peace and in compassion come

The Lamb of God who takes our sins away.
Just *Agnus Dei* was their exordium:
One measure was for all, and one desire,
So that in harmony seemed all and some.
"Master, can what I hear," did I inquire,
"Be spirits?"—''Thou hast said it," he replied,
"And they go loosening the knot of ire. "—
"Now who art thou cleaving our smoke aside,
Who art discoursing of us even as though
Thou didst by calends still the time divide?"—
Speech by a single voice was uttered so:
Whereat the Master said: "Thy answer be
To ask if here the pathway upward go. "—
And I: "O creature that art cleansing thee,
To return beautiful to Him who made,
Shalt hear a wonder if thou follow me. "—
"I'll follow thee far as I may," it said,
"And if the smoke still make our seeing vain,
To keep us joined shall hearing serve instead."—
"Swathed in the bands that Death unbinds again,"
Began I, "do I go the upward road,
And hither came I through the eternal pain;
And since enfolds me so the grace of God,
Showing His will that I behold His court
By way quite other than our modern mode,
What man thou wast ere death do thou report,
Concealing naught, and tell me if I go
Right for the pass; and let thy words escort."
"Lombard was I, called Marco; and did know
The world's concerning, and that virtue love
Whereat each one has now unbent the bow:
For mounting up do thou straight forward move."—
Thus answering, "I pray thee," added he,
"To pray for me when thou shalt be above."—
And I to him: "I pledge my faith to thee
To do that which thou era vest; but I burst
With inward doubt till from it I am free.
Elsewhere suggested, it was simple first,
But now confirmed by words which thou hast said,
Redoubled, and to know the cause I thirst.
The world in very deed is forfeited
To vice by virtue all, as thou dost say,
And is with evil big and overspread:
But put thy finger on the cause, I pray,
That I, discerning it, let others know
Whether the blame to heaven or earth to lay."—
Voicing his deep sighs in a cry by woe
Wrung from him, he began: "The world is blind,
Brother, and sooth thou comst from there below.
All causes are by you who live assigned
To Heaven above, as if its motion still
Did of necessity all natures bind.
Marco Lombardo: a great figure in his day, who left a reputation for sagacity, wit, brusque candor, liberality, honor. Jf he was prone to ire, he probably had good reason
If this were true, your freedom of the will
Would be destroyed, and it would not be right
To have or joy for good, or grief for ill.
The Heavens do your first impulses excite,—
I say not all; but grant that this I said,
For good or evil there is given you light
And free volition; which to battle led
Against the stars, though weary it commence,
Finally conquers all, if rightly fed.
Though free, ye are subject to omnipotence
And better nature, which doth in you mold
The mind, exempt from starry influence.
Hence if the present world go uncontrolled,
In you the cause, let it be sought in you:
And true intelligence I now unfold.
Forth from the hand of her Creator, who
Loves her before she be, in maiden guise,
With gleeful laughter and with tears of rue,
Issues the innocent soul, in nothing wise
Save that from her blithe Maker, she again
Blithely turns thither where her pleasure lies.
Cheated at first, she tastes the savor vain
Of trivial good, and runs to that desire,
Her love by guide unbended or by rein.
Hence law by way of bridle we require;
Require a king discerning from aloof
Of the true city of God at least the spire.
Chewing the cud Laws are,—but who to put them to the proof? *(ruminating) is* None: since the shepherd, he who goes before, *the business of ,,,,,* t *the Pastor. The* Can chew the cud but cleaveth not the hoof. *deft hoof, which* -whence folk who see their leader striking for *does not easily* . D *slip, symbolizes* That having which they greedily pursue,
Pruce Being fed with that, hunger for nothing more.
magistrate. But Well canst thou see that governance untrue *the Pasfor has j c &use* is that hath made the worid maligii *usurped me functions of the* And not that nature is corrupt in you. *Magistrate The Church of Rome Falls in the Mire* 215
Rome, that redeemed the world, once gave to shine Two suns, which both the one and the other course
Made manifest,—the worldly, the divine.
The one hath quencht the other; and perforce,

The sword together with the crazier wed,
I11 can but come of it till they divorce,
Since, joined, the one doth not the other dread.
Consider well, if thou believe not so,
The fruit, for every plant is known by seed.
In the land laved by Adige and Po,
Valor was once in vogue, and courtesy,
Ere Frederick had quarreled with his foe;
Now can fare through it with security
Any whom sense of shame may set at strife
From speaking with the good or drawing nigh.
Survive still, to rebuke the manners rife,
Three veterans, and long appears the road
To them, till God conduct to better life:
Conrad, named of Palazzo, Gerard good,
And Guido of Castello,—better say
The loyal Lombard, after the French mode.
The Church of Rome, declare thou from this day.
That would in double government engage,
Falls with its burden in the miry way. "—
"O Marco mine," said I, "thy words are sage;
And now I see why Levi's children should
Have been excluded from the heritage.
But who is Gerard, that example good,
Thou sayest, of a generation spent,
Who lives to upbraid our barbarous period?"—
"Cheat me thy words, or make experiment, In that thou, speaking Tuscan," he replied,
"Seemst of good Gerard unintelligent.
I know him not by any name beside,
Unless 'twere from his daughter Gaia drawn.—
I come no farther; so be God your guide.
This somewhat indefinite allusion doubtless involves a compliment to a great lady who inherited and increased the honor of a stainless name. Any other interpretation is both baseless and graceless
Already through the smoke the splendor yon
Is whitening,—the Angel is there,—before
He has perceived me, I must needs be gone."-
So he turned back, and would not hear me more.
XVII
Profitable Discourse During The Second Night
Recall to mind if ever shut thee in,
Reader, a cloud upon the Apennine,
Wherethrough thou sawest but as mole through skin;
How, when the dank, dense vapors discombine,
And slowly fall away, the solar sphere
Comes struggling in again with feeble shine;
And to thy fantasy it will be clear
Immediately, how I saw once more
The sun, that was already setting here.
To the sure footsteps of my Counselor
Matching my own, from such a cloud I thus
Emerged to rays now dead on the low shore.
O power of fancy, oft withdrawing us
So from without, we show indifference
Though a thousand trumpets round are clamorous,
Who moves thee if impel thee not the sense?
Moves thee a heaven-informed illumining,
Led down by will or starry influence.
Appeared the trace in my imagining
Of her, the pitiless, who changed, some say,
Into the bird that most delights to sing;
And here my intellect in such a way
Was lockt within, that nothing was descried
Of any object that outside it lay.
In my raised fantasy, one crucified
Rained down thereafterward, of scornful mood
And rancorous in mien, and so he died.
Around him great Ahasuerus stood,
Esther his wife, just Mordecai, he who
In word and deed was of such rectitude.
And as this image of itself withdiew,
Collapsing like a bubble when it wants
The film of water it was fashioned through,
Sunset of secona day. Terrace of the WrallifW
Procne or Progne), see Canto ix, IB. Dante follows Ovid. There is a.more common version of the myth that makes Philomela the nightingale Haman (Book of Esther). TheVulgate in one place terms the scaffold a "cross" Lavinia, whose mother had killed herself at a false report of the death of Turnus, JEneid Ascent to the Terrace of the Slothful
Uprose a youthful maiden in my trance,
Bitterly weeping, and she cried: "O Queen,
Why wouldest thou be naught in petulance?
To lose Lavinia not, thyself hast slain:
Now thou hast lost me; she who mourns am I,
Mother, for thee, ere for another's teen. "—
And even as slumber breaks, when suddenly
Upon closed eyelids strikes the morning light,
And, broken, wavers ere it wholly die,
So fell away from me this fancied sight,
Soon as there struck upon my face a glare
That, matched with what we know, seemed infinite.
When I had turned to see the way to fare,
I heard: "Here go ye up!" in accents blest
Withdrawing me from every other care,
Making my will so eager in request
To know the speaker, and to look and see.
That, until face to face, it cannot rest.
But as before the sun, excessively

Resplendent, veiling so its form from sight,
Thus was the power deficient here in me.
"This is a spirit divine, who tow'rd the height,
Without our prayer, points where we should be hieing,
And wraps himself about with his own light.
He deals with us as self to self replying;
For who awaits the prayer, and feels the need,
Malignly leans already to denying.
To such inviting let our feet be sped:
Now press we up ere darkness round us be,
For else we cannot until dawn is red."—
When so had said my Leader, I and he
Together toward a stairway turned our feet;
And soon as I had reacht the first degree,
My face was fanned as by a pinion's beat,
And I heard say: "Blest the Peacemakers are,
Because by evil anger not beset."—
The Seven Roots of Sin 219
Now were uplifted over us so far *Second night*
The parting beams whereon the night pursues,
That upon every side shone forth a star. "Alas, why are my sinews grown so loose?"
Within me I began to murmur, for
I felt my power of limb was put in truce. Come were we where ascended now no more
The stairway up, and there we fast were stayed,
Even as a vessel moored upon the shore; And for a little while I gave full heed
If aught were heard within the circle new;
Then to my Master turned about, and said: "Inform me here, beloved Father true,
What fault is in this circle purified?
Though pause the feet, let not thy word so do."— And he to me: "The love of good, denied *"AccidwC (cf.*
Its due activity, is here restored; ££ *jy*
Here the ill-slackened oar again is plied. *Spiritual indif*
Wouldst thou more clearly comprehend my word, *!TMoTcn*
Be but attentive and, although we wait, *physical sloth)*
Thou shalt derive some profit and reward. *a-Y*
Neither Creator, no, nor thing create, T''
Son," he began, "was ever void of love,— z excessive might, is prone to rove, tends to primal goods the appetite, In secondary things self-moderator, It cannot be the cause of ill delight; But when it turns to evil, or with greater *When love of*
Or less than proper zeal, on good is bent, *ZtdM*
The creature works against its own Creator. *or when love of*
As seed in you of all that's excellent, gjg"'*good"*
Thou mayest infer that Love must needs have served,
And of each act that merits punishment.
Now, since there never was a love that swerved
From goods that proper to its person be,
From their own hatred are all things preserved;
And since no being independently
Can be conceived, cut from the First away,
From hating Him is all affection free.
Hence if, distinguishing, I rightly say
It is your neighbor's harm you love, takes root
This love in triple fashion in your clay.
There are who, seeing their neighbor underfoot,
Hope to excel, and for this reason, down
From his high pinnacle would have him put.
There are who power, grace, honor, or renown
Fearing to forfeit, if another rise,
Crave the reverse, and on his fortune frown;
Then those who seem to chafe at injuries,
Greedy for vengeance, so that it behooves
Them evil to another to devise.
Yonder below are wept these threefold loves:
Now of the other do I thee to wit,
That to the good in faulty measure moves.
Vaguely each one conceives a benefit
Wherein the mind may rest, and yearns thereto;
Whence each endeavors to attain to it.
If languid be the love inciting you
To look upon it, or to make pursuit,
This Cornice pains you on repentance due.
There's other good wherein there is no boot:
It is not happiness, is not the good
Essence, of every good the fruit and root.
The love that yields unduly to such mood
Is up above bewept in circles three;
But how it were tripartite understood,
I leave unspoken, to be sought by thee."— *Here the Will to Sin Is Purified*
221 *Note*

The discourses of Love and Free Will explain the radical difference between the classification of sins in Hell and that which is set forth here (cf. Inferno xi). In Hell specific sinful deeds are punished; here the Will is purified. Thus the generic vice which Dante calls Avarice may be the occasion of a great variety of specific sins. (To repent of a given sin is one thing; to have the crooked Will so straightened that Love is awakened for the corresponding virtue, is quite another. The avaricious, for example, desires to continue his cleansing and straightening process until unselfish generosity becomes a passion in him.

Second night:
Terrace of the
Shthful
Philosophical discourse continued
"Form,"—i.e., nature: fire lends to rise to the sphere of fire (c/. *close of Par. i)*
xvin
Love And Free Will

Having made end now to his argument,
Into my face the lofty Teacher flung
A searching look, if I appeared content.
And I, with a new thirst already

stung,
Was mute without, and said within: "Perchance
I trouble him by questioning too long. "—
But that true Father, who took cognizance
Of the shy wish that would no word afford,
By speaking, heartened me to utterance.
Whence I: "My vision is so well restored
In thy light, Master, that I clearly see
The whole scope and the import of thy word.
I pray thee, therefore, to expound to me
The Love whereto thou tracest, Father kind,
Every good action and its contrary."—
"Direct to me the keen eyes of the mind,
And the error will be manifest to thee,
r,, Of those who would be leaders, being blind.
The soul, to love created prone and free,
Is mobile to all objects of delight,
When roused by pleasure to activity.
From something real your perceptive sight
Shapes forth an image and displays in you,
So as to make the spirit turn to it;
And if, so turning, she incline thereto,
That inclination is Love, is Nature's bent
Through pleasure striking root in you anew.
Then, even as fire has motion of ascent,
By virtue of its form which makes it wing
To where it dwells more in its element:
So the rapt soul doth into longing spring,
A spiritual motion, never still
Till she rejoice in the beloved thing.
Ethics Based on Freedom of Will 223
Now may be evident how very ill
They view the truth, who would aver to thee
That all love in itself is laudable,
Because its matter may ideally
Appear good always: but not every seal
Is good, however good the wax may be. "—
"Thy words, and my wit following, reveal
Love and its nature to me," answered I,
"But therefore all the greater doubt I feel;
For if Love offer from without, and by
Another foot the spirit travel not,
She has no merit, go she straight or wry. "—
And he to me: "As far as pierces thought,
Myself can tell: beyond that fix thy mind
On Beatrice, that faith in thee be wrought.
Every substantial form that is conjoined
With matter, and yet from it cut away,
Holds inward virtue of specific kind,
Which, save in act, is not brought into play,
By its effect alone in evidence,
Like life in plant evinced by the green spray.
Thus, whence originates intelligence
Of first ideas, is unknown to thee,
And bent of the primordial appetence,
Which are in you as study in the bee
To make its honey; and such primal bent
Of neither praise nor blame receives the fee.
Now, that with this may all desires consent,
The power that counsels is innate in you,
And ought to hold the threshold of assent.
This is the principle wherefrom accrue
The grounds of your desert, as gathering
And winnowing the false loves from the true.
Who to the bottom went in reasoning,
Took notice of this inborn liberty,
Thus morals to the world delivering.
Assuming, then, that from necessity
All love is kindled rightly or amiss,
To hinder it ye have ability.
This noble virtue is called by Beatrice
The Freedom of the Will; take heed aright jf she begin to speak to thee of this."—
*For this compli-*The slow moon tow'rd the middle of the night,
cated series of Shaped like a bucket all ablaze, more wan
allusions I must r, *refer the curious* Now made the constellations to our sight,
If" '*Stud-*Ln counter to the heavens that pathway ran
ies in Dante," Fired by the setting sun, which he of Rome
in, 71-73 gees 'twxt Sardinian and Corsican; *The modern* When he, that noble shade by fame of whom
UrthjlLr91' Pietola every Mantuan town outwent,
Had put aside my fardel burdensome:
So that I, who explicit argument
And lucid to my questioning had found, Remained like one who rambles somnolent.
The purgation But from this somnolence I was unbound
of the Slothful All of a sudden by a multitude
Toward us from behind now coming round.
Of old Ismenus and Asopus viewed
Such hurrying throng at night their banks beside, *Their patron god* If Thebans but in need of Bacchus stood,
As these who round that Cornice curve their stride,
From what I saw of those approaching me,
On whom good will and right affection ride. *The voices in the* They were soon upon us, for that great company
teMiffZeZf WaS?ommg at a *TM,* and lameQt
Two in advance cried out alternately:
"Mary with haste to the hill country went,"
And "Caesar, that he might Ilerda gain,
Struck at Marseilles, then sweeping Spainward bent."—
"Quick, quickly, lest the time be spent in vain
Through little love!"—then cried the others,—"So
Well-doing zeal may make grace green again."—
"O people, in whom keen zeal redeemeth now,

Perchance, delay and negligence in you
By lukewarmth in well-doing shown below,
This man who lives (I surely tell you true!)
Would fain go up, if shine again the sun;
So tell us where is nearest passage through."—

These words were spoken by my Guide; and one
Among those spirits answered: "Follow us,
And thou shalt find the opening anon.

We are so full of zeal for running thus,

We cannot stay; pardon, we therefore cry,
If this our duty seem discourteous.

San Zeno's abbot at Verona I,

Beneath good Barbarossa's empire, whom
Yet Milan cannot name without a sigh.

And one has foot already in the tomb

Who shall erelong that monastery rue,
And rue the having had there master-dom,

Because his son, in body lame, there-to

Mind lamer still, and who was born amiss,
He put in office of its pastor true."—

I know not whether yet he held his peace,
So far beyond us he was hurrying,
But gladly I remember hearing this.

And he who was my help in every-thing

Now said: "Turn hitherward and look,—two more
Are coming onward, giving sloth a sting."

"Dead were the folk whom ocean opened for,"
They, bringing up the rear, were crying thus,
"Ere Jordan lookt on its inheritor,"—
And,—''Those who found it too laborious
To bide the issue with Anchises' son,
Gave themselves up to life inglorious. "—
Then, when so distant were those shades that none
Could more be seen of all that multitude,
My mind began upon new thoughts to run,
Albert, lord of Verona, had made the priorate a berth for his lame natural Those lukewarm Children of Israel who were left in the wilderness, and those followers of jEneas who chose to stay in Sicily The medley of Whence many more were born, a motley brood; *tto-dream And* so one upon another teem,

I lapsed with closed eyes into drowsihood, Transmuting meditation into dream.

XIX

A Repentant Pope (adman V)

It was the hour wherein the heat of noon,
By Saturn haply, or by earth undone,
Can warm no more the coldness of the moon;
When geomancers see before the dawn
Their Greater Fortune rising eastward through
A course she will not long go darkling on;
I saw in dream a stammering woman, who
Was squint of eye, and of distorted feet,
Bereft of hands, and sallow in her hue.
I gazed at her: as from the sun streams heat
Into the limbs made chilly by the night,
Even so my gazing served to liberate
Her tongue, and erelong wholly set her right,
And with the pallor of her features blent
The flushes that to love are requisite.
Thereon her speech became so eloquent,
And so her song began to charm mine ear,
That scarce could I away from her have bent:
"Sweet Siren I, who witch the mariner
Amid the billows," she began to sing,
"So full of pleasantness am I to hear;
I turned Ulysses from his wandering
By power of song; who listen to my strain
Seldom depart from me, all-solacing. "—
Her parted lips had not yet closed again,
Ere for her quick confusion, at my side,
A Lady holy and alert was seen.
"0 Virgil, Virgil, who is this!"—she cried
Indignantly; and he was drawing near
With looks but to that modest Virtue tied.
He seized the other one and laid her bare,
Rending her garb, the belly to display;
This waked me with the stench arising there.
Before dawn of the third day: Dante's Dream This woman, whatever her name, is the original of her who is "of so frightful mien as to be hated needs but to be seen" Dante, who knew Homer only by tradition and comment, confuses the Siren with Calypso There is dramatic contrast between this dream of Virgil's negligence and his real watchfulness

Eying the Master good, I heard him say:

"Thrice have I called thee; rise and come, to find
The opening where goes thy passage-way."—

I rise: lo! round the sacred mountain wind
The Cornices in open day; and now
We go our way with the new sun behind.

Following after him, I bore my brow

Like onewho makes himself, o'erbornewith thought, Into the half-arch of a bridge to bow; *The mice of an* When "Come, here is the passage!"—this I caught *Ang* In accents mild, of such benignity

As in this mortal region hear we not.

With open wings that seemed of swan's-down, he
Upward directed who had spoken thus,
Between two walls of solid masonry.

Thereon with moving pinions fanned he us,
Affirming that the mourners shall be blest,
Their souls endowed with solace plenteous.

"What ails thee that thou earthward rivetest

Thy glance?"—began to say to me my Guide,
When somewhat past the Angel we had pressed.
And I: "With such misgiving am I plied
By novel vision of compulsive stress,
So that my thoughts as by a spell are tied."—
"Hast seen," said he, "that ancient sorceress?
She who alone is now bewept up yond,
And seen how man is loosed from her duress?
Be it enough,—beat heels upon the ground,—
Lift eyes toward the lure up, that with vast
Circles, the Eternal King is whirling round."—
Like hawk that, eying first his feet, at last
Turns to the call and spreads his pinions out,
By longing yonder drawn to break his fast;
Such I, and such, far as affords a route
The cloven rock to them who upward go,
I went where starts the circling round about.

A Worldly Prelate, a Repentant Pope 229

When opened to me the Fifth Cornice, lo! *Fifth Terrace:*
People who wept upon it there, nor stirred *Avarice*"
From lying prone, with faces turned below.,.,, "My soul hath to the pavement cleaved!" I heard
Their voices uttering with such deep sighs,
That one could hardly understand the word. "O ye elect of God, whose agonies
Are made by justice and by hope less grim,
Direct us where the lofty stairs uprise."— "Come ye exempt from lying prone of limb,
And would mount upward by the quickest way,
Let your right hand be ever tow'rd the rim."— Reply was made thus from not far away
To this prayer of the Poet; wherefore I
Marked something which the speaker failed to say, And thereon to my Master turned mine eye;
Wherefore with cheerful sign he gave assent
To what my looks were craving wistfully. When I could act according to my bent,
I said, and stood above that being there,
Whose words already rendered me intent: "Spirit, whose weeping ripens thee to bear
Fruit without which to God is no returning, Suspend awhile for me thy greater care.
Who wast thou? Why your backs thus upward turning?
When I go yon whence moved my living feet,
Can I do aught to satisfy thy yearning?"—"Shalt learn," said he, "why Heaven esteems it meet
We turn our backs to it; but meanwhile know
I was successor to Saint Peter's seat.
'Twixt Sestri and Chiavari doth flow
A river fair, whose title of renown
Springs from my race. A month sufficed to show How heavy the Great Mantle weighs on one *Mournful words*
Who seeks to guard it from the miry sty, *pope T6Pe'1*""
So that all other burdens seem but down.
Ah me! too late conversion here I sigh:
But when I gained the Pastorate of Rome,
Then learned I life for what it is, a lie.
There for the longing heart I found no home,
Nor in that life a loftier ascent;
So love of this sprang up in me therefrom.
Till then I was a spirit malcontent,
Alien from God, devoted all to gain,
Whence thou beholdest here my punishment.
The effect of avarice is here made plain
In purging of converted souls: upon
The Mountain nowhere is more bitter pain.
Even as our eye was not uplifted yon
To Heaven, but fixed upon the things of earth,
So Justice here has sunk it earthward down.
As avarice quenched our love to all of worth
So that our power of doing good was spent,
So Justice binds us here in utter dearth
Of freedom on this ledge, thus impotent:
So long as please our Father just and good,
So long we stay immobile and distent. "—
I had knelt down, and would have fain pursued
The conversation, but he seemed to know
By hearing, of my reverent attitude:
"What cause," said he, "has bowed thee downward so?"—
And I: "By reason of your Dignity
My upright conscience urged the posture low."—
He is no longer "Make straight thy legs; rise, brother!"—answered he,
Ifafa "Err not; because I fellow-service hold
Bride Under one Power with others and with thee.
If thou that holy Gospel word of old
Which saith, 'They neither marry,'ever weighed,
Why thus I speak thou mayst full well behold.
Now go: I would not have thee longer stayed,
For while thou tarriest my tears I stay,
Whereby I ripen that which thou hast said.

Only Alagia Left to Pray for Him 231

I have a niece there named Alagia,
Good in herself, if but our family
By ill example lead her not astray:
And she alone on earth is left to me. "— *Wife of the Malaspina who befriended the Poet in 1306. The speaker leaves Dante to infer why the lady is mentioned. See close of Canto viii* XX

The Founder Of A Great Royal House *Third day:*. Counter to better will

strives will in vain: *morning hours,* Whence I, for his content, with discontent *fifth Terrace, .where Avarice is* Dry from the water drew the sponge again.
purged I moved, and with my Leader onward went Along the cliff through gaps none occupy,
As by a wall hugging the battlement;
Because that folk distilling through the eye
The ill wherewith the world is all possest,
On the other side too near the margin lie.
This terrible Thou old She-Wolf, may curses on thee rest, *Z1L PoTaTL* That more than aU the other beasts hast Prey, *beginning (Inf. i)* Because thy hungry maw gapes hollo west!
O Heaven, in whose revolving, people say,
Conditions are transmuted here below,
When comes he who shall drive this wolf away?
We went along with paces few and slow,
And I attentive to the utterance
Of shadows weeping and lamenting so; *Examples of the* When on in front of us I heard, by chance, *corresponding Uq* blessed Mary "—even as makes her moan *virtue* ."
A childing woman; and in continuance,
"What poverty was thine may well be known
By thy poor entertainment at the inn
Where thou didst lay thy holy burden down."— *Refused the* Then: "Good Fabricius, who wouldest win *ptrThui* Tne meed of V""1116 linkt with poor estate, Far rather than great opulence with sin!"—
These words were of delight to me so great,
That I pushed on, more knowledge to possess *thr NdowrL* at sou wnence they seemed to emanate.
*into their win-*It went on speaking of the largesses *tZ %Z6dis-*a Nicholas to the girls, their maidenhood *honor* Thus leading in the path of righteousness.
"O soul abounding in report so good, Tell who thou wast, and why alone," I said,
"By thee these worthy praises are renewed?
Thy words shall have a meed well merited,
If I return to finish the brief race
Of mortal life that tow'rd the end is sped."—
"I'll tell thee, not that I from yonder place
May hope relief," he said, "but since there shoot
Forth from thee ere thy death such gleams of grace.
I was of that malignant plant the root,
Shadowing so all Christian lands that they
Yield niggard harvesting of wholesome fruit.
But ah! if Bruges and Ghent and Lille and Douay
Were potent, there would light on it swift doom;
And this of Him who judges all I pray.
I was called there Hugh Capet: from me come
The Louises and Philips every one
Who recently in France hold masterdom.
A mere Parisian butcher called me son.
When ceased the ancient monarchs to exist,
Save one, betaken unto orders dun,
Then found I tightly clenched within my fist
The bridle of the realm, with power that goes
With multitude of friends, and new acquist;
So to the widowed diadem arose
The head of mine own son; from whom took birth
The consecrated bones of all of those.
Till the Great Dowry of Provence caused dearth
Of shame among the kith and kin of me,
They did no harm, although of little worth.
Began by fraud and by rapacity jA
Their rapine then; and after, for amends,/""" *fvh Hugh Capet: founder of Vie dynasty now the bane of France, Flanders, Italy Would be called today a great rancher or "packer"*
Charles came to Italy, and, for amends, /
Made Conradin a victim; then a prey
Of Thomas, thrust to Heaven, for amends.)
death the last of the Hohenstaufen and St. Thomas Aquinas r, Charles of Valois
Charles, the second king in Naples of the house of Anjou called "the cripple of Jerusalem!'Par. xix) The outrage done to Pope Boniface by agents of Philip the Fair (IVth) The destruction of the Order of the Temple by Philip. Cf. Browning's "The Heretic's Tragedy"
In the daytime they praise the virtue; at night they stigmatize the vice
I see a time, not distant from this day,
That shall lead forth another Charles from France,
Both him and his the better to betray.
Unarmed he goes alone, but with the lance
Wherewith Iscariot jousted, and that same
Within the bursting paunch of Florence plants.
He thence not any land, but sin and shame
Shall win, so much the heavier therethrough
That he the lighter reckons all such blame.
The other, pluckt once from his ship, I view
Vending his daughter in the market place,
As corsairs with the other bondmaids do.
0 Avarice, since thou hast brought my race To hold its issue at so cheap a rate,
What further canst thou do for our disgrace?
That past and future ill appear less great,
I see the Fleur-de-Lis Alagna gain,
And in His Vicar Christ incarcerate.
1 see how there they mock Him yet again,

I see the vinegar and gall renew,
And between living thieves I see Him slain.
I see so pitiless the Pilate new
That, yet unsated, he without decree
Into the Temple steers his greedy crew.
When, O my Lord, shall I rejoice to see
The vengeance that doth in thy counsels hide,
Calming thine anger in thy secrecy?—
What I was saying of that only bride
Of the Holy Spirit, prompting thee to pray
Some comment of me, that is still replied
To all our orisons while lasts the day;
But in the place thereof, when night comes on
We ring the changes on a counter-lay:
We tell the tale then of Pygmalion
Who traitor, thief, and parricide was made
By gluttony for gold; and harp upon
Poor Midas, how he covetously prayed,
And what fulfillment followed to his bane,
Wherefore men laugh forever at his greed
We all record then Achan the insane,
Who seems, because he took the accursed thing,
Wrung by the wrath of Joshua again;
Sapphira with her spouse to judgment bring;
Then praise the hoof-beats Heliodorus bore;
And Polymnestor's shame doth all enring
The Mountain, for the murdered Polydore;
Lastly we cry: 'Tell us, for thou dost know,
Crassus, the savor of the golden ore!'—
Sometimes we speak, one loud, another low,
According as affection may be spurred
To make the pace of speaking fast or slow;
Wherefore, if I alone erewhile was heard
Citing the good whereof we tell by day,
None else at hand was lifting up the word."—
Departed from him, we had gone our way,
And on the thoroughfare I spent my breath
To overcome it far as in me lay,
When now behold! the Mountain shuddereth
As to its fall; whence over me is driven
A chill, as over him who goes to death.
Such shock was surely not to Delos given
Before Latona coucht therein, to be
Delivered there of the twin eyes of Heaven.
Uprose a paean simultaneously
Such that the Master nearer to me trod,
Saying: "Fear not while I am guiding thee."—
All shouted: "Glory in the highest to God!"
For so the neighbor voices seemed to say,
From whom the paean might be understood.
Like to the shepherds who first heard that lay,
We stood there without motion, all intent,
Till ceased the trembling, and it died away.
2 Maccabees iii, 25 The other examples can readily be found) Apollo and Diana
Again we on our holy journey went,
Eying the shades upon the ground below,
Returned now to their ritual lament.
No ignorance with eagerness to know
Ever within me such a battle fought,
Unless my memory err, as to and fro
Appeared then to be struggling in my thought:
Nor did I, for our haste, to question dare,
Nor of myself could I discover aught;
So faint and pensive did I onward fare.
The Earthquake Explained 237 XXI
The Poet Statius
The natural thirst unsatisfied for aye
Terrace of the
Save with that water for whose boon was fain *Avaricious: forenoon of the*
The lowly woman of Samaria, *third day*
Tormented me, and by the encumbered lane,
Haste goaded me behind my Leader on,
And I was grieving for that righteous pain; When lo! in manner even as Luke sets down
That in the way to twain did Christ appear,
From the tomb's mouth of late arisen and gone, A shade appeared and came behind us where
We were intent the prostrate crowd to view,
And spoke to us before we were aware, Saying: "My brothers, peace be unto you."—
And Virgil, turning with me suddenly,
Gave back the word of greeting that is due. "May the true court in peace establish thee
In council of the blest," then Virgil said,
"Though to eternal exile dooming me."— "How?" said that spirit, while we onward sped,
"If ye are shades God will on high not deign,
Who has so far up by His stairway led?"— "But note the marks," my Teacher said again,
"Which the Angel traces and this man displays,
Well shalt thou see he with the good must reign. But because she who spins through nights and days
Had not yet from the distaff drawn the twine
That Clotho there for each, compacting, lays, The soul of him, thy sister-soul and mine,
In coming upward, could not come alone, Not seeing in the fashion of our eyne.
I, therefore, from wide-throated Hell was drawn
To show him the way onward, and shall show
As far as by my school it can be done.
Iris, the rainbow Dry vapor, according to Aristotle, caused wind, lightning, thunder, earthquakes The soul desires its punishment
until wholly

purified of its sinful disposition. (See note after Canto xvii)

But tell us why the mountain, if thou know,
So quakt erewhile, and all appeared to cry
With one voice, to its wave-washt foot below?"—
So questioning, he hit the needle's eye
Of my desire, and by the hope withal
My thirst was made less hard to satisfy.
The spirit began: "There is nothing here at all
That were not subject to the holy grace
Of the mountain, or that were exceptional.
Exempt from permutation is this place;
In what from Heaven back to itself doth flow,
And naught beside, may we causation trace:
Because not any rain, nor hail, nor snow,
Nor dew, nor frost can fall, or do offense,
Above the little triple stairway; no
Clouds there appear, or rarefied or dense,
No lightning, nor the daughter of Thaumas fleet,
Who often, yonder, changes residence;
Parcht vapor does not rise aloft one whit
Beyond the aforesaid triple stairway forth,
Whereon the Vicar of Peter hath his feet.
More or less quaking may perchance have birth
Down yonder; but up here it never could
By wind, I know not how, enwombed in earth.
It quakes when any spirit feels its mood
Made pure for setting forward, or aloof
Moves to ascend, by such a cry pursued.
Of purity the will alone gives proof;
Quite free for change of cloister, this intent
Takes by surprise the soul to her behoof.
She first wills well, but divine government
Sets will against desire, which, as before
It craved for sinning, craves for punishment.
And I, who have five hundred years and more
Beneath this torment lain, but now could trace
Free will for threshold of a better door.
Three Loving Poets 239
Hence didst thou feel the quake, and spirits of grace
Didst hear along the Mountain celebrate
The Lord,—ah! may He send them up apace."— He said; and since joy is proportionate
In drinking, with the thirst to be allayed,
My gain by him I could not say how great. "I see the net now," my wise Leader said,
"That snares you here, and how ye are set free,
Wherefore it quakes, and whereat glad ye are made. Now tell me who thou wast, I beg of thee,
And in thy words I pray thee be it told
Why thou layest here so many a century."— "When the good Titus in the time of old, *Paradiso vi,*
Helpt by the King Supreme, avenged each wound %I«f; *m'*
Whence issued forth the blood by Judas sold, With name most durable and most renowned *The name of*
I yonder lived," that spirit answering said,
"And passing fame, but not yet faith had found. So sweet a music from my soul was shed
That from Toulouse Rome beckoned me away,
Where I deserved brows myrtle-garlanded. There people call me Statius to this day: *The Poem about*
Of Thebes I sang, and great Achilles' might, 4SJ»e
But with my second load fell by the way. The seeds that raised my genius to its height
Were sparks from that celestial flame shot forth,
Whence more than a thousand have been set alight: The *Mueid,* I mean, that mothered me from birth,
The nurse that suckled me in poesy;
Without it were I not a drachma worth. To have lived when Virgil lived, would I agree
To penance of one sun more than I owe,
Ere from my place of banishment set free."— Turned Virgil to me, he discoursing so,
With "Be thou silent," in his tacit glance;
But there are limits to what will can do: *The sweet and* For tears and laughter are such pursuivants ittXJ upon passions out of which ey rise,
Pod That truest will has weakest vigilance.
I could but smile, with meaning in mine eyes;
Whereat the shadow paused, and lookt me straight
Into the eye, where most expression lies.
"So mayst thou well such labor consummate,"
It said, "tell wherefore I but now descried
A laughter-flash thy face irradiate?"—
Now am I caught on this and the other side:
One bids "Be still," and the other "Speak to me!"
Whence I was comprehended when I sighed.
"Thou needst," my Master said, "not fearful be
To speak, but tell, and let thy words attest
What he besought with such anxiety. "—
"O ancient soul," said I, "thou marvelest
Perchance, because my smile thou sawest shine;
But I will move more wonder in thy breast!
This one who guides on high these eyes of mine,
That very Virgil is, from whom you drew
The power to sing of men and the di-

vine.

If else thou thoughtest of my smiling, eschew

That thought as false; those words thou spakst but now

Of him, believe me, were the reason true."—

To kiss my Teacher's feet he bent his brow;

"Brother," the Master urged with tenderness,

"Do not; thou seest me shadow, even as thou."—

Then Statius rising said: "Now canst thou guess

The sum of love that burns in me for thee,

When I can so forget our emptiness,

Treating a shadow as reality."— *Sin of Statins the Reverse of Avarice* 241 XXII

The Three Poets Converse As They Walk

Behind us had we left the Angel now *Third day, late*

Who up to the sixth round had turned our quest, *cTnHo'the*

Having erased a stigma from my brow; § *Terrace:*

And had announced to us that they are Blest *statiua with*

Who long for righteousness in all they do,— *Dantt*

But saying it with "thirst" without the rest. *For » rell cf*

And, lighter than at other passes through, *xxic*

Following those swift spirits up above,

I went without fatigue. Then did renew Virgil Jus speaking: "Worth-enkindled love

Can kindle in us love reciprocal, its ardor being revealed. In proof whereof, Among us when descended Juvenal

Down into the Infernal Limbo, where

He made thy feeling known to me withal, Never did man to unseen person bear

More love than did my heart toward thee bend,

So that now short to me will seem the stair. But tell me, and forgive me as a friend

If I give rein to overconfidence,

And talk we heart to heart now to the end: Oh, how could Avarice find residence

Possibly, in a bosom such as thine,

Replete with wisdom through thy diligence?"— These words made Statius at first incline

To smile a little; then replied he thus:

"Each word of thine to me is Love's dear sign. Often indeed do things appear to us

That offer for suspicion grounds deceiving,

Since their real causes are not obvious. Thy question proves it to be thy believing

That Greed in th'other life had been my curse,

Perchance because of the round where I was grieving.

Know, then, that my offense was the reverse

Of Avarice; my prodigality

Thousands of courses of the moon amerce.

And if I had not, pondering upon thee,

Set right my conduct, misdirected first,

Where thou exclaimst against humanity

Almost in wrath: 'To what, accursed thirst

For gold, dost thou not mortal longing guide?'

I should be rolling in the tilts accurst.

Then saw I that the hands might be too wide

Of wing in spending, and repented thence

Of that and of my every sin beside.

Among the Because of ignorance of this offense,

SSS *!£* How mayshall arise devoid of hair, *for their sym*-In life and death bereft of penitence!

ic *s air* know that sin, in opposition square

Rebutting other sin, dries up its green

Together with the opposing trespass there.

Wherefore if I, to purge myself, have been

With those who weep their Avarice in throngs,

I suffered it for contradictory sin."—

"Now when thou sangest of the cruel wrongs

Of war that wrought Jocasta's double woe,"

The Singer said of the Bucolic Songs,

"The chords there toucht with Clio do not show

Thee yet as of that Faith a devotee,

For want whereof good works are not enow.

What candles or what sun, if so it be,

So pierced thy darkness that thy sails were spread *St. Peter, as at* After the Fisher of the eternal sea?"— *end of Par.* "Thou first directedst me," he answering said,

"Parnassus-ward, to drink upon its height,

Then on my way to God thy light was shed

Thou diddest like to him who walks by night,

Bearing the torch, not for his proper good,

But to the after-comers giving light,

Virgil the Cause of Salvation of Statins 243

Tien saidest thou: 'The world is all renewed; *The Cumcean*

Justice returns, and man's primeval spring, *Edoaue w*

And out of Heaven descends another brood.' Poet was I, then Christian, following

Thy guidance; but that thou the better view

My sketch, I set my hand at coloring.

The world by now was teeming with the true

Religion, by the sowers of the Lord

Eternal, scattered every country through; And thy words, toucht upon above, concurred

With the new gospelers in such a wise

That I became a hearer of the Word.

They came to seem so holy in mine eyes

Then, when Domitian persecuted sore,

That tears of mine accompanied their cries; And while I lingered upon yonder shore

I succored them, whose upright manners made

All other sects seem worthless; and

before I, poetizing, yet the Greeks had led

Far as the Theban streams, baptized was I;

But hid my Christian faith, because afraid 7 Long while appearing Pagan outwardly;-/

And for that lukewarmth did I circling fare

The fourth round more than the fourth century. Do therefore thou, who unto me laid bare

That good wherein, I say, is great reward,

While for ascending time is yet to spare, Tell me where Terence is, our elder bard,

Cecilius, Plautus, Varro, if thou know:

Tell if they are condemned, and in what ward."— "These, Persius, and I, and many moe,"

My Leader said, "are with that Greek confined,,.

Prime nursling of the Muses, there below In the first girdle of the prison blind.

Still oftentimes do we discourse upon

The mountain, haunt of nurses of our mind.

The fifth Hour is now driving the chariot of the Sun: it is about 11 o'clock The emblematic fruit-tree which the gluttons cannot climb

Euripides is ours there, Antiphon,

And Agathon, Simonides, and more

Of Greeks whose foreheads once the laurel won.

There see we people sung by thee of yore,

Antigone, Deiphile, Argeia,

And there Ismene, mournful evermore.

There see we her who pointed out Langeia;

There is Tiresias' daughter, Thetis there,

And with her sisters there Deidameia. "—

By this time silent both the poets were,

Eager to gaze about them far and wide,

From the walls liberated, and the stair;

And four of the Day's handmaids now abide

Behind, the fifth still pointing up the bright

Horn of the chariot-pole; whereon my Guide:

"Methinks it now behooves us turn the right

Shoulder toward the outer verge, intent

To round, as we are wont to do, the height."—

By custom in such manner led, we went

Our way with the less fear of going wrong,

Because that noble spirit gave assent.

In front they, and alone went I along

Behind, hearing their words, which gave to me

Intelligence about the craft of song.

But their kind talk was broken by a tree

That midway in the road we encountered now,

With fruitage smelling sweet and gratefully.

As fir-tree tapers upward, bough on bough,

So this one appeared downward tapering,

Methinks that none thereon might climbing go.

fhere where our way was closed, a water spring

L Down from the lofty cliff was falling clear,

V And on the upper foliage scattering.

Tne poets twain unto the tree drew near,

Whereon a voice cried out the branches through:

"Dearth of this viand ye shall have to bear."—

Examples of Abstemious Living 245

'Mary was more concerned," it said anew,

"To grace the wedding feast with plenitude,

Than for her mouth which now entreats for you.

3f water the old Roman womanhood

Were satisfied to drink; and Daniel nurst

Wisdom within him by despising food.

Golden in beauty was the world at first;

To appetite it made the acorn sweet,

And every brook like nectar to the thirst.'

Honey and locusts were the only meat

That John the Baptist in the desert knew; i

Whence now he is in glory, and so great /

As by the Gospel is revealed to you."-

' *Terrace of the gluttonous: about noon of the third day This phrase of the Miserere Psalm li, IS) is appropriate to those whose sin has been intemperance in food and drink The dreadful tale is told by Josephus The Latin for man is printed on the human* XXIII

Dante Meets An Old Boon Companion

Because these eyes of mine yet never stirred

From the green foliage, like such an one

As wastes his life to hunt the little bird,

My more than Father said to me: "My son,

Come on now; for the time assigned had need

To be allotted for more benison."—

Then turned I face and foot with equal speed

After those speakers sage, so eloquent

As made it cost me nothing to proceed.

And hark! now singing heard, with weeping blent:

"Lord, open thou my lips!"—Such intonation

As must beget both rapture and lament.

"What hear I, Father?" was my exclamation;

And he: "Shades who are hastening, perchance,

So as to cancel out their obligation."—

As pilgrims rapt in thought, by travel-chance

Meeting an unknown face along their ways,

Cast, without lingering, a backward glance,

So came behind us at a swifter pace

And passed, a crowd of souls as if in flight,

Devout and tacit and of eager gaze.

The cavern of the eye disclosed no light,

Pallid each visage, and so hunger-pined

Over the bone the skin was fashioned tight.

I cannot think that such an utter rind
Was dried on Erisichthon's skeleton
By fasting, when it most appalled his mind.

"Behold!" my thoughts within were running on,
"This is the folk who lost Jerusalem,
When Mary struck her beak into her son."—

Each eyepit seemed a ring without the gem:
Who OMO reads in face of man, might well
Here in each countenance make out the M.
tVho ever could believe that from the smell
Of apples or of water there could grow
Such craving, knowing not how this befell?
still was wondering what pined them so,

The cause that rendered them so scurvily
Withered and meager being yet to know,

When, look now, from its deep skull cavity
A spirit made its eye upon me keen,
Then cried aloud: "What grace is this to me!"

Never should I have known him by his mien,
But something lingered in his utterance
That in his lineament had canceled been.

This spark enkindled to my inward glance
Something familiar in his altered look,
And I recalled Forese's countenance.

"Ah, do not mind," he prayed, "the scurf that took
The fresh complexion of my skin away,
Nor yet the lack of flesh I have to brook,

But tell me truth of thee, and who are they,

Yon spirits twain by whom thou'rt hither led?
Ah, tarry not, speak, speak to me, I pray!"—

"Thy face, bewept by me when thou wast dead,
Gives me for weeping now no lesser rue
Beholding it disfigured so," I said.

"By hope of Heaven, then tell what withers you:
Bid me not speak while marveling, for ill
One speaks, by other craving stricken through!"—

And he to me: "By the Eternal Will
Falls virtue to the water and the plant
Behind us, that emaciates me still.
All of these people who lamenting chant,
For being out of measure gluttonous,
Grow holy here through thirst and hunger gaunt.
Craving for food and drink is stirred in us

By fragrance from the fruit, and from the spray
That sprinkles over all the verdure thus.
face. The limbs of the M are clearer for the disappearance of the eyes (cf. Par. xviii)
Cf. Virgils reference to this shadowy "flesh" of the spirits, Canto Hi, 3133. Also the recognition of Ser Brunetto, Inf. xv

And not once, as we circle round this way,
But many times our penance is renewed.
Penance I say, who solace ought to say:

For to the tree that same solicitude

Leads us, that prompted the glad Christ to cry
'Eli,' when he redeemed us with His blood."—
"Not yet five years from that day forth," said I,
"When for a better world thou tookest flight,
Forese mine, have until now rolled by.
If you repented If sooner ended were in thee the might
CSkk Of sinnmg, *&n* the hour had supervened *more. See* That weds again to God the heart contrite, *Belacqua's* How then art thou arrive(i up hither, friend? *explanation,* r' *Canto iv* I thought to find thee on the slope below, Where time doth dissipated time amend."—
"My Nella, with her tears that overflow,
Hath brought me," he replied, "so speedily
To drink of the sweet wormwood of this woe,
The stormy mice With pious prayers and tears withdrawing me *f %ieaks* Up from the *hSiside* where tne p»ple wait, *through Forese* And from the other circles setting free.

Dearer to God, and of more estimate,

My widow whom so well I loved, as there
She more alone to good is dedicate.

More modest in its dames beyond compare
Is the Barbagia of Sardinia,
Than the Barbagia where I left her.

O brother dear, what wilt thou have me say?
My foresight by a future is possest,
When not yet very old shall be this day,

When warning from the pulpit is addrest
To the unblushing women Florentine,
Who go about displaying paps and breast.

What Pagan women, aye, or Saracen,

Have stood in need, to make them covered go,
Of spiritual or other discipline?
The Mount That Straightens Crooked Sticks 249

But if these unabashed ones did but know

What holds in store for them the hastening sky,
For howling would their jaws be open now;

For if herein my foresight do not lie,

They will be sad ere yet his cheek have down
Who now is quieted with lullaby.

Now brother, pray, be more concealment none:
Look, not I only, but these people all
Are gazing there where veilest thou the sun."—

Whence I to him: "If thou to mind recall
What once to one another were we two,
The present memory will yet appall.

That one who goes in front of me withdrew

Me from that life the other day, when round
The sister of him yonder appeared to you
(I pointed to the sun). Through the pro-

found
Midnight he led me from the dead apart,
With this real flesh that after him is bound.
Thence having drawn me, comforts he my heart
To circle up the Mountain, that again
Straightens you whom the world had wrencht athwart.
He speaks of going with me until when
I shall be there where will be Beatrice;
Without him there must I perforce remain.
He Virgil is who sayeth to me this
(And him I showed); that other shadow, know,
Is he for whom shook every precipice
Recently, when your Kingdom let him go."— *Third day: early afternoon. Terrace of the Intemperate*

We shall meet her in the Heaven of the Moon Par. Hi) The reader is urged to read Longfellow's notes on this lovely canto This Boniface was an archbishop of Ravenna,—not, of course, to be confused with the Pope so often mentioned

XXIV

Cheerful Abstainers From Good Cheer

Neither for talking did we lag behind,
Nor lagged our talk, but stoutly on we went,
Like vessel urged along by favoring wind.
And shades that seemed by double death forspent,
Beholding me alive, were all betraying
Deep in their eyepits their astonishment.
I, going on with what I had been saying,
Said: "Peradventure he doth upward go,
For sake of some one else, with more delaying.
But tell, where is Piccarda, if thou know;
And mention any in this multitude
Of note, among those gazing at me so. "—
"My sister,—if most beautiful or good
I know not,—in her crown is triumphing
On high Olympus in beatitude."—
So said he first, then: "No forbidden thing
Is giving names here, so obliterate
Is our resemblance by the dieting.
This," pointed he, "is Bonagiunta, late
Bonagiunta of Lucca; and farther out,
That face more than the rest emaciate,
Once put his arms the Holy Church about;
He was from Tours, and atones the Vernage wine
And Lake Bolsena's eels, by doing without."
And many another name did he assign;
And all seemed pleased, for not one somber look,
Despite the naming, saw these eyes of mine.
There saw I bite the void and hunger brook
Ubaldin of La Pila, and Boniface
Who shepherded much people with his crook.
I saw Lord Marquess who of old had space
For drinking with less dryness at Forli,
With craving still unsated ne'ertheless.
But as he does who scans selectingly,
So did my choice on him of Lucca fall,
Who seemed most eager to have speech with me.
I heard him murmur, what I know not all,
About Gentucca, where he most was wrung
By Justice that so withers them withal.
"O soul," said I, "that seemest so to long
To speak with me, give pleasure to my ears
And to thy heart by loosening thy tongue."—
"A maid is born, nor yet the wimple wears,
Who shall make pleasant to thee," did he say,
"My city, whatsoever blame it bears.
With this my presage shalt thou go thy way;
And did my murmur error in thee move,
Facts will explain it at some future day.
But tell me, do I speak with him who wove
The rimes in the new manner, that begin,
'Ladies who have intelligence of love'?"—
"I am of those who, when Love breathes within,
Take note," I answered, "and shape heedfully
My cadences to those he dictates in."—
"O brother mine," exclaimed he, "now I see
What bar held back from the sweet manner new
Guittone, and the Notary, and me.
I see distinctly how your pens pursue
The one who dictates, following his bent;
The which was certainly of ours untrue.
And who most looks to find them different,
Can naught else trace 'twixt one and the other style;"—
And holding here his peace, he seemed content.
Even as the birds that winter by the Nile
Go flocking through the welkin now, then fly
With quicker wing that they may go in file,
Thus all that multitude of people I
Saw turn their faces, while their steps they pressed,
And, light by will and leanness, hastened by.

In his throat Referring probably to a lady named Gentucca, who had shown some kindness to the Poet in his exile A canzone of Dante's "New Life," well translated by Rossetti

Because we did not, like you, pen the dictates of the heart. Gf. the conversation with Oderisi, Canto xi Prophecy oj the violent death of his brother, the famous Corso Donati

And, as a weary runner lets the rest
Of his companions go, that he may walk
Until abate the panting of his chest,
So did Forese let the holy flock

Pass by, and, pausing with me, said: "When more
May we thus face to face together talk?"—
"I know not," said I, "when my life is o'er,
Though not so speedily can I arrive
But that my heart is sooner on the shore;
Because the place where I was made alive,
More stript of good from day to day, I wiss,
To utter ruin is foredoomed to drive."—
"Take heart; I see him most to blame for this
Dragged at a horse's tail along," said he,
"Toward the never pardoning abyss.
At each bound goes the beast more rapidly,
Ever increasing, till it strikes amain
The body, and leaves it mangled hideously.
Not often shall those wheels revolve again,"
He raised his eyes to heaven, "ere is made clear
To thee, that which my words cannot explain.
Now stay behind, because the time so dear
Is in this kingdom, that too much I lose
Going at even pace thus with thee here. "—
As sometimes cavalier at gallop goes
Forth from a troop of horse, to make his worth
Renowned by first encounter with the foes,
So he with longer strides departed forth;
And I remained there with those two behind,
Who were such mighty marshals here on earth.
And when he had passed on so far that blind
To follow him mine eyes grew, as, I trow,
To follow on his words had been my mind,
Appeared, with many a laden and living bough,
Another tree, not very far away,
Because my road curved round on it but now.
Warnings against Self-indulgence 253
Beneath were folk with lifted hands, and they
Cried out toward the leaves, I know not what,
Like fond and eager little ones who pray, And that one whom they pray to answers not,
But holds aloft and does not hide their boon,
That it may be more longingly besought. Then, as if disappointed, they were gone:
So reacht we the great tree that doth deny
So many a tear and many an orison.
"Go your way onward without drawing nigh;
The tree is higher up whence Eve devoured
The fruit, and whence this plant was reared on high."Thus spoke some one amid the fronds embowered;
Whence Virgil, Statius, and I, close pressed
Together, moved along the cliff that towered. "Recall those cloud-begotten ones unblest, *The Centaurs*
Who being drunken," so it re-began, *0M-Met-®*
"Strove against Theseus with their double breast; Those Jews the draught proved weaklings, man for man, *Judges vii, 4-7*
Whence Gideon did their company disdain,
When he went down the hills tow'rd Midian."— Hugging the inner of the margins twain,
Concerning sins of appetite we heard,
Followed of old by miserable gain. Then, to a solitary path transferred,
A thousand steps and more had each of us
Wandered immerst in thought without a word. "Ye three alone, what go ye thinking thus?"—
I started when a sudden voice so said,
As starts from rest a creature timorous. To see who this might be, I raised my head;
And never yet in furnace was the hue
Of glass or metal such a glowing red,
As one I saw who spoke: "So please it you
To mount aloft, here must ye turn aside:
This way goes he who would his peace pursue."—
To look on him was sight to me denied:
Whence turned I in my Teacher's steps to fare,
Like one who goes with hearing for his guide.
And as, from herbs and flowers, the harbinger
Of early dawn, the zephyr of the May
Steals odors that make balmy all the air,
Even such a breeze I felt directly play
Upon my brow, and felt myself caressed
By plumage breathing of ambrosia.
And heard proclaimed thereafter: "They are blest
Whom Grace so much illumes, that appetite
Kindles not overmuch within their breast,
Hungering ever in accord with right. "— *How Can Shades Pine for Food?* 255 XXV
The Mental Physiology Of The Shades
Now since the Sun had left the circle of noon *Third day:*
To Taurus, and the Night to Scorpio, *AamtVfa'*
Henceforward the ascent brookt hindrance none. *Seventh Terrace,* Wherefore, as people on their journey go *tiefahtiturh*
And tarry not, whate'er beholding, while *away*
The spur of need is urgent on them; so Now one by one we entered the defile,
Taking the stairway where the narrow lane
Compels the climbers to go single file. And, like the little stork, for flying fain,
Lifting its wing, and, daring not to fly
From off the nest, letting it droop again; Such, with desire kindled and quencht, was I,
And nothing further than the movement made That will to speak is indicated by.
"Do thou discharge"—my gentle Father

said,

Forbearing not, although we swiftly went,

"The bow of speech bent to the arrowhead."— Then opened I my mouth, made confident,

Beginning: "How can there be withering

Of bodies with no need of nourishment?"— "Wouldst Meleager's plight to memory bring,

How by a wasting brand he wasted was,

This would not seem," said he, "so hard a thing; And wouldst thou call to mind how in the glass

Tremble your forms whenever tremble ye,

What seems hard would seem lightly brought to pass; But that thy will be satisfied in thee,

Lo! here is Statius, whom I call and pray

That of thy wounds he now the healer be."— "If here where thou art present I display

The eternal view," responded Statius, "Be my excuse I cannot say thee nay.—

Son, if thou well receive,"—began he thus,

"And if thy mind consider this my word, 'Twill make the 'How' thou askest, luminous.

Ne'er drunk up by the thirsty veins, but stored

The purest essence of the blood remains,

Like viands that thou takest from the board;

And power informing in the heart obtains

To shape all human organs, being that flood

Which, to become them, courses through the veins;

Digested still, descends where it is good

To leave unsaid; thereafter trickles thence In natural vessel on another's blood, *The blood of the* Where both together have their confluence. *beteTMJhatof* Passive is one,—but the other active, through *the female.* The perfect place whence pours its influence, *passive* Begins to operate when joined thereto, Coagulating, quickening the whole

That it for shaping to consistence drew.

The vegetative This active principle, become a soul

TtortZtt ofaplant but»far fferent *only an incident* That it halfway and that is at the goal),

"STM *tepaa* to move and to be sentient *embryo* Like the sea fungus, then to organize The powers whereof it is the rudiment,

Dilates, my son, and spreads the force that lies

Within the heart of the begetter now,

Where Nature would the organs all devise.

But how grow child from animal?— That 'How'

Seest thou not yet; that is the problem great

Which once misled a wiser man than thou,

Averroe Who by bis teaching thought to separate

Soul from potential intellect, for no Organ he saw thereto appropriate.

The Prime Open thy breast to coming truth, and know *Mover (Ood)* That when the organizing of the brain *breathes a soul into the embryo* Has been completed in the embryo, *The Shade an Emanation from the Will* 257

Toward it turns the Primal Motor then,

By Nature's so great art made debonair,

Breathing nejopirit full of power to drain Whatever virtue it finds active there

Into its substance, and one soul there grows,

Living, and feeling, and of itself aware. To make less marvelous what I disclose,

Consider how the Sun's heat becomes wine,

Joined to the juice that from the vine outflows. This soul from out the flesh doth disentwine

Whenever Lachesis hath thread no more,

And latent bears the human and divine: So voiceless each and every other power, *The faculties of*

But will and memory and intelligence *senae muU*

Far keener in their working than before. Incontinent the spirit falls prepense

To one or the other shore in wondrous wise,

And first takes knowledge of its pathway thence. Soon as the region round about it lies,

Virtue informative beams round it there,

As in the living limbs in shape and size. And as, when saturate with rain, the air

By the refraction of the solar rays

Is deckt with variegated colors fair,

Even so upon the circumjacent haze

A wraithlike form is printed by control

Of shaping soul that in the region stays; And as the flamelet's little aureole

Follows the fire upon its shifting flight,

So its new form accompanies the soul. Because thus rendered visible, the sprite

Is called a shade; and organs of each sense Fashions thereafter, even to that of sight.

So thence proceed our words, our laughter thence,

Thence do we fashion forth the tears and sighs

Whereof the Mount may give thee evidence.

First words of a hymn containing a prayer for purity Words of Mary to the Angel, Luke i. Si Ovid, Met. ii. Cf. Par. xxxi, 32-33

According as desires within us rise

Or feeling, takes the shade eonfigurement:

And this is what occasions thy surprise. "—

Now were we come to the last punishment,

And now toward the right-hand were we starting,

And were upon another care intent.

There from the cliffside arrowy flames are darting,

And from the shelf breathes up a blast thereon,

Hurling them back, a pathway thus disparting;
Whence it was needful to go one by one
On the open side, so that I felt dismay
Of burning there, and here of falling down.
"To rein the eyes tight up, along this way,"
My Leader said, "must now be our concern,
Because for little one might go astray. "—
Then from among those flames that hotly burn,
Came singing: "God of clemency supreme!"—
Which filled me with no less desire to turn;
Then saw I spirits walking through the flame:
Wherefore apportioning my sight I go,
Now looking to my steps, and now at them.
They cried aloud: "A man I do not know!"—
As soon as they had to the end pursued
That hymn; then recommenced, with voices low.
This done, anew they shouted: "In the wood
Diana stayed and banished Helice,
For Venus had deflowered her maidenhood."—
Then recommenced the song; then would it be
The praise of wives and husbands who were pure.
As virtue bids, and married chastity.
And in like mode, methinks, they must endure
The while they burn within the fiery blast:
With diet such as this, with such a cure,
The wound of sin must be healed up at last.
Dante's Shadow Amazes the Shades 259
XXVI
Dante Meets Two Modern Predecessors
While, one before the other, thus we paced
The border, often the good Master said:
"Take heed; let not my warning go to waste!"—
Smote me the Sim on the right shoulder-blade,
Now glittering throughout the Occident
And whitening the azure; and I made
The flame seem ruddier where with it blent
My shadow; and of such a token I
Saw many a shade take notice, as they went.
Such an occasion did they profit by
For speech of me; and they began to say:
"His body seems the fiction to belie."—
Then certain of them, far as in them lay,
Were making tow'rd me, always with concern
Never to issue from the fiery way.
"O pilgrim, who no less, perchance, dost yearn
To go, though reverent the rest behind,
Answer me, for in thirst and fire I burn:
Nor but to me be thy reply confined;
For greater thirst for it must these beset,
Than for cold water Ethiope or Ind.
Tell us how formest thou a barrier yet
Against the Sun, as if thou haddest not
There entered where the toils of Death benet?"
So hailed me one of them; and I, no doubt,
Had made me known, but that I was intent
Upon a novel thing that came about:
For, midway through the burning element,
Facing this company, a people hied
Who made me stop to gaze for wonderment.
I saw there hasten up from either side
Each shade to kiss a shade, for dalliance
Unresting, with brief greeting satisfied.
Terrace of the Sensual. Third day,—late afternoon Not the mere eidolon described in Canto xxv
So pausing, as their dusky troops advance,
Emmet encounters emmet, nose to nose,
Their road and fortune to espy, perchance.
No sooner does the friendly greeting close,
Or ever the first footstep passes by,
Strive these to lift up louder cries than those:
"Sodom and Gomorrah!" the newcomers cry; *The"falaavacca"* The rest:
"Pasiphae enters the cow, of *Inf. xii, 13*
that the bul l unto her lust *Ue* »_
As cranes to the Riphaean mountain brow
Might fly in part, part to the sandy plain,
These shunning frost and those the sun, so now
One people goes and one comes on amain,
And weeping they return to their first chants
And to their more appropriate refrain;
And close about me as before advance
The very same who had entreated me,
With will to listen in their countenance.
I, who now twice had seen their urgency,
Began to speak: "O spirit brotherhood
Secure of peace, whenever it may be,
These limbs of mine, neither mature nor crude,
Left I down yonder on the earth behind,
But bring them here with all their joints and blood.
I go hence up to be no longer blind:
A Lady is on high who wins us grace
Whence through your world I bring my mortal rind.
But so may be your fond desire apace
Fulfilled, so harbor you the heavenly height
Most ample, which is Love's full dwelling place,
Tell me, that yet on paper I may write,
Who may ye be and what that multitude
Behind your backs, and going opposite?"—
More stupefied, of more bewildered mood,
Is never the hill peasant, if perchance
He enter town in rustic garb and rude,
Than every shade became in countenance;
But when they did their wonder well restrain
(Which in high heart has brief predominance),

That one who questioned first, began again:
"Blest thou who, that the better thou mayst die,
Winnest experience of our domain!
That people who went hence, offended by
That wherefore Caesar suffered once the blame
When 'Queen!' amidst his triumph rose the cry;
Whence in their parting from us, they exclaim
'Sodom!' as thou hast heard, in self-despite,
And make the burning hotter with their shame.
Our own transgression was hermaphrodite;
But since we heeded not the human code,
Following like the brutes our appetite,
Departing, we, in self-reproachful mode,
Ourselves pronounce the name of her who so
Did bestialize herself in beastlike wood.
Our deeds now, how far guilty, knowest thou:
Wouldst thou, perchance, by name know who we be,
There is no time to tell, nor should I know.
I grant, indeed, thy wish concerning me:
I'm Guido Guinizelli, purged by fire
Through penitence before th' extremity. "—
As, in the frenzy of Lycurgus' ire
Against their mother, the two sons became,
Such became I (but do not so aspire),
When I had heard himself the father name
Of me, and other better men than I,
Who sweet and gracious love-rimes used to frame:
And reft of hearing I went thoughtfully,
Long while agaze at him, and nothing said,
Nor for the fire did I approach more nigh.
As soon as of beholding I was fed,
I offered myself all to do him grace,
With such a vow as makes one credited.
And he to me: "Thy words have left a trace
Upon my spirit charactered so clear
That Lethe cannot dim it nor efface.
But if it be a true avouch I hear,
What is the cause of thy avowal, pray,
By word and look that thou dost hold me dear?"—
And I to him: "Your every dulcet lay,
Which, if our modern use endure so long,
Will render dear their very ink for aye. "—
"He yonder, brother," back to me he flung
With finger pointing to a spirit before,
"Was a better shaper of his mother tongue.
In love-rimes and romantic tales of yore
Surpassed he all, and let fools prate who view *Giraut de* Him of Limoges as the superior.
Bomeil -Iey fold by rumor more than by the true,
And in that way their fixt opinion mold,
Ere art or reason have been listened to.
Thus with Guittone many did of old,
Basing his praise upon *they say, they say,*
Until at length with most the truth controlled.—
Now if thou have such charter that the way
Into that cloister is vouchsafed to thee
Where Christ is abbot of the college, pray
A Paternoster unto him for me,
As far as here may boot the utterance,
Where will to sin remains no longer free."—
Then to give place to others who perchance
Fast followed him, he vanisht in the fire,
As fishes bottomward through water glance.
Thereafter I drew forward somewhat nigher
To him who had been pointed out, to pray
That he vouchsafe his name to my desire.
And thus he graciously began to say:
"Your courteous request delights me so,
I cannot from you, will not, hide away.
I am Arnaut who weep and singing go;
Contritely for past folly I repine,
And blithely see the hoped-for morning glow.
I pray you now by Influence Divine
That guides you to the summit of the stair,
Be timely mindful of this pain of mine. "—
Then hid he in the fire that makes them fair.

Arnaut Daniel, Provencal poet often referred to by Dante, who gives his words in the Provencal tongue, preserving with exquisite art the rime and cadence

XXVII

The Will Of The Pilgrim Of Eternity Is Purified

Third and lust As when the earliest rays of dawning quiver *7MoLtain%.* Where shed His blood the M»ker of the light, *beginning of* High Libra lamping over Ebro-river, *Canto n)* j Ganges-wave at noontide burning bright,
So hung the sun; and day being nearly o'er,
Appeared to us God's Angel benedight.
Standing without the flame upon the shore,
He sang: "Blest they who pure in heart abide!"-
In voice melodious, than ours far more.
Then: "No one farther goes, souls sanctified,
Unbitten by the fire; be thither sped,
Not deaf to chanting from the farther side."—
As we drew nearer to him, this he said:
And, listening, I such became in mien
As he who in the burial pit is laid.
Up started I, with clasping hands, and keen
Glance at the fire, and vivid memory
Of burning human bodies erewhile seen.
My kindly Escorts turned about to me,
And Virgil thus addrest me: "Son of mine,
Here is no death, though well may tor-

ment be.

Recall, recall! when layest thou supine

On Geryon's shoulders, still I safely led;

And how then now, less far from the Divine?

What though a thousand years within the bed

Of this same fire thou didst abide, believe

It could not hurt a hair upon thy head.

And if perchance thou deem that I deceive,

Draw nigh it, and with proper hands assay

Upon the border of thy garments. Give

Fear to the wind,—put every doubt away;

Turn and come hither with security."—

Yet against conscience did I rooted stay.

Dante Passes through the Purging Fire 265

Seeing me stand yet rooted stubbornly,

"Now look, my son," exclaimed he with a sigh,

"There is this wall 'twixt Beatrice and thee."—

As opened Pyramus his dying eye

At name of Thisbe, and gazed at her, while flew

Over the mulberry the purple dye;

So turned I, when my stubbornness withdrew,

To my wise Leader, by the name beguiled

That ever wells in memory anew.

Whereon he shook his head at me, and smiled:

"What, would we tarry here?"—as when we win

With proffered apple an unwilling child.

Then in advance of me he entered in

The fire, entreating Statius to come last,

Who for a long way back had been between.

When I was in, I would have gladly cast

Myself in molten glass for solacement,

So beyond measure was the burning blast.

To comfort me, my kindly Father went

Ever discoursing but of Beatrice,

Saying: "Her eyes seem now upon us bent."—

Beyond, a voice was singing, and by this

Conducted, and to this attentive quite,

We issued forth where mounts the precipice.

"Come, all ye of my Father benedight!"—

Bang from within a light there manifest

So that I could not look, it was so bright.

"Night comes," it added, "and goes the sun to rest;

Then quicken up your pace and do not stay,

While yet not wholly darkened is the west."—

Straight upward through the rock mounted the way,

Directed so that I, before me there,

Cut off the sinking sun's last level ray.

And both I and my Sages grew aware

Of sunset, by my shadow vanisht thence,

When we had made brief trial of the stair.

And ere within one dim circumference

The wide horizon mingled sea and shore,

And Night held sway with all her influence,

Each of us on a stair was bedded; for

The mountain-law deprived us of the will

And of the power of there ascending more.

Just as, while ruminating, goats grow still,

However bold and nimble they had run

Over the heights before they browsed their fill,

Husht in the shade while blazes hot the sun,

Watcht by the herdsman leaning on his rod,

Who, leaning thus, attends them every one;

And as the shepherd, stretcht upon the sod,

Watches by night his quiet flock beside,

That no wild beast may scatter it abroad:

Even so did we at such an hour abide,

I like the goat, they shepherdlike, all three

Hemmed in by lofty rock on either side.

Little without could there be seen by me;

But in that little saw I more intense

The stars, and larger than their wont to be.

So musing and so gazing, somnolence

Fell on me, such as oftentimes before rThey come about, gives tidings of events. That hour, I think, when through the eastern door First on the mountain Cytherea beams,— Who fired with love seems burning evermore,— *Dante's third* A Lady young and fair I saw, in dreams, *dTMmLeahPrnd* o througn a meadow land appeared to go *Rackd—the* Gathering flowers, and singing said, meseems: *thfconvU? UJi* any ask my name'then let him knoW *Hve* That I am Leah, and I move alway

Fair hands to wreathe myself a garland so.

Here at my glass I joy in my array;

But never does my sister Bachel rise

Up from her mirror where she sits all day.

Lord of Thyself! 267

She yearns to look in her own lovely eyes,

As I to deck me with my hands am yearning:

Her, seeing, and me, doing satisfies."—

Through splendors of the dawn already burning (That rise to pilgrim hearts so much more sweet

As less remote their hostel, home returning),

The shades of night were now departing fleet;

And slumber having with them fled away,

I rose, seeing my great Masters on their feet.

"That sweet fruit which, through many a branching spray,

Ye mortals go seeking with little ease,

Shall set at peace thy hungerings today. "—

Virgil began to me in words like these,

And never were there guerdons that could cope

With suchlike rapture-giving largesses.
Such longing upon longing for the slope
Came over me, at every step I could
Perceive my wings becoming fledged with hope.
When all the stairs were traversed, and we stood
Upon the uppermost, did Virgil turn
His eyes on me with wistful fatherhood;
"Son, thou hast lookt upon the fire eterne
And temporal, and comest to a place
Where, of myself, no further I discern.
I brought thee here by intellect and grace;
Henceforth let thy good pleasure guide thy going:
Thou art beyond the steep, the narrow ways.
Look how the sun is on thy forehead glowing,
Look at the grass, the tender shrubs, the bloom
That here the soil is willingly bestowing.
Until the lovely eyes rejoicing come,
Which weeping made me come to lead thee thence,
Here canst thou sit and canst among them roam.
Await no more my word or influence:
Upright is now thy will, and sound, and free,
And wrong to disobey its bidding: whence
Lord of thyself I crown and miter thee."— *Soon after tunrite on the fourth day. Dante, no longer guided but followed by the two great Masters, is walking on the level upland Now Classc, from the Roman name of the port oj Ravenna (Clattis)* XXVIII
The Earthly Paradise Crowning The Mountain
Now eager for exploring the divine
Evergreen forest dense, that screened the day,
So newly-risen, for these eyes of mine,
I leave the mountain-brow without more stay,
And slowly, slowly through the plain advance,
That everywhere breathes fragrance of the May.
A soft air, subject to no variance,
Continually stroked me on the brow
As lightly as when gentle zephyr fans;
And tremblingly responsive, every bough
Was bending all its foliage what way
The Holy Mount cast the first shadow now;
Yet did they not so violently sway
That any little bird on topmost limb
Was fain forsake the practice of his lay,
But might, while chanting the full joy in him,
Welcome the breath of morn the leaves among,
That ever bore a burden to his hymn:
From bough to bough goes gathering such song
Through the pine forest on Chiassi's shore,
When forth by Eolus Scirocco is flung.
So far already through the woodland hoar
My lingering feet had borne me, that I knew
Where I had entered into it, no more;
When lo! a brooklet cut my pathway through,
Rippling along toward my left, and bending
The grasses that along the margin grew.
All waters here in purity transcending,
Would seem commingled in comparison
With this whose limpid wave conceals no blending,
Although it darkly, very darkly run
Beneath perpetual shade, impenetrated
Ever by radiance of moon or sun.
Matilda Gathering Flowers 269
My footsteps tarried, but mine eyes elated
Passed to alight beyond the rivulet
On the fresh May profusely variegated; And there appeared (as when a thing is met *The Lady*
All of a sudden, leading thought to stray *yresaged by Ow*
For the great wonder, and all else forget) *as Rachel pres*
A Lady, who went her solitary way *aBes Beatrice*
Singing and culling flower from flower, whereof
The coloring made all her pathway gay. I said: "Pray, Lady fair, in rays of love
Basking, if I may trust thy countenance,
Which mirror of the heart is wont to prove, Now be it thy good pleasure to advance
Toward the margin of this brook, and sing,
So that I better understand thy chants.
In place and mode thou dost to memory bring
Proserpina, that time when forfeited
Her mother her, and she herself, the spring."— As turns upon the floor with even tread
A lady in the dance who hardly sets
Foot before foot, even so above the bed Of scarlet and of yellow flowerets,
She turned to me with maidlike innocence
And drooping eyes, and to the rivulet's Border approaching, did so recompense
My praying, that the dulcet melody
Was borne to me, together with the sense. When she was where the grass begins to be
Bathed by the ripples of the beauteous river,
She raised the guerdon of her eyes on me. I think there glowed so bright a luster never
Beneath the lids of Venus, by her son
Empierct with dart from his unwilling quiver. She smiled, erect upon the margin yon,
Trailing manifold colors with her hands
Of flowers upon the highland never sown.
Three steps of river hindered more advance;
But Hellespont, where Xerxes passed of yore
(A bridle still to all human arrogance),
Was never by Leander hated more
Because 'twixt Sestos and Abydos swelling,
Than that by me for barring passage o'er.
"Ye are newcomers," she began her telling,

"And so my smiling in this place elect
For human nature as a native dwelling,
Psalm xcii, i, Perchance awakens in you some suspect;
zWn *Joe*-But the Psalm *Delectasti* sheds a ray *turaTna"(Thou,* Of light that may discloud your intellect.
mg'hdthh And tnou m front' who didst entreat me, say»
Thy work) Wouldst thou hear more?—By thy solicitude
Prompted, I came to do it quite away.
"— *See the long note* "The water," said I, "and the murmuring wood *at end oj canto* Impugn within me new belief, thereto
In contradiction, as I understood."—
Whence she: "How from their proper cause ensue
The things occasioning thy wonderment,
Will I declare and purge thy inward view.
The Good Supreme, sole in itself content,
Created man for good, and peace eterne
Pledged him by giving him this tenement.
Here, by his fault, short while did he sojourn;
By his own fault, to travail and to woe
Did innocent joy and pleasant pastime turn.
That the disturbances produced below
By exhalations of the land and sea
(That after heat, as far as may be, go)
Might wage no war upon humanity,
Rose heavenward up so high this mountain here,
And is above the guarded gateway free.
Now since, in circuit with the primal sphere,
The universal air is rolling round,
While it remains unbroken anywhere,
Streams of Oblivion and Remembrance 271
This motion strikes the summit, disembound
In living ether all, and makes the dense
Forest, being a thicket, to resound.
Within the smitten plant has residence
Power to impregn the breeze, and this henceforth,
In whirling, sheds abroad that influence.
Conceived and childed so on yonder earth
Are various trees of virtue various,
According as its clime and soil have worth.
Rightly considering the matter thus,
That without visible seed some plants take root
In yonder earth, should not seem marvelous.
And thou must know that where thou setst thy foot
The holy upland every seed contains,
And never yonder can ye pluck such fruit.
The water that thou seest wells not from veins
Which vapors, by the cold condensed, restore,
Like river that now loses breath, now gains,
But from a fountain constant evermore;
And will divine replenishes that source
By all that forth its double rivers pour.
On this side, it flows downward with the force
That takes man's memory of sin away;
The other, that of all good done, restores.
It is called Lethe here, as Eunoe
On the other side, nor doth the working speed
Till of the taste of both ye make assay.
This every other savor doth exceed.
Now, though thy thirst may be so satisfied
That of more telling there be little need,
A corollary will I grant beside,
Nor deem I the less dear to thee my granting,
If it beyond the pact be amplified.
Who anciently the golden age were chanting,
And its felicity, about this place
Dreamt peradventure, while Parnassus haunting.
The Poet must sometime have dwelt by a torrent near its source in the mountain snoio, which, melting in the sun and freezing at night, keeps the breast of the stream summer-long swelling and subsiding
Here without guile took root the human race;
Here is all fruitage, here the prime unbroken;
This is the nectar they unite to praise.
"— Then looking to my Poets for a token,
I noted how with smiling mien they brooked
The parable that lastly had been spoken; Then to the Lady fair again I looked.

Note

This is one of the many cantos wherein Dante tries to rib his poetry with positive science,—unscientific as much of it proves to be.

In Canto xxi, ll. 40-57, Statins had explained to Dante that above the Gateway of Purgatorio proper,—the uppermost of the three mystic steps whereon the Vicar of Peter has his feet,—there is no earthquake, nor rain nor hail nor mist, in short, no climatic alteration or meteorological change, such as the lower parts of the mountain, being purely natural, are subject to. Here, however, Dante sees a running stream, feels a breeze upon his brow, hears a soughing in the forest whose leaves and sprays are all bent toward the west under the steady stress of the eastern tradewind. All this appears to contradict what Statins had told him, so that he is full of doubt and wonder. Accordingly when the beautiful Lady (Matilda, Canto xxxiii, l. 119) invites him to ask questions, he begs her to explain this contradiction.—The substance of her explanation is as follows: "My smiling is explained by the Ninety-second Psalm, 'For Thou, Lord, hast made me glad through Thy work.'" As to the wind (ll. 97-99), "this passage," says Moore, "describes the exemption of the Earthly Paradise from the storms generated on the lower earth by the exhalations which, proceeding from the water and the earth, rise as far as they can, following the heat by which such exhalations are drawn up." (Studies in Dante, I, 131.) Here, as everywhere, Dante followed the science of his time, which itself followed Aristotle's *Meieorologica.* But the wind here on the upper mountain is due to a very different cause: the revolution of the Primum Mobile (Milton's "that first moved," Par. Lost, B. iii, 483), *la prima votia,* or first moving sphere. It is this that, carrying with it the upper air from east to west around the stationary earth, causes the steady current or tradewind which bends the leaves all one way and makes the forest murmur like that on Classe's shore (la Pineta di Ravenna). As to the water:— In many places (e.g., Purg. Canto v, ll. 109-123; Canto xiv, ll. 31-36) Dante deals with the action of the moisture in the air, forever replenishing the rivers at their sources in the mountains. But here the two streams, Lethe and Eunoe, issue at two sides from a fountain, steady and sure, that is constantly fed by direct interposition of the Will of God. Thus Dante's doubts are solved, but the Lady volunteers a "corollary," identifying the Earthly Paradise with the Age of Gold of the Poets, two of whom are present and are pleased.

The Forest Full of Light and Melody 273 XXIX

The Mystic Procession Of The Church Triumphant

"The Lady, in the manner of a lover, *Vulgate Psalm*

Resumed her singing, when her words were done: *xxxx Wquorum*

"Blessed are they whose sins are covered over."— *peccata"* And as the nymphs were wont to go alone

Among the woodland shadows, with endeavor

Some to behold, some to avoid the sun, She then, against the current of the river,

Followed the bank, and I with her abreast,

Brief paces with brief paces matching ever. Between us not a hundred steps were paced,

When both alike the margins made a bend,

So that toward the East again I faced. Nor yet, so going, had we far to wend

Before the Lady fully turned about

Toward me,saying: "Look, brother,and attend."— And lo! a sudden luster ran throughout

Every quarter of the forest vast,

So that of lightning I was put in doubt. But since the lightning, as it comes, is past,

And this still brightened more and more the wood,

"What thing is this?"—within my thought I cast. Then did a melody delightful flood

The illumined air, whence holy ardor made Me fain to reprobate Eve's hardihood;

For there, where both the Earth and Heaven obeyed,

The woman only, and but just created,

Would underneath not any veil be stayed; Whereunder, had she but devoutly waited,

So should I that ineffable content

Have sooner had, and had it unabated. While I amid so many first-fruits went,

Of the eternal joy, and all upstrung,

And evermore on greater joyance bent,

In front of us, the verdant boughs among,

The air as if by fire enkindled grew,

And the sweet sound was now perceived as song.

O holy Virgins! now did I for you

Hunger or cold or vigils never shun,

Need goads me to implore the guerdon due.

Pour forth for me thy waters, Helicon,

Urania sustain me with thy chorus,

To put in rime things hard to think upon!

The wide tract of the middle distance bore us

The show of seven trees of gold, not far

Beyond, in false presentment there before us;

But when so near approacht to them we are,

That common traits which lead the senses wrong

Forfeit by distance no particular,

The force that makes discourse of reason strong

Perceived at length that candlesticks were they,

And heard "Hosannah" in voices of the song.

Aloft was flaming now the fair array,

Far brighter than the Moon who lamps the skies

At midnight in her monthly course midway.

Thereon I turned about with wild surmise

To the good Virgil, who thereto replied

With like amazement in his startled eyes.

Thence turning back my vision, I descried

Those high things moving on to us so slow

They would have been outstript by the new bride.

The Lady chided me: "Why yearning so

Only to gaze upon each living light,

That what comes after them thou dost forgo?"

Then, as behind their leaders, came to sight

A people in white raiment,—never seen

Was here upon the earth so pure a white.

The water on my left was full of sheen,

Reflecting back the left-hand side of me

As in a mirror, when I lookt therein.

When I had gained such place upon the lea

That separated me the brook alone,

I stayed my steps, the better thus to see,

And saw the flamelets forward move, a zone

Of painted air behind them leaving, so

That they appeared like painters' brushes drawn;

And thus the air above remained aglow

With seven stripes, containing every hue

Of Delia's girdle and Apollo's bow.

These pennons farther than my range of view

Were streaming rearward; by my estimate

Ten steps asunder were the outer two.

Under so fair a sky as I relate,

By two and two came Elders twenty-four,

Their brows with flower-de-luce incoronate.

They all were singing: "Blessed thou before

The daughters all of Adam; blessed be

Thy loveliness forever and evermore. "—

Now when no more the chosen company
Footed the flowers and tender herbage seen
Upon the margin opposite to me,
As follows light on light in the serene
Heaven, came after them four living things,
Each one incoronate with frondage green.
Every one was feathered with six wings
Studded with eyes; the eyes of Argus thus,
If living, might be full of visionings.
I lavish no more verses to discuss
Their form, O Reader! other charges bind
So, that perforce I am penurious.
But read Ezekiel, and call to mind
How he beheld them from the quarter cold
With cloud approaching, and with fire and wind;
As thou shalt find it in his pages told,
Such were they,—save as to their pinions, John
Varies from him, and with the saint I hold.
The lunar and solar spectrum Books of the
Old Testament
The Gospels The Gryphon who draws the Car of the Church typifies the union of the Divine and the human in the Saviour. The middle stripe of the seven colors is between his wings Love
Hope
Faith
Guided by Prudence, who sees past, present, future The beloved physician, St. Luke St. Paul
Within the space among those four came on,
Triumphal, rolling on two wheels, a Wain
That forward by a Gryphon's neck was drawn.
Up he extended both his wings between
The middle striping and the three and three,
That none took hurt from being cleft amain.
How high they rose no human eye could see;
Where he is bird his limbs of gold are wrought,
The others white, but mingled ruddily.
With car so beautiful Rome honored not
Or Scipio or even Augustus,—nay,
Poor were the Sun's to such a chariot,
The chariot of the Sun which, driven astray,
Was burnt at Earth's devoted orison,
When Jove was just in his mysterious way.
At the right wheel, in dance came whirling on
Three ladies: one of such a ruddy glow
As haply in the fire were seen of none;
Such flesh and frame the second one did show
As out of emerald she had been made;
The third appeared like freshly fallen snow.
Now by the white appeared they to be led,
Now by the ruddy lady, by whose lay
The others timed their swift or tardy tread.
Beside the left wheel four made holiday
In purple raiment, following as guide
One in whose head three eyes lookt every way.
Behind all those described thus, I descried
Two aged men clad with a difference,
But like in bearing grave and dignified.
One seemed adept in the experiments
Of high Hippocrates, whom Nature made
For th' animals she holds in preference;
The other, who was carrying a blade
Gleaming and sharp, showed care so opposite
That, though this side the stream, I was afraid.
Thereafter saw I four of humble plight;
And behind all an aged man alone
Walking in trance, but yet acute of sight.
These seven, like the company first shown,
Were habited in white; yet not like those
Around the forehead wore a lily crown,
But rather flowers of crimson, and the rose:
Onlooker would have sworn, if near them not,
That they were all aflame above their brows.
When over against me was the Chariot,
Thunder was heard; whereby that worthy band
Was interdicted further march, methought,
There with the vanward ensigns brought to stand.
Minor Epistles
and Apoca-
lypse (Revela-
tion of St.
John the
Divine)
See the long note at the end of this canto The symbolical Seven Candlestick guided as Charles's Wain here guides the
XXX
The Reproaches Of Beatrice
When the Septentrion of highest Heaven
That set or rising never knew, nor pall
Of any cloud save that of sin, had given
To every creature there processional
Such due direction as is ever sought
From that below by homing pilots all,—
When that stood still, the people true of thought
First come 'twixt Gryphon and Septentrion,
As to their peace turned to the Chariot.
"Come with me, with me, Bride, from Lebanon,"
Cried one like Messenger from Heaven, in song
m Thrice over, and so the others every one.
And as the blest, when the last trump has rung,
Shall each rise lightly from the funeral urn
With Hallelujah on requickened tongue,
So on the Car Divine did I discern
A hundred at such Elder's call upstand,
Angels and ministers of life eterne.
"Blessed be thou that comest!" cried that band,

Filling the air with flowers along the way,
"O give ye lilies all with liberal hand!"—
How often have I seen at break of day
The region of the East all roseate,
And else the limpid sky in fair array,
While overshadowing mists so mitigate
The rising splendor that these eyes of ours
Encounter it awhile with gaze sedate,—
So in the bosom of a cloud of flowers
Flung in the air and drifting to the ground
From the angelic hands in blossom showers,
In veil of white, with olive fillet crowned,
Appeared to me a Lady in mantle green,
With color of living flame invested round.
Vanishing of Virgil 279
And to my spirit that so long had been
Out of her presence, which did ever move
Me to stand trembling and abasht of mien,
Virtue descending through her from above
Attested, without witness of the eye,
The great tenacity of early love.
No sooner smote my sight the virtue high
Which had already pierct me through the breast
Before my early boyhood had gone by,
Than to the left as trustfully I pressed
As to the mother does the child, distraught
By terror or by grief, to manifest
To Virgil: "In my pulses beats no jot
Of blood that does not quiver; I perceive
The early flame beneath the ashes hot. "—
But gone was Virgil, leaving me to grieve,
Virgil, to me a father passing dear,
Virgil from whom salvation I retrieve,
Nor all that lost our ancient motherTiere
Availed to keep my cheeks, though cleansed with dew,
From being stained again with many a tear.
"Dante, because Virgilius withdrew,'
Do not weep yet, not yet a-weeping fall:
Another sword has yet to pierce thee through."—
As stands at stern or prow an admiral
To inspect the service, and to cheer the men
Upon the other ships to prowess all,
At the left margin of the chariot,—when
I turned about on hearing mine own name
Which here indeed I cannot choose but pen,—
I saw the Lady, she before who came
Veiled underneath the angelic festival,
Direct her eyes to me across the stream.
Though, circled with Minerva's coronal,
The ample veil descending from her head
Gave forth but faint glimpse of her form, withal
-How didst thou deign to come unto the Mount?
Knewest thou not that man is here in bliss?"—
Mine eyes fell down into the limpid fount,
But seeing myself reflected, did I turn
Back to the lawn again with bashful front.
As to the child appears the mother stern,
So she appeared to me; for bitter food
Is pity, and tart in flavor, though it yearn.
She held her peace, and the angel multitude
Ptalm xxx, 1-8 Chanted: "In Thee, Lord, do I put my trust,"
But beyond "set my feet" did not conclude.
As, on the back of Italy, the gust
Slavonic doth the living rafters sheathe
With drifted snow soon frozen to a crust,
Which melts and trickles down if only breathe
The land where shrink the shadows, and appears
Like wax that liquefies the flame beneath,—
So I remained with neither sighs nor tears
Before the song of them who chanting go
After the notes of the eternal spheres.
But when I heard their tuneful pity flow
More sweetly than as if it were exprest:
"Lady, why dost thou break his spirit so?"—
The ice that was about my heart comprest,
To breath and water changing, gusht forth hot
Through lips and eyeswith anguish from my breast.
Still from the same side of the Chariot,
Turned she to that compassionate array
Her words, her attitude yet moving not:
"Ye keep your watch through the eternal day
So that nor night nor slumber robs from you
One step the world may walk along its way;
Dante Accused before Angels 281
Thus to my answer greater heed is due That yonder weeper understand me, whence
Of equal measure may be guilt and rue.
By work not only of the wheels immense
Guiding all seeds toward their destined places
According as the stars rain influence,
But by the guerdon of celestial graces,
Which have so lofty vapors for their showers
That nevermore our sight their fountain traces,
Such, virtually, was this friend of ours
In his new life, that issue marvelous
Was to be lookt for from his native powers.
But all the wilder and more mischievous
Is an unweeded garden grown to seed,
The more the soil is rank and vigorous.
Whiles I sustained him with my face indeed,
The light of my young eyes upon him

turning;
And tow'rd right issues followed he my lead.
When I had crossed my second threshold, spurning
That earthly life, the heavenly to inherit,
Then he forsook me for another yearning.
So, when arisen out of flesh to spirit,
Waxing in beauty and in worth, I grew
Less precious to his mind, and of less merit;
And his feet wandered by a way not true
After false images of good, pursuing
Promises unredeemed with payment due.
To summon him away from his undoing,
The invocation of no dream or vision
Availed to me,—so little was he ruing.
He fell so low, no means for the remission
Of sin in him yet in my power was lying,
Save showing him the people of perdition.
For this I gained the portal of the dying,
And to that one who led him here were spoken
My supplications mingled with my sighing.
High fiat of the Almighty would be broken
Were he to traverse LethS without scoring
Due payment of such viand, certain token
Of deep repentance with hot tears outpouring."— *Note*

No sooner has the divine Chariot come to a standstill, than there arise upon it a hundred ministers and messengers of eternal life, singing and flinging up a cloud of flowers, in the midst of which appears to the poet a Lady clad in the tricolor of the Christian virtues. Her robe is of the hue of living flame, and her mantle green, but of these the poet seems only to have a glimpse, for she is all shrouded in a white veil flowing down from the head where it is filleted with the frond of Minerva,—the olive garland, symbol of wisdom and peace. His pulses all astir with the tokens of the old flame (veteris vestigia flamimr), the poet turns to share the transport with his wise guide, his beloved father; but Virgil, who has never failed him in distress, is not permitted to be a partaker of his joy. With a subtle suggestion of man's first forfeiture of Paradise, the poet betrays a pathetic weakness, making us aware that even in this supreme moment of revelation and attainment, his strongest sentiment is that of regret for his lost master. A great flood of human feeling rolls over him, the "light of higher eyes" is darkened, and he yearns backward even as Orpheus did after the vanishing shade of his Eurydice.

This is the most humanly significant moment in the poem. Virgil signifies for him all grace of art, all serenity of reason, all human amenity,—all that the Parthenon typifies in contradistinction from the Cathedral of the Christian. It is not without a pang that the poet can give up all this, even at the moment of the fulfillment of his unexampled quest, even now when he stands at last in the presence of Beatrice. Probably many readers will share Dante's sense of bereavement in the loss of the gentle Pagan Sage.

At this moment when his face is darkened with tears of vain regret, in the hush of song, in the lull of the angelic festival, a woman's voice, terrible in its sweetness, stabs him with his name, as with premonitory sting of the sword by which his tears are yet to flow:

"Dante, because Virgilius withdrew,
Do not weep yet, not yet a-weeping fall:
Another sword has yet to pierce thee through."—

Henceforth, in this and the following canto, images of war predominate. The Lady's attitude is one of command,—like an admiral she stands on the left or Old-Testament side of the Chariot. The warm color of her inner vestment is now wholly shrouded by the long flowing white veil, through which he can divine her form as through a glass darkly. There is some cheer in the touch of green (fior del verde) in the olive garland; love being hidden, he must make the best of faith and hope. With queenly sternness, like one who *Structural Imagery of Poem* 283 keeps back her hottest words, she bids him look well at her as she declares herself by name:

"I am indeed Beatrice!"

Dante! Beatrice! It was not thus he had dreamed in the New Life that her name should be linked with his!—With superb irony, referring to his besetting sin of pride, she demands:

"How didst thou deign to come unto the Mount?"

Instead of looking at her as she bids, he lets fall his eyes, but seeing his shamefast features reflected in the clear brook, he is fain to turn them to the grassy margin, where they rest upon the color of Hope.

Taking advantage of a pause, the Angels now intone the Psalm, "In Te, Domine, speravi,"—"In Thee, O Lord, do I put my trust" (Ps. xxxi), or in the Catholic version of the Vulgate (Ps. xxx), "In Thee, O Lord, have I hoped."

The divine compassion of the angel voices melts all the ice which had congealed about the heart of Dante, who is seized with an agony of contrite tears. This passion of tears is emphasized by the sublime similitude of the freshet from the snowy Apennines. It is a narrow criticism which has pronounced this similitude to be "too elaborate." Its elaboration is calculated, like everything else in this poem, to support the design. Perhaps this is the only long poem in literature in which all the decoration subserves a structural purpose. The matter is so important that it must here be dwelt upon for a moment.

Dante, Virgil, Beatrice, each one alongside of the personal and the human, symbolizes a whole system of ideas. Virgil represents that partial vision of truth which it may be given to human philosophy to attain. Beatrice represents that seeing of God face to face, that perfect revelation of truth, which to the thought of the poet is summed up in the word Theology. The nebula of ideas of which the man Dante is the type is nothing less than the whole sinful but aspiring nature of man stumbling on the altar steps that lead from Nature up to the highest possible knowledge. Prom his brow the seven P's, each emblematic of a whole category of sins, have been erased one by one by the angels who guard the successive cornices by which be has climbed the mountain that straightens those whom the world made crooked (Canto xxiii, 1.126). But the merely formal cancellation of sin typified by this action does not satisfy the conscience. Divine Justice requires a deeper participation,—a breaking up of the ice about the heart,—what Protestant Theology was afterward to emphasize as Conversion. Hence before the final rite of immersion in Lethe, which is to blot out, not sin merely, but the very remembrance of sin, Beatrice must sharply recall to Dante's mind his offenses against her, in order that he may make confession before men and angels with every evidence of contrition. The confession which Dante so solemnly makes is by no means merely symbolic, but truly personal: hence the necessity of recording his own name. He is about to partake of that "sweet oblivious antidote" which shall

"Purge the stufft bosom of that perilous stuff
Which weighs upon the heart,"
and in making this pathetic confession he is performing the most spiritually consoling act of his life. The importance then of the inward breaking up as preliminary to all outward, formal absolution cannot be too strongly emphasized.

It was Dante's purpose, as is shown by his letter to Can Grande, to blend in his poem the personal and human experience with the universal. Nowhere more than in this canto is the allegory fused with the personal fact. All is personal and all is symbol. This canto and the next form together a personal record of thrilling spiritual significance. Here the allegorical mode in art reaches its utmost height. One may perhaps feel that the delineation of Virgil is on the whole more sympathetic than his delineation, after this point and throughout the Paradiso, of Beatrice. So one may prefer the marble splendor and pure symmetry of the Parthenon to the pinnacles and dim religious light of the Cathedral. A liberal criticism will recognize in each an ultimate outreach of human faculty. Dante's art is incomparably more ample than that of the Cathedral builders, who render perfectly the terrors and mysteries of religion, but in the matter of human interest fall into the grotesque. Dante's classic taste keeps the grotesque within bounds, so that he is able more than they, and more than any other artist, to render the beauty of holiness, while never getting away too far from human nature and experience, necessarily the subjects of all acceptable art.

The Poet Humble and Contrite 285

XXXI

Dante's Bitter Confession cO thou who art yon side the sacred river," *The cutting edge*

Aiming her speech at me by thrust, that through *pTMfsethDeante*

The cutting edge alone had made me quiver, *intolerably sweet*

Pursuing without truce began she anew-*reTofht9*

"To such a heavy charge is requisite *life in thefore*

Thine own confession: speak, speak, is it true?"— *Zi'thY1* So great the perturbation of my wit, *angeU*

Though my tongue moved, it was with such delay

That first my voice had died away on it. Granting short shrift, she urged: "What dost thou say?

Answer me, for the memories that gnaw

Are not yet by the water purged away."— Together intermingled shame and awe

Constrained my lips to shape forth such a "Yes"

As could be heard only by her who saw. As crossbow, tightened up with too great stress,

Is shattered when the arrow forth is flung,

Which strengthless from the target falls, no less Was I beneath this heavy charge unstrung,

Pouring forth tears and sighs, and so undone

The faltering voice was slow upon my tongue. "In thy desires of me that led thee on

To love the Good Supreme," then did she say,

"Beyond which aspiration there is none, What thwarting trenches or what cables lay

Across the avenue of thy advance,

That thou hadst need to strip thy hope away? And what allurements in the countenance

Of others, or what advantage didst thou spy

That thou shouldst linger for their dalliance?"— After the heaving of a bitter sigh

My lips for utterance were almost sealed

And with great effort shaped out a reply.

Weeping I murmured: "Present things that yield
Fallacious joy, allured my steps aside
Soon as your countenance became concealed."—

And she: "Hadst thou been silent, or denied
What is confest, the record would allege
Thy guilt no less, by such a Judge descried.

But when the sinner's scarlet cheeks are pledge
Of self-accusal, in our Court and Fane
The grindstone is whirled back to blunt the edge.

Howbeit, in order that thou now sustain

Shame for thy fault, and be of stouter soul
When thou shalt hear the Sirens sing again,

Awhile the sowing of thy tears control,

And hearken how my flesh when laid away
Ought to have led thee to the countergoal.

Never did Nature, never Art convey

Such rapture to thee as those features fair
That held me, and are scattered in decay,

And if my dying left thy soul so bare

Of joy supreme, what mortal hankerings
Ought ever have allured to baser care?

At the first shaft of perishable things

Thou oughtest truly to have soared aloof

With me from such concern; nor should thy wings
Have been weighed downward to abide the proof
Of further strokes, whether of dainty maid
Or other vanity of brief behoof.
For two or three the fledgling may be stayed,
But in the sight of the full-plumaged bird
Vainly the bolt is sped or net is laid."—
As children stand abasht without a word,
But listening with eyes upon the ground,
Conscious and sorry for the fault incurred,
So stood I; and she said: "Since thou hast found
Pain in the hearing, lift thy beard,—thou must
Receive, by looking, yet more grievous wound."—
Drinks Forgetfulness of Fault 287
With less reluctance is an oak robust
Wrencht up by gale that scours across the sprays
From Libia, or stricken by our Alpine gust, Than did I at her word my chin upraise;
And when by "beard" invited to the viewing,
Full well I felt the venom of the phrase. And my uplifted eyes, their gaze renewing,
Plainly distinguisht those primordial creatures
How they were pausing from their blossom-strewing; And these mine eyes, as yet uncertain teachers,
Showed Beatrice turned to the Animal
That is one single Person in two natures. Beneath her veil, beyond the stream withal,
She seemed beyond her ancient self to go
More than outwent she here the others all. The nettle of remorse there prickt me so
That what once most with love seductive drew
Now most of all things seemed to be my foe. Such self-conviction gnawed my conscience through,
I fell undone; what then upon me passed,
That knows she best who gave me cause thereto. When heart revived my outward sense at last,
Appeared the Lady whom I had found alone, *Matilda draws*
Above me, saying: "Hold fast to me, hold fast!"— £g JjEJf Me throat-high in the river had she drawn, *takes away*
And, haling me behind her, was she light Swt *of*
As any shuttle o'er the water gone. *personal sin*
When I drew nigh the margin benedight,
"Purge me," so sweetly did I hear the sound,
Remember it I cannot, much less write. The Lady fair then put her arms around
My head, and plunged me under, so embraced,
Till fain to drink the water; then she crowned The whole by leading me, thus rendered chaste,
Within the measure of the lovely Four,
Who each with guarding arm my shoulder graced.
Dante sees the mystery of the union of the human with the divine nature, not directly, but reflected in the emerald eyes of Beatrice
"Here we are nymphs, and stars in Heaven; before
Beatrice down to life on earth had gone,
We were ordained each one her servitor.
We lead thee to her eyes; but those three yon,
Whose vision searches with profounder quest,
Will sharpen to their jocund light thine own."—
So first they sang; then to the Gryphon's breast
Led me along with them; and at that spot
Toward us turned, was Beatrice at rest.
"Take heed," said they, "to spare thy gazing not;
Thou art before the emeralds at last,
Whence Love of yore his arrows at thee shot."-
A thousand ardors, hotter than fire blast,
Held mine eyes fixed upon the eyes ashine
Which were in turn upon the Gryphon cast.
The Animal wherein two natures twine
Was gleaming there,—so in mirror gleams the sun,-
Now in the human, now in the divine.
Think, Reader, how I marveled, seeing yon
The Creature standing, as if inanimate,
Yet being transmuted in its eidolon!
While yet both full of wonder and elate,
My soul was breaking fast upon the food
That quenching causes thirst insatiate,
The other Three came forth, their attitude
In dancing their angelic roundelay
Approving them to be of nobler brood.
"Turn, Beatrice, O turn," so ran their lay,
"Thy holy eyes upon thy servant leal
Who moved his steps to thee from far away.
Of thy grace to us, graciously reveal
Thy smile to him, so that he may discern
The second beauty which thou dost conceal."—
O splendor of the living light eterne,
What dreaming poet ever has so paled
In shadow of Parnassus, or at its urn
Revelation of Heavenly Beauty 289
So drunken, that his heart would not have failed
Endeavoring to render thee, how fair,
Beneath the harmony of heaven unveiled
When opening thy beauty to the air?
Vision seen in the Earthly Paradise on the morning of the fourth day Too intense personal vision reproved by the Church. Possible reference to the traces of the early flame (xxx, 68) Behind the right wheel of the Car XXXII
Allegory Of *I* He Evil Days Of The Church
So steadfast and att entive was my eye

To satisfy my thirst decennial,
All other sense did in abeyance lie;
And so her holy smiling made me fall
In the old toils, that my indifference
Inclosed me on every side as with a wall;
When force perforce my sight was shifted thence
Tow'rd my left hand by those Divinities,
Because I heard from them a "Too intense!"—
And that condition of the sight, which is
In eyes but lately smitten by the sun,
Canceled awhile my vision after this.
But when my sight was for the less rewon
(The less compared with that superior
Splendor from which perforce I had withdrawn),
Turned on the right flank face about, once more
The glorious army stood to me revealed
With sun and with the seven flames before.
As changes front, 'neath cover of the shield,
A squadron with the standard, while yet not
The body of the army can have wheeled,
The knighthood of the heavenly realm that brought
The van up, all had wheeled and passed us by
Ere the front beam had turned the Chariot.
Back to the wheels did then the damsels hie,
Whereat the Gryphon moved his blessed charge
So that no feather of him shook thereby/
The Lady fair who drew me, to the marge,
And Statius and I fell in withal
Behind the wheel that curved with arc less large;
And thus, while passing through the forest tall,
Void by her fault who pledged the Snake amiss,
Our feet to angel music timed their fall.
Car of Church Bound to Tree of Empire
291
Three flights might carry along as far as this
An arrow, haply, loosened from the string:
At such remove alighted Beatrice.
I heard them one and all there murmuring
"Adam!"—then circled they about a tree
Bare on each bough of bloom and burgeoning.
Its foliage, which spreads accordingly
As it is towering upward, would for height
To Indians in their woods a marvel be.
"Blest art thou Gryphon, that thou dost not smite
With beak this tree that to the taste is sweet,
For anguish follows on such appetite."—
So round the sturdy tree the rest repeat;
Whereat the Animal of natures two:
"Thus to fulfill all justice it is meet."—
And, turning to the wagon-pole, he drew
It up beneath the widowed trunk,—whereon
That which came from it left he bound thereto.
Even as, when falls the great light of the sun
Downward, commingled with that radiance far
Which beams behind the heavenly Carp, anon
Burgeon our trees, and each its singular
Color renews, before the sun has set
Yoke on his coursers under other star:
So did the tree, of fronds so naked yet,
Revive and open out into a hue
Less than of rose and more than violet.
What hymn that throng then sang, I never knew,—
A matter not intoned in human chants,—
Nor could I bear the melody all through.
O could I picture sinking into trance
Those cruel eyes, of Syrinx hearing tell,
Those eyes that paid so dear long vigilance,
Into what drowsihood hereon I fell,
Like painter from the life would I portray:
Who would, must know to image slumber well.
Tree of Knowledge. The cross, whereof the wain-pole is symbol, was fabled to be of the wood of this tree This tree, grafted with the cross, blossoms anew, as in spring when the sun is in the Ram just behind the sign of the Fishes, our trees renew verdure and bloom The tale with which Hermes lulled Argus Matilda Theology left to guard the Church, surrounded by the Seven Virtues
Whence pass I to my waking, and I say
A dazzling splendor rent the veil from me
Of slumber, and a calling: "Rise, why stay?"—
As, to see blossoms of the apple tree
That makes the angels eager to be fed,
And marriage feasts in Heaven eternally,
Peter and James and John were upward led,
And, overcome, recovered at the word
Of Him who broke the slumbers of the dead,
And saw their band to what it was restored
By loss of Moses and Elias too,
And changed again the raiment of the Lord;
So I recovered, and so did I view
Above me standing that compassionate Guide,
Who my first steps along the river drew.
"And where is Beatrice?"—perplext I cried;
"Sitting beneath the foliage freshly sprung,
Upon its root behold her," she replied.
"Behold around her the companion throng;
The others with the Gryphon upward speeding,
Singing a sweeter and a deeper song."—
And if she spoke more words than the preceding
I know not, so mine eyes were fixt upon
Her who had shut me off from other heeding.

Alone upon the bare earth sat she down,
Left there as warder of the Chariot
I saw made fast by Creature two-in-one.
The seven nymphs a ring around her wrought,
And in their hands the seven lampads lay
That Aquilo and Auster extinguish not.
"Here art thou forester but a brief day,
And of that Rome where Christ is Roman, then
Shalt thou a burgess with me be for aye.
Whence, for the benefit of erring men,
Observe the Car, and what thou canst descry,
Having returned to earth, take heed to pen."—
So Beatrice commanded, and so I,
To very foot of her commands devote,
Whither she willed gave all my mind and eye.
Never with fall so swift the lightning smote
Out of a heavy cloud-bank, when it showers
Down from that bourn which stretches most remote,
As now beheld I through the leafy bowers
Swoop down the bird of Jupiter amain,
Rending the bark and the fresh leaves and flowers,
Thereon with all his might smiting the Wain;
Whereat it reeled, like ship storm-buffeted,
Wave-tost to starboard and to port again.
I saw a she-fox glide with stealthy tread
Quite into the triumphal Car thereon,
And she appeared with wholesome food unfed.
But for so foul a fault, with malison,
My Lady put her to such flight as bore
The fleshless framework of her skeleton.
Then, by the course that he had come before,
I saw the eagle swoop into the ark
Of the Chariot, and leave it feathered o'er.
And out of Heaven a voice of sighing, hark!
Such sighs as from a grieving bosom steal:
"How badly art thou fraught, my little bark!"—
Thereon the earth seemed cleft twixt wheel and wheel,
And thence I saw a dragon issuing,
That upward through the Chariot thrust his tail;
And like the wasp withdrawing forth the sting,
He with malignant tail drew forth amain
Part of the floor, and went off wandering.
As fertile soil takes grass, the rest again
Took on the plumage, given to satisfy
Intent perchance benevolent and sane,
And both the wheels were overrun thereby
So quickly, and the chariot-pole o'errun,
The lips are longer parted with a sigh.

Allegorical view of the history of the Church The Roman Eagle Merely Donation of Constantine, Inf. xix, 115-118 The schism between Greek and Roman Church, or perhaps Islamism Corrupting gifts Corrupt relations of Papacy and French Monarchy. The scourging of the whore doubtless refers to the outrage upon the person of Pope Boniface (Canto xx, 85-90). Dante perhaps here personifies in himself the enemies of Philip the Fair Removal of Papal See to Avignon. The strange animal must be the Car bestialized by the heads, representing the mortal sins

The holy structure, thus transformed, anon
Heads over all its different portions bore,
Three on the pole, at every corner one.
The three were horned like bullocks, but the four
With single horn had each the forehead crowned:
Monster like this was never seen before.
Secure as citadel on lofty mound,
Sitting upon the Car appeared to'me
A wanton whore, darting her oglings round.
And, as her warder, lest she taken be,
Was standing at her side a giant brute,
And now and then their kissing did I see.
But since her roving eye and dissolute
Was turned on me, that savage paramour
Did scourge her from her head unto her foot.
Then jealously and fierce with anger, tore
The Monster loose, and dragged so far withal
That with the forest shielded he the whore
From me, and shielded the strange Animal.

Beatrice Prophesies a Better Day 295

XXXIII

The Poet Made Pure For The Ascent To The Stars

"O God, the heathen are come into Thine own!"
So did the weeping maids, now three, now four
Alternately, sweet psalmody intone;
And heavily sighed Beatrice, and wore
A listening look of such a plaintive grace
That Mary at the Cross changed little more.

But when the other virgins had given place
For her to speak, now upright on her feet,
She made reply to them with blazing face:
"A little while and me ye shall not meet;
And yet a little while," again she said,
"And ye shall look upon me, sisters sweet."—
Then sent she all the seven on, and made
To follow after, merely by a sign,
Me and the Lady and the Sage who stayed.
So went she, and had taken, I opine,
Scarcely ten paces, through the woodland faring,
When with her piercing eyes she smote on mine:
"Approach," commanded she, sedate of bearing,
"In order that, if I discourse with thee,
Thou mayst remain within an easy hearing."—
When I was with her, as I ought to be,
"Brother," said she, "why art thou diffident
To question, seeing that thou walkst with me?"—
As befalls people over-reverent
In speaking in the presence of the great,
Whose chattering teeth the living voice prevent,
So I, inapt for sound articulate,
Began: "You know, my Lady, what beseems
To me, because you know my poor estate."—
"I would not have thee henceforth by extremes
Of fear and shame," she answered, "made to quail,
Nor would I have thee speak like one in dreams.
Seventy-ninth
Psalm
Gospel of John xvi, 16. AUegorically, the restoration of the Church The Lady Matilda; the sage Statins Dante addresses
her as if she
were a royal
personage:
Canto xxx, 70,
Par. xvi, be-
ginning
Following the Know that the vessel rent by dragon-tail, *Torraca) Was* and is not: but be the guilty aware *So the ardent* That Divine Vengeance fears no coat of mail.
vilhallbe"" ot always shall remain without an heir *answered; the* The Eagle that emplumed the Chariot, whence *shall come.* t grew a monster and then a prey: I bear *The DXV,* Sure witness, and foretell an influence *whatever be the* /». Iji A i" j A *date foretold,* -" stars already close at hand to give *may be an ana-* An era free from all impediments, *Uader,or it may* Wherein One, a Five-hundred Ten and Five, *be the emblem of* God-sent, shall with the harlot do to death *Christ*
That giant who doth now with her connive.
Perchance in cloudy talk I waste my breath,
Like Sphynx and Themis, unpersuasive thus,
Since in their mode the mind it darkeneth;
But fact erelong will be the Œdipus
Of this enigma, the hard knot untying,
Nor be to fold or field injurious.
Do not let the Mark thou: and even as I am prophesying,
miqhty hinder o do tlou teacn to those who run the race *thee from telling* Of life, which is a hastening to dying; 2 *of"philip* kear m mmd, when thou the writing trace, *the Fair is such* Not to conceal how thou hast seen undone *ZfojitedisTM* The Plant,that twice was pillaged in this place.
obedience of our Whoever robs or rends it, malison *r JMre* Of very deed upon High God is casting,
Who hallowed it to purpose of His own.
For tasting it, in pain and longing wasting
Five thousand years and more, the first soul sighed *First by the J?ot* Him who punisht on Himself that tasting.
Demi, now by _.,, Philip the Fair lay wit must slumber, having not descried *(the giant)* How for a special reason passing high
„7,.,. Rises the Tree, and has the top so wide.
Worldly joys , ' f stain, as did And did thy vain conceits not petrify *tmas"the* Like Elsa water round thy mind, were not *mulberry* Their joy a Pyramus to the mulberry, *Dante Has Forgotten His Estrangement* 297
So many circumstances would have taught
The justice of the interdict Divine
Upon the Tree, symbolically wrought.
But though I see that intellect of thine
Grown stony, and so windowless and blind
To radiance wherewith my teachings shine,
Yet, if unwritten, painted on the mind,
Pray bear them, by what token palmers do
Their staves with frondage of the palm entwined."—
And I: "As to the seal the wax is true,
Holding the form and pressure evermore,
So is my memory now stampt by you.
But why do your desired words outsoar
The utmost pinion of my sight, that so
I fail of them, the more I strive therefor?"—
"It is," she said, "to enable thee to know
The school that thou hast followed,—to display
How lamely it can follow where I go;
And that thou mayst perceive your human way
As far from the Divine, as is remote
From Earth the Heaven that highest speeds away."—
Whereat I answered her: "I have forgot
That ever I estranged myself from you;
And qualms of conscience for it have I not."—
"And if it has been blotted from thy view,
Now recollect," her smiling answer went,
"How thou hast drunk of Lethe but anew;
So that, if smoke of fire is argument,
Thus to forget affords clear evidence
Of error in thy will elsewhere intent.
Be that as may, my oracles from hence
Shall be unveiled, far as to lay them

bare
May be not unbefitting thy rude sense. "—

Par. xxvi. In remembrance of the pilgrimage The penetrating intellect of Dante must have more than distrusted the jejune scholastic philosophy Canto xxviii, 121 and following lines Evidently the Poet meant the three,parts of the Poem to be of equal length. He has now slightly gone beyond the

With slower paces and with greater glare
The sun in the meridian circle glowed,
That with the point of view shifts here and there,
When,—as is wont to halt upon his road
Whoever as a Leader goes before,
Finding strange thing or vestige,—so abode
The seven ladies by a shadowy shore:
Green foliage and glooming branches throw
Such shadow over mountain torrents frore.
In front, methought I saw Euphrates flow
And Tigris, from a single starting-place,
And separate, like friends at parting slow.
"O light, O glory of the human race!
What flood is this that gushes here away
Out of one fount, and separates apace?"—
To such a prayer reply was made me: "Pray
Matilda that she tell."—As one who scatters
Suspicion of some fault imputed: "Nay,"
Said the fair Lady,—"this and other matters
Were told him by myself, and sure am I
That they were not concealed by Lethe waters."—
And Beatrice: "Perchance some care more high,
Which often renders inward vision dim,
May have bereft him of his memory.
But lo! where Eunoe doth overbrim;
Lead thither, and with wonted aid of thine,
Let fainting virtue be revived in hirn,"—
Like gentle spirit that would not decline,
But willingly makes other will her care,
Whenever that is manifest by sign,
So, laying hold on me, the Lady fair
Moved forward, and with grace all womanly
To Statius said: "Do thou come with him there."—
Were ampler space, O Reader, left to me
For writing, I would sing in partial strain
Sweet draughts whereof I ne'er would sated be;

Dante Drinks Remembrance of Good
299

But since all sheets are full that I ordain *limit set by the*
This Second Canticle of mine unto, *zThS*
The discipline of art now draws the rein. From that most holy water I withdrew
Reanimated, like new plants that are
Renewed again with leafage ever new,
Pure and prepared to mount from star to star.—

PARADISO

Ascent Of Dante With Beatrice

Pervades the universe the glory of Him Who moveth all, and shineth more intense
In one part, in another region dim.
Within the Heaven that of his effluence
Partaketh most, I found myself, discerning
Things which no tongue can tell, descending thence;
Because the mind, approaching its own yearning,
Plunges engulfed in so profound a sea,
That for the memory is no returning.
Nathless, whatever in my memory
I could entreasure of the Kingdom blest,
Henceforth the matter of my song shall be.
O good Apollo! for the final quest
Inform me with thy power, till I be found
Fit for the laurel which thou lovest best.
So far one summit of Parnassus bound
All my desire, but now the twain beneath,
Needs must I enter the last wrestling-ground.
Into my bosom enter thou, and breathe
As when thou didst pluck Marsyas amain
And from the scabbard of his limbs unsheathe.
O Power Divine, if thou wilt lend me a strain
Such as may body forth the Realm above
Whose shadowy vestige lingers in my brain,
Shalt see me to the laurel of thy love
To crown me with those leaves, a pilgrim come,
Wreath which thy theme shall make me worthy of.
So seldom, Father, do we gather some
For triumph or of bard or emperor,—
Of human wills fault and opprobrium,—

301 *Prologue, lines 1 to 36 The mailer of my long Invocation to Apollo Influence of the tun at the Vernal Equinox, when the circles of the Equator, the Zodiac, the Equinoctial Colure cross the circle of the Horizon "Here" refers to Italy: "yonder1* to *the Summit of Purgatory Earthly Paradise*

Ascent through the Sphere of Fire

That the Peneian frond should all the more
In the glad Delphic God enkindle joy,
When it sets any one athirst therefor.
From little spark beacons great flame on high:
Perchance for me with voices more

elate
Shall prayer arise, that Cyrrha may reply.—
Rises to mortals up through many a gate
The lantern of the world; but from that line
Wherein four circles with three crosses meet,
With better course and in a better sign
It issues forth, and stamps with imprint clear
And tempers the world's wax to its design.
Almost this gate had made it evening here
And morning yonder; there was all aglow
And darkness covered this our hemisphere,
When, turned about toward the left-hand, lo!
Beatrice who was gazing on the sun:
Never did eagle fasten on it so.
And just as ever from the former one
Issues a second ray and upward flies,
Like pilgrim turning homeward, journey done,
So did her act, informing through the eyes
Mine own imagination, give me grace
To fix the sun beyond our wonted wise.
Much is permitted yonder, in this place
Debarred our powers, thanks to the spot, of yore
Fashioned and fitted for the human race.
This not so long nor little yet I bore,
But that I saw it sparkling round me nigh
As iron pours molten from the furnace door;
And of a sudden day to day thereby
Seemed to be added, as if He who can
Had with another sun adorned the sky.
Fixed where the everlasting circles ran
Were the rapt eyes of Beatrice, and mine
Withdrawn from Heaven were turned her own to
scan.
Music in Sphere of Fire 303
Gazing at her, I grew within divine
Like Glaucus, tasting of the herb and thence
Peer of the other gods beneath the brine. No word transhumanizing represents:
The example then to him sufficient be
Whom Grace reserves for like experience. If I was merely what Thou recently
Createdst, Love, who governest the skies,
Thou knowest, who with Thy light upliftedst me! Now when the wheel Thou dost eternalize
By being desired, made me on it intent
By music Thou dost tune and harmonize, So kindled then appeared the firmament *The Spheral*
By the sun's flame, that never rain nor stream *uslc*
Flowed over into a lake of such extent. The newness of the sound and the great gleam
Kindled my wish their causes to assign
To poignant longing, never so extreme. Whence she, who could my question well divine,
The perturbation of my mind to lull,
Parted her lips and took the words from mine, Beginning thus: "How dost thou make thee dull *First words*
With false imagination, not perceiving ce
What would be clear wert thou less fanciful. No longer art thou on earth, though so believing,
But lightning from its region never flew
Such flight as thou, thy proper home retrieving."— If disencumbered of my first doubt through
Such little words as these, more smiled than phrased,
I was the more benetted with a new,
And said: "I almost ceased to be amazed;
But now is wonder upon wonder piled
How through these lightsome bodies I am raised."— Then she began, with sigh of pity mild,
Bending her eyes upon me with such glance
As mother casts on her delirious child: *The harmony of the universe "Descent and fall to us is adverse"*
"All things whatever observe ordinance
Among themselves; here doth that form prevail
Which keeps the world with God in consonance.
Here creatures high are hot upon the trail
Of the Eternal Worth, which is the goal
Whereto the rule fore-mentioned doth impel.
The ordinance in question doth control
All natures, which through fates of different sorts
Neighbor, both near and far, their Primal Soul;
Wherefore they shape their course to different ports
Of the vast sea of being,—each with boon
Of instinct that informs it and supports.
This bears away the fire toward the moon,
This force doth mortal hearts forever move,
This bind the earth together and attune.
Not merely things created empty of
Intelligence, this mighty crossbow hurls,
But those endowed with intellect and love.
The Providence that shapes all ends, enfurls
That Heaven in dateless quiet with its light,
Wherein that sphere which is most speedy, whirls.
And thither now, as to appointed site,
Bears us along the vigor of that cord
Which aims at happy mark its arrow-flight.
As character does not indeed accord
At all times with the artisan's intent,
The stuff being deaf to the creative word,
So may the creature from the course he went,
Though thus impelled, as free will may inspire,
Incline sometimes to follow other bent
(In the same manner as we see the fire
Fall from the cloud), if down to earth

amiss

Be wrenched the primal thrust through false desire.

Thou shouldst not wonder, judge I well of this,
At thy ascending, more than at a rill
Plunging to foot of lofty precipice.
All Natures Tend Godward 305

A marvel it would be if with thy will

Unclogged, thou wert to settle to the base,
As if on earth a living fire were still."—

Thereon tow'rd heaven she turned again her face.
The warning The promise Order of verbs reversed to suggest instantaneous action Heaven of the
Moon
II
Heaven Of The Moon 0 ye who in your little bark till now,

Eager for listening, have made your way
Behind my vessel with the singing prow,

Turn to your native shore while yet ye may:
Do not put out to sea, lest haply there
By losing me, ye should remain astray.

None ever coursed the water where I fare:
Minerva breathes, Apollo pilots me,
And all nine Muses point me to the Bear.

Ye other few, with neck stretcht yearningly
For bread of angels whereon ye are fain
To live while here, nor ever sated be,—

Your ship may well put out upon the main,
Following close upon my wake before
The salt-sea water returns smooth again.

Those glorious ones at Colchis who of yore

Saw Jason made a plowman, no such burning
Amazement felt, that ye shall not feel more.

The concreate and everlasting yearning

For the Realm Deiform bore us well-nigh

As swiftly as moves heaven to your discerning.
1 gazed on Beatrice, and she on high:

And in such time perchance as cross-bow shot
Alights and is unloosened and let fly,

I found myself arrived where sight was caught
Compulsively by something marvelous:
Whence, since my doing could be hidden not

From her, she faced me, blithe as beauteous:

"Lift up thy grateful mind to God!" she said,
"Who with the prime star has united us."—

Around us there appeared to me to spread

A cloud smooth, dense, consolidate, and bright
Like diamond whereon the sun is shed.

Into the pearl of everlasting white We glided, even as water though unstirred
Is penetrated by a ray of light.
If I was body (and here it seems absurd
That one bulk brookt another, as must be
If body into body glide!) more spurred
Should be the longing of our hearts to see
That Essence where we shall behold the plan
Of our own nature blent with Deity.
There shall be seen what now by faith we scan,
Not proved, but primal truth self-evident
And by direct cognition held by man.
I answered: "Lady, with devout intent

I render thanks to Him who did ordain
That from the mortal world I should be sent.

But tell me, what those dusky marks which stain
This body, whereby on earth below the while
People are prone to fable about Cain?"—

"And if," she answered with a little smile,
"Where key of sense effects no opening
Mortal opinion may so far beguile,

Surely the shafts of wonder should not sting
Thee longer, since even following the sense
Thou seest that reason has too short a wing.

But tell me, what is thine own inference?"—

And I: "Methinks what here seems different
Is brought about by bodies rare and dense."—

"Well shalt thou see what credence thou hast lent
To error," she answered, "giving heed unto
What I adduce in counter-argument.

The Eighth sphere shows forth many a light to you
Which in their quantity and in their kind
May be observed from different points of view.

If only rare and dense herein combined,
One single virtue in all were absolute,
Now more, now less, now equally assigned.
Mystery of the union of the human with the Divine Spots in the
Moon
The smile of
Beatrice
Dante's former opinion The correct view (scholastic reasoning) For the argument here see note at end of this canto

But Virtue different must needs be fruit

Of fundamental forms, and these, save one,
Thy reasoning would pluck up by the root.

Besides, if rarity produced that dun

Thou mootest, or this planet through and through
Is perforated, leaving matter none,

Or otherwise, as fleshly bodies do

The fat and lean apportion, so would this
Alternate leaves within its book renew.

Supposing true the first hypothesis,

The sunlight in eclipse would be descried
Right through, as through whatever orifice.

This false, consider we the other side,

And if I chance to find an error there
Then thy opinion will be falsified.

Now if this rareness find no thor-

oughfare,
There needs must be some limit hindering
The counter-penetration of the rare;
Thence will the ray of other body spring
Reverberated backward, in such kind
As back from leaded glass comes coloring.
But thou wilt say that here appears more blind
The radiance than in regions othersome,
From being reflected further from behind.
The Expert-Such an objection may be overcome
Zlrf M) Experimentally, if thou wouldst try
That fountain of all human masterdom.
Take mirrors three, and two of them set by
At equal distance, and between the twain
The other further off, before thine eye.
Turning toward them, let a light remain
Behind thy back, kindling the mirrors three
And smitten by them all to thee again.
Whereas the further light will seem to thee
Less ample as to size, yet will it show
An equal luster, of necessity.
Heavenly Influences Modified 309
Now, even as the ground beneath the snow
Is stript of previous color and of cold
Beneath the beating of the warm rays, so Thy mind, being stript of error fold on fold, *Influences of*
Will I inform with light so crystalline *the &""*
That it shall quiver now thou canst behold. Within the Heaven that harbors Peace Divine *Primum mobile*
Circles a body in whose virtue lies
The being of whatever it enshrine. The following heaven, which has so many eyes, *Fixed stars*
Imparts that being through various types, and these
Distinct from it, which yet it doth comprise. The other spheres in different degrees
Dispose of their distinctive elements
According to their seeds and purposes. Thou seest these universal instruments
Thus drawing from above, while raining down
From grade to lower grade their influence. Look at me finding pathway for thine own
Arrival at the truth thou art fain to scan,
And know henceforth to keep the ford alone! The breath of blessed Movers needs must fan *Celestial in*
Motion and influence of holy sphere, *tdligenees* As craft of hammer moves by artisan.
And that same Heaven the many lights make fair,
From the Deep Mind that/gives it whirl and thrust
So takes the image and so seals it there. And as the soul within your human dust
Makes different members work in unison,
Distributed through each in measure just, So doth the Mind deploy its benison
Multiplied through the starry firmament,
But turns upon Itself, remaining One. Each different power makes mixture different
With precious body rendered quick thereby,
Wherewith, like life within you, it is blent.
By glad endowment of the Nature High,
This mingled virtue through the body glows,
As gladness lights the pupil of the eye.
From this proceeds whatever difference shows
'Twixt light and light, and not from rare and dense:
This is the intrinsic principle whence flows
The dark and bright, as by its excellence."— *Note*

The astrological theory of the time was that the starry heavens, although of one substance, vary in quantity and kind, and to these differences correspond the diverse influences they are supposed to exercise on the earth and on human affairs. The same principle, it is argued, must apply to the spots in the moon. These appearances proceed from causes much deeper than mere rarity and density.

III

Spirits Of Women In The Lunar Heaven

The sun that erst with love had warmed my breast
Had now the fair sweet face of truth, by proof
And refutation, rendered manifest;
And to confess, so far as was behoof,
Myself corrected thus and confident,
My head for speech was lifted more aloof.
But something gleamed on me, whence so intent
To gaze thereon my baffled vision grew,
That my confession out of memory went.
As through transparent polisht glass, or through
Still and pellucid waters, of too mean
A depth to have the bottom lost to view,
Come back the contours of our faces, seen
So pallidly that pearl on forehead white
Is caught as quickly if the eye is keen,—
Such faces, fain for speaking, came to sight;
Whence I in counter-error fell thereby
To what befell the fount-enamored wight.
The instant that aware of them was I,—
Reflected images by my surmise,—
To see of whom they were, I turned mine eye;
But, seeing nothing, went with my surprise
Straight to the light of her, my Leader sweet,
Whence smiling kindled in her holy eyes.
She said: "No wonder if with smiles I meet
This exhibition of thy childish mind
Unwilling yet to truth to trust its feet,
But turns thee back in vain, after its kind.
True substances are what thou dost

perceive,
Here for some forfeiture of vows assigned.
Whence talk with them, and listen, and believe;
For that which gives them peace, the one true Fire,
Suffers their feet its purlieu not to leave. "

Heaven of the Moon

Marvelous vision: Dante mistakes spirits for reflected images The smile of Beatrice

Dante addresses the spirit Piccarda Donati (see Purgatorio xxiv, near the beginning; also the prediction of the fate of Cor so Donati in same canto) Remiss in execution of vows Degrees of beatitude

And to that shade who seemed most to require
Question with me, began L tow'rd it bended
Like one bewildered by too great desire:
"O spirit born to bliss, with radiance blended
Of life eterne in sweet felicity
That, tasted not, is never comprehended,
Thou wilt be gracious to content in me
The craving for thy name, and for your lot."—
Whereon with smiling eyes and promptly, she:
"To just desire our charity doth not
Deny the door, more than His love doth so
Who wills His Court all in His image wrought.
I was a virgin sister there below;
And if thou recollect, it will appear
That greater beauty doth not hide me: know
I am Piccarda, relegated here
Together with these others who are blest,
And myself blessed in the slowest sphere.
All our affections, kindled as may best
Conform to pleasure of the Holy Spirit,
Rejoice being fashioned after His behest.
And this low-seeming lot that we inherit,
Is given to us because we did our vow
/ Make in some manner void, or did defer it."—
"Your wondrous faces shine, I know not how,"
Was my reply, "with some diviner grace,
Transmuting them from what we knew ere now:
Whence was my memory of laggard pace;
But what thou tellest helps me to make clear
Thy features which now better I retrace.
But tell me, ye whose blessedness is here,
Do ye desire a loftier place above
To grow in vision or become more dear?"—
Her flitting smile lit up the faces of
Those others; then she spoke so blithesomely
She seemed to kindle with first fire of love:
"Brother, the influence of charity
Contents our will, alone solicitous
For what we have,—no craving else have we.
Did we desire a place more glorious,
Then our desires would be at variance
With will of Him who here assigneth us;
These circles have no room for dissonance,
As thou shalt see, for herein love is fate,
If thou behold its nature not askance.
Nay, 'tis the essence of this blessed state
To dwell within the Will Divine alone,
Whereby our wills with His participate.
So that throughout this realm, from zone to zone,
We pleasure the whole realm without surcease,
And please the King who in wills us with His Own;
His will is consummation of our peace;
And everything is moving to that sea,—
All it creates as nature gives increase. "—
Then only was the truth made clear to me
That everywhere in Heaven is Paradise
Where Grace Supreme rains not in one degree.
But, as will happen, should one food entice,
Other than that wherewith we have been fed,
Returning thanks for that, we crave for this,
Such was my case in what I did and said
Seeking to learn what web it was whereof
She had not drawn the shuttle to the head.
"Life perfect and high worth enheaven above,"
She said thereto, "a Lady among the blest,
Under whose rule in your world women love
To robe and veil, till death to watch and rest
Beside that Spouse, accepter and rewarder
Of vows which love conforms to His request.
To follow her, of maiden weeds discarder,
Fleeing the world and in her habit dressing,
I pledged me to the pathway of her Order.

"La sua volontate i nostra.pace" Santa Clara of Assist Violence done to Piccarda by Corso Donati

The great Constance, mother of the great Frederick The three blasts of Swabia are Frederick Barbarossa, Henry VI, and Frederick II (one of the most interesting men of his century). For the fate of her grandson, Manfred, see Purg. iti

Thereafter men more used to ban than blessing
Ravisht me from the cloister sweet:

God knoweth
What my life then, without mine own confessing.
This other splendor on my right who showeth
Her beauty to thee, luminously burning
With all the light that in our circle gloweth,
Takes to herself these words myself concerning:
A sister she, and so from her was riven
The veil by hands its holy shadow spurning.
But when she back into the world was driven
Despite her wish and wont legitimate,
She never from her heart the veil had given.
This is the radiance of Constance great,
Who to the Second Blast of Swabia
Bore the Third Puissance, and ultimate. "—
So spake she, and in chant began to say
Ave Maria, and chanting from me stole
As through deep water sinks a weight away.
My vision, straining to pursue that soul
To the utmost, when she vanisht into bliss,
Turned to the mark of a more longed-for goal,
Reverting wholly round to Beatrice;
But such a lightning flasht she on my look
That first my sight endured it not; and this
So gave me pause that question I forsook.

IV

Solution Of Perplexing Questions

Between two foods alike to appetite
And like afar, a free man, I suppose,
Would starve before of either he would bite;
So would a lamb, between the hungry throes
Of two fierce wolves, feel equipoise of dread,
So hesitate a hound between two does.
Whence by my doubts alike solicited
By sheer necessity, blame can be none
Nor commendation, if I nothing said.
And I said nothing; but desire upon
My face was pictured, questioning as well,
Set forth more fervently than words had done.
Beatrice did as once did Daniel
Taking Nebuchadnezzar's wrath away,
Which first had rendered him unjustly fell,
And said: "I see how two desires have play,
Each so compelling that the eagerness
Stifles the very breath of what 'twould say.
Thou urgest: 'By what justice can duress
Imposed by others, if persist good will,
Render the measure of my merit less?'
Perplexes thee another question still:
'Do souls rejoin the stars, as it would seem,
And the idea of Plato thus fulfill?'
These questions balance equally the beam
Of thy desire; and therefore will I first
Treat that which is in venom most extreme.
Not he of Seraphs most in God immerst,
Not Moses, Samuel, nor either John
Thou choosest, nor yet Mary, I say, can thirst
In any other heaven to have their throne
Than do these spirits whom thou didst discern,
Nor more nor fewer years of being own.

A canto of scholastic reasoning Dilemma of
Buridan's ass
Beatrice reads in Dante's face the two questions All in the same Heaven The appearances in the various spheres emblematic Plato's error

All make the Primal Circle fair, and earn
Life of sweet bliss in different measure here,
Through feeling more or less the breath eterne.
Not as allotted here did they appear
Within this heaven, but as a sign intending
The least exalted though celestial sphere.
My words perforce unto your wit are bending,
Which grasps but by perception of the sense
What then it worthy makes for comprehending.
The Holy Scriptures, condescending hence
To your conceit, with foot and hand endue
The Deity, with mystic difference;
And Holy Church so represents to you
Michael and Gabriel with human traits,
And the other who gave Tobit health anew.
That which Timaeus of the soul debates
Is different from that seen here so far,—
For seemingly he thinks it as he states.
He says the soul returns to its own star,
Whence nature actuated its descent,
Giving it in the flesh an avatar.
And in his doctrine haply more is meant
Than meets the ear, and may have sense whereto
Befits it not to be irreverent.
If, for the influence they rain on you,
He means one must approve and disapprove
These wheels, perchance his bow hits something true.
This principle, ill comprehended, drove
Almost the whole world formerly astray
In naming Mars and Mercury and Jove.
The other dubitance that gives thee stay
Empoisons less, for its malignity
Could never lead thee from myself away.
That Justice here should seem unjust to be
In mortal vision, is an argument
Of faith, not heretic iniquity.

Can the Will be Farced? 317

But that ye, humanly intelligent,
May penetrate into this truth the more,
As thou desirest, make I thee content.

If it were violence that he who bore *Violence done*

In no wise aided him who used the might, to *hunum* "

These souls could claim no pardon on that score; For will is never quencht in will's despite, *Due to laxity*

But doth as nature ever doth in fire,

Though hundred tempests buffet left and right. For, little or much as it may yield, desire

Abets the violence: and these did thus, Free to their sanctuary to retire.
Had but their will been whole and vigorous,

Like that which fastened Lawrence to his grill

And ruthless to his hand made Mucius, Then up the road whence they were dragged, their will *Not all the*

Would have impelled them, soon as they were free;

But all too rare is will so inflexible.
And by these words, if thou hast duteously

Gathered them up, is quasht the argument That would yet many a time have troubled thee.
But now another cross-entanglement

Puzzles thine eyes, wherethrough thou couldst not find
An issue for thyself, until forspent.
I have for certain put into thy mind

That never could speak false a soul in bliss,

Since to the source of truth forever joined; Then mayst have understood Piccarda amiss *Analysis of the*

That Constance to the veil was ever true: *Piccarda about*

So that she seems to contradict me in this. *Constance*

Many a time, my brother, urged thereto

By hope of scaping peril, under stress,

Men have done what they ought not, would not do; Even as Alcmaeon,—who by prayer express

Of his own sire, his mother life refused,—

Not to lose piety, grew pitiless.

Think, pray, when come to this, that force is fused
With will together, and so the two are blent
That the offenses cannot be excused.

Will absolute doth not to ill consent:

Consenting just so far as it may rue,
If it resist, some greater detriment.

Therefore Piccarda, saying what is true,
Means absolute volition; I, however,
The other,—whence in truth agree we two."—

Such was the rippling of the holy river

Out of the fountain whence all truth flows over,
Setting at rest both my desires forever.

"Divine one, O belov'd of the First Lover,"

I straightway said, "whose words are in me burning
And flooding till I life on life recover,

Not deep enough the channel of my yearning
For thanks of mine coequal with your favor;
Let Him reply who can and is discerning!

I see our mind unsated still with savor
Of any truth, till of that truth aware
Beyond which is no light that doth not waver.

Therein it rests, like animal in lair

When it attaineth; and it can attain,
Else frustrate every craving for it were.

Whence like a shoot doubt ever springs again

At foot of truth; and so from height to height
Doth nature urge us summitward amain.

This doth assurance give me, this invite

To ask with reverence of another theme,
O Lady, wherein truth is dark to sight.

Fain would I know if man may ever dream
With good to so amend vows forfeited,
They shall not in your balance kick the beam."—

Beatrice gazed at me with eyes that sped
Flashes of love, divine of radiance,
So that my vanquisht force of vision fled,

And I became as lost, with bended glance.

Sacrifice of the Will Absolute 319
Vows And Free Will; Ascent To The Heaven Of
Mercury

"If my love beam upon thee blazing hot

Beyond the measure that is absolute

On earth regarded, do thou marvel not, Seeing that such intensity has root

In perfect vision, which doth ever move

Tow'rd the good apprehended, sure of foot. I see how shines already from above

Into thine intellect the Eternal Light

That needs but to be seen to kindle love; And if some other thing your love delight,

Naught is it but some vestige of that same

Effulgence, comprehended not aright. Thou askest whether men for vows they maim *Commutation of*

May pay such other service as to gain

Exemption of the soul from any claim?"— So Beatrice began this further strain;

And even as one discoursing, who would not

Break off, took up the holy theme again: "The gift most precious to Creative Thought,

Most signal of God's bounties, and the one After the pattern of his goodness wrought,
Was Freedom of the Will,—a benison *Free will*

Wherewith all creatures of intelligence

Both were and are endowed, and they alone. Now will appear to thee by inference

The high worth of the vow so framed, supposing

That with thine own consenting, God consents; For, between God and man the bargain closing, *The vow sacri*

Of what I call this treasure an oblation *ees*

Is made in sooth, made by its own proposing. What may be offered then in compensation?

Weening to use well what thou offerest,

Thou seekest for thy plunder consecration.

Now art thou assured concerning the main quest:
But since herein doth Holy Church acquit,
Which seems against the truth I manifest,

Thou canst not choose but still at table sit

Awhile, for the tough viand thou hast chewed
Wants further aid for thy digesting it.

Take what I tell thee in receptive mood
And hold it fast; it is the very vice
Of wit to lose what has been understood.

Pertain to essence of this sacrifice

Two elements: one what it treats about,
The other from the covenant takes rise.

The latter never can be canceled out
Save by fulfillment; and already so
I spoke about it as to banish doubt;

Hence had the Hebrews still to offer, though
Some thing whereof the sacrifice was made
Might be commuted, as thou shouldest know.

The former, which as matter I portrayed,
May well be such that no offense is done
If with some other matter counterweighed.

But willfully let on his shoulder none

Shift burden, without sanction of the Power
That turns the white key and the yellow one.

And folly all commuting deem, before

The thing remitted in the thing ye essay
Shall be contained, as in the six the four.

Therefore whatever by its worth may weigh
So much as can make every balance swing,
Can never be redeemed with other pay.

Let men deem not the vow a trifling thing:
Be loyal, and in being so not blind
As Jephthah was in his first offering,

Who did worse honoring the vow unkind,

But should have said: 'I sinned'; like foolish plight
The mighty leader of the Greeks entwined,
Heaven of Mercury 321

Whence rued Iphigenia her beauty bright,

And made for her both wise and simple rue,

So many as hear report of such a rite!
Christians, be graver in your moving; do *Application of*

Not featherlike to every wind consent, *the le"m*

And ween not every water washes you. Ye have the Old and the New Testament,

The Shepherd of the Church to shape your aim:

Therewith for your salvation be content. If sorry greed aught else to you proclaim,

Be men, and be not silly sheep, that so

The Jew among you laugh you not to shame. Behave not like the lamb who doth forgo

The mother's milk, and wantonly delight

In making of himself a mimic foe."—
Thus Beatrice to me, just as I write;

Then all in longing up to that expanse

Where most the world is quickened, turned hersight. Her silence and transfigured countenance

Imposed like silence on my eager wit,

Though ready with new questions to advance. And as the mark is by the arrow smit *Slipping into*

Before the cord forgets to quiver, thus Jkst"

Into the Second Kingdom did we flit.
I saw my Lady there so rapturous

As to the luster of that heaven she drew

That even the planet grew more luminous. And if the laughing star was altered too,

What then became I, by my native mood

Ever susceptible to something new!
As in clear pool where the still fishes brood, *The approach*

Aught dropping in impels the finny drove "' *new ptn '*

To dart toward it, deeming it their food, So saw I there a thousand splendors move

To meet our coming, and every one was hymning:

"Behold one who will multiply our love."—

And every shade of them, now nearer swimming,
Appeared as with effulgent glory fraught
Streaming out of its rapture overbrimming.

If what is here begun proceeded not,

Think, Reader, what an agonizing dearth

Of knowing more would be within thee wrought;

And from thyself infer how these gave birth

To yearning in me to hear each circumstance Concerning them, when they revealed their worth. *Dante U* "O happy-born, whom sovran Grace thus grants amw *by a* rj.o see *e* thrones triumphant and eterne

Ere thou abandonest thy militance,

By light that ranges through all heaven we burn
Enkindled so; and therefore, if thou please,
Content thy heart with light from out our urn."—
One of the souls devout spoke words like these
To me; and Beatrice: "Speak, speak out free
And trust to them as to divinities."—
The poet doet "Well I perceive how thou art nesting thee

In thine own light, and drawing it again
Through eyes that coruscate so laughingly.

But who thou art, blest soul, I cannot ken,

Nor wherefore thou art graded in the sphere
That is in alien radiance veiled to men.
"—

Thus spoke I straight toward the luster fair
That first addrest me; whereupon it

grew
By far more radiant than it was whilere.
Then like the sun concealing himself through
Excess of light, when heat has gnawed away
The tempering shade to heavy vapors due,
Concealed himself from me in his own ray
The holy shape for very jubilance;
And thus fast folded did in answer say
In fashion as the following canto chants.

speak Justinian Speaks VI

A Philosophy Of History: The Function Of Rome In Human Redemption

"When Constantine had wheeled the Eagle away Against Heaven's course, where it was following
That ancient who espoused Lavinia,
Two centuries and more saw hovering
The Bird of God at Europe's border line,
Near to the mountains whence it first took wing;
And, overshadowing with wings divine,
Governed from hand to hand the world of man,
And in due turn alighted upon mine.
Caesar was I, and am Justinian,
Who, to the primal Love obedient,
Winnowed the laws, and bolted to the bran.
And ere yet wholly on that labor bent
Did I a single nature in Christ misdeem,
Not more, and with such faith remained content;
But blessed Agapetus, the supreme
Shepherd of souls, directed me and drew
To the pure faith, discoursing of the theme.
Him I believed, and what by faith he knew
Now clearly see, as seest thou every pair
Of contradictories both false and true.
When with the Church my footsteps moving were,
I gave me single-minded to the laws,
Inspired by Grace Divine to that high care;
Committing weapons in the imperial cause
To Belisarius mine, so comforted
By Heaven's right hand that I had leave to pause.
Here then to thy first question comes to head
My answer; but its terms make apposite
That something as a sequel should be said,
That thou mayest see with what amount of right
Against the hallowed ensign move both they
Who make it theirs and who against it fight.

The soul of Justinian the lawgiver speaks Conversion and work of Justinian Victorious flight of the Roman eagle from the time of Mneas on

Think what large reverence we ought to pay
Its prowess, starting from the moment when
Died Pallas to secure it sovereign sway.
In Alba 'twas, thou knowest, a denizen
Three hundred years and more, until the close
When fought the three to three for it again.
From Sabine rape down to Lucretia's woes
Thou knowest how with seven kings it went
Subduing round about the neighbor foes.
Thou knowest how, borne by Romans eminent,
'Gainst Brennus, against Pyrrhus it o'ercame,
And against others, prince or government;
Torquatus, and that Quinctius who took name
From hair unkempt, Decii and Fabii so
Wrought deeds that gladly I embalm their fame.
It laid the pride of the Arabians low,
Who passed in train of Hannibal among
The rocky Alpine peaks whence pours the Po.
It led to triumph while they yet were young
Pompey and Scipio, and bitterly
Wrought to that hill beneath which thou art sprung.
Then near the time when heavenly harmony
Would tune the world to concord with its own,
Caesar laid hold of it at Rome's decree;
And what it wrought from Var to Rhine is known
To Isere, to the Saone, and to the Seine,
And every valley brimming up the Rhone.
Its prowess, issuing from Ravenna, when
It leapt the Rubicon, so swiftly flew
That follow it could neither tongue nor pen.
It wheeled the legions back to Spain; then threw
Them on Durazzo; and smote Pharsalia
So that to torrid Nile was felt the rue.
Antandros and the Simois it saw,
Its starting point, where Hector sleeps so fast;
Then, woe to Ptolemy, roused beak and claw;
Thence fell, like thunderbolt on Juba cast;
Then wheeling back into your West it came
On hearing the Pompeian trumpet-blast.
What the next bearer with it did, proclaim
Brutus and Cassius in the hellish deep,
And Modena and Perugia wail the same.
Ever doth wretched Cleopatra weep
Because of it,—she, fleeing on before,
Took from the adder suddenly black sleep.
With him it coursed far as the Red-sea shore;
With him composed the world in peace so great
That barred on Janus was his temple door.
But what the standard that I celebrate
Had done before and was about to do
For mortal man in every subject state,
Dwindles away, beclouded to the view,
If one in hand of the third Caesar seek
With vision clear and with affection

true;

For Living Justice, moving me to speak,
Gave it, in person of that emperor,
The glory vengeance for just wrath to wreak.

Now marvel here at what I tell thee more:
Later it flew with Titus, doing again
Vengeance on vengeance for the sin of yore.

And after, when the Lombard fang would fain
Bite Holy Church, beneath those eagle wings
Came to her aid victorious Charlemagne.

Now mayst thou judge of their endeavorings
Accused above; the people I accuse
Have been the cause of all your sufferings.

Against the public standard one would use
The yellow lilies; one to party lines
Confine it,—hard the criminal to choose.

Under another ensign Ghibellines

May ply and ply devices,—for amiss
Follow it who from justice discombines.
The Eagle executes Divine Justice for man's sin, and does vengeance on the Jews Application of the lesson to Dante's time "That last infirmity of noble mind" Noble unselfishness of Romeo, minister of Count Berenger of Provence

And let that younger Charles not trample this,

He and his Guelfs, but fear the claws that wield
Force to flay tougher lion-fell than his.

Children have oft bewailed by flood and field
The father's fault, nor let him ever ween
His lilies to be quartered in God's shield.

This little planet is made passing sheen

With the good spirits who have striven that fame
And honor follow them; whenever lean

The truant wishes toward such an aim,
Then true affection needs must radiate
Upward to Heaven less vividly aflame.

But that our guerdon is commensurate
With worth, is part of our beatitude,
Seeing it nor too little nor too great.

Whence Living Justice sweetens so the mood
Of love in us that no perversity
Can tangle it in any turpitude.

Voices diverse below make melody;

So in this life of ours each various grade
Benders among these wheels sweet harmony.

And from within the present pearl is rayed
The light of Romeo, whose labors great
And generous were shabbily repaid.

But those of Provence cannot gratulate

Who wrought against that noble minister:
Evil to them who other's good abate!

Four daughters, Queens, had Baymond Berenger,
And he who crowned them was no citizen
But Romeo, a lowly pilgrimer.

By crooked counsel moved, the Master then

Calls to account the servant just, who clears
His credit,—seven and five for every ten.

Then he departed poor and stricken in years;
But if the world could know the heart he bore
Begging his bread and eating it with tears,

Much as it praises, it would praise him more."— VII

Mystery Of The Redemption

"Hosannah, holy God of Hosts, Thou who
Dost all the blessed fires that are burning
Within the Kingdom with Thy light outdo!"—

Even so, in time to its own music turning,

That being on whom two splendors form a crest,
Chanted, as well I saw, the while discerning

How he began to dance with all the rest,
And like swift sparklets with velocity
And sudden distance veiled them from my quest.

Within me I was saying doubtfully:

"Tell it to her, tell it my Lady, whose
Distillments are so sweetly slaking me;"

But reverence, whereby I cannot choose

But mastered be at sound of "Be" or "Iss,"
Bowed me again like one whom slumber sues.

But little while so left me Beatrice

Till, with a radiant smile of such a kind
As would have put a burning man in bliss,

She said: "By my unfailing sight I find

The question how a vengeance that was just
Could justly be avenged, perturbs thy mind;

But if I speed to thy release, so must

Thou listen well, because these words of mine
Will guerdon thee with reasoning august.

By not submitting to a curb benign

Upon his power of will, that man ne'er born
Damning himself, condemned thus all his line,

Whereby the human race below forlorn
Lay many a century in error great,
Until the Word Almighty did not scorn

Going down to join in Person increate,
By the sole act of His eternal love,
That nature from its Maker alienate.
He reverences the very syllables of her name The smile of
Beatrice
His question stated FaUofMan "For God so loved the world" The just.penally Why did not God let man ransom himself? That which distills from God is permanent, free, and in the divine likeness

Now turn thy look to what I reason of:

This nature, which its Maker made

His own,
Did as created pure and sinless prove,
But it was exiled by its fault alone
From Paradise, for that it wandering
From way of truth and life astray had gone.
Thus, by the adopted nature measuring,
The penalty upon the cross exacted
Did never any yet so justly sting;
And likewise never was such wrong enacted,
Considering Who suffered, and the worth
Of Him in whom this nature was contracted.
Thus from one act diverse effects took birth;
The same death pleased the Hebrews and the Lord:
Opened the Heavens thereat, and shuddered earth.
No longer deem then difficult the word
When it asseverates that vengeance just
Was afterward avenged by a just sword.
But now I see how thought on thought is thrust
Upon thy mind, entangled in a skein
Whence it awaits release with eager trust.
Thou sayest within: 'Yea, what I hear is plain,
But it is hidden from me why God chose
This only way our ransom to attain.'
My brother, this decree from eyes of those
Lies buried deep, whose wit is not mature
Within the flame of love that ripening glows.
Nevertheless as at this cynosure
Mortals long gaze, though little they discern,
Will I declare why this way was the truer.
Bounty Divine, that doth all envy spurn
Away from Him, sends burning sparks therefrom,
So lighting up the loveliness eterne.
That which distills without a medium
From Him, has then no end, for permanence
Gives form and pressure where His seal has come.
That which rains down without a medium thence
Is wholly free, since not beneath the bar
Of changing secondary influence.
Things please Him most that in His likeness are,
For the All-irradiant sacred glow must be
Most living in the things most similar.
These coigns of vantage all humanity
Inherits, and if one of these it wants
Falls force perforce from its nobility.
Sin only is man's disinheritance,
Rendering him unlike the Highest Good
And less blancht therefore by its radiance,
And never he gains his former altitude
Except he fill the guilty void again,
Just penalty for pleasure ill-pursued.
Your nature, sinning in your Sire amain,
From such advantages as these was barred
Even as from Paradise; and such the stain
That in no manner could they be restored,
If thou with subtle wit the matter heed,
Except by passing one or the other ford:
Either that God's sole clemency concede
Redemption, or that human foolishness
Should expiated be by human deed.
Now let thine eye pierce into the abyss
Of the eternal counsel, close intent
As possible to my discourse of this.
Man could, within his finite limits pent,
Never atone, his pinions downward weighing
With meekness and thereafter obedient,
Far as he planned to soar by disobeying;
And this is why, though man himself would pay
His own atonement, he was barred from paying.
Whence Deity must needs in His own way
Bring man in perfect life again to birth,—
In one way, or indeed in both, I say.

By the fall man lost his freedom and divine likeness, thus becoming sub to death

Why human atonement might not suffice

Necessity of the Incarnation

The elements not distilled directly from the divine, but through the secondary influences of the stars

But since the doer's deed is graced with worth
The more in measure as it more infers
The heart of bounty whence it issued forth,
Bounty Divine that stamps the universe,
Was fain to put in force His every mode
To liberate you from the primal curse;
Nor was nor shall be, since the first day glowed
Till the last night, so high and glorious
A progress on the one or the other road:
For, giving Self, was God more bounteous,
So making man sufficient up to rise,
Than if He simply had forgiven us;
Nor any other method might suffice
For justice, had the Son of the Most High
Not humbled Him, assuming mortal guise.
And now, with all thy yearning to comply,
Let me turn back to make one matter clear,
That we may see it together, eye to eye.
Thou sayest: T see the water, I see the air,
The fire, the earth and all their mixtures stay
But little while, then to corruption fare,
Yet nothing but created things were they;'
Wherefore, if what I have averred is

sure,
They ought to be secure against decay.
The angels, brother, and the country pure
Wherein thou art, may be called generated
In all their being, as they are, mature;
But the elements whose names thou hast related,
And all the things that from their minglings flow,
Informed with power that was itself created.
Created was the matter in them so,
Created the informing influence
Within these stars that sweeping round them go.
Pluckt out from their potential elements
By light and motion of the holy fires
Are souls of every brute and of the plants.
Direct and Indirect Creation 331
But the Supreme Benignity inspires
Your soul directly, and enamors her
With Him, whom she forever then desires.
And furthermore thou mayest hence infer
Your resurrection, if thou think once more
How human frames divinely fashioned were
When our first parents both were framed of yore." *Morning and evening star Evidence of the ascent* VIII
The Heaven Of Venus
The world was in its peril wont to hold
That the fair Cyprian was raying out
Wild love, in her third epicycle rolled;
Wherefore the ancient people went about
In antique error, not alone to pay
To her the sacrifice and votive shout,
But Cupid and Dione honored they,
This as her mother, that one as her son,
Telling how he in Dido's bosom lay;
And named from her with whom I have begun
That planetary star which, now at brow
And now behind the shoulder, woos the Sun.
I had no sense of rising there till now,
But of our being there my Lady's favor
Gave proof, because I saw her fairer grow.
And as in flame we see the sparkles waver,
Or as within a voice a voice discern
One holding note, one shaking out a quaver,
So in that radiance other torches burn
In circle speeding variably fast,
Methinks in measure of their sight eterne.
Never from icy cloud so swift a blast
Swept, seen or unseen, that the interim
Would not have seemed long-drawn before it passed.
To one who should have seen approaching him
Those lights divine as they forsook the gyre
Begun among the lofty Seraphim.
And from among the foremost of that quire
Rang forth Hosannah, so harmonious
That ever to rehear it I desire.
Then one of them drew near alone, and thus
Began: "We all with eagerness are burning
At thy good will to give thee joy of us.
Of one orb, of one circling, of one yearning
With the Celestial Princes are we rolling
To whom once thou, from worldly matters turning:
'Ye the third Heaven by intellect controlling;'
And to delight thee shall a quiet space
Be no less sweet, our love is so ensouling."—
After mine eyes had sought my Lady's face
With reverence, and she of her assent
Had satisfied them, and assured her grace,
Then to the light which did such hope present,
I turned about, and,—''Tell me, who are you?"
Inquired in tone of tender sentiment.
Ah, when I so had spoken, how it grew
Transfigured to my vision, and enhanced
In size and brilliance, joy and joy thereto!
"The world," he answered, thus enradianced,
"Held me short while, and had it longer been
Much harm that will befall had never chanced.
I am concealed from thee behind a screen
Of gladness that irradiates me round,
As swathes a creature its own silken sheen.
Much didst thou love me, with good reason fond;
For had I stayed below I would have shown
More of my love to thee than in the frond.
That left bank which is watered by the Rhone
When it has drunk the Sorgue up, would have held
Me in good time the master of its own;
And that horn of Ausonia, citadeled
By Bari, Gaeta, and Catona, and where
Tronto and Verde in the sea are quelled.
Already gleamed the crown above my hair
Of that dominion which the Danube purges
Abandoning its German banks; and fair
Trinacria, which on occasion merges
Pachynus and Pelorus in one gloom
Over the gulf that Eurus chiefly scourges
The courteous spirit quotes the first line of a canzone of Dante Charles Martel, heir presumptive to many kingdoms The poetry of the map The Sicilian Vetpers (a.d. *1282) The father Charles, the Cripple of Jerusalem, had but the one virtue (cf. Canto xix, 127-119) How can a bad son descend from a good father Arguing in the manner of a professor at Paris or Bologna* (Not through Typhceus, but through sulphur fume),
Would for her sovereigns be looking still,
Who should through me from Charles and Rudolph come,
Had not the subject folk, by lordship ill

Exasperated, been provokt to cry
Insurgent in Palermo: 'Kill them, kill!'
And had my brother been forewarned thereby,
He now were fleeing, lest it work him woe,
The greedy Catalonian poverty.
For he or his must make provision so,
Forsooth, his overladen bark aboard,
That none shall further lading seek to stow.
His nature, niggard from a generous lord,
Should be supported by such retinue
As would give little heed to till or hoard. "—
"Since I believe the lofty joy that through
Me courses from your words, my lord and friend,
As to my own is patent to your view
Where all good has beginning and has end,
The gladder I; glad also that my wish, you
By looking into God can apprehend.
You make me blithe; but put aside the tissue
Of doubt whereby your words have veiled my mind:
How from sweet seed can bitter fruitage issue?"—
So I; and he to me: "If I can find
An answer setting truth in evidence,
Thou'lt have before thee what is now behind.
The Good that turns the whole and that contents
The Realm thou mountest, in these bodies vast
Makes active virtue of its Providence;
And Mind in Itself perfect has forecast
The natures not alone, but has in charge
Along with them their welfare first and last.
Whence whatsoever thing this bow discharge
Alights to predetermined end, like dart
Unerringly directed to the targe.
If not, the Heaven where thou a pilgrim art
Would so in its effects come short of goal
That they would not be beautiful, but thwart,
Which could not be unless the minds that roll
These stars were in default, defaulting too
For leaving them at fault, the Primal Soul.
Dost thou require more proof that this is true?"—
"Not so; it is impossible, I see,
That Nature weary in aught of need to do."—
"Now say, were't worse for man," continued he,
"Were he on earth unsocial?"—"It were so,"
I answered; "that is obvious to me."—
"And can he be so if he live below
Without diversity of offices?
If well your master write about it,—No!"—
So he by inference drew up to this:
"Therefore perforce the roots of what is done
Among you are diverse; whence not amiss
Is one born Solon, Xerxes one, and one
Melchisedech, another who would fly
Fanning the welkin, losing thus his son.
Revolving Nature well her craft doth ply
Stamping her seal on wax of mortal clay,
Nor takes account of hostel, low or high.
Whence it occurs that Esau falls away
At birth from Jacob, and Quirinus rose
From Sire so mean that sired him Mars, they say.
Careers of children would conform to those
Of their begetters, like to like in kind,
But that Divine prevision overthrows.
Now frontest thou the truth that was behind;
But that thou know my joy in thy behoof,
With corollary will I cloak thy mind.
If she find Fortune from herself aloof,
Ever will Nature, like another seed
Out of its region, come to evil proof.
Uniformity of ion with father would make social life impossible The corollary: an application of the lesson
And if the world down yonder would take heed
To what the rudiments of nature teach,
Following these, well would her people speed.
But ye pervert him to a priest, whose reach
Of nature fitted him for a belted knight,
And make a king of him who fain would preach:
Therefore ye wander from the way of right."— *Cunizza* 337 IX
A Great Lady And A Poet Prophesy
After thy Charles had thus, O Clemence fair, *Clemence the*
Enlightened me, he told the frauds, he said *ffkT*
That his posterity would have to bear; *speaker*
Adding: "Be silent till the years are sped;"
So that I naught can say, save that of right
Tears for these wrongs of yours shall yet be shed. And now the spirit of that holy light
Had turned toward the Sun, that plenteous
Fountain of good to all things requisite. Ah, souls deluded, creatures impious,
To wrench your hearts from such a blessed state,
Your brows tow'rd vanity directing thus! And lo! another of those splendors great *Cunizza da*
Drew nearer, while its will for my content *Romano*
Seemed from its features forth to radiate. The eyes of Beatrice were on me bent
As heretofore, and to the thing I sought
Gave me assurance of her sweet assent. "Soon be thy longing to fulfillment brought,
Blest spirit," said I, "and give me certitude
That in thyself I can reflect my thought."— Whence the new light, from deep beatitude
Wherein it had before been singing, said

In manner of one delighting to do good: "In that depraved Italian region spread *The March of*

Between Rialto sitting by the sea *Treriso*

And where the Brenta and Piava head, Rises a hill, not very loftily,

Whence there came down a flaming brand of yore,

Of that fair countryside the enemy. *Ezzelino (Inf.*

From one root with it I arose, and bore '

The name Cunizza, and here am overbowed

With splendor, since this star prevailed the more.

Remorse for sin But gladly conscience has to me allowed *f2f(Purgn* The cause of this mvlot, witbout dismay, *xxxi)* Though hard the saying, haply, to your crowd. *Folco (or Foul-*This precious jewel of pellucid ray

miles, first' ur heaven adorning and to me most near,

troubadour, tlien Left great renown, and ere it fade away *bishop* Shall be quintupled this centennial year. Ah, let man look to make him excellent

That the first life bequeath a second here!

So reason not the rabble turbulent

Which Tagliamento and Adige include,

Nor yet for being scourged are penitent.

But at the pool shall Padua with her blood

Soon stain the water of Vicenza red,

Since against duty harden they their mood.

One plays the lord and struts with lifted head

Where Sile and Cagnano lately met,

For trapping whom the snare is being spread.

A treacherous Feltro shall weep with bitter wailing yet op For treason of her impious pastor,—nay

Such caitiff never was in Malta set!

Capacious must the bucket be that day

Which of the Ferrarese shall hold the gore,—

And weary he who ounce by ounce should weigh,-

That this obliging priest will have to pour

To prove him factious; gifts like this are due

To match the life that land is noted for!

Above are mirrors—thrones as called by you—

Whence God in judgment doth upon us shine

So that seem good to us these sayings true."—

Herewith she held her peace, and gave me sign

Of being turned to other heed, whirled on

As heretofore along the dance divine.

The other joy, already known as one,

Swam into vision as a thing illumed,

Like a choice ruby smitten by the sun.

Folco of Marseilles 339

Brightness up there by rapture is assumed

Like laughter here on earth; but they who live

Below are shadowed as the soul is gloomed.

"All-seeing God," said I, "to thee doth give *Dante prays the*

Vision so inwardly with Him imbued, *30ul, l Fco io .... reply to his un*

Can no desire from thee be fugitive. *spoken question*

Therefore thy voice that gives beatitude

To Heaven, in concert with those fires divine

Who with their six wings make themselves a hood, Why does it leave me in desire to pine?

Surely I would not wait thy questioning

Could I indwell thy spirit as thou mine!"— "The widest vale of waters issuing," *The poetry of*

With these words his discourse to me began, *the map*

"Out of that sea the earth engarlanding, Between contrasting shores so wide a span

Spreads to the sun, that what was just before

Horizon, soon appears meridian. I was a dweller midway on that shore

Twixt Ebro and Magra which, with passage short

Bars to the Genoese the Tuscan door.

For rise and set of sun of one report

Would be Buggea' and my native town,

Whose blood once warmed the waters of the port. Folco they called me where my name's renown

Was noted, and this heaven is stampt by me

As on me once its influence rained down. More burned not Belus's daughter, balefully

Both to Sichaeus and Creiisa too,

Than I while it became my locks; nor she, The Rhodopeian maid who had to rue

Demophodn's deceit; Alcides not

When Iole into his heart he drew. *He can speak*

Yet nowise grieve, but smile we in this spot, *'eneTof his*

Not at the fault which ne'er returns to mind, *time of sin*

But at the Worth that ordered and forethought. *(Pur-» Here ends the shadow cast by Earth The golden florin with the stamp of the lily Profitable study of ecclesiastical law*

Here we behold the skill which has assigned

Itself so fair result,—discern the Good

Which with the world above atones mankind.

But that thou bear away in plenitude

Fulfilled those wishes native to this sphere,

With something further I perforce conclude.

Thou wouldest know who in this radiance here

Beside me scintillates, as in pure stream

A sunbeam tremulous in water clear.

Now learn that rests at peace within that beam

Rahab, and that our order, made her own,

Bears signet of her in degree supreme.

Into this heaven, where ends the shadowy cone

Cast by your earth, all other souls before,

She, in Christ's triumph, was received alone.

Meet was it in some heaven forevermore

Leave her as palm of the victorious hope

Achieved with one palm and the other; for

She lent her aid to the first glorious scope

Of Joshua upon the Holy Land,

That little stirs the memory of the Pope.

Thy City, the plantation of his hand

Who turned his back on his Creator first,

And from whose envy spring your woes, doth brand

And scatter far and wide that flower accurst

Whereby the shepherd into wolf is turned,

So that the sheep and lambs are all disperst.

The Gospel and the doctors great are spurned,

And only the Decretals studied well

For this,—as by their margin is discerned.

On this the Pope and cardinals do dwell:

Never on Nazareth is fixt their scan,

Where opened once his pinions Gabriel.

But holy parts of Rome, both Vatican

And other, chosen as the burial spot

Of the army whereof Peter led the van,

Soon shall be purged of the adulterous blot."— *The Devout Astronomer* 341

X

Heaven Of The Sun: Starry Garland Of Sages

Tlie primal and unutterable Worth

Gazing upon His Son's benignant face

With Love which both eternally breathe forth, M!ade all things that revolve through mind or space

With so much order that whoso looks aright

Can never want some image of His Grace.

Then, Reader, lift straight up with me thy sight *xhe intersection*

To the high wheels, where the two motions come *of the Equator _,..,,,,. and the Eclip* 1 o that point where they each on other smite, *tie (cf. Canto %,*

And there begin to enjoy His masterdom *37-39)*

Who loves His work within Him with such love

As never to withdraw His eye therefrom. Look, how that circle oblique, the bearer of

The planets, is at present branching thence

To appease the world that calls them from above; And were their road not bent, much influence

In Heaven would be unfruitful, and down here

Almost all virtue drained to impotence; Did it at less or greater angle veer

From the right line, deficiency were dire

Both up and down, in either hemisphere. Now on this foretaste of the heart's desire,

Remain, O Reader, on thy seat to brood,

For it will charm thee long before thou tire; I set it forth; do thou partake the food;

For I have made me scribe of such a theme

As claims the whole of my solicitude. The Minister of Nature all-supreme, *The Sun, to*

Who with the worth of Heaven the world is sealing *Vhich Dante ....,,. had impercep*

And measuring our time out with his beam, *tibly arisen*

Joined with that region named above, was wheeling

Along the spirals of that thoroughfare

Where daily earlier is his revealing;

And I along with him, but unaware

Of the ascending, more than one perceives

Thought in the mind before its advent there.

'Tis Beatrice herself who leading gives

From good to better, so immediately

Her act no vestige of duration leaves.

Within the sun where I had entered, see

How brighten spirits into recognition,

By light, not color, manifest to me!

What though I summon genius, art, tradition,

That splendor could be imaged nevermore,

But faith may see,—ah, let us crave the vision!

No wonder our low fancy cannot soar

To such an altitude, for never yet

Was eye that did not quail the sun before.

So bright was the fourth family, here set

By the High Sire, imbuing them with bliss,

Showing how He doth breathe, and how beget.

"Give thanks to Him," began now Beatrice,

"Thank Him who of the angels is the Sun,

Who by His Grace has lifted thee to this!"—

So ardently subdued to orison

Devoted, heart of mortal yet was not,

So eager for divine surrender none,

As at these words my own desire was hot; And so my love to Him was wholly plighted

That Beatrice was in eclipse forgot.

The smile of Nor this displeased her; but her eyes so lighted

Beatrice With laughter, that the splendor of her mien

Drew off to other things my mind united.

J For other living lusters, passing keen,

Centered upon us like a chaplet round,

Still sweeter in their voice than bright in sheen.

Tlie garland of The daughter of Latona thus enwound

souls is hke the Is seen at moments when so teems the air

halo around the ...

moon It holds the thread wherewith her zone is bound.

Manifold are the jewels dear and fair

In Court of Heaven, whence I returning come,

And none to carry them away could dare;

Of these the carols of those light were some:

Who takes not wing up thitherward to fly

May better ask for tidings of the dumb!

When, chanting so, those blazing suns on high

Had wheeled about us thrice, in radiance

Like stars the steadfast pole forever

nigh,
Ladies they seemed, who break not from the dance,
But stop in silence listening for the chord
Whereto their tripping steps again advance.
And from within one light came forth this word:
"Since radiance of Grace, enkindling so
True love to be the multiplied reward
Of loving, doth in thee so brightly glow,
Leading thee up that stairway where none save
To reascend can ever go below,—
Whoever should deny thee if thou crave
Wine from his flagon, would be free no more
Than water seeking not the level wave.
Thou wouldest know what blossoms now enflower
This garland, circling with blithe roundelay
The Lady beautiful, thy heavenly dower.
Lamb of the holy flock was I, whose way
Is shepherded by Dominic, and here
Fair is the fattening if they do not stray,
The brother to my dexter hand most near
Was Albert of Cologne, my master best,
And I was Thomas of Aquino there.
And if to name and number all the rest
Thou cravest of me, let thy look awhile
Circle up here along the garland blest.
That other splendor issues from the smile
Of Gratian,—one and the other court he lent
Such aid as Heaven with rapture to beguile.
Dancing the successive stanzas of the ballata Speaks the great
Dominican
theologian,
Thomas Aqui-
Albertus Magnus Gratian Peter Lombard Solomon Dionysius Orosiut Boethius Siger of Brabant, who lectured at Paris on Theology The Bride is throughout the Poem, of course, the Church
And of our chorus the next ornament
Was Peter, who gave Holy Church his mite
Like the poor woman of the Testament.
The fifth and loveliest of our circle bright
Breathes from such love that all the world below
Looks eagerly for tidings of its plight:
Within it is the lofty spirit, so
Imbued with wisdom that, if truth be true,
No second rose so much to see and know.
Next it the radiance of that taper view
Which, still in mortal flesh, did best divine
The angelic nature, and its service due.
Next in that little light see, smiling, shine
That advocate of Christian ages whose
Fair Latin edified Saint Augustine.
Now, if in sequence as my praise pursues
From light to light, thy mental eye is veering,
Thou cravest for the eighth, and canst not choose.
Therein the sight of Good Supreme is cheering
The holy soul who renders evident
The world's deceit to whoso well give hearing.
The body whence on earth it hunted went
Lies in Cieldauro, and from torture came
Into this peace and out of banishment.
And yonder see the fervent spirits flame
Of Isidore, of Bede, of Richard who
In contemplation more than man became.
This one, wherefrom to me returns thy view,
Shines from a soul to thought so dedicate
That death, he thought, too slowly on him drew:
This is the light of Siger, beyond date,
Who in the Street of Straw once lecturing,
Had enviable truths to demonstrate."—
Then as a chiming horologe doth ring
To rouse the Bride of God to matin-song
Unto the Spouse, His love soliciting,
The Holy Chime 345
Where one part draws another and thrusts along
With tintinnating note harmonious
Whence love in well-tuned spirit waxes strong,— The glorious wheel I saw revolving thus
And render voice to voice, in concord blending
With sweetness never to be known of us, Save in that place where joy is never-ending.

XI

The Canto Of St. Francis

O mad solicitude for mortal things,
Alas, how all the reasonings are vain
That make thee heavily beat down thy wings!
One played the clergyman, one followed gain,
One aphorisms of Hippocrates,
One strove by violence or craft to reign,
One throve by theft, one by juristic pleas,
One in the pleasures of the flesh enwound
Was wearing out, and one gave up to ease,
While I, set free from all that dreary round,
Aloft in Heaven, with Beatrice at hand,
So passing glorious a welcome found.
When every member of that circling band
Had gained the point where he had been before,
He stayed, as stays the taper in the stand.
And now I heard the former voice once more
Within that luster, while yet more intense
Became the brilliance of the smile it wore:
"As I am kindled in His effluence,
So, gazing into the Eternal Light,
I trace thy thoughts back to their rudiments.
Thou doubtest, and wouldst have me sift aright

My utterance, and in plain language bring
The matter to the level of thy sight
Where lately I said,—'Where is good fattening,'
And where I said, 'No second ever was,'
And here is need of clear distinguishing.
The Providence which rules the world with laws
Mysterious, so that every mortal eye
Is baffled ere it to the bottom draws
(So that to wed with Him who espoused her by
The blessed blood with loud proclaim, the Bride
Might go with greater nuptial loyalty,
And with more self-security beside),—
Ordained two princes who should both attend her,
One upon either hand to be her guide.
All fire seraphical was one defender;
The other one with wisdom all aflame,
Light to the world cherubic in its splendor.
Of one I mean to speak, for both may claim
Our praises, whichsoever one intending,
Because their labors had a single aim.
Between Topino and the stream descending
The hill that blest Ubaldo erewhile chose,
A fertile slope is from the mountain bending,
Whence hot and cold upon Perugia blows
Through Porta Sole; while behind it groan
Gualdo and Nocera their heavy woes.
Where drops the highland less abruptly prone,
A sun upon the world began ascent,
As somewhiles out of Ganges dawns our own.
Wherefore let any, when this place is meant,
Say not 'Ascesi,' which were short to say,
But, fitlier to speak, say 'Orient'!
He, from his rising not yet far away,
Began to give the world some handsel of
The comfort-giving virtue of his ray;
And, still a boy against his father strove
For such a Lady, men unbar the door
As willingly to death as to her love;
And in the spiritual court, before
His father's face, united with her stood,
Whereon from day to day he loved her more.
Reft of first husband she in widowhood
Till after the eleven hundredth year,
Contemned, obscure, awaited him unwooed;
Nor aught availed that men of her should hear
As with Amyclas found unterrified
By voice of him who struck the world with fear;
Francis
Dominic
One of the geographical descriptions which the Poet loves (cf. ix, 82-93) Assisi, supposed to be derived from "Ascesi? I rose He loved the Lady Poverty, but the father opposed the match Sealed by the
Church
Sealed by the
Holy Spirit
Nor aught availed her faith and courage tried,
So that, let Mary at the foot remain,
She mounted up where Christ was crucified.
But lest too enigmatic be my strain,
From my long parable shalt thou infer
That Poverty and Francis are these twain.
So blithe and so harmonious they were,
Their love, their wonder, their communion sweet
In all around set holy thoughts astir;
Whence venerable Bernard first thought meet
To go unshod, and after so great peace
He ran, and running blamed his lagging feet.
O wealth untold, good fruitful of increase!
Giles bares his feet, Sylvester his behind
The Bridegroom, such the Bride's peculiar grace.
Then with his Lady and with the house assigned,
All with the humble cord begirded now,
Went forth that Father and that Master kind;
Nor did he cravenly abase his brow
As son of Peter Bernardone, or feel
Cast down by strange contempt. But his stern vow
With regal dignity did he reveal
To Innocent the Pope, by whom was granted
For his religious order the first seal.
As multiplied the poor folk who had panted
To follow him whose life-work marvelous
Were better in the glory of Heaven chanted,
This Master-shepherd's holy zeal for us
Was sealed with crown of the Eternal Spirit
A second time through Pope Honorius.
Then preached he to the Soldan proud (to merit
The palm of martyrdom he would have borne)
Christ and his followers; but since to hear it
He found unripe that folk, who put to scorn
Salvation, and lest vain should be the quest,
Returned to harvest of the Italian corn;
'Twixt Tiber and Arno on the rocky crest
From Christ's own hand the final seal he won,
Borne for two years upon his limbs imprest.
When God, allotting him such benison,
Vouchsafed to draw him to the meed above
That he had gained by being a lowly one,
Unto his brethren, as right heirs thereof,
Bequeathed he all his wealth, his Lady dear,
Bidding them hold fidelity in love;
And from her breast the lofty spirit clear

Desired to pass to its own realm divine,
And for its body willed no other bier.
Judge now the worth of one who could combine
With him to pilot over the high seas
The Bark of Peter by the starry sign!
Such was our Patriarch; and they who please
To follow him, obeying his command,
Take on such freight of good commodities.
But now so greedy is become his band
For novel fodder, nothing can withhold
The sheep from roaming through wild pasture-land;
And these, the more by distant lure cajoled,
And truant more from him in field and wood,
Emptier of milk return they to the fold.
Some truly, boding evil likelihood,
Cleave closely to the Shepherd, but so few
That scanty cloth would furnish every hood.
Now, if I fail not of my meaning true,
If an attentive listener thou art,
And if thy memory the words review,
Will thy desire be satisfied in part,
For thou wilt see what plant they chip away,
And thou wilt take the reprimand to heart:
'Where is good fattening, if they do not stray.'"— *Sealed with the stigmata of tlte Crucified Ood Judge of the worth of my master Dominic, worthy colleague of such a saint Degenerate friars The greet Doctors of the Divine forming a double hah of circling and singing flames Speaks the Franciscan Doctor Seraphicus, St. Bonaventura, in praise of Dominic* xn
The Canto Of St. Dominic
Before the final cadence ceased to sound
Forth from the blessed spirits radiant,
Began the holy millstone to whirl round,
But of full circling something yet did want,
When now another ring around it fuses
And matches dance with dancing, chant with chant,
Chant that as passing far excels our muses,
Our sirens, in those mellow flutings blew,
As the first sunbeam by reflection loses.
As curve two bows the filmy cloud-rack through,
Both parallel in line and color, done
As Juno bids her maid the picture do,
The outer taking birth from the inner one
In hues reechoed like that wandering voice
Consumed by love, as vapor by the sun,
Giving mankind a signal to rejoice
That what God promised Noah shall abide,
Whence deluge nevermore the world destroys:
So the two garlands bright about us plied
Of roses an eternal coronal,
And the cuter to the inner so replied.
Then, when the dance and lofty festival
Both of the flaming lights and of the quires
Light beside light jocund and blithesome, all
Of one accord grew quiet, song and fires (Even as the eyelids cannot choose but shut
Or lift themselves again as will requires),
From one of the new lights a voice came out,
Which made me, needle to that pole, incline
My body round toward its whereabout;
And it began: "The Love that makes me shine
Prompts me to laud the other Leader great,
For whose sake here is spoken fair of mine.
Life of Dominic 351
Each with the other should be celebrate
That, as united they were militant,
Their glory may together radiate. The army of Christ, at cost exorbitant
Equipt anew, was moving slow of pace
Mistrustful, and too few the flag to plant, When He who kings it over time and space
Provided for His knighthood jeopardied,
Not for their worth, but only of His Grace; Coming, as said, to succor of His Bride
With champions twain, whose prowess and behest
Rallied the stragglers who had turned aside. Where first the winds breathe gently from the west
To open the fresh foliage of spring,
Whence smiles Europa being newly drest, Not far from where the waves are thundering
Wherein the sun, because his course is great,
Somewhile from man concealed is slumbering, There Calahorra sits, the fortunate,
Protected by the great escutcheon where
The lion doth succumb and subjugate. *Royal arms*
Therein was brought to birth the lover dear *$ CaMe*
Of Christian Faith, athlete in holiness,
Kind to his own, to enemies severe. Such life-power in his mother did possess
The infant spirit at its first creation
As to transform her to a prophetess. Fulfilled at holy font the declaration
Between him and the Faith, of sacrament
Wherein each pledged the other with salvation, The woman who for him had given assent
Beheld the admirable fruit, in dream,
Of him and of his heirs; and with intent That what he was he might in grammar seem,
A spirit went bearing the possessive word
Of his Possessor hence to christen him,
And called him Dominic: for I record
The story of the husbandman whom Christ *No other word* Chose for his aid in vineyard of the Lord.
rimTlriihth!? True messenger ne seemed and friend of Christ, *name of Christ* For the first love obtaining mas-

terdom *aid CeUewheTe)* In *m,* was tne first counsel given by Christ.
His nurse discovered him, awake and dumb,
Many a time recumbent on the ground,
As who should say, 'To this end am I come!'
0 thou, his father, Felix truly found!
And thou, his mother, verily art Joan,
If that interpretation be the sound.
Not as men now are spent for worldly boon
Authorities in Following Thaddeus and the Ostian,
medmne and jjut loving tne true manna, very soon *canon law (the T% i Decretals). Cf.* He grew a mighty teacher, and began *0ofctX8agC* About the *vhieysad* to be vigilant,
Where bleach the vines if bad the husbandman; And of the Seat that once to righteous want
Benigner was (not by her own offense *Boniface the* But that of her degenerate occupant!),
He begged,—not two or three for six dispense,
Not income of first vacant benefice
Not tithes, of God's own poor the competence,—
But leave against the world, that goes amiss,
To battle for the Faith, from seed whereof
Sprang twice twelve plants that garland thee with bliss.
Then, both with learning and with zealous love,
By apostolical authority,
Like torrent urged by fountain up above,
Dasht in among the shoots of heresy,
Smiting with greater vehemence, the more
Resistance proved to be refractory.
From him thenceforward various runnels pour
To irrigate the Catholic garden spot,
Making its bushes greener than before.
If such was one wheel of the Chariot
Wherein rode Holy Church for her defense
Over the field where civil strife was hot,
Clearly shouldst thou perceive the excellence
Of the other wheel, which Thomas had discussed
Before I came, with courteous eloquence.
But where the outmost rim was wont to thrust
Its pressure, is the track deserted,—so
That now there is the mold where was the crust.
His household, who set forward straight to go
With feet upon his prints, are turned again
So that they set the heel upon the toe;
And by the harvesting will soon be seen
How bad the tillage, when the tare will rue
Because it is excluded from the bin.
Yet, whosoever search our volume through
Leaf after leaf, might chance some page upon,
Reading, 'To what I was remain I true!'
But from Casal or Acquasparta none,
Whence come they who the writing so apply
That one lets loose, and draws it tighter one.
The effluence of Bonaventura am I,
From Bagnorea, who did evermore
Put last the left-hand care in office high.
Here, of the earliest of the barefoot poor,
Illuminato and Augustin, made dear
To God while circled with the cord of yore.
Hugh of Saint Victor is among them here,
And Peter Mangiadore, and Peter of Spain
Who in twelve books down there is shining clear,
The Prophet Nathan, Metropolitan
Chrysostom, Anselm, that Donatus who
Stooped to the first art, a grammarian;
Here is Rabanus, here beside me too
Shines the Calabrian abbot Joachim,
Gifted with spirit of prophetic view.
The two wheels of the Chariot of the Church A violent shift of metaphor! Dante, like Shakespeare, often defies the rules of the rhetoricians The household of Francis going back on their tracks Acquasparta relaxed the Rule of the order; Casale would have made it more rigid The other lights of the outer wreath of saints
In rivalry such Paladin to hymn,
Moved me with courtesy-enkindled mood
Friar Thomas, by the fair discourse of him,
And with me prompted all this Brotherhood."— XIII
St. Thomas Aquinas Gives A Lesson In Relativity
Let any fancy, who would fain not balk
At what I now beheld, and hold the sign Firm as a rock before him while I talk, Fifteen stars that in various quarters shine And so the sky with their effulgence steep,
They pierce the densest cloud-rack vespertine;
Fancy that Wain whereto the bosom deep
Of our own Heaven suffices night and morn,
Punctual to the wain-pole's mighty sweep;
Fancy thereto the opening of that horn
Commencing at the axle's point, whereby
The Primal Wheel is still revolving borne;
Fancy these made two clusters in the sky
Like that one which the daughter of Minos made
When, chilled, she felt herself about to die,—
One cluster with the other garlanded
And in such fashion whirling both the two
That one was leader and the other led:
Then will he have some shadow of the true
Star clusters, as in counter-dance they gleam,
Circling the point that I was rooted to,
Since these outstrip the things we see or dream,
As does that Heaven which is the swiftest o'er us
The moving of Chiana's oozy stream.
Not Bacchus, not Apollo was their

chorus,
But Persons three in being all divine,
In one, divine and human, to restore us.
The song and circle measured, turned in fine
To us those holy lusters, more by token
Passing from heed to heed with joy benign.
'Mid those concordant powers was silence broken
Then by that light whence the achievements of
The marvelous mendicant of God were spoken:
The double garland of saints; astronomical comparison (cf. the comparison beginning Canto xii) The horn is the constellation of the Little Bear See note about the Chiana, Inf. xxix St. Thomas Aquinas now explain his attribution of highest wisdom to Solomon Adam and Christ, bot/i direct creations of the Divine, must have been superior in wisdom to Solomon "A religious hymn breathing the sense of mystery that surrounds the Divine" Ton,oca)
"One sheaf being thrasht," the words fell from above,
"And that its grain is to the garner gone,
To beat the other beckons me dear love.
Thou thinkest of the bosom whence was drawn
The rib wherewith to fashion the fair face
Whose palate cost the world so dear a pawn,—
And of that lance-pierct bosom, by whose grace
Sin past and future was so compensated
That the atonement in the scale outweighs,—
Thou thinkest man may be illuminated
By no more light than was infused in those
By that same Power who both of them created:
And hence thy wonder when my story goes
That the Fifth Light with knowledge so profound
Was gifted, that 'No second ever rose.'
Open thine eyes now and behold how bound
Is thy belief with what I shall reply,
Both in the truth like center in the round.
That which can die, and that which cannot die,
Are nothing save the splendor of that Word
In love begotten by our Father High;
Because that Living Light which is transferred
So from its Source, it may not be undone
From it or from that Love which is their third,
Its mirrored rays by its own benison
In nine subsistencies together brings,
Itself eternally abiding One.
Thence passes through successive lowerings
To the ultimate potential elements,
Producing naught but brief contingent things;
And these contingent things I take in sense
Of things from seed engendered animal,
Or void of seed, through heavenly influence.
The wax of these, and that which molds it all,
Are variable, since less and more hath shined
Beneath the stamp the idea original;
Whence comes about that, after its own kind, The selfsame tree bears worse and better fruit,
And ye are born endowed with various mind.
Now were the wax exactly worked to suit,
Did stars supreme their influence assemble,
The luster of the seal were absolute;
But Nature mars,—wherein she doth resemble
The craftsman who about his labor goes
And keeps the knack, although his fingers tremble.
Yet if the fervent Love seal and dispose
Clear insight of the Primal Power, achieved
Perfection on that substance fully shows.
Dust of the ground, made worthy thus, received
Full animal perfection once therethrough;
Thus wrought upon, the Virgin once conceived.
So that I give my sanction to thy view
That human nature never yet has been,
Nor can be, such as in those persons two.
Now if no farther forward should I win,
'How then consider him without a peer?'
Upon this question would thy words begin.
But to see clearly what is not yet clear,
Think who he was and why petitioning
When he was bidden ask the guerdon dear.
Thus have I spoken but exhibiting
That he was king, and asked for plenitude
Of wisdom to become a worthy king,—
Not for the number of the multitude
Moving these spheres, nor if *necesse* chained
With a contingent ever could conclude,
Nor if prime motion is to be maintained,
Nor if in semicircle could be drawn
Triangle, save right angle be retained.
Whence, taking this with my discourse foregone,
A kingly prudence is that peerless prize
The shaft of my intention hits upon.
The application: warning against ignorant reading and map judgment) 'Donna Berta o Set Martino"
And if on 'rose' thou turnst discerning eyes,
Thou wilt perceive that it is spoken of
Kings,—who are many, and but few the wise.
Thus qualified, in what I said above
Agreement with thy view is found complete

As to our primal Sire and Him we love.
Let this be ever lead upon thy feet
To make thee like a weary man move slow
When *Yes* and *No* the inner vision cheat;
For he among the fools is very low
Who affirms or who denies in either kind
Without distinction of the *Yes* and *No,*
Since often to false bias are inclined
Opinions men too hastily attain,
And mere conceit then trammels up the mind.
His putting forth from shore is worse than vain
Who wanting skill goes fishing for the true,
Since as he went returns he not again;
Melissus gives the proof of this to view,
And Bryson and Parmenides, who reckt
Not of their goal, however fast they flew.
So with Sabellius, Arius, and each sect
Of fools who were as swords to Scripture pure,
Distorting features otherwise correct.
Let folk in judgment never be too sure,
As when into the field the peasant goes
To reckon up the ears not yet mature;
For I have seen beneath the winter snows
The wild brier rugged seem, and troublesome,
And then upon its summit bear the rose;
And once I saw a gallant vessel come
Straight over-seas, completing her emprise,
To perish entering the port at home.
Seeing one thieve, another sacrifice,
Let not Dame Joan and Gaffer John presume
To penetrate them with divining eyes,
For one may rise, the other fall to doom."— XIV
The Spiritual Body. Galaxy Of The Cross In Mars
From center unto rim, or back about,
Vibrates the water in a rounded vase,
As smitten from within or from without.
Into my mind came suddenly the case
That here I moot, soon as the effluence
Of glorious Saint Thomas held his peace.
Because of likeness in the incidence
Of his discourse and that of Beatrice,
Whom it pleased after him thus to commence:
"This man has need (yet does not tell you this
Either by voice or thinking) to pursue
Another truth to where it rooted is.
Inform him if the light which doth endue
Your substance with its blossom, will remain
As now it is forevermore with you;
And if it shall remain with you, explain
How ye can bear it and conserve your sight
When ye shall be made visible again. "—
Just as, impelled by urgence of delight,
They who are wheeling in the dance as one,
Lift up the voice and make the movement light,
So at the prompt devoted orison
The holy rings gave proof of rapture new,
Turning in wondrous choral unison.
Whoso laments our death down here, therethrough
To win new life above, did never see
Refreshment here of the eternal dew.
That ever-living One and Two and Three
Reigning in Three Two One beyond all date,
Unbounded and all-bounding Trinity,
Did each among those spirits celebrate
Three times, with such melodious utterance
As were fit meed for merit passing great.
The voice of Thomas had come from the rim; that of Beatrice flows back from the center The mystery of the glorified body after the raurrection
And where divinest was the radiance
Of the inner ring, a quiet voice replies
(To Mary such the Angel's voice perchance!):
"Long as the festival of Paradise
Shall have continuance, so long our love
Engarments us with such a radiant guise.
Its brightness will keep pace with movement of
Our zeal, and zeal with vision, which is full
As it has grace its proper worth above.
When with the glorious holy flesh the soul
Shall be reclothed, our personality
Will dearer grow, since wholly beautiful.
Thereby will wax the light, that largess free
Vouchsafed us by Supremest Excellence,
Light which enables us His Face to see;
Wherefore the vision needs must wax intense,
The fervor wax that from the vision came,
And wax the radiance proceeding thence.
But even as a firebrand, darting flame,
Is by its living glow victorious
So that its visible form remains the same,
So will this luster now enswathing us
Be vanquisht by the flesh, that now from sight
This many a day by earth is covered thus.
Nor can we weary of so great a light;
Strong shall the bodily organs be concerning
All that may minister to our delight."—
So ready and with such an eager burning
To cry "Amen" appeared to me both quires,
As for the mortal body showed their yearning,
Not for themselves alone, but for their sires
And mothers and perchance for others dear
Ere they became imperishable fires.
And lo! a luster all around, of sheer
Surpassing splendor dawned upon the view,
Like an horizon that is growing clear.

.Ajad. even as at early nightfall, new
Gleamings begin to spot the sky again,
While true appears the vision, yet not true,
Methought up there, beginning to grow plain,
Novel existences, a circling host
Outside of those circumferences twain.
O very sparkling of the Holy Ghost,
Smiting mine eyes with such an instant flare
They might not brook it, in the luster lost!
But Beatrice showed so smiling and so fair,
It must be left with visions that elude
The memory, which cannot follow there.

Therefrom mine eyes, resuming aptitude

To lift their lids, showed me with her alone
Lifted to loftier beatitude.

That I was lifted to a higher zone

Was told me by that star's enkindled smile
Which ruddily beyond the common shone.

In that deep language of the heart whose style
Is one in all, to God I here addrest
Oblation for the gift bestowed the while;

Nor yet was consummated in my breast
The sacrifice, before I knew the prayer
To be propitious and with favor blest,

For with a rubeate glory past compare

Showed splendors forth, within two rays of light,
Such that I cried: "O Sun that makes them fair!"

As, 'twixt the two poles of the world, gleams white
The Galaxy with less and greater stars,
Putting in doubt the very erudite,

Thus, constellated in the depth of Mars,
Fashioned those rays the venerated sign
Formed in a round by crossing quadrant bars.

Here conquers memory all wit of mine:

Because that Cross was lamping so with Christ
I cannot find similitude condign;
The smile of Beatrice always marks the rise into a higher sphere Thervddy Heaven of Mars
Imagine the "Milky Way" in the form oj a Cross For the rime cf. Canto xii Hymn of the
Warrior-Saint)
Because the
eyes of Beatrice
reflect the
Divine (cf.
Purg. xxxi,
the closing
strain)

But whoso takes his cross and follows Christ
Shall yet forgive me what I leave unsaid,
Seeing that dawnlight flashing with the Christ.

From arm to arm, and between base and head,
Lights were in motion, brightly scintillant,
Passing and counterchanging as they sped.

So swift and slow and level and aslant

Are seen here, ever altering their mien,
The atomies of bodies long or scant

Adance upon the ray that cleaves the screen
Of shadow often, which for their defending
Men cause by handicraft to intervene.

And, as the harp or violin, with blending

Of many chords, sweet tinkling makes to him
Who hears the music without comprehending,

So from the lights there shining bright or dim
Gathered along the Cross a melody
That raptured me, oblivious of the hymn.

High laud it was,—so much was clear to me,
Because "Arise and conquer" was the strain
Which still I heard uncomprehendingly.

So charmed was I therewith that until then

Naught had there ever been that could impose
On me the fetters of so sweet a chain.—

Perchance too bold appear such words as those,
Disparaging the charm of those fair eyes
Gazing wherein my longing has repose.

But whoso comprehends how as they rise
Those living seals of all things loveliest
Augment, nor had I turned to that emprise,

May excuse me from the accusation, stressed.
But to excuse me, thus my truth approving;
For here is not cast out the rapture blest,

Becoming ever purer upward moving.

XV

Dante's Ancestor Begins The Sketch Of The Men And Manners Of Old Florence

Benignant will, resolved into the blest

Love whence forever benefactions flow, As greed in wicked will is manifest, Laid silence on that tuneful lyre, and so Withheld those holy chords from sounding on,
That Heaven's right hand now twitches, now lets go.
How can be deaf to righteous orison

Those Beings who, to open wide the door
For my petition, paused in unison?

'Tis right he should eternally deplore

Who, out of love for what does not abide,
Forfeits that other love forevermore.

As through the pure and tranquil eventide
A flash is seen from time to time to race,
Setting the calmest eyelids staring wide,

Appearing like a star that changes place,

Save that, where first enkindled is its light
Nothing is missed, and it goes out apace,—

So shot from the arm extending to the right
To bottom of the cross, a star of them
That make the constellation there so bright;

Downward it ran along the radiant

stem
Like fire in alabaster shining through,
Nor from the fillet once broke forth the gem.

Such love the shade of old Anchises drew,
If credit we our poet passing great,
When in Elysium his son he knew.

"0 kinsman mine! Grace incommensurate
Upon thee shed! to whom, as unto thee,
Was ever opened twice the Heavenly gate?"—

So spake that light; whence thereto eagerly
I turned,—then to my Lady,—in such wise
That from both quarters awe came over me;

The light of Dante's greatest ancestor falls down the shaft of the mystic cross like a 'shooting star" The Great Book in which he reads, the Mirror in which they gaze, are images of the Divine Mind

For such a smile was glowing in her eyes
That, with mine own, methought I touched the bound
Both of my grace and of my Paradise.

Thereafter, blithe of look and blithe of sound,
That soul to salutation added speech
Past my conception, it was so profound;

Of choice concealed he not what he would teach,
But force perforce, because the lofty sense
So overshot the mark of mortal reach.

But when the bow of burning love less tense
Became, and his discourse came down and stood
Upon the plane of our intelligence,

The first expression that I understood
Was: "Benediction on Thee, Trine and One,
For guerdoning my kinsman with such good!"—

"A grateful and long fast," he followed on,
"From reading the Great Book where black on white
Is set down ineffaceably, my son,

Hast thou now satisfied within this light
I hail thee from, thanks to her favor who
Clad thee with plumage for the lofty flight.

Thou deemest that thy thought to me flows through
From the First Cause, even as from unity,
If that be known, the five and six to you,

Not asking who I am, nor why in me
Appears a gratulation more elate
Than elsewhere in this jocund company.

Thou deemest true: in this life small and great
Are gazing in that Mirror whence, before
Thou thinkest, thy reflections emanate.

But that the Holy Love mine eyes adore
In vigil never broken, hunger-spent
With sweet desire, may be fulfilled the more,

O let thy voice, secure, glad, confident,
For will and yearning find the fitting word
Whereto is predetermined my consent. "—

Thereon I turned to Beatrice, who heard
Before I spake and gave assent, whereby
The growing wings of my desire were stirred.

"When dawned on you the Prime Equality,
Love and intelligence for each of you
Became of equal poise,"—so answered I;

"Because the Sun that lit and warmed you through
Holds in its heat and light such balance fit
That all comparison falls short of true.

But mortal wing of will and wing of wit,
For reason well apparent to your sight,
Fail of the balanced pinions requisite.

Whence I, who with the heart alone requite
Thy dear paternal welcome, feel my lame
Mortal disparity of will and might.

I do entreat thee, living topaz-flame,
Set as a gem upon this jewel choice,
To satisfy my craving with thy name. "—

"O leaf of mine, who made me even rejoice
Expecting thee, thy root behold in me!"—
Beginning thus, replied to me the voice;

Then said: "That soul who gave thy family
The surname, and has round the Mountain gone
On the first terrace, a long century,

Was thy great-grandfather, and was my son:
Befits that respite thou for him bespeak
From his long travail, with thy orison.

Florence, encircled by her wall antique,
Whence tierce and nones are tolling evermore,
Lived peaceable and temperate and meek.

Her arm no clasp, no crown her forehead bore,
No silken petticoat, with girdle gay
More tempting to the eye than she who wore.

Not yet did little daughter's birth dismay
The father; not too early did they mate,
Nor yet was dowry ruinous to pay.

Dante humbly urges the inadequacy of mortal wit to discourse with a being in whom deed balances desire The father of Dante's greatgrandfather tells of the social condition of Florence in the eleventh century Hills from which travelers from the north got the first view of Rome and of Florence Great citizens in their day (cf. Inf. xvi, 37, and next canto) A woman of doubtful reputation, and a man whom Dante detested

No house was then of children desolate;
Not yet Sardanapalus came to show
What in a chamber he can perpetrate.

Not yet outflown was Monte Mario
By your Uccelatoio,—which as outflown
In soaring up, shall be in falling low.

I saw in belt of skin and clasp of bone
Bellincion Berti, and his lady quit
The mirror with complexion still her own;
I saw the Nerli and the Vecchio fit
The leathern jerkin with good countenance,
With spindle and with flax their ladies sit.
0 happy women! each yet in advance
Sure of her burial, and none beguiled
Of comfort in her bed because of France.
One, keeping watch above her cradled child,
Would soothe it with the babbling idiom
Whereto the fathers and the mothers smiled;
And one, the thread from distaff drawing home,
Gathered her brood and prattled fables how
Came Trojans to Fiesole and Rome.
A marvel then Cianghella's brazen brow,
Or Lapo Salterello, as complete
As Cincinnatus and Cornelia now.
To life of citizen in house and street
So fair and quiet, to so great a fame
For neighbor loyalty, to home so sweet,
My mother gave me, calling Mary's name;
And so, within your ancient Baptistry,
Christian and Cacciaguida I became.
Moronto and Eliseo brothered me;
My Lady came from Valley of the Po,
Whence was thy surname handed down to thee.
1 followed Kaiser Conrad then, with so
Good service that he belted me a knight,
So much my prowess made his favor grow.
Beneath his banner followed I to fight
That ill-famed law whose folk usurp control,
To pastors' shame, of what is yours by right.
There disentangled by those caitiffs foul Was I from the delusive world, whose quest
Infatuate debases many a soul,
Vrid came from martyrdom unto this rest."—

Second Crusade, preached by St. Bernard (1147) Dante addresses his ancestor as if he were royal ("you" instead of "thou") Modem Florence is the city oj the Baptist, as the ancient ims the city oj Mars XVI

"old, Unhappy, Far-off Things"
O petty our nobility of blood!
If thou prompt men to make their boast of thee
Down here, where faints our yearning for the good, Never shall this seem wonderful to me,
For where desire is not perverted, yea
In Heaven itself, I felt such vanity.
In truth, thy cloak so quickly shrinks away,
That, add we not a frequent piece thereto,
Time with the shears goes round it day by day. With *You,* which Rome at first permitted, *You,*
Wherein her children now least persevere, Proudly began I my discourse anew,
Whence Beatrice, a little distant here,
By smiling called to mind that dame who coughed At first recorded fault of Guenevere.
"You are my Father," so began I soft,
"You fill me for discourse with courage high, You lift me far above myself aloft.
So many rivulets are pouring joy
Into my heart that happy is my tongue
Seeing I can bear and not be rent thereby.
Tell then, beloved root whence I am sprung,
Who were your forebears, what the years foregone
That signalized themselves when you were young. Tell me about the sheepfold of Saint John,
What were the numbers and who were the folk Within it who the highest places won?"—
As if by breathing of the wind awoke
Flame in a coal, so did I see that blaze
Kindle at the caressing words I spoke,
And growing ever fairer to my gaze,
With sweeter accent gentlier it said,
But in no dialect of nowadays: *Causes of Moral Decline of Florence* 369
"From the first *Ave* to that childing-bed
Whereon my mother, now ensainted, through
Delivering of me was comforted,
Five hundred times and fifty and thirty drew
This circling fire to its own Lion apace,
Beneath his paw to kindle up anew.
My sires and I were native to that place
Where the last ward first intersects the course
Of the hot runner in your annual race.
Enough about my elders this perforce:
For as to whence they came and who they were,
Silence is more becoming than discourse.
All those at that time competent to bear
Weapons, the Baptistry and Mars between,
Numbered a fifth of them now living there.
But the community, where intervene
Campi, Certaldo, and Figline now,
Pure to the humblest artisan was seen.
O how much better let such neighbors plow
Around Galluzzo, and let your border lie
At Trespiano, rather than allow
Their entrance, so to be offended by
The stench of Aguglion, and Signa's clown,
Who has for jobbery so sharp an eye.
Were folk who most on earth have fallen down
Not stepmother to Caesar, but instead
Benignant, like true mother to her son,
One, made a Florentine by truck and trade,
Would have turned back to Semifonte again,
Where went about his grandsire begging bread.
Still would the Counts on Montemurlo reign,
The Cerchi be in Acone's parish still,
Perchance the Buondelmonte on Greve's plain.
When mingled populations overfill
The city, evermore begins its woe,
As added victual makes the body ill.

580 x 686+
(the number of
our days re-
quired for the
revolution of the
planet Mars)
gives about 1091
as the birth-year
of Cacciaguida
The city lay between the Church of St. John and the Ponte Vecchio with the mutilated statue of Mars That is to say, if the clergy had kept hatids of

And the blind bullock falls more headlong low
Than the blind lamb, and more one sword will cleave,
And often deeper than the five will go.
If Luni and Urbisaglia thou perceive,
How they have gone, and likewise pass away
Chiusi and Senigallia, to believe
That in like fashion families decay
Will seem opinion neither strange nor new,
Seeing that even cities have their day.
All your affairs are mortal, even as you,
The very brevity of life concealing
In some the creeping steps of death from view;
And as the lunar heaven, forever wheeling,
Covers and bares incessantly the shore,
So fickle Fortune is with Florence dealing.
Hence what I tell should seem no fable-lore
Concerning the renowned Florentines
Whose fame through lapse of time is known no more.
I saw the Hugos, saw the Catellines,
Filippi, Greci, Ormanni, Alberichi there,
Illustrious citizens in their declines,
And saw, as mighty as they ancient were,
With one of La Sannella, of Area one,
Ardinghi and Bostichi and Soldanier.
Above the gateway newly weighed upon
By felony so heavy in its shame
That from the bark shall soon be jettison,
The Ravignani Dwelt then the Ravignani, from whom came
dArghAhe good Count Guido down, and whoso to this hour
Gualdrada from Has taken lofty Bellincione's name.
Mtincione jje of Lft P,. wisely fc power
Already, and the Galigaio claimed
Sword-hilt and pummel gilt in hall and bower.
Greatly the pale of Minever was famed,
Sacchetti, Giuochi, Fifanti, and Barucci,
And Galli,—and others by the bushel shamed.
Origin of the Factions 371
Che parent stock whence budded the Calfucci
Was great already, and to curule chair
Already drawn Sizii and Arrigucci. *h,* mighty did I see them who despair
Because of their own pride! and the Balls of Gold
In all her prowess made our Florence fair. So likewise did the ancestors of old
Of those who, when your see is vacant, find Fat profit by abiding in the fold.
That haughty breed, so dragon-fierce behind
The fugitive, but let your teeth be seen
Or purse belike, seem lambs, they grow so kind, "Was on the rise, although from people mean,—
Whence Ubertin Donato felt disgrace
When his wife's father made them kith and kin. Down from Fiesole to market-place
Had gone now Caponsacco,—Judah there
And Infangato, burghers in good grace. Incredible, yet true, what I declare:
The little circuit had an entrance way
Called after them whose emblem is the Pear. All wearers of the fair insignia
Of the great Peer, whose name and valor grim
The feast of Thomas calls to mind today, Knighthood received and privilege from him;
Though with the populace today unite
That man who guards the scutcheon with a rim. *Giano della* Gualterotti and Importuni were at height;
And had they for new neighbors suffered dearth *The mmei*
More tranquil would the Borgo be tonight. *whose murder*
The house from which your tears have had their birth, *%umddmonte*
Because its just resentment killed your joyance *for slighting*
And with the blood of many stained the earth, *is /Ae tradi.* Was honored in itself and its alliance: *Hand origin of*
O Buondelmonte, by what evil daring
G a7Mj
Didst flee at others' prompting its affiance! *Ghibelline The old banner showed a white lily in a red field; the Ouelfs reversed the colors. See the. plates of the tu,o shields*
Glad would be many who are now despairing,
If God had to the Ema relegated
Thyself, when first toward the City faring.
But meet it was that Florence consecrated
A victim, while her last peace was prevailing,
To that bridge-warding marble mutilated.
With folk like these, nor yet were others failing,
Did I see Florence in such deep repose
That she had no occasion yet for wailing;
I saw her people glorious with those,
And just, so that the Lily never stood
Reversed upon the lances of her foes,
Nor dyed vermilion yet by party feud.
"— *Note*

It has not seemed desirable to fill the margins with references and explanations. Those interested in the history of old Florence will know where to look. For biographical information and anecdote Toynbee's Dictionary is the obvious repertory. The reader will find profit in looking up Bellincion Berti and his daughter, the good Gualdrada (Inf. xvi, 37). The historical student soon perceives that the viewpoint in these cantos is very much that of an old Tory. The new families, like the Cerchi, were often useful citizens. And the institution of the guilds is nowhere here referred to, although economically, politically, socially, even intellectually, of primary importance and immeasurable influence.

Autobiography of Dante 373 XVII

Dante's Exile And Justification

As who makes fathers chary of undue
Promise to children, questioned Clymene
If what he heard against himself was true,
Even such was I, and such perceived to be
By Beatrice and by the Holy Lamp
Who previously had changed his place for me.
Then said my Lady to me: "Do not damp
The flame of thy desire, but let it soar
Well making manifest the inward stamp;
Not that thy words may make our knowledge more,
But that thou mayst acquire the habitude
To tell thy thirst that we for thee may pour."—
"Dear parent stock, raised to such altitude
That, as to earthly minds is evident
No triangle may two obtuse include,
Thus do contingent things before the event Exist for thee, still gazing where take head
All times together with the present blent;
While in the company of Virgil led
Up and along the spirit-healing slope
And down throughout the region of the dead,
I heard discourses grievous in their scope
Touching the remnant of my life, although
Well squared against the blows of Chance by Hope:
Wherefore my will were well content to know
What fortune is approaching to molest;
For bolt foreshadowed strikes a lighter blow."—
So to that selfsame light that had addrest
Beforehand me, I said as willed to say
By Beatrice, and mine own will confest.
Not with blind riddles which in former day
Ensnared the credulous, ere yet was slain
The Lamb of God who takes our sins away,

Pope Boniface
Eighth
Dante's fellowexiles, so unworthy that he shakes them off

But with clear utterance and language plain
That fatherly affection made reply,
In his own smile withdrawn and shown again:
"Contingency, which is embounded by
The volume of your matter, is beheld
All pictured forth before the Eternal Eye,
Yet not thence of necessity compelled,
More than the vessel down the current steering
Is by the mirror in the eye propelled.
Therefrom comes, even as comes upon the hearing
Sweet organ music, to my sight the course
Of time already now for thee preparing.
As through stepmother proof to all remorse
Hippolytus from Athens fled of old,
So out of Florence shalt thou go perforce.
Already this is willed and sought,—nay hold
It good as done by him who plans thy fall
Where every day the Christ is bought and sold.
The hue and cry will hound as usual
The party wronged; and yet shall vengeance give
A witness to the truth dispensing all.
Thou art to forfeit as a fugitive
All held most dear: of arrows thou must bear,
This first the bow of banishment lets drive.
Thou shalt make proof what salt and bitter fare
Is bread of others, and what toils attend
The going up and down another's stair.
But what will heaviest thy shoulders bend
Will be the senseless company malign
With whom thou wilt to such a pass descend,
Who, ingrate all and maddened, will combine
In fury against thee; but thereafter soon
Their forehead will be red for it, not thine.
Their brutishness will in their very own
Deeds be avoucht, nor will thy fame be blurred
In having made a party all alone.

Dante in Exile 375 ?irst hospitality shall be conferred
On thee by kindness of the Lombard great, *Bartholomew*
Who on the ladder bears the sacred bird, *tntof'vZona* WTio will to thee be so considerate *and Can*
That of the wish and boon between you two, *fcTM£ della*
First will come that which else is granted late. Beside him shalt thou see that hero who
Took from this mighty star at birth such mold That his emprise will be renowned therethrough. His worth the nations do not yet behold
Because his age is tender,—years but nine These wheeling spheres have round about him rolled. But ere the Gascon cunning undermine *Clement V and*
The noble Henry, sparkles of his worth *Henry VU* In scorn of lucre and of toil shall shine.
So his magnificence shall yet show forth,
His foes will not be so predominant
That they could keep report of it from birth.
On him and on his favors do thou plant
Thy trust; through him shall many change degree,
Altering state, both rich and mendicant.
And bear thou written in thy memory
Of him, but tell it not,"—and he revealed
Things past believing, even of those who see.
Then added: "Son, these glosses may be sealed
To what was told thee; snares are waiting thus
Behind few circles of the spheres concealed.
Yet be not of thy neighbors envious,

Seeing thy future life will long outlast *Dante's fame*

The forfeit of their deeds perfidious. "— *predicted*

Soon as that holy soul to silence passed, Showing the pattern had been woven above

The web whereof myself the warp had cast,

Did I begin like one misdoubting of

His course, who craves advice from one of those

That, seeing, do correctly will, and love: *Were it not prudent to be "a timid friend of truth"? "lascia pur grattar dovi la rogna" Dante must speak out*

"Well see I, Father, how my time of woes

To deal me such a buffet spurs along

As is the heavier when one heedless goes;

Whence it is good with foresight to be strong,

That, though bereft me be the dearest prize,

I forfeit not the others by my song.

Down through the world of bitter tears and cries,

And up the mountain side from whose fair height

Uplifted me my Lady with her eyes,

And afterward through Heaven from light to light,

Have I learned that which will, if I respeak,

For many have disrelish infinite;

And if to truth I prove a friend but weak,

I tremble lest my fame the forfeit pay

With those who are to call this time antique."—

At this the light wherein the treasure lay

Which I had found there, flasht with such suffusion

As golden mirror in the solar ray.

"A conscience darkened,"—then he made conclusion,—

"With self-shame, or another's, this being sung

Will wince indeed at every harsh allusion.

Nathless away be all dissembling flung,

And be thy vision wholly manifested,

And let them wince who feel their withers wrung;

For though thy word be grievous when first tasted,

It will forever after leave behind

A vital nourishment, if well digested.

This cry of thine shall do as doth the wind

That buffets most the topmost mountain crown:

Which no small pledge of honor wilt thou find.

For this among these Wheels, and up and down

The Mountain, and within the Vale of Woe,

Are shown thee spirits only of renown;

For restive is the hearer's mind, and so

Recalcitrant to faith, it holds aloof

From instances buried its ken below,

And from all else except explicit proof."— *Illustrious Souls in the Cross of Mars* 377 XVIII

How The Souls Form The Mystic Symbol Of Justice In The Temperate Star Of Jove

Now in his inward thought with joy replete

Was that blest Mirror, and I savored mine

By seasoning the bitter with the sweet; And the Lady leading me to the Divine

Said: "Shift thy thought to see my link unbroken

With him who lightens every load malign."— Thereat I turned to look at the fond token *The consoling*

Of my Consoler, and what love I viewed " *Beatrice*

In the holy eyes is here perforce unspoken, Partly that words would be misunderstood.

Partly that memory is unreturning

If others guide not to such altitude.

This only can I tell that point concerning,

That, rebeholding her, my own affection

Grew fetterless and free from other yearning. While the Eternal Joy without deflection

Rayed upon Beatrice, and mirrorwise

From her fair face appeased me by reflection, Subduing me with light of smiling eyes,

"Turn round and hearken," thus to me she said,

"Not in mine eyes alone is Paradise!"— As sometimes in the visage here is read

The inclination, if of so much force

That the whole soul thereby is riveted, So turning to my great progenitor's

Sanctified radiance, the wish I found

Yet somewhat further with me to discourse. Then he began to speak: "In this fifth round

Of branches on the Tree that from the crest

Sends life-sap down and never sheds a frond, Are souls who, ere they came among the blest,

Were in the world below of so great fame

Could noble Muse no richer theme request.

Observe the arms o' the Cross, and those I name

Will at the signal in such mode proceed

As in the cloud its fulminating flame. "—

I saw along the Cross a luster speed

At name of Joshua: to ear and eye

The word did not anticipate the deed.

And at the name of Maccabaeus high

Another spiral whirling flasht amain,

And that which whipt the top was holy joy.

Likewise for Roland and for Charlemain

Did my enraptured gaze two lights pursue,

As eye doth after flying falcon strain.

Afterward William drew, and Renouard drew,

And great Duke Godfrey drew mine eye by fire

Along that Cross, and Robert Guiscard too.

Then mingling with the other lights, the Sire

Whose spirit had discoursed with me made known

His artistry among the heavenly quire.

To my right hand I turned me at that tone,

My duty to behold in Beatrice

Either by language or by gesture shown,
The smile of And all her past and recent wont at this
Beatrice mark-Her look outrivaled, with so bright a ray
mg ascent to .." the Heaven of Her eyes were shmmg, and so full of bliss.
Jupiter nd as DV greater comfort in essay
Of righteous doing, man becomes aware
Of virtue waxing in him day by day,
So, wheeling in a wider circle there,
A heaven of more extended scope I knew,
Seeing that miracle become more fair.
For now a shift of color met my view,
As when a woman's countenance, oppressed
With blushful shame, resumes its pallid hue,
Such, when I turned about was manifest
Dawning in the white star of temperance,
The sixth that had received me to its breast.
I saw within that Jovial radiance
The flying sparks of love that there abound
Shaping our language out before my glance.
As birds, rejoicing in their pasture ground,
Start up together from a river dell
And gather in a flock, now long, now round,
So holy creatures in the lights that dwell,
Were flitting and were chanting, fashioning
Their flock to figures,—D and I and L.
First sang they, to their own notes fluttering,
Then, having fashioned one or the other sign,
Would hold their peace awhile and stay their wing.
O Pegasea, glorifier divine
Of human wits, their life to render long,
As towns and kingdoms they, by aid of thine,
Brighten me with thyself to tell in song
Their shapes as I deciphered them in Heaven,
In these brief verses let thy breath be strong!
These then displayed themselves in five times seven
Vowels and consonants: I noted down
The members as they seemed by utterance given.
DILIGITE JUSTITIAM, first noun
And verb of all the figure were enscrolled,
QUI JUDICATIS TERRAM, followed on.
These in the M of the fifth word did hold
Such settled order there, that Jupiter
Seemed to be silver patterned out with gold.
And other lights I saw descending where
The apex of the M appeared their goal,
Chanting, I think, the Good thatdraws them there.
Then, as by stirring of a burning coal
Innumerable sparks are upward sped,
Prophetic omens to the simple soul,
So thence thousands of lights seemed spirited
To mount aloft, some lower and some higher,
By their enkindling Sun distributed;
"Love Justice, you that are judge) of the earth" The medieval capital M resembles the Florentine lily, the high medial upward point of which, slightly changed, gives the figure of an heraldic Eagle
And lo! when settled into place each flier,
I saw an Eagle as to head and breast
Delineated by that patterned fire.
He there who paints has none to guide, but best
Guideth Himself, and from Him we divine
The secret of the molding of the nest.
The other blessed flock, content to twine
A lily flower at first upon the M,
With a slight flutter filled out the design.
Sweet star, what jewels, and how many of them,
Informed me that our Justice is the birth
Of that sixth heaven whereof thou art the gem!
Wherefore I pray the Mind wherein thy worth
And motion start, that He take note whence come
The fumes that dim thy radiance on earth;
That he once more be wroth with all and some
Who buy and sell within the Temple-door
Built round with miracles and martyrdom.
O heavenly host on whom I gaze, implore
For them who still are here on earth, each one
Misled by ill example!—War of yore
Was waged by dint of sword, but now 'tis done
Merely withholding, now here, and now there,
The bread the pitying Father grudges none.
But thou whose writ is only made to tear,
Reflect that Peter and Paul are living yet,
Who died for the vineyard thou art stripping bare.
Well mayst thou urge: "I have my heart so set
On that ascetic who in royal hall
Was danced into the martyr's coronet,
That I know not the fisherman nor Paul."— *Yearning to Probe Divine Justice* 381 XIX
The Discourse Of The Symbolic Eagle
The image fashioned by the engarlanding
Souls who in sweet fruition took delight,
Stood fair before me, spreading either wing. Each seemed a little ruby where a bright
Sunbeam appeared so burningly to sink
As to Same back again upon my sight. And what I now am bound to tell, by ink
Was never traced, by ear was never heard,
Nor entered into heart of man to think: For lo! I heard and saw that beaked Bird

Give voice to / and *MY,* though understood

Were *we* and *our* as men conceive the word. So it began: "Through being just and good

Raised am I to that glory far transcending All mortal yearning for beatitude,

And left remembrance of my great intending

Upon the earth, but wicked people there

Follow the story not, although commending."— As many an ember makes us feel the glare

Of one sole heat, so rang one melody

From many loves out of that image fair: Whereon I prayed: "O flowers perpetually *Dante prays*

Blooming from Joy eternal, breathing forth *fait* jXn

Your odors that one fragrance seem to me, So breathing, banish from me the great dearth

Which makes me for so long in hunger pine,

Finding not any food for it on earth. Well know I that, though Justice the divine

Be in another Heavenly kingdom glassed,

Yours looks without a veil on the design. Ye know how eagerly do I forecast

The hearing, and ye know what is that doubt

Which is within me such a long-drawn fast."—

As from the hood the falcon issuing out

Conceals not her desire, but makes her fair,

Lifting her head and fluttering about,

So in my sight became that emblem, where

Praises of Grace Divine were interwound

With songs familiar to the happy there.

Then it began: "Who turned the compass round

The world, and Who in its circumference

Set much both clear to sight and too profound,

Could not in all the Universe condense

His Worth so far but that His infinite

Wisdom remained in overplus immense.

In proof whereof, behold that first proud Wight

Among all creatures supereminent,

Falling unripe, through not awaiting light;

Therefore too scanty a recipient

Appears each lesser nature for that Good

Which has no bound but by self-measurement.

From this it follows that our sight, which should

Out of that Mind supernal radiate

Wherewith all things whatever are imbued,

Can by its nature have no power so great

But that its origin sees far afield

Beyond the narrow limit of your date.

Therefore no vision to your world revealed

Can plumb eternal Justice to the ground,

Just as the ocean to your eye is sealed;

Awhile from shore ye may the bottom sound,

And out of soundings in the unplumbed sea

We know it still is there, though never found.

Save from the never-clouded Source, may be

No light, but rather everywhere is shade,

Venom and shadow of carnality.

Now amply is the covert open laid

That kept the living Justice from thy sight,

Whereof thou hast so frequent question made.

Virtuous Heathen 383

'For,' saidest thou, 'on Indus-bank a wight *The problem:*

Is brought to birth, where none is to direct *ri7uous heathen*

To Christ, nor who may read of Him, nor write, *be condemned?* And all his acts and wishes are correct

As far as human reason may perceive,

Whether in word or life without defect; Faithless he dies, nor baptism can receive:

What is this justice which condemns the man?

What is his fault if he do not believe?'

Now who art thou to mount the bench and scan,

A thousand miles from what thou wouldst discuss,

With thy short vision reaching but a span? Surely for him who cavils with me thus,

Were not the Scripture over you, the food

For subtle questioning were marvelous. O earthly animals! O spirits rude!

Never the Primal Will was self-betraying,

Nor altered from Itself the Supreme Good. Weighed is your human justice with Its weighing,

By no created goodness is It led,

Rather from It created good is raying. "— As wheels the mother-stork just overhead

When she has given her nestlings all their fill,

And they look up toward her comforted, So thither was my brow uplifted still,

And circling so the blessed image flew

On wings propelled by force of many a will. Wheeling it chanted, adding thereunto:

"My notes thou hearest heeding not their sense,

So mortals by Eternal Justice do."—

When quiet was that glowing effluence

Of Holy Ghost, still in the heraldry

That gained the Romans world-wide reverence, *Thf stormv* , *# voice again*

"Up to this Kingdom," it resumed to me, *strikes the high*

"Rose never one who had not faith in Christ jf *1ak u* -ii Tt i *rime on*

Before or since they nailed Him to the tree. *Christ) Philip the Fair*

Charles of Naples. Evidently the Book kept in Roman numerals Frederick, King of Sicily, whose misdeeds will crowd the page The Venetian ducat and the florin were the standard coins everywhere

But many, mark, who cry aloud

Christ! Christ!
Shall be less near Him at the Great Assize,
By very far, than some who know not Christ.
The Ethiop shall such Christians stigmatize
When the two colleges apart are led,
One poor, the other with the eternal prize.
To Christian monarchs what will not be said
By Persians, when the Book is open placed
Upon whose page their evil deeds are spread?
There 'mid the deeds of Albert shall be traced
That which will start the moving pen once more
To show the Realm of Prague become a waste;
There seen how men along the Seine deplore
The doing of that counterfeiter accurst
To perish by the bristle of the boar;
There seen the arrogance that sets athirst,
Driving both Scot and Englishman insane,
Whence both anon across the border burst;
There the soft life and lust of him of Spain
And the Bohemian,—never known to them
Was prowess, or held ever in disdain.
There to the Cripple of Jerusalem
Shall with an / the good be credited,
While the reverse is rated at an *M.*
There shall the greed and cowardice be read
Of him who wards the fiery Island,—tomb
Where the long journey of Anchises led;
And to denote him paltry, let the doom
In curt abbreviations be set down,
Infinite matter in a little room.
And foul to all be noted the renown
Of uncle and of brother, who deflower
Illustrious lineage, and each a crown.
And he who holds in Portugal the power,
And Norway shall be shown; and Rascia there
Who saw Venetian coin in evil hour.
Wicked Christian Kings 385
O blest were Hungary, if she would bear
No buffets longer; and Navarre in bliss
If her own mountain but a rampart were! *Henry of Luti*
And let each one recall, in proof of this, *iittle'King? who*
How Nicosia and Famagosta groan *keeps pace with*
Already for their beast, and take it amiss *.powers " in evil*
That he beside the others hold his own."— *doing The voice of the Just, blending in the neck of the Eagle, issue like the sound of falling water, or of musical notes* XX
The Eagle Continues To Discourse
When he who sheds through all the world his ray
Is from our hemisphere descending so
That everywhere the daylight fades away,
The sky, ablaze with him short while ago,
Is suddenly rekindled to our ken
By many lights that answer to one glow:
And I recalled this heavenly action when
The ensign of the world and of its head
Grew silent in the blessed beak again;
For all those living luminaries, made
Brighter than ever, were beginning chants
Out of my memory to lapse and fade.
O sweet Love, veiled in smiling radiance,
How ardent didst thou seem in those canorous
Flutes that breathed only holy meditance!
After the bright and precious brilliants o'er us,
Wherewith I saw the sixth heaven glittering,
Had made an end of their angelic chorus,
It seemed to me I heard a murmuring
Stream that runs limpid down from stone to stone
Showing the plenty of its mountain spring.
And as upon the cittern's neck the tone
Assumes its form, and in reed instrument
The vent-holes mold the breathing through it blown,
Thus, brooking no delay, incontinent
Did that soft murmur of the Eagle float
Up through the neck, as if it were a vent;
There became voice, and issued from the throat
Out through the beak, with words in unison
With longing of the heart whereon I wrote.
"That part in me which sees, and braves the sun
In mortal eagles," it prelusive said,
"Should now attentively be gazed upon;
For of the fires whereof my form is made,
Those are in all their grades of most renown
Wherewith the eye is sparkling in my head.
Who midmost as the pupil glitters down,
He was the Holy Spirit's laureate
Who bore about the Ark from town to town;
Now knows he his song's merit adequate,
So far as subject to his will's control,
By the reward which is proportionate.
Of five who curve along my brow, that soul
Neighboring nearest to the beak of me
Did the poor widow for her son console;
Now knows he dear the ransom is if we
Follow not Christ, by the experience
Of this sweet life, and of the contrary.
"Who next, along on the circumference
In question, follows on the upward way
Delayed his death by very penitence;
Now knows he that Eternal Judgment may
Be altered never, though a worthy prayer
On earth below tomorrows the today.
The next, to set the Pastor in the

chair, 1ll fruitage gathering from good intents,

Made Greek himself, the laws, and me down there;

Now knows he that the evil consequence

Of his good deed gives him no cause to grieve,

Although the world go all to ruin thence.

Next in the downward curve dost thou perceive

Him who was William, whom those lands regret

Which weep that Charles and Frederick still live;

Now knows he how the love of Heaven is set

On a just king, and the effulgency

Of his appearance makes it patent yet.

Down in the erring world who would agree

That Trojan Rhipeus in this round were fit

The fifth among the holy lights to be?

Dante's wonder that Rhipeus and Trajan are redeemed

Now knows he much whereof our human wit

In Grace Divine can catch not any gleam,

Although his vision cannot fathom it. "—

Like to the lark that in the morning beam

Upsoars, first singing and thereafter still,

Rapt with the sweetness of her song supreme,

Such seemed the imaged Emblem of the Will

Eternal, in accordance with whose bent

Created things their final ends fulfill.

And notwithstanding that my wonderment

Showed through me like the color through the glaze,

Yet could it not abide the time content,

But forced by virtue of its weight the phrase

Forth from my lips,—''What wonders these!" Oh thence

I saw great revelry of flashing rays!

Thereon with kindling eye still more intense,

To me the Blessed Emblem made reply,

To hold me not in wondering suspense:

"I see that thou believ'st these things, since I

Report them to thee, but dar'st not avow,

For, though believed, they are hidden from the eye.

Thou doest like that one who may well allow

A thing in name, but who cannot define

Its essence if another show not how.

The Kingdom of Heaven suffers force benign

From living hope and loving fervency,

Able to overcome the Will Divine;

Not as man over man wins victory,

That which is craving to be quelled they quell,

And, conquered, conquer through benignity.

The brow's first living soul and fifth may well

Astonish thee, because thou seest with those

Adorned the region where the angels dwell.

These left their bodies not, as men suppose,

Gentile, but Christian, each in firm faith cleaving

To crucifixion's past or future throes.

Exceptional Cases of Redemption 389

For one from Hell, whence none returns retrieving

Good will again, did yet his bones resume,—

And living hope this guerdon was receiving,—

The living hope whence vital power should bloom

Through prayer to God for his upraising made,

So that his will could move to change his doom.

The glorious spirit whereof this is said,

Short while abiding in the flesh on earth,

Put faith in Him who had the power to aid,

And so belief enkindled on his hearth

True love, that when returned he to the grave

He was found fit to come unto this mirth.

So deep a fountain yielded grace to save

The other soul, no eye, however bright,

Of any creature pierced its primal wave;

And so in righteousness was his delight That our redemption in the future, more

And more by Grace was opened to his sight:

Wherefore he put his trust therein, nor bore

Thenceforth the stench from heathendom arising,

Reproving the perverted folk therefor.

To him, a thousand years ere solemnizing

Of baptism, those three maids thou sawst, who wheeled

Beside the dexter wheel, stood for baptizing.

Predestination! Ah, how far afield

Thy root from vision of their intellect

To whom the First Cause is not all revealed!

And be ye, mortals, closely circumspect

In judging, forasmuch as we, who see

The very God, know not yet all the elect;

And in such lack is our felicity,

For in this good our own good we refine

So that with Will Divine our wills agree."

Thus by that emblematic form divine,

To make me feel the limits of my vision,

Was dealt to me delightful medicine.

As on the chorded lute the good musician

Pinching the strings supports the singer good,

Thus making more delightful the rendition,

So I remember, while he thus pursued,

Beholding those two blessed lusters dance

Accordant, as the eyes in winking would,

Moving their flame lets with that utterance.

Ladder of Contemplation 391 XXI

Heaven Of Saturn

Already on my Lady's countenance

Mine eyes were bended, and my mind withdrew

With them from every other circumstance;

Nor was she smiling, but began thereto: *Ascending to*

"Were I to smile thou wouldst become like fair *the Heaven of iSaturn, aea*Semele, when she dust and ashes grew; *trice withholds*

Because my beauty on the Palace stair *the smsl'*

Eternal, shining in more bright relief

As thou hast seen, with our ascending there, If not attempered, would be past belief

Effulgent, so that thy poor mortal sense

Would be but as the thunder-blasted leaf, liaised are we to the Seventh Splendor, whence,

Now warmed beneath the Lion's burning breast, Rains down its mitigated influence.

Let thy mind follow where thine eyes request,

And let them mirrors be for that reflection

Which in this mirror shall be manifest."— Whoso could know how great was the refection

Mine eyes found in her features sanctified,

When drawn away perforce in new direction, Might comprehend, by weighing the one side

With the other, how delighted I became

To do the bidding of my heavenly Guide. Within the crystal that doth bear the name

The world around of its bright Leader, who

So ruled that perished every deed of blame, 1 saw a Ladder all of golden hue *The Golden*

Burnished with light, and lifted up so high

Mine eyes were unavailing to pursue; Then saw so many splendors downward fly

Along its rungs, all light the stars distill

Had, it appeared to me, been shed thereby.

Ladder

And as, at bidding of their nature's will,

Jackdaws together flock at break of day,

Bestirring them to warm their plumage chill;

Thereafter there are some who fly away

Without returning, others fly off where They started from, and others, wheeling, stay:

In such a fashion came together there,

Methought, that scintillating company,

Soon as it lighted on a certain stair;

And one, which nearest us appeared to be,

Became so bright, I murmured in my thought:

"Well I perceive thy love that signals me."—

But she, by whom the How and Where is taught

Of speech and silence, pauses, whence aright

I do, against desire, inquiring not.

Whence she who saw my silence in the sight

Of That One to whose seeing all is shown,

Bade me,—''Appease thy yearning appetite!"—

Dante humbly And I began: "No merit of mine own

asks two Renders me worthy that thou make reply,

questions of the "m *r J' spirit* But for her sake who bids me ask, made known,

O soul in blessedness, enshrouded by

The joyance that doth round about thee glow, What places thee so near me; and tell why Within this wheeling sphere keeps silence so The dulcet symphony of Paradise Devoutly sounding through the rest below."— *The eyes oj*

"Thy mortal eye and ear are both amiss," *beZ'theile?* He answered, "here aloft no songs are sung *his muddy* For the same cause that smiles not Beatrice. *tZvZl* Down on the sacred ladde rung by rung

the music So far descended I to make thee graced

With words, and with the radiance round me flung;

Nor was it greater love that made me haste,

For equal love, or more, burns up above,

As makes the flaming clearly manifest;

St. Peter Damian 393

But we, as prompted by Exalted Love,

To serve the purpose of the world so burn:

'Tis love allots,—thou seest the mode thereof."—

"Full well, O holy lamp, do I discern

How love, left free, may in this Court suffice

For following the Providence eterne;

But ever this is baffling to mine eyes:

Wherefore among thy consorts thou alone

Hast been predestinate to this emprise?"—

Before I uttered forth the final tone,

The light an axis of its middle made,

Rapidly whirling as in mill the stone.

Thereon the loving spirit in it said: "Focused on me is radiance divine Piercing the mesh of that around me shed, Whereof the virtue and my sight combine To lift me so above myself, I see The Fount Supreme whence doth this luster shine. Thence comes the rapture all aflame in me, For to my vision as it grows more bright I match a flame of equal clarity. But soul in Heaven with most access of light, *The mystery of*

Seraph whose eye is most on God intent, *Predestination*

Could to thy question not reply aright, For it is gulfed in the arbitrament Unfathomed, of eternal law's control, Where all created sight is vainly bent.

Carry this back to every mortal soul

On thy return, that men no more presume

To lift their feet toward so high a goal.

The mind that here is flame, on earth is fume;

Consider then if it below can do

That which it cannot do, though Heaven assume."—

His language such a limit round me drew,

From every further question I forbore,

Except to humbly ask him, "Who were you?"—

The beautiful site of the monastery oj

Fonte AveUana on Monte Catria St. Peter
Damian
The stormy voice Astounds the
Poet himself
"Crags rise in Italy 'twixt shore and shore,
And from thy fatherland not far away,
So high, the thunderstorms below them roar,
Making a hump whose name is Catria,
And there a hermitage was consecrate
Which used to be a place for men to pray."—
With words like these did he inaugurate
The third discourse: "On Godly service bent,
I grew so used to feed on lenten cate
Which had but olive juice for condiment,
That here I passed the seasons hot and cold
Lightly, in thoughts contemplative content.
That cloister once bore fruitage manifold
Unto these heavens, but now it yields no more,
As must perforce hereafter soon unfold.
There Peter Damian was the name I bore;
Peter the Sinner was I in the fane
Of Our own Lady on the Adrian shore.
To me did little mortal life remain,
When called to take, against my own accord,
That Hat which shifts from bad to worse again.
Came Cephas, the great Vessel of the Lord
Came lean and barefoot, taking bit and sup
From whatsoever hospitable board.
Now serving-men are needed to hold up
Fat modern pastors, one on either side
And one before and one behind to prop.
Their furs o'erflow the palfreys which they ride (How much, O Patience, hast thou yet to bear!)
So that two beasts go underneath one hide."—
Flames saw I at such cry from stair to stair
Descending and whirling round in multitude,
At every whirl becoming still more fair.
Around this soul they flocking came, and stood,
And lifted up such a resounding shout
That here there could be no similitude,
Nor, thunderstricken, could I make it out.
Stricken with bewilderment, the Poet is reassured by Beatrice St. Benedict 395
XXII
St. Benedict; Dante's Natal Constellation
Plunged in bewilderment I turned me thence
Round to my Guide, even as a little child
Runs ever where he feels most confidence; And promptly as a mother's cadence mild
Is wonted to give courage to her son
Pallid and gasping,—so her words beguiled My fear: "Enfolds thee not the benison
Of Heaven where all is holy? and canst thou doubt
That zeal for good prompts what in Heaven is done? What perturbation had been brought about
Both by the singing and my smiling eye,
When thou hast been so startled by the shout? Wherein, if thou hadst understood their cry
Which is a prayer, already would be clear
The vengeance thou shalt see before thou die. Smites never down in haste the sword from here,
Nor tardily, excepting in his view
Who waits for it in longing or in fear.
But look about thee now to something new;
Thou shalt see spirits most illustrious,
Turning thy face round as I bid thee do."— Compliant to her wish, I turned me thus,
And saw a hundred little globes of fire
By interchange of light more beauteous. Like one who blunts the edge of his desire
Within himself, became I, diffident
Of question, lest I overmuch aspire.
And the most lustrous and preeminent
Among those pearly lights began to advance,
To make my wish concerning it content. Within it then I heard: "Could but thy glance *Speaks St.*
Like mine perceive our interflaming Love,""
Thy tacit thought would have found utterance; *Monte Cassino, one of the most venerable monuments of the Christian world Dante's prayer to Benedict The Heavenly*
Ladder
But lest thou linger from the goal above
I will make answer even to the scope
Of the request thou art so chary of.
Where lies Cassino on the mountain slope,
Up to the very summit dwelt of yore
The folk perverse who in delusion grope;
And I am he who first up thither bore
The name of Him who brought the human race
The Truth enabling us so high to soar:
Then shone upon me so abounding Grace
That from the impious worship which misled
The world, I drew each neighbor dwelling place.
These other fires were men whose spirits fed
On Contemplation, kindled by that heat
Whence holy flowers and holy fruits are bred.
Here Romuald and here Macarius meet
All my good brethren of the cloister who
Kept steadfast heart and stayed their truant feet."
And now I spoke: "The love thou givest to view
Talking with me, and the benevolence
Which I perceive aglow in all of you,
Dilate as genially my confidence
As the sun doth the rose, till she uncase
Her petals and exhale her perfume thence.
Wherefore I pray,—and tell me if

such grace,
O Father, may perchance upon me shine,—
That I may see thee with uncovered face."—
"Brother, up in the final sphere divine,"
Said he, "shall thy exalted wish be granted,
Where all the others are fulfilled, and mine.
There is mature and perfect and unscanted
Every desire; and in that realm of day
Alone all parts eternally are planted;
For it is not in space, nor doth it sway
On poles; and thither doth our ladder go,
Whence it is fading from thy sight away.
Degenerate Religious Orders 397
The Patriarch Jacob saw it long ago
Extend its upper reaches Heavenward yon,
When angels up and down seemed thronging so. But now to clamber thither raises none *The "dread*
His feet from earth, and, though my Rule remain, *Toice"* a5,al"
Waste is the paper it is written on. The abbey walls, that used to be a fane,
Are become robber dens, and every cowl
A sack that doth corrupted meal contain. But heavy usance levies smaller toll
Counter to will Divine, than fruits that curse
With such insanity the monkish soul. What Holy Church may have to disemburse
Belongs to them who in God's name invoke;
Not to one's kindred, nor to others worse. The flesh of mortals is so frail that folk
Make good beginnings there, which do not hold
Till acorns ripen on the sapling oak. Peter made his beginning without gold
Or silver, I with fast and orison,
And Francis humbly set about his fold. And scanning the beginning of each one,
And then where it has wandered, thou wilt see
How white has been converted into dun. But Jordan backward turned, in verity,
And ocean at God's will in flight perdue,
More wondrous were than rescue here would be."— He spoke, and turned to his companions, who
Surrounding him, together closed their throng,
Then upward like a whirlwind all withdrew. My gentle Lady urged me then along *Ascent to the*
With a mere wafture up that mystic stair, en o/ "
So was her power upon my nature strong; Nor in our rising and descending here
By natural law, has ever been a flight
So swift as with my pinion to compare.
Splendid invocation to his natal constellation,—The Eternal Twins In the year 1265 the Sun was in Gemini from 18th May to 17th June. The exact day of Dante's birth is not recorded Speaks Beatrice
Survey of the
Solar System
Reader, as I to that devout delight
Hope to return, for whose sake I deplore
Ofttimes my sins, and on my bosom smite,
Thou wouldst have pluckt thy finger nevermore
Out of the fire, ere I beheld the Sign
After the Bull, and was within its core!
O glorious stars, whose influences shine
Pregnant with power, to whom is honor due
For whatsoever genius may be mine,
With you was dawning, darkening with you
He who is Sire of all mortality,
When my first breath of Tuscan air I drew;
And then, when gift of Grace had made me free
Of the high wheeling sphere wherein ye roll,
Your very region was assigned to me.
To you devoutly now suspires my soul,
Virtue soliciting and consecration
For the hard passage to the final goal.
"Thou art so near the Ultimate Salvation,"
So Beatrice began, "that it is meet
To have eyes keen and purified from passion.
Hence, before deeplier immerst in it,
Look down below and see what world expanse
I have already put beneath thy feet;
So that thy heart with utmost jubilance
Confront the Triumph of the multitude
Who through this ether-sphere blithely advance."—
Then one and all the Seven Spheres I viewed
With backward gaze, and saw this globe of dust
Such that I smiled at its poor likelihood;
And to his counsel I most largely trust
Who holds it cheapest; and who turns him thence
To other thoughts may well be reckoned just.
Latona's daughter kindled on my sense
Without that shadow making her appear
Such that I held her once both rare and dense.
The Seven Planets 399
Hyperion, I could endure up here
The radiance of thy son, and markt how move
Maia and Dione round about him near. Tlaence I perceived the tempering of Jove
Father and son between, and thence the mode
Of all their variations as they rove. Tlience to me all the seven planets showed
How vast they are, how swift they are, and how
Far. far apart they are in their abode. With the Eternal Twins revolving now,
I saw our madding little threshing floor *"Faiuola che ti*
Spread out from river mouth to mountain brow: *la tantoferocl"* Then turned I to the beauteous eyes once

more.
xxin
Vision Of The Host Of The Redeemed
As birdling the beloved leaves among
Having reposed with her sweet nestling brood
While night has over all her mantle flung,
Who, that she may adventure for their food,
Delighting in hard toil, and that she may
See the loved pledges of her motherhood,
Anticipates the hour on open spray,
And fired with eagerness awaits the light,
Vigilant ever until break of day:
Beatrice So was my Lady standing at full height
expectant ert and watchful, lifting up her face
Thither where most the sun retards his flight;
Whence I, observant of her eagerness,
Became like one who wistfully doth pant
For his desire, and so takes heart of grace.
But now the interval of time was scant,—
I mean of my suspense until aware
That more and more the heaven grew radiant.
The Harvest And Beatrice said: "Behold the army fair
of Christ Of Christ Triumphant,—all the harvest raised
By whirling influence of every sphere."—
It seemed to me that all her features blazed
And such a flood of rapture filled her eye
That I must pass it by perforce unphrased.
As at still midnight when the moon is high
Trivia smiles among the nymphs eterne
Who brighten every quarter of the sky,
Above a thousand lusters saw I burn
One Sun, enkindling round it all and some,
As does our sun the other lights supern.
And that illuminating Masterdom
Shot down a living splendor so intense
Into mine eyes that they were overcome.
"Hymning the holy smile" 401
Oh, Beatrice, dear gentle influence!
Now said she to me: "Thou art here controlled
By force wherefrom there can be no defense. Herein the Wisdom, here the Power behold,
That frayed from Heaven to Earth a thoroughfare
For which the yearning was so long of old."— As fire, expanding beyond bound, doth tear
The cloud asunder, and swiftly earthward fall
Against its proper nature, through the air, So found my spirit in that festival
Enlargement, and the bound of self forsook,
Nor what it then became can now recall. "Open thine eyes," resumed she then, "and look *Dante's eyes*
Upon my very nature; thou hast seen *aUUof*
Things that enable thee my smile to brook."— *Beatrice* I was like one who feels the spell again
Of a forgotten vision, and doth try
To bring it back to memory, in vain,
When I received this proffer, worth so high
Tribute of thanks as could not be effaced
Out of the chronicle of time gone by.
Not all the tongues by Polyhymnia graced,
That both from her and from her sisters drew
Their lyric milk most honied to the taste, Could tell a thousandth part of what is true,
Hymning the holy smile of Beatrice
And on her holy face what light it threw. Whence; in depicting Paradise, at this
The sacred Poem leaps perforce the theme,
Like one whose way is cut by an abyss. But whoso notes its weight will never deem
Me blamable if mortal shoulder bear
But tremblingly a burden so supreme.
For little bark can be no passage where
Cf. beginning of
The wave is cleft by my adventurous prow, *Canto* '
Nor yet for pilot who would labor spare.
The Sun of Heaven shows just so much light as the mortal eye can bear The Virgin Mary Mother The splendor and music of Qabriel
"Why so enamored of my face art thou,
And turnest not to the fair garden-close
Blooming beneath the rays of Christus now?
The Word Divine became in yonder Rose
Incarnate; yonder are the lilies white
Whose fragrance did the way of life disclose."—
So Beatrice: and I, submitting quite
To what she urged, again free scope allowed
To the contention of my feeble sight.
Just as mine eyes, themselves beneath a shroud
Of shadow, have beheld a flowery lea
Laughing in light that streamed through rifted cloud,
So many a splendid throng now seemed to be
Lit from above by burning radiance, though
No fountain of those flashings could I see.
O Power benignant who dost mark them so,
Thou hadst withdrawn thee upward to give way
Before mine eyesight baffled by the glow!
The mention of the Rose whereto I pray
Morning and evening, utterly subdued
My soul to contemplate her greater ray.
When with her quality and magnitude
As she transcended here up there transcending,
That living star had both mine eyes imbued,
Behold athwart the heaven a torch descending,
Formed like a coronet, wherewith it crowned her.

About her in a fiery circle bending.
Whatever melody is sweet hereunder
Most wooingly to wake the heart's desire,
Would seem a cloud-bank rended by the thunder
Compared to the resounding of that lyre
Engarlanding the Sapphire beauteous
Whose holy azure tints the Heaven of Fire.
"I am the Love angelic circling thus
The lofty rapture of the womb, that blest
Hostel of Him who was desired of us;
And I shall circle until thou followest
Thy son, O Lady of Heaven, diviner making
The Sphere supreme because thou enterest."—
So now the circling melody was taking
The seal, and all the other lights in fine
With name of Mary into song were breaking.
That regal mantle which doth all entwine
The rolling worlds, and hath its appetite
Most quickened in the breath and deeds divine,
Held far remote from us and at such height
Above my standing place its inner shore,
That vision of it dawned not on my sight.
Therefore mine eyes did not have power to soar
After the flame incoronate, who rose
Up to her Son where He had risen before.
As little child toward the mother throws
Its arms up, soon as it with milk is fed,
And grateful love in such a transport shows,
When each and all of those fair splendors shed
Their light upstretching, so an infinite
Love toward Mary in the act I read.
Before me still remained those splendors white,
And "Queen of Heaven" they all so sweetly chanted
That present with me yet is the delight.
Oh, how great plenty is laid up unscanted
In those abounding coffers that of old
Were husbandmen upon the ground they planted!
There live they, glad in treasure manifold
Which in captivity at Babylon
They gathered up with tears, forsaking gold.
There triumphs, under the exalted Son
Of God and Mary, now victorious
And with the council old and new, that one
Who holds the keys of gate so glorious.
Probably the ninth sphere, "that first moved" (Primum mobile) They had received "the Kingdom of God as a little child" St. Peter Beatrice prays Jar Dante Cf. the comparison at end of Canto x XXIV
St. Peteh Examines Dante Concerning Faith
"0 chosen fellowship of the Lamb Blest
At the great supper where He feeds you so
That your desire is ever set at rest,
Since Grace Divine doth on this man bestow
Foretaste of viands from your feast above,
Or ever death cut short his time below,
Give heed to his immeasurable love,
Bedew him somewhat: ye are quaffing bowls
Brimmed from the fount that he is dreaming of ."-
So Beatrice besought; and those blithe souls
Flasht out like comets streaming in the sky,
Whirling in circles round determined poles.
And even as wheels in clock escapement ply
In such a fashion geared that motionless
Appears the first one, and the last to fly,
Likewise those wheeling carols let me guess,
By variable measure of the dance
Or swift or slow, their wealth of blessedness.
The carol that seemed fairest to my glance
Was flaming forth such plenitude of bliss
That none was left of greater radiance,
The fairest carol And swept three times encircling Beatrice
Accompanied with singing so divine
That fantasy in me falls short of this:
I write it not, my pen must skip the line,
For hues of fancy would too coarsely glare,
Let alone words, on drapery so fine.
"O holy sister, thy compelling prayer
Devout, and with so fervent feeling made,
Detaches me from yonder circle fair."—
After the blessed fire its motion stayed,
Did it directly to my Lady turn
Breathing forth what I have already said.
sweeps around Beatrice
And she replied to it: "O light eterne
Of the great peer to whom our Master gave
Keys he brought down of this delight supern,
Xiivite this man, on questions light or grave
As pleases thee, about the Faith to tell
Wherethrough thou once didst walk upon the wave.
If loves he, hopes he, and believes he well,
Is hidden not from thee who hast thine eye
Where all things seen as in a picture dwell.
But it becomes him thus to testify
For the true Faith, that it be glorified,
Seeing this Realm is citizened thereby. "—
As arms the bachelor, whose tongue is tied
Until the Master doth the question stir,
To sanction it with proof, not to decide,
Even so did I, hearing these words from her,
Equip me all with answer in advance
In such a shrift to such examiner.
"Speak up, good Christian, give it utterance, What thing is Faith?"—Where-

at I raised my brow
Whither was breathing forth that radiance,
And then turned round to Beatrice, who now
Wafted prompt signals to me that I lift
The inward sluice gate and my creed avow.
"May Grace, which is vouchsafing to me shrift
In presence of the chief Centurion,"
Began I, "mold the expression of my drift.
Father, as wrote the truthful pen thereon
Of thy dear brother who set the feet of Rome
In the right path with thee, Faith's benison
Is substance of the things we hope will come,
And of invisible things the evidence:
Its essence such appears to me in sum."—
Then heard I: "Rightly dost thou catch the sense,
If comprehending why he classed it now
With substances and now with arguments."—
The light of St. Peter
Picture of an examination such as the Poet had undergone at the University
Definition of Faith drawn from St. Paul
Faith is the substance,— that which stands under and supports Hope Faith based on Scripture
Divine because attested by miracle
"*This is arguing in a circle, objects the examiner*
And I thereon: "The deep things which allow
That glimpses of themselves should here be shown
Are so concealed from mortal eye below
As to exist there in belief alone,
Whereon our hope sits, founded high aloof,
Whence Faith is by the name of substance known;
From which belief is laid on us behoof
To argue without seeing more than it,
Wherefore it takes the notion on of proof."—
Then heard I: "If whatever men admit
For doctrine were so understood on earth,
No room would there remain for sophist wit."—
This was from that enkindled Love breathed forth,
Subjoining then: "Right well dost thou rehearse
The carats of this coinage and the worth:
But tell me if thou hast it in thy purse?"—
And I: "That have I, both so bright and round
That of its stamp to me no doubt occurs."—
Thereafter issued from the light profound
Glowing above, this utterance thereto:
"This precious gem, wherein all worth we found,
Came to thee whence?"—And I: "The ample dew
Of the Celestial Spirit, which is shed
Over the Ancient Parchments and the New,
Is argument that hath within me bred
Belief so strong that, set against its force,
All demonstration seems to me but dead."—
I heard thereon: "The old and the new course
Of argument with such conclusion fraught,
Why dost thou hold it for divine discourse?"—
And I: "The very proof is to be sought
In th' after-works, whereto might never be
Hot iron yet on Nature's anvil wrought."—
"Who vouches, pray," it was replied to me,
"That these works were performed?—Thou wouldst attest
The very text affirming it to thee."—
"Though without miracles the world confest
Christianity, this were a hundredfold
More wonderful," I answered, "than the rest;
For poor and hungry once into the wold
Didst thou go forth to sow there the good plant,
A bramble now, which was a vine of old."—
The high and holy Court, then celebrant,
Made a "Praise God" throughout those circles ring
In such a melody as there they chant.
And that great Lord who, thus examining,
Had so far drawn me now from spray to spray
That near the topmost frondage poised our wing,
Resumed: "The Grace whose dalliance doth so play
Upon thy soul, thus far to conference
Hath opened thy lips duly; and I pay
My commendation to what issued thence;
But now to tell thine own belief is meet,
And why it captured thine intelligence."—
"O holy Father, soul with so complete
Discernment of thy faith, thou didst outfare,
Anigh the Sepulcher, more youthful feet,"—.
Began I,—''thou wouldst have me here declare
The very essence of my prompt believing,
And also have the grounds of it laid bare.
And I reply: by faith am I receiving
One God, sole and eterne, the Heavens all
Who moves (Himself unmoved) by love and craving.
And for such faith have I proofs physical
And metaphysical, nor am denied
The verity that showers from here withal
Through Moses, Psalms, and prophecies, beside
The Evangel, and what you Apostles writ
When by the fiery Spirit sanctified.

In three Eternal Persons, and to wit
One Essence I believe, so One and Trine
That *are* and *is* the syntax must admit.
The conversion of the world through the agency of a few humble men would have been more wonderful than a miracle
Dante's own belief and its grounds The light of St. Peter now encircles Dante as it had first encircled Beatrice
This, the mysterious state of the Divine,
Doth many a time the Gospel teaching leaven,
Which stamps upon my mind its seal and sign.
This is the focus whence the spark is driven
Which then doth into living flame dilate
And shine within me like a star in Heaven."—
Even as a lord who hears good tidings, straight
The story ended, presses to his breast
The servant whom he would congratulate,
So, by his singing rendering me blest,
Three times encircled me, when ceased my voice.
That apostolic Light at whose behest
I spoke: so did he in my words rejoice.
uSe mai continga che il poema sacro"
409 XXV 5T. James Examines The Poet Concerning Hope tf ever it happen that the Sacred Song, Whereto both Heaven and Earth have so set hand
That it has made me lean for seasons long,
Slaould foil the cruelty that keeps me banned
From the fair sheepfold where, a lamb, I lay,
Hated of wolves that harry all the land,
With other voice, with other fleece, that day
Returning Poet, will I from mine own
Baptismal font accept the wreath of bay;
There entered I the Faith that renders known
The soul to God; and after, by her worth.
Did Peter, as I said, my brow enzone.
Then usward moved a radiance that took birth
Out of that sphere whence issued the first Head
Of those Christ left, his vicars here on earth.
And my own Lady, full of rapture, said:
"Look, look, behold the Baron for whose grace
Galicia below is visited."—
As, circling nearer to the nesting place
And cooing to his mate, alights the dove,
And both pour forth affection, in like case
I saw one great and glorious Prince with love
And welcome by that other grandeur greeted, Praising the food which feeds them thereabove. But when the gratulation was completed, Silent in front of me they both stopt short,
Enkindled so, mine eyes fell down defeated.
Then Beatrice smiled forth what I report:
"Illustrious Life, who didst in bounty write
The perfect gifts of our Imperial Court,
Do thou make Hope resound upon this height,
For thou dost hope as often typify
As Jesus granted to the three most light. "—
These lines, too few, express the Poet's hope deferred Froissard also terms St. James a "Baron." He was believed to be buried at Santiago dc Compostela, "The Jerusalem of the West"
Beatrice, smiling, addresses the light oj St. James Cheering wordi of the Apostle to the Poet Beatrice answers for Dante as to the second question, that he might not appear to boast Definition of Hope
"Be of good cheer and lift thy head on high,
For all ascending here from mortal stress
Must in our mellowing rays to ripen lie. "—
The Second Fire did with this comfort bless;
Whence to the hills I raised mine eyes, before
Bowed heavily by radiant excess.
"Since of his grace desires our Emperor
That thou meet face to face before thy death
His baronage within the secret door,
That, seeing this Court truly, thou draw breath
Till in thyself and others thou relume
The Hope which well below enamoreth,—
Tell what hope is, and how therewith abloom
Thy spirit, and tell whence it came to thee:"
So speaking, did the Second Light resume.
And she who with compassionate sympathy
To so high flight my fledgy wings beguiled,
With answer thus anticipated me:
"Church militant has not a single child
Richer in hope, as read we in the fire
Of that Sun which throughout our host has smiled;
And hence it was vouchsafed to his desire
To come from Egypt to Jerusalem
To see, before the limit of his hire.
The other two points,—since thou askest them
Not for thy knowing, but that he report
To men this virtue as thy dearest gem,—
To him I leave; he will not find them thwart
Nor matter of boast; let him reply thereto,
Nor may the grace of God in him come short."—
I answered even as willing pupils do
The Master, who are glad, when competent,

That their proficiency be brought to view:
"Hope is the expectation confident
Of future glory, fountain that doth stream
From Grace divine and merit that forewent.
Coming of St. John 411
Stars many cause this light on me to beam, *Dante first*
But who first made it through my bosom shine *tTpfJnT*
Was supreme singer of the Guide Supreme. *next from the*
So speaks he in his Psalmody divine: je *of*
'Hope they in Thee who know thy name,—' and who
Can know it not, having like faith with mine? Thou then didst so bedew me with his dew
In thine Epistle that I am full, and pour
On others rain that showers from both of you."— "While thus I spoke, within that living core
Of fire there quivered forth a flash of light
Quick as chain lightning. Whereupon once more It breathed: "The love wherewith I flame so bright
For that same Virtue still my comforter
Unto the palm and issue of the fight,
Again on thee whose joy abides in her
Moves me to breathe; and I would fain be told
What is it Hope gives promise to confer?" And I: "The Scriptures, new as well as old,
Set forth the emblem whence I understand
The bliss of souls, God's friends, the double-stoled: Isaiah promises that all shall stand
In their own land with double raiment on,—
And this sweet life is their own fatherland; Far more distinctly does thy brother John,
Where he is treating of the robes of white, Make manifest to us this benison. "—
Now first, my words being ended, from the height
"Hope they in Thee" a voice was heard to say,
The carols all responding; then a light
Among them shot forth so intense a ray
If the Sign of
That, if the Crab held one such diamond, *%£%* Jjg
Winter would have a month of one sole day. *as the light of*
As winsome maiden rises with a bound *vrinter night*
To go and join the dancing, honor due *would be abol*
Giving the bride, and from no motive fond, *ished The pelican, supposed to feed tier brood with her own blood, is an emblem of Christ in medieval art*
Compare Dante's desire to see the glorified body of St. Benedict, Canto The Poet cannot see Beatrice
So saw I drawing near the other two
The brightened splendor, where they wheeled along
As it became their burning love to do.
It mingled with their measure and their song;
And gazing on them did my Lady rest
Even as a bride unmoved and still of tongue.
"This, this is he who lay upon the breast
Of our own Pelican; to him the award
Of the great trust was from the cross addrest."—
My Lady thus; not more was her regard
Moved to withdraw itself from its delight
Before these words of hers, or afterward.
Like one endeavoring to view aright
The eclipsing of the sun a little space,
Who through long gazing grows bereft of sight,
Such, by that latest fire, became my case,
While it was said: "Why dost thou dazzle thee
To see a thing that here can have no place?
My body is on earth, and there will be
With all the rest, until our number grow
Such as to tally with the eterne decree.
With the two robes in blessed cloister glow
Only those two great Splendors who ascended;
Bear this report back to your world below."—
And at this voice the flaming whirl was ended,
And therewithal was brought to quiet close
The trinal breath harmoniously blended,
As when, avoiding risk, or for repose,
The oars, that smote till now upon the wave.
All pause together when a whistle blows.
Alas! how much the mind in me misgave
When I turned round to look on Beatrice,
At having no power to see her, although I clave
Close to her side, and in the world of bliss.
Dante Blinded by the Light of the Saint
413 XXVI
St. John Examines Him Concerning Love
While I was trembling for my sight, forspent
By the effulgent flame, there issued thence
A breathing voice that made my heed intent,
Saying: "While thou recoverest the sense
Of vision which thou hast burnt out on me,
Let conversation serve for recompense.
Begin then, and declare where centered be
Thy heart's desires; and let assurance stand
That dazzled and not dead is sight in thee,
Because the eyes of the Lady, through this land
Divine conducting thee, irradiate
The power that was in Ananias' hand. "—
I said: "To these mine eyes, which were her gate

To enter with fire that ever burns me so,
Let balm come at her pleasure, soon or late.

The Good whereto these courts contentment owe
Is Alpha and Omega of the scroll
That Love is reading me, or loud or low. "—

The selfsame voice, first lifted to control
My fear when dazzled suddenly, to large
Discourse of reason called again my soul:

"Nay, but thy sieve more finely must discharge,"
So it resumed, "and needs must thou reply,
Who aimed thy arrows at so high a targe?"—

"By teachings of Philosophy," said I,
"And by authority descending hence
I bear perforce the print of love so high,

For Good, as such, when brought in evidence,
Makes love flow forth to it in fuller stream
As it embraces more of excellence.

Hence to the Essence which is so supreme
That every good outside it to be traced
Is but an emanation from its beam,

St. John assures the Poet that Beatrice vrill do for him what Ananias did for Paul Primal good necessarily enkindles Love Aristotle taught
that the world
is moved by the
desire of all
things for Ood
"omne bonum," "all good," in the Vulgate The Apocalypse The homely words "teeth," "biting," are in accordance with the Poet's proposed intention to write in everyday language such as even mere women of the people use (muliercula)

More than to any other needs must haste
In love the soul of every one not blind
To truth whereon this argument is based.

This truth has been unfolded to my mind
By him who demonstrates to me what drew
The primal love of all the eternal kind.

It is unfolded by the Author true
To Moses, speaking of His proper worth:
'AH goodness will I set before thy view. '

Thou too unfoldest it at setting forth
To cry Heaven's secret in that herald word,
The loftiest of all heralding to earth."—

"By human understanding," then I heard,
"In concord with authoritative writing,
Thy sovran love is looking Heavenward.

But further, if thou feelest other plighting
That draws thee Godward, by thy words attest
With just how many teeth this love is biting."—

Not hidden from me was the purpose blest
Of the Eagle of Christ; nay, whither he would guide
My declaration became manifest.

"All of those bitings," therefore I replied,
"Of force to turn the heart to God alone,
Combine to make such love in me abide:

Because the world's existence and mine own,
His death that I might live forevermore,
And what I hope with every faithful one,

As well as the aforesaid living lore,
Drew me from love perverse wherein I drowned,
And of right love have set me on the shore.

My love for blooms embowering the ground
Of the eternal Gardener, is strong
In measure as His gifts in them abound. "—

Soon as I paused, a strain of sweetest song
Rang through the Heaven, and my Lady said,
"O Holy, Holy, Holy!" with the throng.

As slumber breaks when vivid light is shed, So runs the spirit of sight to meet the burning
Splendor, through tunic, after tunic sped
Until the waker flinch,—for undiscerning
Is consciousness before the sudden day
Till judgment to his succor is returning,—
Thus from mine eyes drove Beatrice away
All motes with luster of her own so bright
That myriads of miles was shed the ray;
Whence better than beforehand was my sight:
And I made question like one in a maze,
Perceiving there before us a Fourth Light.
My Lady answered: "Shrouded in those rays
The first soul that was made by Virtue Prime
On his Creator doth in rapture gaze."—
Even as the treetop bows from time to time
Beneath the passing breeze, then rises slow
To place again through native power to climb,
While she was speaking did I waver so,
And then grew confident, though struck with awe,
Such will to question set me all aglow.
And I began: "O fruit that ripe, not raw,
Alone hast been produced, O Father of yore
To whom each bride is daughter and daughter-in-law,
Devoutly as I may do I implore
Thy speech with me; thou seest that I have stayed
My utterance to speed thy speaking more."—
Sometimes a covered animal is swayed
So that its feeling necessarily
Is by its undulating wrap betrayed;
And so the primal soul gave me to see,
Transpiring through his screen of radiance,
How blithesome he became to pleasure me.
Then he breathed forth: "Without thine utterance
Can I more readily detect thy yearning,
Than canst thou any surest circumstance,
The return of the Poet's eyeright scien-

tifically described, as science was then understood The light of the first created human soul How the Poet detected the joy of Adam Dante'i four questions, historical, theological, philological The third question is first answered: because our First Parents unshed to be "as gods, knowing good and evil" (So the Vulgate) Adam states that he remained in Paradise but seven hours! This was tradition

Because in the True Mirror this discerning,
Which forms of all things images sublime,
And naught such mirror unto Him is turning.
Thou wouldest know what ages since the time
God placed me in the lofty Paradise,
Where taught thy Lady so long stair to climb,
And how long it was pleasant to mine eyes,
And the true reason of the scorn divine,
And the idiom I used and did devise.
Now, not the tasted tree, O son of mine,
Was solely cause of so great banishment,
But only overstepping of the line.
Down there, whence by thy Lady Virgil went,
Four thousand and three hundred circles and two
Of sun, I yearned for this high Parliament;
And on the solar pathway to my view
Nine hundred times the lights all reawoke,
And fifty, and still breath on earth I drew.
Long silent were the accents that I spoke
Before the work not to be consummated
Was undertaken first by Nimrod's folk;
For never aught by reason fabricated
Endured, because of human choice renewing
As heavenly influences operated.
The use of speech by man is nature's doing;
But nature lets you shape it thus or so
As suits the fashion you may be pursuing.
Before I sank down to the Eternal Woe,
Men gave the name of 'Jah' to the Chief Good
Whence comes the rapture round me all aglow;
Then called Him 'El' as fitted to their mood;
For mortal fashions are like leaves that cling
To branch, and fall in swift vicissitude.
The Mount above the wave most towering
Held me, with life first pure, and then undone.
From the first hour to that next following
The sixth, at altered quadrant of the sun."— *Indignation of St. Peter* 417 xxvn

Ascent To The Crystalline Heaven: A Splendid
Vision, Set Between Two Rebukes To Men

"To Father, Son, and to the Holy Ghost
Glory," began with sweetness exquisite
Intoxicating me, the Heavenly Host.
Seemed what I witnessed with so deep delight
A laughter of the Universe; for this
Elation entered through both ear and sight. O Joy supreme! 0 inexpressive bliss!
O life of love and peace in ample store!
O wealth secure exempt from avarice! Above my enraptured eyes the torches four
Stood kindled, and the one that first had come
Began to grow more vivid than before, And to take on such look as might assume
Bright Jupiter were he and ruddy Mars
Transformed to birds, with interchange of plume. *The light of* The Providence allotting to the stars s-*PeteT.. . grows ruddy*
Of heaven their function and their office due,
Had stilled the quiring of the blessed cars, When I heard say: "If I transform my hue,
Marvel not, for behold incarnadine
While yet I speak will grow the others too! He who on earth usurps that place of mine,
That place of mine, that place which now doth lie *St. Peter de*
Vacant in presence of the Son Divine, *nounces Pope* iii-*Boniface as an*
Has turned my sepulcher into a sty *usurper*
Of blood and filth, so that the Evil One
Who fell from here is comforted thereby."— With such a crimson as the adverse sun
Paints on the cloud at morn or eventide,
Did I behold all heaven suffused thereon. And as a modest lady doth abide
Sure of herself, but through another's shame
At the mere hearing becomes mortified, *The same "dread voice" that speaks in Milton's "Lyeidas" Clement V was*
a Gascon; John
XXII from
Cahors
As Cacciaguida had done (Canto xvii, final lines), so Peter commands the Poet to speak
So Beatrice changed semblance; and I deem
That such eclipse took place in Heaven perchance
When suffered the Omnipotence Supreme.
Thereon proceeded forth his utterance
With voice so greatly altered that behold!
Was not more changed his very countenance:
"The Bride of Christ was nurtured not of old
On blood of mine and that of Linus good
And Cletus, to be used for acquist of gold;
But for acquist of this beatitude
Did Sixtus, Pius, and Calixtus weep,
And Urban, and thereafter shed their blood.

Nor purposed we the Christian folk to keep
To right and left of our successors,—these
Stigmatized goats, the others favored sheep;
Nor were confided to my hand the Keys
To be an emblem on a banneret
For war on the baptized; nor do I please
To figure as a signet that is set
On privileges venal and untrue,
Whereat my frequent blush is burning yet.
From here aloft in all the folds a crew
Of ravening wolves in shepherd garb is seen:
Vengeance of God, why dost thou lie perdue?
To drink our blood Gascon and Cahorsine
Are making ready. Alas, must needs the end
Of fair beginning be indeed so mean?
But lofty Providence that once did fend
Rome's empire of the world with Scipio,
Will quickly here, I deem, some succor lend.
And thou who must return once more below
Through mortal load, open thy mouth, my son,—
Fail not to say what I fail not to show. "—
As when our atmosphere is snowing down
In flakes the frozen vapors, when the horn
Of the Sky-goat is gilded by the sun,
Such swarming flakes in triumph upward borne
Seemed those who with us there had sojourn made,
And now awhile the ethereal sky adorn.
My sight was following what their wraiths displayed,
And followed till the vastness manifold
All power of penetrating farther stayed.
Whereon my Lady, seeing me withhold
From gazing up, commanded me: "Now cast
Thine eye down at the distance thou hast rolled."—
I saw that, so revolving, I had passed
From the first hour I lookt, the whole arc through
Which the first climate makes from midst to last,
Hence could the wild course of Ulysses view
Past Cadiz, and well-nigh the hither shore
Whereon Europa so dear burden grew.
And further surface of this threshing floor
Had been uncovered, but the sun sped, turning
Beneath my feet, removed a Sign and more.
Now my enamored spirit always yearning
After my Lady, to bring back and sate
Mine eyes on her, was more than ever burning.
All Nature ever made, or art, of bait
To catch the eye and captivate the thought
In human flesh real or delineate,
This, though united, would appear as naught
To the diviner beauty piercing through me
When now her smiling face I turned and sought.
The power wherewith I felt that look endue me.
From the fair nest of Leda tore me away
And to the fleetest heaven of all updrew me.
So uniform its parts I cannot say
Which one had Beatrice chosen for my place,—
Full of exceeding life and lofty they.
Then she, who saw my longing, of her grace
Began with smile of so blithe innocence
That God appeared rejoicing in her face:

An upward fall of snow Dante had revolved with the Twins through 90 of the "first climate" and could now see that.portion of the earth from the Eastern Mediterranean to where Ulysses voyaged the Atlantic (Inf. xxvi). Cf. the close of Canto xxii The nest of Leda by metonymy for the Twins, Castor and Pollux The Crystalline Heaven, "that first moved" Here are the roots of Time The daughter is the human race. The Sun is the father of mortal life (Canto xxii, 116)

"The nature of the World which holds suspense
The center and makes all else around it fare,
Doth here as from its starting point commence.
And in this Heaven there is no other Where
Than in the Mind Divine, wherein both move
The Love that turns and Power that sheds the sphere.
Engird it with one cincture light and love,
As it engirds the others; He alone
Who girdles it is governor thereof.
No other measures motion all its own,
But by this mete are measured all the rest,
As ten by its half and by its fifth is shown.
And how in such a vessel Time can nest
Its roots, its foliage in the others grow,
Henceforward may to thee be manifest.
O Greed, who overwhelmest mortals so
Beneath thyself that none has masterdom
To lift his eyes again from out thy flow!
Will does indeed in men to blossom come;
However long-continued rain and reek
Convert to blighted fruit the perfect plum.
Only in little children are to seek
True faith and innocence; then both too soon

Vanish before the down is on the cheek.
Many keep fast while yet they babble and croon,
Who swallow, when the tongue is free to play,
Whatever food under whatever moon;
And many while they babble love and obey
Their mother, who when they can speak aright
Long for the dawning of her burial day.
Even so the skin grows swarthy, which was white
At the first aspect, of the daughter fair
Of him who ushers morning and leaves night.
But lest thou shouldst as at a marvel stare,
Consider none on earth is governor,
Whence human household strays from thoroughfare.
But before January be no more
In winter, by the hundredth part neglected
Down there, so shall these upper circles roar
That Fortune, who has been so long expected,
Shall whirl the stern about where lies the boom,
So that the fleet will run the course directed;
And perfect fruit will follow on the bloom."— *Roughly estimated, the error in the calendar amounted to a hundredth of a day every year He first catches this revelation from the eyes of Beatrice A Spaceless Point of surpassing brilliance The nine orders of Angels Though the rainbow were a complete circle* XXVIII
The Heavenly Intelligences
When she who doth imparadise my mind
Had ended the veracious charge she brought
Against the life of wretched humankind,—
As one whose eye has in a mirror caught
The image of a torch behind him, long
Before he has it or in sight or thought,
And turns to verify if right or wrong
The mirror speak, and finds it to agree
With truth, as chimes the meter with the song,
So did I, as I call to memory,
On looking in those eyes with beauty burning
Wherewith Love made the noose for snaring me.
And, as I shifted round my look, discerning
The contents of that volume, read aright
With eye that is intent upon its turning,
I saw a Point which radiated light
So piercing that the vision, fired thereby,
Is closed perforce by vividness so bright.
That star appearing smallest to our eye
Would seem a moon beside its light intense,
As star is matcht with star along our sky.
Perchance in distance equal to that whence
Halo engirds the light that has impearled
Its color when the vapor is most dense,
So distant round the Point a circle whirled
Of fire so swift its motion had outpaced
That which goes quickliest around the world;
Round this another circle swept in haste,
Round that a third, a fourth the third enwound,
The fourth a fifth, and that a sixth embraced;
The seventh came afterward so wide of bound
That Juno's herald, though complete, would run
Too narrow to engirdle it around;
Likewise the eighth and ninth; and slowlier on
Did each one move according as accrued
Its number farther from the point of One;
And shone that flame with clearest plenitude
From the Pure Spark at shortest interval,
I think because more with its truth imbued.
Perceiving me become the anxious thrall
Of dubitance, my Lady spoke this word:
"From that one Point hang Heaven and nature all.
Look at that circle which doth next engird
The Point, and know it has such eager haste
For the enkindled love whereby 'tis spurred."—
But I made question: "If the world were based
Upon the order yonder wheels disclose,
Enough were what has been before me placed;
But in the world of sense one sees and knows
The orbits to be ever more divine
The more their distance from the center grows.
Whence wouldst thou still the longing that is mine,
Within the wonderful angelic Fane
Which light and love and these alone confine,
I need to hear thee furthermore explain
Why copy is not here with pattern vying,
Since I unaided gaze thereon in vain."—
"Suffice not thy own fingers for untying
Such knot, there is no wonder, seeing it
So tangled has become for want of trying."—.
My Lady thus; and then: "Take what seems fit
For me to tell, wouldst thou be satisfied,
And going round it sharpen thou thy wit.—
The spheres corporeal are strait or wide
According to the virtue less or more
Which throughout all their regions is supplied.
Superior good wills weal superior,
And if like perfect organs it dispose,
Holds larger body weal in larger store.
The Poet's scientific notion of space and therefore of time) seems

here upset and reversed Apparently the sensible universe reverses the pattern The larger corporeal circles are more excellent; in the world now suddenly revealed the order is reversed, so that the sphere "that first moved? corresponds to the smallest circle of intelligences Referring to pictures of the winds on old maps (cf. Shakespeare: "Blow winds and crack your cheeks") The squares of the board reduplicated by arithmetical progression

Therefore this sphere which carries as it goes
All the universe beside, must correspond
To that small circle which most loves and knows.

Hence if thou seek to measure with thy wand,
Not the appearance, but the excellence
Of substances to thy discerning round,

Of more with greater wondrous congruence,
As of the less with lesser wilt thou seek
In every Heaven, with its Intelligence. "—

Then as remains serene and cleared of reek
The hemisphere of air, soon as the blast
Is puffed by Boreas from the gentler cheek,

Whereby the cloudy rack that overcast
The welkin is dissolving, and the blue
Of Heaven in all its beauty smiles at last,

So cleared was I of all confusion through
The lucid answer that my Lady made,
And like a star in Heaven appeared the true.

Thereon, when her discourse to me was stayed,
As iron rays forth sparkles under stress
Of fire, such sparkles now the circles rayed.

Each spark did with their blazing coalesce,
And running into thousands manifold
More than the duplication of the chess.

From quire to quire I heard Hosannah rolled

To the fixed Point which holds them to the *Where*
From evermore, and will forever hold.

And she, of my perplexity aware,

Said: "The first gyres enlighten thee concerning
The Seraphim and Cherubim, who fare

After their bonds so swiftly, because yearning

To grow as like the Point as most they may,—
And so they may, exalting their discerning.

Those other loves that whirling round them play
Are Thrones, wherein God's grace is manifest,
For that the primal triad ended they.

And thou must know that one and all are blest
According as they penetrate the true,
Wherein all understanding is at rest.

Herein perceive we how the act of view

Is source wherefrom beatitude draws being,
Not act of love thereafter to ensue;

And merit is the measure of this seeing,—

Merit begot by Grace and right endeavor:
Such are the steps progressively agreeing.

The second triad, burgeoning forever
To flower in this sempiternal spring
Which the nocturnal Bam doth ravage never,

Is here perpetually caroling

Hosannah, sounded with three melodies
Whence orders three with trinal rapture ring.

This priesthood musters three divinities:

The Dominations first, the Virtues then,
And third the order of the Potencies.

Next, all but ultimate, in dances twain,

Are Princedoms and Archangels wheeling on;
Rejoicing Angels last in sportive train.

Upward are gazing all these orders yon,
And down prevail so that to the divine
They all are drawing as they all are drawn.

Such zeal to contemplate these orders nine
Showed Dionysius, that coincided
His definitions and his names with mine.

Thereafter Gregory from him divided;

Wherefore that saint, first opening his eye
Within this Heaven, himself with smiles derided.

And that on earth a mortal might descry

Such inward truth, need not astonish you,
Since learned from him who saw it here on high,

With much more of these circles that is true."— *Love flows from knowledge The constellation Aries appears in our sky at the time of the falling leaf Dionysius learned the truth from St. Paul*

XXIX

Creation And Nature Of Heavenly Intelligence *The letting sun* When, by the Ram and by the scales o'erbrooded, *and the rising* The twinborn children of Latona f air *full moon at the* , *Equinox,—the* In one horizon girdle are included, *one under the* Long as the zenith balances them there *Ram, the other* .
under the scales Until both swerve from that circumference *(Libra)* Unbalancing and shifting hemisphere,
So long, with smiles lighting her countenance,
Paused Beatrice, concentering her ken
Upon the Point that had subdued my glance.
"I tell and do not ask," began she then,
"What thou wouldst hear; by vision I assist
Where centers every Where and every When.
Why the Angels Not to possess Himself of good acquist,
were erected Which cannot be, but in the splendor of
His glorious declaration, 'I Exist,'
Outside time Beyond all limits, and all time above,
and space p pleased Hini(in His own eternity,

Unfolded in new loves the Eternal Love.
Nor yet before as if inert lay He,
Since nor before nor after moved the flow
Of spirit divine to brood upon this sea.
Pure form or Matter and form, combined and simple, so
Zlth intelligence Came *mio* bein8 flawless and unblighted, *(Angels); matter* Like arrows three from triple-corded bow; *%t%!repassive* And » glass, amber, crystal may be lighted *in character; the* So that between the earliest radiation *foaTmiter* f effulgence all remains united, *is found in ere*-Even so the Father's threefold operation *ated things, es*-All at a flash its being consummated *penally in man ...*
Without an interval in the creation.
Order was constituted and created
In substances; and the world's crowning grace
Were these, wherein pure act was generated.
Iure potency retained the lowest place; Midway did act and potence interweave
Such withies as can never disenlace.
Jerome wrote to you that we must believe
The angels to have been created ages
Before the other world; thou mayst perceive,
However, if thou but peruse the sages
Through whom the Spirit spoke in Holy Writ,
The very truth displayed on many pages;
And also reason gets a glimpse of it,
Which that Prime Movers for so long could be
Without their perfect work, could not admit.
Now where these loves were formed is known to thee,
And when and how; and in thy longing hence
Already are extinguisht ardors three.
Ere they reach twenty who to count commence,
So quickly of the angel host a part
Disturbed the lowest of your elements.
The rest, who stayed, began to ply this art
Which thou beholdest,—so beatified
That never from their circling they depart.
The Fall originated in the pride
Accursed of that One whom thou hast seen
Crushed by the weights of all the world beside.
Those whom thou seest here have humble been
To acknowledge them as from that Goodness kind
Which made them apt for knowledge so serene;
Wherefore illuminative Grace combined
With their own merit to exalt their view
So that they have a full and steadfast mind.
I would not have thee doubt, but hold it true
That grace accepted thus is merited
By laying open the longing heart thereto.
Henceforth, so have my words been harvested,
Canst round this Sacred College take thy fill
Of contemplation without further aid.
Memory cannot
be predicated of
beings outside
of time and
space, who
never forget
They do not "look before and after and sigh for what is not" The stormy voice again Common nicknames in Florence: "Lapo" corresponds to "JakJ' (Jacopo) (cf. xiii, 139)
But since on earth your schools attribute still
To the angelic nature, memory Together with intelligence and will,
I will speak further to make clear to thee
The truth, confused by men below who indite Prelections fraught with ambiguity.
These substances, since first they drew delight
From God's own face, wherefrom is hidden naught, Have never turned away from it their sight;
Whence they have vision intercepted not
By concept new, and need not undertake
To call back memory through divided thought. So men down there are dreaming, wide awake,
Weening, or weening not, truth to declare; But in the one more guilt and shame partake.
Below ye travel not one thoroughfare
Philosophizing; so far does the love
Of show delude you, and its specious air.
Yet even enduring this, the Heavens above
Are less indignant, than when set aside Is Holy Writ or idly prated of.
What blood was spent to sow it far and wide
Is given no heed, nor how their prayer is heard Who in humility by it abide.
Each is agog to shine, and ply absurd
Inventions, and these form the staple theme
Of preachers,—of the Gospel not a word! During Christ's passion, some would have us deem
The moon turned back again and canceled through The intercepted sunlight; and some dream
That of its own accord the light withdrew,
And hence would this eclipse alike appear To Spaniard and to Indian, as to Jew.
So many a Lapo and Bindo every year
Breeds Florence not, as fables of this kind
Are bawled out from the pulpit, far and near; i that from pasture, flatulent with wind, The silly sheep flock, witless of salvation; Yet is it no excuse that they are blind.
tirist did not say to his first congregation:
'Preach to the world with idle utterance,'
But laid for their behoof the true foundation;
ad. that had from their lips such resonance,
That, to enkindle faith, their battle quest,
The Gospel formed their buckler and their lance.

ow preachers sally forth to break a jest,
Buffoons who, so they may provoke a grin,
Puff out their cowls and reck not of the rest;
iut could the people see what bird of sin
Is nestling in the hood-tail, they would guess
What kind of pardon they are trusting in;
Vhence in the world so waxes foolishness
That, seeking not approof of any sign,
Men jump at promise of indulgences.
lereby St. Anthony makes fat his swine,
And others also, far more swine than they,
Paying their scot with counterfeited coin.
3ut since we have gone very far astray,
Let us look back to the straight thoroughfare,
So with the time to shorten up the way.
The angelic nature runs up such a stair
Of number, scaling so remote a height,
Never could tongue or thought pursue it there.
.nd Daniel's revelation, read aright,
Shows, in the thousands he enumerates,
That definite number is withheld from sight.
The Primal Light, which all irradiates,
By modes as many is received in these
As are the splendors whereunto it mates.
And since love follows on the act that sees,
Therefore the sweetness of their love is spoken,
More or less fervent in diverse degrees.
St. Anthony puts the hog under his feet as a symbol; his monks now degenerate to the hog Number of the angels countless
Let this the height henceforth, and breadth betoken
Of Worth Eternal, fashioning great store
Of mirrors whereupon its light is broken,
One in Itself remaining as before."—
uDa questo passo vinto mi concede"

431 XXX

The Celestial Rose

Tien, eastward ho! six thousand miles perchance
Noon blazes, and toward the level bed
The shadow of this world already slants,
he deep of central heaven above our head
Grows so suffused that here a star and yon
Begins to pale the radiance it shed,
nd, as the brightest handmaid of the sun
Advances, so are quencht the heavenly graces
Star after star, even to the fairest one.
Jot else the Triumph that forever races
Around the Point which overcame me quite,
Seeming embraced by that which it embraces,
Vas imperceptibly immerged in light;
Whereat to turn mine eyes on Beatrice,
Love laid constraint on me, and lack of sight.
ould what is said of her as far as this
All in one single act of praise conclude,
It would but serve the present turn amiss.
rhe beauty that I saw doth so elude
Our measure, that its Maker, I surely deem,
Alone can taste its full beatitude.
I yield me vanquisht at this pass supreme;
Comic or tragic poet overborne
Was never thus by crisis of his theme.
For, as to dazzled sight the sun of morn,
So doth her sweet remembered smile erase
My memory, of its very self forlorn.
From the first day when I beheld her face
In this life, even until the present viewing,
My song yet never faltered on her trace;
But now I must give over from pursuing
Her beauty in these cadences of mine,
Like every artist taskt beyond his doing.
Such as I leave her to a more divine
Renown than any that my trumpet grants,—
Which now concludes its arduous design,—
She said, with leader's voice and vigilance:
"Quitting the widest sphere of the concrete
We reach the heaven that is pure radiance:
Radiance of intellect with love replete, Love of true good replete with ecstasy,
Ecstasy far exceeding every sweet.
The Host of Here both the one and the other soldiery
ttl ani Of Paradise, and one host of the two
that of the Redeemed Robed as at Final Judgment, shalt thou see."—
As when a sudden lightning routs the crew
Of visual spirits, putting them to flight
So that the clearest things are canceled through,
So beamed there all about me living light,
Leaving so thick a veil around me closing,
That I saw nothing for that glory bright.
"The Love wherein this heaven is aye reposing
Is wonted so to welcome those who come,
Duly the taper for its flame disposing. "—
No sooner had this brief exordium
Within me penetrated, than I knew
Myself upraised beyond my masterdom;
And I rekindled with new power of view
Such that no light could be so unalloyed
But that mine eyes were tempered thereunto.
And I saw light in river-form with tide
Of fulgent fire between two margins streaming,
Which wondrously with flowers of spring were dyed.
Out of that current living sparks were teeming
And flashing from the flowers with hues intense

Like very rubies from gold patines gleaming.

Thereon, appearing drunken with the scents,

They plunged again into the wondrous eddy,

And as one sank another issued thence.

"The lofty wish aflame in thee already For knowledge of this vision, in like wise

Extends my joy as its increase is steady;

But thou must of this water of Paradise

Drink deep, to slake a thirst that so consumes."-

Thus spoke to me the sunshine of mine eyes,

Adding: "The river and the smiling blooms,

The plunging and emerging jewels bright,

Are types of truth that in their shadow looms;

Not that these things are hard to see aright,

But on thy part there is inaptitude

Since not yet so exalted is thy sight."—

There is no child far later than it should

Awakening, with face toward the breast

That plunges with more hunger-stricken mood,

Than did I, that mine eyes might mirror best

That vision, bending me my fill to take

Out of that flood which pours to make us blest.

No sooner had I felt its ripple slake

Mine eyelids, than both margins seemed to yield

From long to large and rounded to a lake.

Then, even as masqueraders are revealed

Quite other than beforehand, letting fall

The alien guise wherein they were concealed,

So changed for me to ampler festival

The flowerets and the flashes, till I saw

Clearly the two Courts of the heavenly Hall.

O splendor of very God, whereby I saw

The Kingdom true in triumph high, increase

In me the power to tell it as I saw!

A light up yonder shows without surcease

The Maker to that creature, who alone

In seeing Him inherits its own peace;

And this light broadens in a circling zone

So far and wide that its circumference

Would be too large a girdle for the sun.

The stream of grace, the flowers, and the ruby-sparks are but symbols Dante's sight exalted to see the reality behind these symbols The identical triple rime upon "saie" *has the same solemnity as that upon "Christ." Cf. Hugh Capet's discourse, Purg. xx, 66-69 Striking upon the outermost surface of the Universe, it gives motion to all the spheres The last words of Beatrice*

Its semblance, all of radiant effluence,

Doth to the top of Primal Motion pass,

Which takes vitality and vigor thence.

And as a hillside makes a looking-glass

Of water at its foot, as if discerning

How fair and rich it is in flowers and grass,

So mirrored, round and round above the burning

On myriads of thrones, beheld I those

Of us who there above have won returning.

And if the lowermost degrees inclose

Luster so large, what amplitude of light

Spread in the outer petals of the Rose!

My vision in the vastness and the height

Strayed not, at home and fully conversant

With essence and with scope of that delight.

There near and far do neither add nor scant,

For where God is directly governing

The law of nature is not relevant.

Into the yellow Rose unwithering,

Whose petals are unfurled with fragrance cast

Of praise unto the Sun of dateless spring,

Like one long silent, moved to speak at last,

Did Beatrice conduct me, saying: "View

The Congregation of white robes, how vast!

Look the wide circuit of our city through!

Look at our benches which are so replete

That here henceforward are expected few!

There where thine eyes are drawn to that great Seat

By the already overhanging crown,

Ere thou shalt at this wedding supper eat,

The soul of noble Henry shall sit down,

Who comes, august, to render straight the way

For Italy, ere she be ready grown.

Blind Greed, who doth her spell upon you lay,

Has made you like the child who, though he pine

With famine, pushes yet the nurse away.

Then shall be Pontiff in the Court Divine

One such that open word and covert deed

Walk not on equal feet to one design.

But little while will God permit him speed

In Holy Office, for he shall be thrust

With Simon Magus, and make, by way of meed,

Him of Alagna bite the baser dust."—

Clement V, who secretly opposed Henry VII while pretending to favor. He of Alagna is Boniface VIII. The best commentary is Inferno xix The comparison with the bee was merely suggested in Canto XXX Ilelice was turned into the Great Bear (the Wain or Dipper), her son into Bootes XXXI

Beatrice, Assumed Into The Celestial Rose, Sends

St. Bernard To Dante

In fashion therefore of a pure white Rose
Unfolded to my view the sacred throng
Whom Christ in His own blood espoused. But those
Who witness as they fly, and tell in song The glory of Him who makes them love, and sing
His excellence who made them fair and strong-
Even as a busy swarm of bees a-wing
That merge in flowers awhile, then speed away
To where their labor sweet is savoring,—
Plunged into the Great Flower, with fair array
Of Petals, and were reascending thence
Where sojourns their own Love for ever and aye.
Their features were alive with flame. intense,
Golden their wings, the rest so white that banks
Of drifted snow have not their innocence.
Alighting on the Flower, to ranks on ranks
They proffered of the ardor and repose
Which they had won by winnowing their flanks.
Nor did the coming in, between the Rose
And That Which dwelt above, of flight so great
Obstruct the vision; still the splendor glows,
For through the universe doth penetrate
In measure of its worth the Light Divine
So that no bar can ever separate.
This safe and happy City, where combine
Both ancient folk and modern crowded so,
Had look and love all turned toward one sign.
O Trinal Light, that in one Star doth glow
Upon their vision with such benison,
Look down upon our tempest here below!
If the barbarians from out that zone
Where spreads forever Helice her span
Revolving with her well-beloved son,—
Coming of St. Bernard 437
If, entering Rome, her mighty works to scan,
These stared in wonder, in that era when
Transcended mortal things the Lateran,— I, who to the Divine had come from men,
From time unto eternity had come,
From Florence to a people just and sane, With what amazement was I overcome!
Truly the wonder and the joy between,
'Twas rapture to hear nothing and stand dumb. And as the wayworn pilgrim grows serene
Gazing around the temple of his vow,
And muses how he shall describe the scene, I, bending on the living light my brow,
Followed along the lines, and sought to trace,
Now up, now down, and round the circle now. I lookt on many a love-persuading face
Deckt with.Another's light, and their own eyes
Smiling, and action of all noble grace. The universal form of Paradise
My glance had gathered as a whole immense, But did no single part yet signalize;
And round I turned with will rekindled thence
To ask my Lady what these matters be
Concerning which my mind was in suspense. One thing I meant, another fronted me:
Weening to look again on Beatrice, A glory-vested Elder did I see.
His lineaments were overspread with bliss
Benignant, kindly was his mien and eye,
Betokening a father's love in this. "And she,—where is she?" was my sudden cry: *Speaks St.*
Whereat he answered: "To fulfill thy yearning *Bernard*
Beatrice urged me from my place on high: Third from supreme the circle, which discerning,
Thou shalt again behold her countenance
Shine down from where her worth a throne is earning."
Without reply I lifted up my glance
And saw her, where a coronal she wore
Woven from out the eternal radiance.
From welkin whence the highest thunders roar
Has never mortal eye so distant been,
Though sunken deep beneath the ocean-floor,
As mine from Beatrice; but 'twas so keen
No distance mattered, since her features beaming
Shone down on me without a blur between.
Dante's prayer "O Lady in whom my living hope is teeming,
to the Heavenly nd wh0 *fafe* once endure to leave the trace
Beatrice
Of thy dear feet in Hell for my redeeming,
In all the worth and beauty finding place
In things thou hast enabled me to see,
I recognize thy virtue and thy grace.
Thou leddest me along from slave to free
By all those ways, by all expedients
Whereby the power to do so lay in thee.
Preserve in me thine own magnificence,
So that my spirit through thy healing, may
Content thee as it slips the coil of sense. "—
Far as she seemed, on hearing me so pray
She smiled and lookt: then to the Fountain-head
Eternal turned her shining eyes away.
"In order," now the holy Elder said,
"That thou complete thy course,—whence holy love
Dispatched me and true orisons have sped,—
Let thy fleet glances through this garden rove,
For better will such sight thy vision steel

Upon the ray divine to mount above.
And she, the Queen of Heaven, for whom I feel
Love's utter flame, will grant us furtherance,
For reason that I am her Bernard leal. "—
Like him who from Croatia, perchance,
Comes to see our Veronica, well known
Through old report, and cannot sate his glance,
zBut thinks within, so long as it be shown,
"My Lord and very God, Christ Jesus Mine,
And were these features once thy very own?"—
Such was I, gazing at that living shrine
Of charity, who in the world below
By contemplation tasted peace divine.
"This blithesome being wilt thou never know,
O son of grace," such was his further note,
"With eyes but fixed here at the bottom so;
But mark the circles to the most remote
Until thou shalt the enthroned Queen descry,
To whom this realm is subject and devote."—
I raised mine eyes; and as the morning sky
Displays a point of the horizon bright
Beyond that of the westering sun, so I,
As going with my glance from vale to height,
Beheld a region at the verge extreme
Surpassing all the other front in light.
And as, where we expect the chariot-beam
That Phaeton guided ill, the glows increase,
Fading away on either hand, the gleam
Illumined so that Oriflamme of peace
In the live center, while on either side
In equal measure did the splendor cease.
And at that center I saw, on wing flung wide,
A thousand jocund angels sweep along,
In glow and ministry diversified.
There, smiling on their games and at their song, I saw a Beauty that was bliss indwell
The eyes of all the other holy throng.
Yet were my wealth of diction parallel
With wealth of fancy, rash were the emprise
The least of her delights to strive to tell.
Then holy Bernard, when he saw mine eyes
Fastened upon the object of his yearning,
His own in her did so imparadise
As to make my desire to look more burning.
Bernard directs the Poet to look up to the Queen of Heaven The quieter tone of this canto, with Us lovely, familiar images of the bees, the . dfl *Northman in* j' *Rome, the pU- grim in the temple of his vow, the Croatian gazing upon the picture of his Saviour, the angels sporting about the beautiful Queen,— is in marked artistic contrast with the splendors and intensity of the Thirtieth Mary Eve Rachel Sara,*
Rebecca,
Judith,
Ruth
For the Diagram see Gardner'! "Temple Primer"
Between hi own death and that of his Lord XXXII
Order Of Places In The Mystic Amphitheater
That contemplator took the office free
Of teacher, while intent upon his bliss,
Beginning with these holy words to me:
"The wound by Mary balmed and covered, this
That woman fair reposing at her feet
Inflicted, opening the cicatrice.
Beneath her third in order has her seat
Rachel, and thou seest at her side
Beatrice. Below these in order meet
Sara, Rebecca, Judith, and that bride,
Great-grandame of the singer who for grief
Of his own guilt the *Miserere* cried:
From rank to rank descending, these in chief
Mayst thou behold, as, naming each one, I
Go downward through the Rose from leaf to leaf.
And from the seventh degree, as from on high
To it, are Hebrew women cutting through
All petals of the Flower successively;
For these, according to the point of view
Whence lookt their faith to Christ, compose a blended
Wall that divides the sacred stair in two.
Upon this side where every petal splendid
Is full in bloom, are seated in their places
All who believed in Christ not yet descended;
And those half-circling ranks, with vacant spaces
On the other side, with happy intuition
To Christ already risen turned their faces.
And just as here the glorious position
Of Heaven's Lady, with the others one by one
Below it, constitute so great division,
So counterposed is that of mighty John,
Who bore the desert, martyrdom in fine,
And, holy still, two years in Hell thereon;
The Ring Fits the Finger 441
And Francis, Benedict, and Augustine,
With others hitherward from row to row
Continue downward the dividing line. Now see high Providence Divine, and know
That one and the other phase of our believing Shall to this garden equally bestow.
And know that down from yonder circle, cleaving
Across, midway on the partitions two,
Sit they, no meed of merit so retrieving, But meed of others, by conditions due;
For these are souls who did the flesh

divest *children*

Before they could make any choices true. This by their countenances may be guessed

And by the tune their childish voices hum, If thou but lookest well and listenest.

Now doubtest thou, and doubting makes thee dumb;

But I will shatter for thee the strong chain

Of subtle thought which is so cumbersome. The boundless amplitudes of this domain

No particle of accident admit,

More than of hunger, thirst, or any pain, For Law Eternal has established it

In what thou seest, that with exactitude

Duly the ring doth to the finger fit. Wherefore this swiftly hasting multitude,

Seeking true life, are not without causation Placed at a higher or lower altitude.

The King through whom reposing is this nation

In so great love and in such Paradise

That none aspires to loftier consummation, All minds creating in his own glad eyes,

At His good pleasure doth with grace endue

Diversely; and here let the fact suffice. And this expressly is made clear to you

In Scripture, by that twin-embrothered pair

Who even in their mother angry grew.

I

Whence fittingly the light supremely fair

May crown us with a chaplet of that grace

According to the color of the hair.

They stand then, not by merit of their ways,

At different stages, only differing

Themselves in primal keenness of their gaze.

So, when the centuries were at the spring,

Sufficient was the parents' faith, along

With native innocence, for rescuing;

And when the centuries were no longer young,

'Twas needful that the males by circumcision

Should have their innocent pinions rendered strong;

But since the era of free grace has risen,

If lacking perfect baptism into Christ,

Such innocence has been kept down in prison.

Look now upon the face most like to Christ

In its fair lineaments, whose radiance bright

Alone can make thee fit to look on Christ."—

I saw rain down upon her such delight

Carried by those intelligences good

Created all for soaring through that height,

That whatsoever I before had viewed

Did never so suspend my soul in wonder

Nor show me of God so great similitude.

And that Love who had flown before thereunder

Singing: "Hail Mary, full of grace benign!''—

Now spread in front of her his wings asunder.

Responses to the minstrelsy divine

Rang through the blessed Court from all and some,

Making all features more serenely shine.

"O holy Father, who endurest to come

For me down here, quitting the blissful quire

Where by divine allotment is thy home,

Who is that Angel who with glad desire

Looks in the eyes of our own Empress yon,

Enamored so, he seems a flame of fire?"—

Great Peers of the Just Realm 443

So turned I to the teaching of that one

Who gathered beauty out of Mary's face

As does the star of morning from the sun. And he to me: "All confidence and grace

Are in him, much as ever was conferred on *The Seraph*

Angel or soul, and willing is our praise, *Gabriel*

For this is he who brought the palm as guerdon

To Mary down, when took without distrust

The very Son of God our fleshly burden. But follow with thine eyes now, for I must

Pursue the theme, and mark the throng of those

Great peers of this most holy realm and just. The twain who most enraptured there repose,

Through being next neighbors to Augusta fair,

Are as the double roots of this our Rose. He who upon the left is next ber there

Is that First Sire by whose audacious taste Mankind is savoring such bitter fare.

That ancient Father of Holy Church, once graced

By Christ with keys of this fair realm, beside

Our Lady and upon her right, is placed. And that one who beheld before he died

All grievous days of her purchased for us

At cost of lance and nails, Christ's own fair Bride, Sits next that Father; and over against him thus

That Leader under whom were fed with manna

The folk ungrateful, headstrong, mutinous. Opposite Peter seest thou seated Anna, *The Poet of the*

So happy in her daughter that no whit £jTM£ -£ "

She moves her eyes away to sing Hosanna. *thought for the*

Our greatest of housefathers opposite *dhfiXn?*

Sits Lucy, who impelled thy Lady down *Let us call him*

When thou wast heading straight toward the Pit. *"narchitect.witk .. _.. i,i an eye to sym*But since Time speeds along thy trance to drown, *metry. "ParaHere* let us pause, like prudent tailor who JK?

exf%fi. Patterns according to the cloth the gown; *only three lines*

And to the Primal Love turn we our view,
So that, on visionary wing upspeeding,
Thou pierce as in thee lies his radiance through.

Yet lest thou, peradventure, while receding,

Flutter thy wings, advancing but in thought,
Let grace be our petition, grace exceeding

Through her with power to help thee must be sought; And do thou follow me with adoration,, 0, That from my word thy heart be severed not."— *dose of Canto v* Here he began this holy supplication:—

I *Prayer for the Eternal Pilgrim* 445 XXXIII

The Prayer Of St. Bernard. The Ultimate Vision

"Daughter of thine own son, thou Virgin Mother, *Compare the*

Of the eternal counsel issued fated, *Invocation* to *Mary by*
Lowlier and loftier than any other, *Chaucer*

To such nobility hast thou translated

Man's nature that its Maker did not spurn

To make Himself the thing that He created. Beneath thy heart was made again to burn

The Love by virtue of whose warmth withal

This Flower has blossomed in the peace eterne. A living torch here art thou to us all

To kindle love, and down where mortals sigh

Thou art a fount of hope perennial. Thou art so prevailing, Lady, and so high

That who wants grace and will to thee not run

Would have his longing without pinions fly. Thy lovingkindness fails to succor none

Imploring it, but often is so free

As to anticipate the orison. In thee is mercy, pity is in thee,

In thee munificence, in thee a host Of human virtues are in unity.

This man, who hither from the nethermost

Pool of the world comes making observation

Of spiritual natures, ghost on ghost,
Now doth to thee of grace make supplication

That he by vision may uplift his being

Still higher toward the Ultimate Salvation. And I, who never burned for my own seeing

More than I do for his, imploring pray

With all my soul, and pray for thine agreeing, That thou drive every mortal cloud away

Which darkens round him, with thine interceding,—

Be the Chief Joy unveiled to him today.

i

Hear, all-prevailing Queen, my further pleading,
Keep his affections through thy vigilance
Sound for him, after vision so exceeding.

Quell by thy watchcare baser human wants:
Lo, yonder, Beatrice with all the blest
Clasping their hands to thee are suppliants."—

The venerated eyes, beloved best

Of God, attent on him who made the prayer,
Showed us her pleasure in devout request;

Then plunged into the Light Eternal, where
We may not think of any creature turning
An eye that penetrates so clearly there.

And I who to the goal of every yearning

Was drawing near, slaked, as was meet for me,
And satisfied the thirst within me burning.

Then Bernard beckoned to me smilingly
To look aloft; but I already grew
Of my own accord as he would have me be;

Because, becoming purified, my view

Now more and more was entering the ray Of the deep Light that in itself is true. *Cf. "In Me*-Thenceforth my seeing was more than tongue can say, Tomw'irwSj Yields our discourse before the Light Supreme, ki/i *how hard*
And violated memory falls away.
mfra . Like mm wh0 *seea* while dreaming, and the dream B Remains thereafter traced upon his feeling, While memory holds thereof no other gleam,
Even such am I; for though the great revealing
Fades almost all away from me, yet flow
Its drops of sweetness in my heart distilling.

Thus in the sun evanishes the snow;

Upon the light leaves by the zephyr drifted
The wisdom of the Sibyl perished so.

O Light Supreme, who art so high uplifted

From mortal thought, still let my mind with some
Of what thou didst appear to me, be gifted,
The Beatific Vision 447

And dower my tongue with so great masterdom
That one sole sparkle of thy glory be
Thereby transmitted to the folk to come;

For by some glimpses caught by memory,

And by some echo in these rimes, perchance Better shall be conceived thy victory. Pierced by the vivid living radiance Methinks I had been lost, if by the sight
Bewildered, I had turned aside my glance;
And I remember, till I could unite

My gaze therewith, my hardihood to dare
The vision of the Goodness Infinite.
0 plenteous grace, whence I presumed to bear

The stress of the Eternal Light, till thirst
Was consummated in the seeing there!
1 saw in its abysmal deep immerst,

Together in one volume bound with love,
What is throughout the universe disperst:

Substance and accidents all thereabove
So interfused in property and mood,
That what I say gives but scant glimpse thereof.
Of this same fusion do I think I viewed
The universal form, for uttering
This word, I feel ampler beatitude.
To me more Lethe doth one moment bring
Than five and twenty centuries for the emprise
Whence Argo's shade set Neptune wondering.
So was my spirit gazing, all surmise,
Steadfast, intent, in absolute repose,
And evermore enkindled through the eyes.
In presence of that radiance one grows
So rapt, it is impossible the soul
Could yield to turn aside to other shows;
Because the Good, which is volition's goal,
All gathers there, and the deficient rest
Outside it, there becomes a perfect whole.
i
Now will my words fall even shorter, in quest
Of my remembrance, than the infant lore
Of him whose tongue is moistened at the breast.
Not that the Living Light I saw gave more
Than one sole semblance to my contemplation,
For it is always what it was before;
But by my gathered strength of observation,
One sole appearance, unto me thus seeing,
Was ever changing with my transformation.
To me within the luminous deep being
Of Lofty Light appeared three circles, showing
Three colors, and in magnitude agreeing;
And from the First appeared the Second flowing
Like Iris out of Iris, and the Third
Seemed fire that equally from both is glowing.
O but how scant, how feeble any word
To my conceit! and this to what I viewed
Is such, to call it little were absurd.
O Light Eterne, who dost thyself include,
Who lovest, smiling at thy own intents,
Self-understanding and self-understood!
That circling which in thee seemed effluence.
Of light reverberated, by my view
L Surveyed awhile in its circumference,
B Within itself of its own proper hue
V Seemed painted with the effigy of man,
Whereat my sight was wholly set thereto.
As the geometer, intent to scan
The measure of the circle, fails to trace,
Think as he may, some feature of the plan,
Such I at the strange vision of the Face:
How the image fits the circle, fain aright Would I perceive, and how it there finds place; *An instant of* But my own wings were not for such a flight—*perfect fulfill-*f/Except that, smiting through the mind of me,
There came fulfillment in a flash of light. *ment "L'Amor eke move il sole e Valtre stelle"* 449
V Here vigor failed the lofty fantasy;
But my volition now, and my desires,
Were moved like wheel revolving evenly
By Love that moves the sun and starry fires.

CPSIA information can be obtained at www.ICGtesting.com
Printed in the USA
LVOW09s2128060114

368315LV00018B/703/P